THEOLOGY FOR A SCIENTIFIC AGE

Being and Becoming – Natural, Divine and Human

Arthur Peacocke

Enlarged Edition

SCM PRESS LTD

0334 02547 8

To fellow members
of the
Society of Ordained Scientists

First published 1990 by Basil Blackwell Ltd

Second, enlarged edition published 1993
by SCM Press Ltd
9–17 St Albans Place, London N1 0NX

Second impression 1996

Typeset by The Spartan Press Ltd.,
Lymington, Hants.
Printed and bound in Great Britain by
Mackays of Chatham PLC, Chatham, Kent

CONTENTS

PREFACE

Anyone who has been at all concerned with the history of the interaction between Christian theology and the natural sciences cannot but view current controversies between the self-appointed 'conservatives' and the pejoratively labelled 'liberals' with an acute sense of *déjà vu*. For again and again Christian theology has had to face up to the challenge of new knowledge about the natural world – and indeed about its historical origins and sacred scriptures – and the heresies of one generation have become the orthodoxies of the next. So much so that, even when the traditional words are used in creeds and worship by a twentieth-century Christian, the content of their belief often bears only a distant genetic relation to what was believed in the context of the thought-world centuries, or even a millennium, ago. For the whole framework in which affirmations of belief about nature, humanity and God are set have changed radically over the centuries, and never more rapidly than in the twentieth.

It is no use pretending that these recent changes have been at all helpful to membership of the mainline churches in the West which have usually been associated with the conservation of past beliefs rather than with intelligent, open inquiry into new modes of expression of commitment to God in Christ through the Holy Spirit, to use traditional terms. The current resuscitation of very conservative positions, both in and outside these churches, is a sign not so much of a recovery of faith as of a loss of nerve before the onslaught of new perceptions of the world.

The understanding of the world which is evoked by the contemporary natural sciences is commonly taken in the West to be inimical to, or at least subversive of, religious belief in general and Christian belief in particular. I am convinced that this widely accepted view is mistaken and that the myth of the gulf between Christian theology and the natural sciences is debilitating to our culture while impoverishing the spiritual and personal life of the

generations who have come to believe it. Study of this interaction, as expressed in my earlier writings* (some of them
listed on p. 350) has impelled me to evolve a theology that has
been refined, as far as it lay within my powers, in the fires of
the new perceptions of the world that the natural sciences have
irreversibly established. Such a theology needs to be consonant
and coherent with, though far from being derived from, scientific perspectives on the world.

In this work the more overt and explicit theme of reflection
on the theological implications of scientific perspectives on the
world is accompanied by a kind of ground bass constituted by a
sequence of traditional 'heads of doctrine', namely: 'Nature'
(Part I, chs. 1–5); 'God' (Part II, chs. 6–10); 'Revelation' (ch. 11);
'Man' (ch. 12); 'Jesus of Nazareth' (ch. 13); 'The Incarnation' (ch.
14); 'The Nature of Man and the Work of Christ' (ch. 15); 'The
Means of Grace, the Church and the End' (ch. 16); and 'The
Trinity' (Postscript). Part III (chs. 11–16) is an expanded
version of the 1993 Gifford Lectures which I delivered at St
Andrews University whose courteous and gracious hospitality I
am glad to be able to acknowledge here. I have been much
helped in this last Part by the comments on earlier drafts of
chapter 12, section 5, and of chapter 13, section 3, made respectively by Professor H. Newton Maloney of Fuller Theological
Seminary, Pasadena, and by Dr George Brooke of the Depart-
ment of Religions and Theology, University of Manchester –
and also by the stimulus provided by graduate students at
seminars of the Chicago Center for Religion and Science.

This presentation has necessarily involved a process of re-
integration of many of my, somewhat dispersed, previous theological reflections (in works devoted primarily to the challenge
of the natural sciences to theology) into what I hope is a more
coherent theology. So I ask the reader to forgive what might
otherwise appear as a tendency to excessive retrospective self-
reference in the notes. In the event, these notes have, more
generally, become somewhat extensive since the process of
integration has required the incorporation into my theology of
the insights of other theologians and scientists, so that many
particular points merited fuller elaboration than was appropriate in the main text – which the reader is, in any case, advised
to follow initially without interruption by reference to the
notes.

For the whole exercise is intended not so much as 'apologetic' but, putatively, as creative theology in response to the comprehensive, indeed dazzling, perspective on the being and becoming of the world and of humanity that the sciences have now unveiled to our generation in this last decade of the twentieth century. I offer these reflections not in any spirit of wishing to disturb those for whom fully traditional formulations and interpretations still have meaning, but to those who would like to follow in the Christian 'Way' but have thought they could not do so with intellectual integrity.

Arthur Peacocke
Oxford, May 1993

*The Introduction to this volume incorporates ideas, and some actual text, drawn from lectures by the author in part published in: *Religion and Intellectual Life*, 2 (1985), pp. 7–26; ibid., 5 (1988), pp. 45–58; *Religion, Science and Public Policy*, ed. F. T. Birtel (Crossroad, New York, 1987), pp. 3–29; *Cosmos as Creation*, ed. Ted Peters (Abingdon Press, Nashville, 1989), pp. 28–43.

Note 'God is neither male nor female, and I have earlier (in *Creation and the World of Science*, Clarendon Press, Oxford, 1979, pp. 141–4) been quite explicit concerning the need to recover and extend the use of both feminine attributes of God and feminine models of God's relation to the world. So I have tried to avoid the use of male pronouns in sentences about 'God'. Sometimes, however, the exigencies of English syntax and euphony have defeated me. I ask the reader to be indulgent to me in these unavoidable lapses and not to attribute any theological significance to them.

The Theological and Scientific Enterprises

1 'SCIENCE AND RELIGION'

There are many indications that the understanding of the world which is evoked by contemporary science is seen in the West as inimical to, or at least subversive of, religious belief – mainly Christian belief. That this impression is induced early on in life was well substantiated, just to take one example, in a report in 1977 on the beliefs of young people:

> Childhood belief is breached with incredible ease on the basis of a simplistic scientism...
>
> In general... what we find... is an uncritical acceptance of a vocabulary of natural science which is... out of date... and is capable of enshrining new myths within itself... Instead of religion our young people have a mild form of science fiction...
>
> [We are]... left with a growing suspicion that one of the crucial processes at work in our modern world is, or has been, the imperialistic advance of a *vocabulary* of rationality, science and individualism... what has got crowded out is a *language* which modern society will regard as valid in which symbols and rituals can be described and expressed.[1]

In a wider context, Lesslie Newbigin, with his long missionary experience in the Third World, has recently reflected upon the shrinking influence of the churches in modern Western culture – which now includes not only the peoples of Europe and North America but also their former colonial and cultural offshoots and those parts of the Third World that are undergoing 'modernization' under the influence of education, the media and invading industries. No-one concerned with the future of the Christian, or indeed any other religion, can avoid facing up to the impact of science on faith.

This encounter is identified by Newbigin as the crucial point at which the gospel is failing to have any impact on 'Western' men and women.[2]

The general level of discussion of issues which involve any relating of scientific knowledge to received Christian belief, or rather to what is widely assumed to be such, remains at a depressingly low level – witness the controversies surrounding so-called 'creationism' in the United States and the relation of a fertilized human ovum to the human 'soul', not to mention the welcoming by even the 'serious' press in the English-speaking world of any controversy among evolutionary biologists as somehow casting doubt on 'Darwinism' and thereby implicitly vindicating 'religion'. Every year when the British Association for the Advancement of Science meets, some journalist or other inevitably resuscitates the myth (and 'myth', in the popular sense of 'untrue story', the historians are now showing it to be) of how the Saint George of science in the person of T. H. Huxley slew the dragon of religious bigotry in the person of the then Bishop of Oxford, Samuel Wilberforce, at its 1860 Oxford meeting.

In a more serious vein, I would hazard the guess that leading Western intellectuals, and particularly the scientists who have this century set the pace for the others, would concur that the natural sciences were *par excellence* the manifestation of the human search for intelligibility. I would also guess that they would recognize too the validity of the human search for the meaning of existence, and some might even concur that religion was one of the fundamental manifestations of the existence of this unfulfilled human longing – along with the arts and non-religious rituals. For in spite of many prophecies, religion has not withered away entirely, even in Western societies, and in many parts of the world it is positively flourishing. The human need to discern meaning and significance for the individual in the universe as understood and experienced has, if anything, been sharpened and the appetite for it quickened by the widening vistas opened up by the sciences. For the perennial challenges of our sense of mortality within the joyful vitalities of existence, of human suffering and yet also of human joy and exaltation in achievement, of our inner transcendence over that on which we reflect and of our vulnerability to the fragility of the fantastically complex organization of our evolved bodies – all these experiences, and much else, continue to fire in us humans longings and aspirations that appear incapable of satisfaction from within the resources vouchsafed to us by the too-monochrome scientific descriptions of our world. So it is perhaps not so surprising, after all, that the investigations of, for example, the Alister Hardy Research Centre at Oxford, have uncovered how widespread in highly secularized late twentieth-century Britain are experiences of awareness of a benevolent non-physical power that appears to be partly or wholly beyond, and far greater than, the individual self. Such experiences are properly designated as 'religious', whatever the official allegiance, or lack of it, of those reporting them to any religious institution.

The form of religion with which the greater proportion of those nurtured in Western societies, in the narrow sense, is acquainted is Christianity. It has shaped our art, music, architecture, customs, laws and inbuilt social assumptions, and through our use of symbols and language still does so shape the inner pattern of our thinking in incalculable ways, even that of those who overtly repudiate it. We may perhaps, after a lifetime's study and immersion in another (for example, Buddhist) culture become sufficiently indigenized that 'God', if there is one, can speak to us through the resources of that culture – but it is extremely unlikely that we shall achieve such a degree of re-enculturation in an average lifetime, and there are very few who actually do so. A shrewd appraisal of what might be a fruitful use of time and energy would suggest that a Western writer seeking to interpret the religious experience of human beings to a Western readership could best do so with reference to their common Christian inheritance, even if it is no longer appreciated by the majority. This is the policy pursued in this book, but in no way is this meant to imply that other non-Christian religions cannot be a path to that reality which is, as I shall argue, God.

Moreover, since the aim of this work is to rethink our 'religious' conceptualizations in the light of the perspective on the world afforded by the sciences, there are at least two further reasons, in addition to the cultural one just proposed, why the relation of Christianity to that perspective has a special significance for all forms of religious experience and cultures.

The first is that Western Christianity in its Catholic, Protestant and Anglican forms (Eastern Orthodox Christianity constitutes a different experience) was the first major religion to encounter the full impact of the natural sciences on important features of the received content of its beliefs. Their systems of Christian belief incorporated many basic affirmations about the relation of God, humanity and nature within a matrix of assumptions concerning the natural world that had accumulated over many centuries of 'natural philosophy', later called 'natural science', or just 'science'. Since it was in England that Newton and Darwin first propounded their ideas, the Church of England in particular had, a little earlier than some other churches, to take the full brunt of the revolution in our thinking about the natural world initiated by these key figures. In this context, it is interesting to note how the relatively conservative reformation of the Church in England was viewed in that formative period for the rise of science, the seventeenth century, by a contemporary historian – Thomas Sprat, the first historian of the Royal Society of London:

> we behold the agreement that is between the present *Design* of the *Royal Society*, and that of our *Church* in its beginning. They both may lay equal claim to the word *Reformation*; the one having compassed it in *Religion*, the other purposing it in *Philosophy* . . . They both suppose alike, that their *Ancestors* might err; and yet retain a sufficient reverence for them . . .[3]

In fact it was on a church of this kind, in a society in which the church, though influential, could and did have its beliefs subjected to wide and open criticism, that the scientific revolution had such a major impact. In fact, the reaction to Darwin in nineteenth-century England was very mixed and recent historical studies show that there was much less antagonism on the part of theologians and more on the part of scientists than the current mythology allows.[4] There is indeed much that can be learnt concerning the interaction between the theological and scientific enterprises from the careful and objective historical study of such interactions between scientists ('natural philosophers') and theologians. Although such historical analysis is not the focus of this study, what follows has, I hope, been informed by it.

The second reason why the Christian religion merits special attention as a paradigm case of a religion operating in the new cultural climate associated with the rise of science is that the Christian religion has had to take up the gauntlet thrown down by what is loosely called the 'Enlightenment'. It, almost alone among the major world religions, has been subject within its own culture to critical, historical, linguistic and literary analysis of its sacred literature and its sources; has had its beliefs exposed to sceptical philosophical critique; its attitudes to psychological examination; and its

structures to sociological inquiry. All this has occurred in the course
of barely three centuries during which the immense economic
upheavals of industrialization have, along with increased freedom
and education, entirely altered people's lives and outlooks.

It is one of the ironic features of this culture in the last decade or
so of the twentieth century that after more than 300 years of a
fecund natural science – one of the supreme achievements of human
reason and curiosity – the search for intelligibility concerning the
nature and origin of the cosmos has plunged human beings irrevocably, and for some unwillingly, into the darker stream of the search
for meaning. An irony it is – for did not this selfsame science,
according to popular mythology, only acquire its freedom even to
seek intelligibility by unshackling itself from the stifling embrace of
a Christianity too much concerned with meaning and too little
concerned with what came to be called the evidence? But the irony
is compounded, for Christian civilization itself, having given birth to
its child of science[5] and having seen that growing infant cut its
umbilical cord, has resorted more and more to an emphasis on
subjective personal experience ('meaning for me') as its basis, only
to find that twentieth-century human beings cannot find such a
resource of meaning in the Christian religion (or in anything else)
unless it is consonant with their understanding of the world which is
itself moulded by that same science.

So after two centuries or more of bickering, or of sullen silence
with demarcation of spheres of interest, these two fundamental
activities, the search for intelligibility and the search for meaning,
that characterize respectively, but not exclusively, science and
religion, find themselves inextricably interlocked with each other in
the common human enterprise of seeking *both* intelligibility *and*
meaning. Each now provides the other with challenges to and
resources for an interaction gradually becoming more fruitful and
wholesome. This judgement on the contemporary scene could be
illustrated from many spheres: the understanding of the human
person as a psychosomatic unity in both science and religion; the
integration of biological evolutionary ideas with the sense of God as
an immanent, ever-working Creator; or reflections on the origins of
the cosmos induced both by astrophysics and cosmology, on the one
hand, and clarification of the Judeo-Christian doctrine of creation on
the other.

The last trumpet in the so-called warfare of science and religion
has long since become silent and those engaged in both enterprises

have today, I think, acquired a new humility – not least because they have come to recognize both the limitations of their presumed knowledge and the dire, indeed evil, social consequences of ultra-dogmatic, over-confident, imperialistic applications of half-truths about their respective quests. For example, the intellectual descendants of the Enlightenment have long castigated religion, with justification, for the wars fought in its name, only to find themselves to have sired in twentieth-century nuclear physics the possibility of global, rather than local, holocaust.

Implicit in this study is the assumption of the significance of the relationship between 'science' and 'religion', not only for the health of each enterprise but also for the future of humanity. For the relationship between these two claimants on human loyalty is probably the most fundamental challenge that faces the mind and spirit of human beings today. It is necessary to be more precise about these terms. By 'science' I shall mean the *natural* sciences, including not only the physical and biological sciences but also the 'human sciences' (psychology, sociology, etc.). That is, by 'science' I shall be referring to *naturwissenschaften* rather than to *geisteswissenschaften* (the 'humanities'[6]). Furthermore, I shall be concerned principally with 'theology' rather than with the more widely ranging area of 'religion'. The distinction is difficult to make precise, but broadly I shall take 'theology' to refer to the reflective and intellectual analysis of the experience of God[7] and, for the reasons mentioned above, principally the Christian forms of that experience, though this inevitably includes much of the Jewish experience too, since this shares the same roots. Such analysis of the Christian experience of God that is the concern of theology necessarily involves a careful consideration of the content of Christian belief, for Christianity, more than most of the major world religions, makes cognitive claims. It affirms, in some sense, the reality of that to which it refers. The sense in which this is so will be discussed later in this chapter.

It is also apparent that scientists, and the general public who utilize the fruits of their claimed knowledge, believe even more strongly that science affirms the reality of that to which it refers. Hence, there is a strong *prima facie* case for re-examining the claimed cognitive content of Christian theology in the light of the new knowledge derivable from the sciences, since both enterprises purport to be dealing with what they regard as realities. If such an exercise is not continually undertaken theology will operate in a cultural ghetto quite cut off from most of those in Western cultures who have good grounds for thinking that science describes what is going on in the processes of the world at all levels. The turbulent history of the relation of science and theology bears witness to the impossibility of theology seeking a peaceful haven, protected from the science of its times, if it is going to be believable. Indeed, theology has been most creative and long-lasting when it has responded most positively to the challenges of its times, as when the Cappadocian Fathers used Greek philosophy to express the categories of Christian theology and when St Thomas Aquinas faced up to and triumphantly utilized the then overwhelming intellectual resources of Aristotelianism to reshape that same theology into a form that endured for centuries. It is in this spirit that we set out on the journey to attempt to shape a contemporary expression of the Christian experience of God in terms – metaphors, models, analogies and symbols – that might be believable and usable by a 'Western' humanity now deeply and irreversibly, and quite properly, influenced by the sciences.

2 ATTITUDES TO SCIENCE AND THEOLOGY

Before going further it is worth reflecting a little on the respective standings of both the scientific and theological enterprises in our Western societies today. Let us take science first.

The standing of science has changed abruptly in the 1970s and 1980s from a general glow of public approval, which was translated politically into generous provision for scientific research, through an increasing hesitation about the long-term social value of science, to a current downright suspicion on the part of many ordinary citizens, who nevertheless continue to reap its benefits in terms of the ease, health and longevity of their lives. This tarnishing of the image of science can be traced back to a succession of public disasters generated by a scientifically-based technology – the thalidomide tragedies, oil spills (of which the *Torrey Canyon* and *Amoco Cadiz* were to prove to be only the first of a long line), acid rain, and the nuclear industry accidents at Long Island and Chernobyl, to mention only a few of the more publicized. Everyone can give their own accounts of more local and personal incidents in which it has seemed that the previously worshipped idol of science, and its offspring, technology, were proving to have feet of clay. The tendency of science to imperiousness in our intellectual and cultural life has been dubbed 'scientism' – the attitude that the *only* kind of reliable knowledge is that provided by science, coupled with a conviction that all our personal and social problems are 'soluble' by enough science. Many popularizers of science – more rarely those most engaged at the frontiers of scientific investigation of the mysteries of the natural world – appear, implicitly at least, to acquiesce in such 'scientistic' attitudes.

These and many other factors have led to a recent increase in anti-scientific attitudes. These are actually not new in Western cultures, for there has been quite a long history of profound dissatisfaction with purported scientific 'explanations' that do not answer the questions human beings actually ask, despite the acknowledgement of many committed scientists that science could not answer them. The Australian philosopher, John Passmore, has studied the development of both scientistic and anti-scientific attitudes with some care. He has some scathing comments on, for example, that presumed pecking order in the prestige of scientists which puts mathematical physicists, dealing with the most abstract entities, at the top (the 'aristoscientists'), followed by those who work with entities (such as molecules and genes) that are a little less abstract to the non-scientist, down to those concerned with obviously accessible phenomena like butterflies and the weather, and finishing with those concerned with people – anthropologists and sociologists, only doubtfully admitted into the club at all. Passmore judged that this hierarchical view generated attitudes of mind that are socially dangerous, even affirming, not irrelevantly to our present themes, that 'the resemblance between the aristoscientist and the mediaeval theologian daily becomes more striking.'[8]

Such attitudes have understandably provoked anti-scientific attitudes. Nevertheless Passmore concludes that

> many of the major charges which have been brought against science cannot be sustained ... I have not pretended that all is for the best in the best of all possible worlds, or denied that science has encouraged, even when it did not generate, attitudes of mind which can have adverse consequences. We are all of us, I think, coming to recognize that fact, scientists along with the rest. Science needed an injection of humility, and has had it ... When it touches on human affairs, science is no longer accorded automatic respect.[9]

Yet in spite of all this scepticism about its social value and antipathy to excessively arrogant claims on its behalf, science still seems to most people, both intellectuals and others, to be the paradigm of what constitutes reliable knowledge. For allowing, as it does, prediction and control in many simple and complex circumstances involving the natural world, what it refers to is seen by most people simply to be 'real' – they cannot afford to ignore it in their dealings with nature. Such a 'naive realism' regards scientific concepts, theories and mechanisms as literal descriptions of the natural world. In this vein Henry Harris, a practising medical scientist, could stress that, although it is true that in physics Einstein's equations superseded those of Newton, yet this

> is no argument at all for the notion that all scientific conclusions are similarly bound eventually to be displaced. I do not believe that it will ever be shown that the blood of animals does not circulate; that anthrax is not caused by a bacterium; that proteins are not chains of amino acids. Human beings may indeed make mistakes, but I see no merit in the idea that they can make nothing but mistakes.[10]

Hence it is not surprising – such is the influence of the media and of some exceptionally good popular presentations of science on television in recent years – that scientific accounts of the world are taken as literally descriptive and as constituting for most people the framework, or stage, of the 'reality' in which they believe their lives to be set and enacted. However, this constitutes a naive philosophy of science and we need to examine the relation between scientific knowledge and the 'reality' it purports to describe. Therefore, before embarking on an inquiry into a believable theology for a scientific age, we must first establish what kind of knowing and what kind of knowledge of 'reality' actually prevails in the sciences. As a working definition, we shall take 'reality' to mean that to which we find we cannot avoid relating in our experiments and experience.

Now the world described by some parts of modern physics, to take just one area, is a very strange one indeed, far removed from any world to which it is possible to extrapolate from our senses, including as it does apparently obscure entities such as electron holes, black holes, gravitational waves, anti-matter, and so on. So we shall have to consider to what it is that scientific terms actually refer. Do they depict reality? This question will be taken up later, in discussing science and theology today (p. 11).

Let us turn now to theology. Almost the only usage of the word 'theology' with which the general public is now familiar is that of politicians who employ it to refer pejoratively to the views of their opponents, thereby intending to characterize them as 'theoretical', 'abstract', 'utopian', 'unrealistic' – all thought to be highly undesirable features – while at the same time signalling that their own opinions and policies are 'realistic', 'practical' and, of course, 'relevant'. Even within the membership of the Christian churches, 'theology' is frequently regarded as the activity of intellectuals of doubtful Christian commitment, pontificating from remote academic ivory towers and isolated from the realities and tensions of the religious experience of 'ordinary' believers living in the 'real world'. This gap between the pew and the study has been much in evidence in recent years in relation to a number of controversies, at least in England, surrounding the doctrines of the incarnation and resurrection. The gulf shows no signs of narrowing, such is the general appallingly low standard of lay adult education in the churches. Yet the content of what 'ordinary' Christians believe is inevitably 'theology', even when it is relatively uninformed. One of the principal causes of the weakness of the churches' mission to Western humanity must be their failure to find a convincing way of expressing their beliefs, that is, of having a theology which is capable of coping with the contemporary cultural and intellectual situation and of out-thinking it. But the unfortunate theologian has to fight on at least one other front – that of his fellow scholars and intellectuals. For in spite of the universality of religious experience amongst human beings,[11] the academic study of the philosophy, history and tradition of such experiences – namely, theology – is still looked at askance by the Western intellectual world, despite massive attempts by many Christian theologians to be in genuine dialogue with new knowledge and social developments.

Furthermore, within theology itself there has been a crisis of authority in the Christian religion which will just as surely overtake other religions as critical education becomes more widespread. The effects of the Enlightenment are, quite rightly, irreversible, and no sacred writings and no sacred tradition can ever again be self-authenticating in the sense of itself validating its own claims to truth. Some fulcrum, some point of leverage, of assessment from outside the written sacred word or the sacred tradition, is needed to assess the truth of their affirmations and the reality of that to which the adherent of a religion commits him- or herself. So theistic religions have to face sharp questions today: Is talk about God valid? Do theological terms refer to reality? These and related questions are of the same kind as those generated about the status of theoretical terms and theories in science and, in a parallel manner, press us into making an assessment of the nature of religious language and its ability, if any, to depict reality. For both science and theology have only the resources of human language to explicate the significance of their experiments and experience. It is this shared necessity that we must now explore a little further in the conviction that examination of the relation between the languages of, and so the status of assertions in, science and theology is no mere 'academic' exercise, but a vital component in the clarification of their relationship. Only so can there be established that *modus vivendi* between science and theology, the lack of which is already proving so debilitating to the moral and spiritual health of late twentieth-century humanity.

3 SCIENCE AND THEOLOGY TODAY: A CRITICAL-REALIST PERSPECTIVE

There have been a variety of philosophies of science in the twentieth century, ranging from the widespread and popular naive realism already mentioned, which was inherited from the last century and was rapidly discredited by the revolutions in physics in the first few decades of this; through instrumentalism and decades dominated by positivism; to a variety of views in the last decade which range from a socially-contextualized view of scientific knowledge through non-sociological but anti-realist positions to the critical realism which is the view espoused here. It is moreover, I believe, also the implicit, though often not articulated, working philosophy of practising scientists who aim to depict reality but know only too well their fallibility in doing so. The arguments for critical realism as a valid and coherent philosophy of science have been widely rehearsed elsewhere.[12] All I propose to do here is to summarize this view, without any attempt at a detailed justification.

This is less easy than might at first appear, for there are many forms of 'realism' concerning science which are all non-naive and so could be described as 'critical' or, at least, as 'qualified'. For, as has been justly observed, 'Like the Equal Rights Movement, scientific realism is a majority position whose advocates are so divided as to appear a minority.'[13] However, the fine distinctions between different forms of non-naive scientific realism (meaning realism with respect to scientific knowledge) are less important for the purposes of our present exercise than its principal, general stance which distinguishes it from earlier, other philosophies of science of this century and also from very socially-contextualized interpretations of the content of science as an almost purely social construct. In spite of the variety of adjectives that may qualify 'realism' as a philosophy of science, there is a common core which I shall, in company with others, denote as 'critical realism'. The position may be summarized thus, in the words of J. Leplin, 'What realists do share in common are the convictions that scientific change is, on balance, progressive and that science makes possible knowledge of the world beyond its accessible, empirical manifestations.'[14] It is aiming to depict reality. For the basic claim made by such a critical scientific realism is that it is the long-term success of a scientific theory that warrants the belief that 'something like the entities and structure postulated by the theory actually exists.'[15] A formidable case for such a critical scientific realism as 'a quite limited claim that purports to explain why certain ways of proceeding in science have worked out as well as they (contingently) have'[16] can, in my view, be mounted, based on the histories of, for example, geology, cell biology and chemistry. During the last two centuries, these sciences have progressively and continuously discovered hidden structures in the entities of the natural world that account causally for observed phenomena.

Critical realism recognizes that it is still only the *aim* of science to depict reality and that this allows gradations in acceptance of the 'truth' of scientific theories. It is a 'critical' realism about entities, structures and processes which figure in scientific theories (the 'terms' of the theories), rather than about theories as such. For the 'reality' of what theories describe is more problematic, since they are concerned principally with the relations between its constitutive terms – and such relations are an aspect of the causal nexus which itself serves to characterize those terms and thereby to justify that reference to them which is the basis of any attribution of reality to them. Only gradually does confidence in theories (and models, see below) increase, as a result of success in explanation, eventually to the point where the entities, structures and processes referred to in them are ascribed some degree of reality. Critical realism recognizes that it is the aim of science to depict reality as best it may – and since this can be only an aim, the critical realist has to accept that this purpose may well be achieved by scientists with but varying degrees of success. So such a critical realism might more correctly be regarded as a programme for the natural sciences, and the extent to which the aim is achieved should be regarded as open to assessment in any particular case. It must never be forgotten that the realism is always qualified as 'critical' since the language of science is, as we shall shortly see, fundamentally metaphorical and revisable, while nevertheless referring.

This last remark reminds us that this position of critical realism as regards the status of scientific propositions inevitably involves some theory of reference.[17] At the very least, what is required is a 'causal' theory of reference to the effect that the referent of a term in a theory is 'that which causes' particular effects or phenomena, or 'that magnitude responsible for the effect or effects' which the experimentalist observes.[18] The new postulated 'particles', 'electrons', say, in J. J. Thomson's Cavendish Laboratory cathode ray tube experiment, were 'that which caused' the spot of light to appear at the end of the tube and to be deflected by electric and magnetic fields. It was, say, the double helical structure of the DNA molecule in M. H. F. Wilkins's X-ray diffraction experiments on DNA fibres that caused the diffraction pattern to have its characteristic diagonal cross form.

Often, a historical sequence can be traced in the use of a theoretical term back to the terminus of a historical-causal chain, the original act of introducing the term into the language, its 'baptism' or dubbing. For the whole process of referring to scientifically postulated entities, structures and processes is often both social and historical, depending on an unbroken history of reference in a continuous linguistic community that stretches back to the initiating experiment or theorizing in which the entities, etc., were first dubbed or, as it is often said, 'discovered'. Such a continuity of reference is entirely consistent with changes in the concepts concerning that which is referred to, as, for example, when the beams of 'electrons', up to this point regarded as particles, gave rise to a diffraction pattern on being passed through a crystal of nickel, and so were then seen also to partake of wavelike properties. In such cases the theory of reference on which a critical realism rests will include an overt social perspective, for this enhances our understanding of the way in which the reality of a referent persists through change in theory and is gradually established in a community by a critical winnowing process. The basic essential for such social reference is adequately provided by the 'causal' links in each experiment – the postulate that there *is* a cause of the phenomena observed, that there is a 'that which causes' the observed effects. Thus it is that science can often be confident of the realities to which its theories refer, but accepting that its language and models concerning these realities are always revisable and subject to change.

It is in this context that we have to be reminded of the use of models and metaphor in science. In general, 'an object or state of affairs is a model when it is viewed in terms of its resemblance, real or hypothetical, to some other object or state of affairs.'[19] Or, with particular reference to science, 'a model in science is a systematic analogy postulated between a phenomenon whose laws are already known and the one under investigation.'[20] Models, which need not be linguistic at all, and metaphors, which are strictly speaking figures of speech, are closely linked, for metaphors arise when we speak on the basis of models.[21] The use of models is fundamental to any developing science and has been widely investigated. The deeply and irrevocably metaphorical character of scientific language does not detract from the aim of such language to refer to realities. Moreover, recognition of the metaphorical nature of scientific language entails an acceptance of its revisability in seeking to explore a world only partially and imperfectly understood – and whose ultimate reality is bound to be elusive since we ourselves are structures in the selfsame world we study.

We have seen that the status of models in science covers the spectrum from naive realism via positivism and instrumentalism to a critical realism. Theology also employs models that may be similarly classified. I urge that a critical realism is also the most appropriate and adequate philosophy concerning religious language and theological propositions.[22] Critical realism in theology would maintain that theological concepts and models should be regarded as partial and inadequate, but necessary and, indeed, the only ways of referring to the reality that is named as 'God' and to God's relation with humanity. Metaphor obviously plays an even wider role in religious language than in scientific. Thus God is variously described, just to take the Judeo-Christian tradition, as Father, King, Judge, etc.; in that same tradition, Jesus is described as the Anointed (Christ), Son of God, Second Adam, the Good Shepherd, etc.; and the third *persona* of the Trinity as Holy Spirit, Paraclete (Advocate, Comforter).

One major difference between the way models are deployed in science and theology is that in the latter models have a strong affective function evoking moral and spiritual response. However, the models stir the will and emotions because of their implied cognitive reference to that which makes demands on our wills and evokes our emotions. But how can such an intuition cope with the philosophical pressure to show how theological propositions actually *refer*, that theological models depict reality?

We have to distinguish between referring to God and describing him; this is crucial to a critical-realist stance in theology. It is at this juncture that, in all religions, *negative* theology and *positive*, affirmative theology meet. The former (the *via negativa*) recognizes that, having referred to God, whatever we say will be fallible and revisable and *ex hypothesi* inadequate; and sometimes goes so far as to say that nothing can positively be said about God. However, this too easily becomes a slippery slope to atheism, so positive theology (the *via positiva*) affirms that to say nothing about God is more misleading than to say something – and that then we have to speak in metaphors. The metaphors of theological models that explicate religious experience can refer to and can depict reality without at the same time being naively and unrevisably descriptive, and they share this character with scientific models of the natural world. We may reasonably hope to speak realistically of God through revisable metaphor and model.

Fortunately there certainly have been, and still are, individuals and communities who affirm they have experienced God. Moreover, in theology, as is in science with respect to its own focus of inquiry, one can have grounds for affirming that 'God' is 'that which is causing, or has caused, this particular experience now (or in the past) in me (or in others)'. Since we wish to avoid describing 'God' as an entity within the causal nexus (not even as the 'First Cause'), and since we shall eventually be recognizing that 'God' is at least personal in some sense, we would be wiser to say that God is 'the One who is encountered in this particular experience now (or in the past) in me (or in others)'. How, in theology, 'that which, the One who, is encountered' in any particular experience is to be identified with what the tradition has named as 'God' is by inferring to the best explanation by application of the criteria of reasonableness that are used generally to assess ideas and, in particular, in appraising scientific models and theories – namely, fit with the data, internal coherence, comprehensiveness, fruitfulness and general cogency.[23]

This kind of critical theological realism takes as central the past and present religious experience of one's own and of others, so that there is also a continuous community and interpretative tradition, in comparison and in contrast with which one's own experience can be both enriched and checked. In that community and tradition, the seminal, initiating experiences of particular individuals, small groups of individuals, and sometimes even whole communities, when God was encountered, will be recalled, especially in liturgical contexts. Using our previous terminology, we would have to say that in the initiating, 'dubbing' experiences, reference was being made to 'God' and since then the community has continuously provided by recapitulation links of referential usage in and through repeated experiences of the same kind. This process enables us today to refer to that which the initiators referred to, even though we may well have revised the models and metaphors which we use to refer to the same reality, namely God. Not all such claimed experiences of God will be perpetuated in a community, but some over the centuries become widely available as a resource and come to enrich the lives of others in the community who have not participated directly in the original seminal experience. Some even become what in Christianity is called 'catholic' in the classical Vincentian sense of what has been believed everywhere, always and by all – although, formulated as propositions, the number that meet such exacting criteria is inevitably small.

This approach to theology recognizes that both the 'positive' way, mediated through the world and the revelation transmitted by the community, and the direct, 'negative' way of contemplation and silence, are ways to the reality that is 'God'. The language used eventually to articulate the 'positive' way can be said to depict the reality of God but not in any unrevisable fashion. It has to allow what the 'negative way' stresses, namely, our incapacity ever to express in human language the nature of that ultimate Being who is called 'God'. It is the aim of theology to tell as true a story as possible. Like science, it too must allow gradations in the degree of acceptance of belief in the 'truth' of theological propositions and that there is a hierarchy of truths – some more focal and central (and defensible) than others. The whole theological enterprise has often been criticized because it has been said to have no way comparable in rigour to that of science in the sifting and testing of its 'data', in this case the content of religious experience and tradition and the scriptures that preserve some of them. However, some philosophers of religion have in fact been able to mount what seems to me to be an effective defence of the warranty of religious belief as expressed theologically.[24] For theology, like science, also attempts to make inferences to the best explanation – or, rather, it *should* be attempting to do so. In order to do this it should use the criteria of reasonableness already mentioned, for these are criteria which at least have the potentiality of leading to an inter-subjective consensus. Some signs that this is not an entirely forlorn hope are provided by the changes that were initiated in the Roman Catholic Church by Vatican II, with its moves towards a greater collegiality in its deliberations, so that we might hope that the constituency of the *sensus fidelium* will eventually be wider than its current hierarchical concentration; and by the development during this century of the World Council of (non-Roman) Churches, which has generated the remarkable Lima document on *Baptism, the Eucharist and the Ministry*, the fruits of a convergence unthinkable even a few decades ago. Furthermore, dialogue between the world's major religions is only just beginning as movements of population have brought them into closer contact in free societies. In all this it must be remembered that consensus is, of course, not a reason for believing a theological statement to be depicting reality: that can come only from successful application of the criteria of reasonableness which warrant inferences to the best explanation. But at least parallels to inter-subjectivity in the scientific and religious communities seem to be emerging with regard to their respective models.

The need now is for theology to develop the application of its criteria of reasonableness in a community in which no authority would be automatic (for example, of the form 'the Church says', 'the Bible says', etc.) but would have to be authenticated inter-subjectively to the point of consensus by inference to the best explanation. This needs to be combined with an openness to development as human knowledge expands and experience is further enriched. When I urge this kind of critically realist aim and programme on Christians, and indeed on the adherents of all religions, I cannot help feeling a little like William Temple who is reputed to have said: 'I pray daily for Christ's one holy, catholic and apostolic Church – and that it may yet come into existence.'[25] That could also be said of the present situation of a critical-realist theology. It has broadly the same intentions as that described by Hans Kung[26] as 'truthful', 'free', 'critical' and 'ecumenical' (both inwardly among the churches and outwardly towards other religions, ideologies and the sciences) – a theology which deals with and interprets the realities of all that constitutes the world, especially human beings and our own inner selves.[27]

There is no hope of obtaining an inter-subjective consensus, even within Christianity, on the basis of an appeal to authority, since there have been, and still are, classical, and entrenched, disagreements between the Protestant, Anglican, Orthodox and Roman Catholic churches about the mode, scope and location of authority for the Christian believer – and no independent way of adjudicating between these positions, if the appeal is only to 'authority'. More importantly for the future of Christianity, an appeal to the 'authority' favoured by any one of these groups of churches cannot hope, in a post-Enlightenment culture, to foster any conviction on the part of even sympathetic inquirers into the truth of Christian affirmations.[28] For any theology to be believable it will have to satisfy the criteria of reasonableness that lead us to infer the best explanation of the broader features of the natural world ('natural theology', traditionally), and of what men and women believe to be their experiences of 'God'. Truths that are claimed to be revealed or are the promulgations of ecclesiastical authority cannot avoid running the gauntlet of these criteria of reasonableness, for they cannot be at the same time both self-warranting and convincing. Any belief system resulting from such a sifting process would inevitably involve a 'hierarchy of truths'; that is, it would explicitly recognize that some beliefs were integral to Christian identity, others less so, and yet others held simply to be not inconsistent with the core of belief but mainly of devotional value for those brought up in certain church traditions.

In spite of what the 'cultured despisers' of Christianity might say, there are 'data' available to the theological enterprise, just as there are to the scientific. These latter are constituted by the broad features of the entities, structures and processes that science is demonstrating as characteristic of the natural world.[29] For theology, the 'data' are constituted by the well-winnowed traditions of the major world religions, among them Christianity which provides our principal source in the West of tested wisdom about how to refer to that which is encountered in those experiences initially dubbed as experiences of God. As John Bowker has put it: 'Religions are a consequence of successive generations testing, correcting, confirming, extending, changing, the accumulating wisdoms of experience.'[30] In this book we are attempting to reflect on some of the principal aspects of the 'accumulating wisdom' of the Christian religion in the light of and in relation to the realities in the world that are referred to and depicted in the natural sciences.

4 THE RELATION BETWEEN SCIENCE AND THEOLOGY

From a critical-realist perspective both science and theology are engaging with realities that may be referred to and pointed at, but which are both beyond the range of any completely literal description. Both employ metaphorical language and describe reality in terms of models, which may eventually be combined into higher conceptual schemes (theories or doctrines). Within such a perspective, it is therefore entirely appropriate to ask how the respective claimed cognitive contents of science and theology might, or should be, related.

Before doing so, however, it is pertinent to point out that this way of asking the question about the relationship between science and theology has itself already been sharpened and made more explicit by the adoption of a critical-realist standpoint. For example, one might adopt the point of view of what is often called the 'strong' programme in the sociology of scientific knowledge, whereby the actual content of scientific cognitive claims is regarded as predominantly socially conditioned.[31] Those having this view would adopt *a fortiori* a similar view of the cognitive claims of theology and then the exercise of relating science and theology would be reduced to that of relating two ideologies and so would itself become a purely sociological inquiry or exercise in the history of ideas. No cognitive claims of either science or theology would be countenanced and the whole question of the relation of science and theology, and even more so that of science and religion, would have been relativized into non-existence. To adopt a critical-realist view of science and of theology is to reject this position, and I think there are good grounds for doing so.[32] However, this does not mean to say that at any one stage in their respective histories the cognitive claims of science and theology are so insulated from society that the cluster of metaphors, models, theories and doctrines that they employ are a 'truth' determined only by 'reality'. That would be entirely inconsistent with the known histories of the two disciplines. Nevertheless, I think it to be the case in science and, I would urge, it *should* be the case also for theology, that any particular state of the

discipline can be shown to have been subjected to a critical winnowing process by application of the criteria of reasonableness I have
described.

I mention the 'strong programme' in the sociology of scientific
knowledge as a somewhat extreme example, inconsistent as it is
with the experience of practising scientists and religious believers,
because it illustrates that any individual's view of the relation of
science and theology is closely dependent on his or her view of their
epistemology and of the ontological status of that to which they
respectively refer. I have delineated elsewhere[33] at least eight putative relations between science and theology, apart from the social
dimension. Thus science and theology may be regarded as non-
interacting approaches to reality; as constituting two different
language systems; as generated by quite different attitudes; as each
subservient to its own 'object' of study and defined only in relation
to it ('nature' for science and 'God' for theology). As R. J. Russell[34]
has pointed out, these positions may be differentiated with respect
to four 'dimensions' of the science–theology relationship, namely:
approaches, languages, attitudes and *objects*. In each of these four
'dimensions', the relation between science and theology can be
construed as either positive and reconciling and so as mutually
interacting, or as negative and non-interacting. This makes a total
of eight ($=4\times2$) different, conceivable relationships between science and theology. It is the first of the four 'positive' relationships
which is the outcome of a critical-realist philosophy of both science
and theology – namely, that *science and theology are seen as
interacting approaches to reality*. To this we will revert below, but
for the moment it is worth pursuing a little further this inquiry into
the general character of the relationships between science and
theology.

In addition to these eight possible relationships, support has been
given by some authors to seeing science and theology as referring to
two distinct 'realms': for example, the natural/supernatural; the
spatio-temporal/eternal; the order of nature/the realm of faith; the
physical-and-biological/mind-and-spirit; and so on. This view, which
is contrary to that adopted here, takes a negative non-interacting
position with respect to all four 'dimensions'.

Instead of allowing only two alternatives in each of the four
'dimensions' (approaches, languages, attitudes and objects) of the
possible relationship between science and theology, it might be
better, Russell has suggested,[35] to envisage a continuum of possi-

bilities in each 'dimension', now conceived as more like axes in a four-dimensional space. The extrema of the axes would have to be designated as the most positive and the most negative positions with respect to each dimension ('positive' in the sense of 'consonant and reconciling'; 'negative' in the sense of 'non-interacting'). Various constellations of perspectives on the relation between science and theology would then occupy different locations in this four-dimensional 'space'. This model serves, at least, to emphasize the richness and complexity of the possibilities of interaction between two disciplines whose epistemologies are themselves subject to such differing interpretations.

I have chosen to steer a path based on a critical-realist appraisal of both science and theology and this brings us back to our earlier question: how are the claimed cognitive contents of science and theology to be related? Might it not be simply that 'theology and science deal for the most part with different domains of the same reality',[36] so that, as the same author continues, 'Science has no access to God in its explanations; theology has nothing to say about the specifics of the natural world.' However, to say the least, the history of theology shows that its development is intimately related to the understanding of the natural, including the human, world that has prevailed at different periods.[37] More pertinently to the present context, since the aim of a critical-realist theology is to articulate intellectually and to formulate, by means of metaphor and model, experiences of God, then it behooves such a theology to take seriously the critical-realist perspective of the sciences on the natural, including the human, world. For on that theology's own presuppositions, God himself has given the world the kind of being it has and it must be in some respects, to be ascertained, revelatory of God's nature and purposes. So theology should seek to be at least consonant with scientific perspectives on the natural world.

Correspondingly, the sciences should not be surprised if their perspectives are seen to be partial and incomplete and to raise questions not answerable from within their own purview and by their own methods, since there are other realities – there is a Reality – to be taken into account which is not discernible by the sciences as such. A critical-realist science and theology cannot but regard themselves as mutually interacting approaches to reality. But we need to examine further the relations between the 'realities' to which each refers. This is the principal objective of the present work.

With an increasing richness and articulation of its various levels, the expansion of our scientific knowledge of the natural world has more and more shown it to consist of a hierarchy of systems in levels of organization, each successive member of which is a whole constituted of parts, often preceding it historically in the series. As we shall see in chapter 2,[38] the science pertinent to each level may well develop non-reducible concepts of its own appropriate and relevant to the specific behaviours, relations and properties that can be seen only at that level. This has the important consequence *inter alia* that we have no basis for any favoured attribution of 'reality' to the different levels in the hierarchy of complexity. Knowledge of each level, or (perhaps better), along each 'vector' of inquiry, has to be regarded as a kind of slice through the totality of reality.

Now human beings are natural parts of the universe and among their commonly reported experiences are those of reaching out to God and of God coming towards them: theology is the intellectual analysis of such experiences in which this traffic is experienced as being in both directions between God and humanity. When human beings are thus experiencing the presence and activity of God, whether or not engaged in explicitly 'religious' and worshipping activities, they are operating at a level in, or 'vector' of, the hierarchy of complexity that is more integrative than any of the levels or 'vectors' studied by the individual natural, human and social sciences. In such human 'religious' activities, whole persons believe themselves to be interacting with each other, with the natural world, and with the transcendent, yet immanent, Creator as the source of all that is – the One who gives them and the world meaning and significance. No higher level or more significant 'vector' of integrated relationships in the hierarchy of the natural could be claimed or envisaged. Theology, we have seen, is about the requisite conceptual schemes (doctrines) and models and associated metaphors that articulate the content of these claimed experiences of God of both the individual and of a historical community.

There appear to be two ways in which this fundamental, integrative, role of theology, the study of humanity-nature-God, might be expressed – ways that correspond to the two modalities of God's relation to all-that-is (both humanity and nature), namely the transcendent and the immanent.[39] If one emphasizes the transcendence of God, the activity and language of the theological enterprise can be regarded as reflecting on that specifically and uniquely human activity, the 'religious', which involves nature, humanity and God in its total integrating purview. This activity then stands at the summit of conceivable integrative complexity and wholeness (and, note, nearest to the level of the human and personal). From this perspective, theology, albeit no longer the medieval 'queen of the sciences', might still possibly be accorded the position of a constitutional monarch. This may indeed be the proper placement for theology when we consider ultimate ontological relationships, the relation of the Being of God to all other derived being.

But when we contemplate God's activity in the world, and so God's Becoming, rather than God's ultimate Being, we also (as we shall see later) have to predicate immanence of God as Creator and to emphasize God's presence to, in, with, under and through all natural events. Thus it may well be that theology should be regarded as an exploration of the ultimate meaning of all levels[40] – that is, as an attempt at interpreting the significance of the various levels of natural reality in the total scheme of things. Any particular levels would be viewed in relation to God's continuous creative activity at all levels through all space and time. We encounter here that difficult requirement of a fusion of the concepts of transcendence and immanence, in this instance, in relation to the role of theology and its relation to science, which will lead us at the end of Part II to speak rather of 'transcendence-in-immanence' and of the 'immanence-of-the-transcendent' to articulate our understanding both of the human person[41] and of God's relation to the world.[42]

All of this implies that, before proceeding with further theological reflection, we must look carefully at the broad characteristics and features of the entities, structures and processes of the world that the sciences are postulating as the currently best explanations of their observations.

PART I

Natural Being and Becoming

CHAPTER 1

Introduction

It has become a commonplace to observe that the last three centuries have witnessed an unparalleled transformation in the way human beings have come to regard the natural world and their relation to it; yet from time to time we need to be reminded of this. One needs only, say, in the English-speaking world, to reread a play of Shakespeare to be reminded of the enormous gulf that separates us from a pre-scientific culture in terms of what it believes is actually in the world and is actually going on in it. As historians such as Herbert Butterfield have amply demonstrated, the advent of the scientific culture 'outshines everything since the rise of Christianity and reduces the Renaissance and Reformation to the rank of mere episodes, mere internal displacements, within the system of mediaeval Christendom.'[1]

Even as a purely social phenomenon, any community of religious believers, in order to communicate at all with their contemporaries, would have to take account of this fundamental displacement, in what Butterfield called human 'habitual mental operations even in the conduct of the non-material sciences'.[2] More significantly, this shift in human 'habitual mental operations' constitutes a challenge to the conceptual schemes whereby the principal theistic religions organize their reflections on their characteristic experiences, that is, their experiences of God. This challenge is particularly cogent for Christianity, which takes with utmost seriousness the reality and nature of the natural world, both because of its doctrine of creation, which it basically shares with Judaism and Islam, but more particularly because of its belief that the Creator God was present in and was manifested through an historical human person, himself part of nature and human history. So the now scientifically observed and understood character of the natural world, including humanity, is today of immense *theological* significance. For what nature is like, what God is like, indeed whether or not God exists, have become interlocked questions that cannot be considered in isolation – in

spite of the tendency of much contemporary theologizing nevertheless to do just this.

However, necessary though the attempt is to work out the relations between nature, humanity and God in the light of the staggeringly new understanding of the world afforded by the natural,
human and social sciences, it is also necessary to enter a word of
caution. For, as has often been remarked, a theology which marries
the science of today is liable to find itself a widow tomorrow, such is
the rapidity with which science changes. There is wisdom in this
charge, but as we have seen, H. Harris has sharply affirmed that
because some, indeed many, scientific ideas become obsolete and
are superseded, this 'is no argument at all for the notion that all
scientific conclusions are similarly bound to be displaced . . . Human
beings may indeed make mistakes, but I see no merit in the idea that
they make nothing but mistakes.'[3]

As I hope became clear in making the case for a critical-realist
view of science, there are solid grounds in many wide areas of the
natural sciences for believing that these sciences are giving us a
reasonably assured account of what the natural world is like and
what has been going on in it. We have to recognize that scientific
language is metaphorical but is none the worse for that in its
attempt to depict reality, and that it does increasingly succeed in
referring to aspects of natural reality, as evidenced by its success in
prediction and control. Even so, the caveat entered concerning the
ephemeral nature of many currently countenanced scientific proposals is a proper one. It warns us that it should be only with the
best-established general features of the scientific accounts of the
world that we should be concerned in our reflections on the relation
of nature, humanity and God.

The rest of Part I will be devoted to delineating certain features of
the accounts of the world afforded by a range of sciences for
consideration later as we come to attempt a formulation of what
might constitute a contemporary and defensible understanding of
nature, humanity and God. Inevitably, the discussion will take place
at a level of generalization which it will be impossible to substantiate in a work of this compass. I can but refer the reader to some of
the works listed in the notes and assure him or her that the broad
features and characteristics of the world of science I attempt to
collate are ones which seem to be widely recognized by authors of
many different philosophical positions and religious beliefs.

CHAPTER 2

What's There?

We are accustomed to looking at the world around us and attempting to identify its furniture. We ask 'What's there in the world? Of what is the world made up? In what does the world consist?' In raising such questions we inevitably reveal a conception of the world in which, as it were, objects are inserted into space at a particular time and all that human beings need to do is to look around and see what 'is there', even though such a looking at the world may now involve the experimentally and theoretically sophisticated methods of the sciences. For a very wide range of the sciences – from chemistry, concerned with the atomic and molecular, to ecology, concerned with ecosystems – this attempt to discern the entities, structures, and processes in the world has been remarkably successful. The presupposition that such questions in such a form may be addressed, as it were, to the world turns out to be not only legitimate but even capable of being answered through experimental science combined with human ratiocination.

1 SPACE, TIME, MATTER AND ENERGY

In the Newtonian perspective, which dominated the mind of the West for two and a half centuries – and still prevails in the general intellectual climate since it corresponds so well with intuitions derived from our senses – the stuff of the world, *matter*, possesses *energy*, and is located in *space* at a particular *time*. Even though by the end of the nineteenth century there had been a profound enrichment and enlargement of our understanding of both matter and energy, these two concepts were still quite distinct and absolute space and time still provided the basic framework in which they were deemed to exist. The concepts of space, time, matter and energy continued to appear to be 'given', self-evident features of the world, *a priori* concepts essential to our thinking. Although, as we shall see, this understanding has been fundamentally overthrown in modern physics, the fact is that it still provides the basic conceptual framework for most of the sciences from the molecular to the ecological. But though the intuitions derived from our sense experience are still useful in these ranges, they cease to be so in the range of the very small, the very large, and the very fast – that is at the sub-atomic particle level, at the cosmological level and for anything moving at speeds close to that of light. The relation between these different ranges and regimes of phenomena is well understood. It may be roughly characterized by the assertion that the understandings of space, time, matter and energy of the 'classical' perspective turn out to be approximations (in most of the sciences concerned with the not very small, not very large and not very fast) of more subtle, and often unpicturable, concepts and entities which are related in ways that were unthinkable before the first few decades of this century. For during that period relativity theory, in its special and general forms, and, even more iconoclastically, quantum theory, together caused a complete revolution in human understanding of the physical world, the consequences of which are still being absorbed into philosophy – and hardly yet into theology.

In Newtonian physics *space* was held to be uniform and three-dimensional, obeying the geometrical laws of Euclid. It was physically inert, infinite in extent, continuous and infinitely divisible. For Newton it had an absoluteness which he thought of as God-given. These premises were overthrown by Einstein, with the possible exception of its infinity and infinite divisibility. Certainly the commonsense notion of juxtaposition cannot be understood coherently when absolute simultaneity is also denied, as it was by Einstein. Indeed, our intuitively separate concepts of space and time become inextricably interwoven and mutually defined in relativity theory, now completely accepted in modern physics. Not only do the space measurements in one system determined by an observer moving relative to it depend on time differences, but also *mutatis mutandis* the time measurements made by such an observer on the same system involve space measurements. So modern relativistic physics adds to our intuitive spatialization of time a dynamization of space.

Time was also a fundamental concept in the classical physical picture of the world – the single dimension in which instants followed each other. Like space, it too was homogeneous, independent of any objects or events 'in' it, inert, infinite, continuous. In the special theory of relativity, absolute simultaneity exists only for events occurring at the same location. Consequently the concept of a great three-dimensional 'now', of world-wide instants, loses all physical significance. However, the succession of events which form causal chains is independent of the choice of frame of reference and, indeed, the concept of *causality* is affected by this initial theory of Einstein only to the extent that we now have to recognize that causal influences can never be transmitted through the universe at a speed greater than that of light. Although the metrical scale of time intervals (the 'dilatation of time') depends on the frame of reference, this is a distortion only from the perspective of the relative motion of the observer. In Einstein's later general theory of relativity, the concept of time is more fundamentally transformed and loses its classical features of homogeneity and uniformity (its dilatation in a gravitational field is not merely related to a particular frame of reference), and its independence of physical content.

In fact, physicists concerned with events on a cosmic scale, or with velocities significantly close to that of light, measure intervals between events in terms of a combined function, 'space-time'. Fortunately, for the greater part of the range of natural events which are the concern of most of the sciences ranging from chemistry to ecology, and much even of astronomy, these considerations do not arise and the natural intuitions we have of an actual 'now' at a particular point in space suffice adequately. However, this does not detract at all from the fundamental reassessment of our concepts of space and time that relativity theory has necessitated; they turn out to be mutually interlocking concepts and, as we shall see, not at all independent of the concepts of matter and energy.

There is another aspect of the reassessment of time that the sciences have forced upon us during the last century and a half. That we experience time as having a direction is not only a part of our psychology, it is also built into our organization as a biological system proceeding from birth to death, and this itself is, in the long run, but a manifestation of the wider irreversibility of all natural processes in the observable universe. Whether or not this experienced directionality is a necessary aspect of the concept of time, or is only a feature of our experience and therefore interpretation of it, has been much, and inconclusively, debated.

Hawking has argued[1] that storage of information in an entity must always involve the expenditure of energy and its consequential partial dissipation as heat, and always involves a net increase in disorder, and so of entropy. So our subjective sense of time (our memories are of the past) runs parallel with the thermodynamic arrow of time, the net increase of disorder (entropy) in all natural processes. He reports calculations that suggest that this increase in disorder (the thermodynamic arrow of time) points in the same direction as the cosmological arrow of time not only in an expanding universe such as ours appears to be, but also (and this is what had to be calculated) in the future universe, if it eventually contracts. Disorder will continue to increase during the contraction – but it is only in the expanding phase, in which we now are, that intelligent beings could exist. This well-defined thermodynamic arrow of time is in fact necessary for intelligent life to operate, since living organisms have to consume food to maintain their organization and convert it into heat, a more disordered form of energy. So, Hawking argues, the thermodynamic, psychological and cosmological arrows of time point in the same direction.

It suffices for our present purposes, namely, discernment of the meaning and significance of such intelligibility as the world yields, to stress that the direction of time in which our lives move, from birth to death, is the same on the cosmic scale as that in which physical and biological forms develop. As is well known,[2] there is very good evidence for the 'hot, big, bang' account of cosmic history, according to which our universe has been expanding to the present time from a highly condensed, extremely hot and compacted state, of dimensions of the atomic order, for about 10–20×10^9 years. (Speculations which modify the validity of such an extrapolation over the first 'instants' of this supposed range of physical time will be discussed later.) So there appears to be a *direction in time* from the sub-nuclear to galaxies and the many forms of matter that constitute them and exist in the space between; and also, on the Earth, a direction in time towards increasing complexity and variety of biological forms up to the myriad intricacies of human society. Time, far from flowing equably and leaving everything much the same (as in the classical Newtonian perspective) is now seen from the perspective of an impressive number of the sciences (thermodynamics, cosmology, astronomy, geology, biology) to be the 'carrier or locus of innovative change'.[3] Over far longer timescales than that of any individual biological life, science now bears formidable witness that new entities, structures and processes come into being that did not previously exist; that is, there is a coming into being of that which was not, as well as changes in, and often the disappearance of, that which is.

Even before the full blossoming of quantum mechanics, with its many anti-intuitive and paradoxical insights into the nature of matter, Einstein's special theory of relativity had rendered impossible the classical notion of *matter* as something impenetrable that fills space. For the interconvertibility, initially required as a mathematical consequence of the theory, and now verified by the electricity coming from any nuclear power station, of mass and energy (the famous $E=mc^2$) also blurred the distinction between space and mass. Furthermore, if a 'particle' of matter is but a certain local configuration of space-time, as it is according to the general theory of relativity, how can it be said to 'move in' a 'space' that itself constitutes its own nature? Einstein's theory undermined the natural distinction between motion and that which moves, a distinction that seems so natural to our ordinary sense perception, and one whose obliteration was completed by subsequent developments in quantum mechanics.

Yet this intuitive, natural distinction, limited though it is by the above considerations, served well enough as the basis for a highly successful methodologically reductionist development in science until well into the twentieth century, whereby the observable structures and entities of the natural world were successively, and successfully, broken down into smaller and smaller component units – first molecules, then atoms, then protons and neutrons. The limit of attainable divisibility continually became smaller and for a long time the units so unveiled could still be conceived of as just small bits of the world – admittedly very small bits but nevertheless essentially tiny particles, easily imaginable by extrapolation downwards from our ordinary sense experience of the macroscopic world. However, as larger and larger energies had, by the nature of the case, to be deployed to penetrate deeper and deeper into the substructure of the world, the interchangeability of matter and energy required by relativity theory became more and more significant.

The other great discovery of the early decades of this century, namely that energy is quantized, that it is transmitted and absorbed in finite, irreducibly small units, had to be incorporated into the perceptions of what was being discovered, 'uncovered' rather, at these deep levels of natural reality. The 'fundamental particles' that emerged had to be thought of, paradoxically, at first as having a wave-like character as well as being particulate. This anomaly was then transcended by quantum field theory at the cost of a loss of naive picturability but with the gain of the discovery of a profounder rationality, now expressible only in the language of mathematics – the only adequate way of dealing with the 'quarks' and 'gluons' and other entities that the physicists postulate. The simple idea of their being a kind of accessible bedrock to the physical world (and so to the biological too), that could be visualized in terms of the categories used to interpret our human sense experience, has proved to be not only naive and simplistic but downright misleading. There is a genuine limitation in the ability of our minds to depict the nature of matter at this fundamental level; there is a mystery about what matter is 'in itself', for at the deepest level to which human beings can penetrate they are faced with a mode of existence describable only in terms of abstract, mathematical concepts that are the products of human ratiocination. It seems likely that this increase in abstractness and unpicturability will never stop as physicists delve deeper into matter and further and further back into the early universe, when the energies pertaining far exceed any achievable in principle on earth (so that the early universe becomes the only available 'laboratory' for such studies). Certainly the experience of science has been always that of finding new conceptual frontiers to cross as each territory yields its secrets.

In the early classical Newtonian world of physics *energy* was at first a concept whose formulation was closely interlocked with what were regarded as the basic categories of space, time and mass, this latter being linked with classical concepts of matter itself. The kinetic energy of a body in motion was proportional to the square of its velocity (change of position in space per unit time) multiplied by its mass, which was supposed to be calculable by summing a property of each of the body's components. But other forms of energy had early to be recognized, such as that possessed by a body in virtue of its location in a gravitational field with the concomitant recognition that the energy of a system could be increased by 'work' (force × distance) being done upon it. Gradually, and especially during the nineteenth century, other forms of energy came to be recognized as interchangeable with these mechanical, kinetic and gravitational forms, namely, electrical, chemical and magnetic forms of energy storage. With Einstein's equating of energy with mass it came also to be recognized that the mass of a body was actually dependent on the binding energies of its components and therefore not a simple sum of quantities characteristic of each component taken separately.

So during the twentieth century we have been witnessing a process in which the previously absolute and distinct concepts of space, time, matter and energy have come to be seen as closely and mutually interlocked with each other – so much so that even the modification of our thinking to being prepared to envisage 'what is there' as consisting of matter-energy in space-time has to be superseded by more inclusive concepts of fields and other notions no longer picturable and expressible only mathematically. Fortunately at the low energies, low velocities and small time and space scales ('low' relative to those needed to penetrate the sub-atomic world and 'small' relative to the velocity of light and to the scale of the cosmos), the classical concepts continue to be adequate to account for our experimental observations and our experience. More significantly for our present purposes, these classical concepts are broadly those operative in a wide range of the sciences – though, of course, even certain macroscopic phenomena only find their explanation in terms of quantum theory (for example, many features of computer hardware) and even relativity theory (for example, the electrical energy from nuclear power stations). However, this should not delude us into thinking that when we pursue the question 'What is there?' to its ultimately accessible limits we are going to come up with answers that are at all picturable and intelligible in terms of our 'common-sense' experience of the world. Even so, this intermediate level, if we may call it that, between the ultra-microscopic and the ultra-macroscopic still constitutes the vast bulk of the natural world and the great majority of the natural sciences concerned with investigating it. The multiple and diverse pictures and features of the natural world so provided are of immense significance for our understanding the content of its structures, entities and processes, and, needless to say, of immense significance also for human beings in interpreting their own world, which itself falls between these extremes. So let us now examine what are the general features which have been discerned in the material entities and structures to be found in the contemporary world through the intensive investigation it has undergone by the natural sciences up to our own day. The processes by which it reached the condition so discerned will be examined in chapter 3.

2 STRUCTURES AND ENTITIES

What would undoubtedly first strike any intelligent being from Mars
or any other planet – were there any such, since all the observable
planets seem to lack life, certainly in any developed form – would be
the enormous diversity in the *structures* and *entities* that exist on
our planet, especially in the millions of species of living organisms
living at present, not to mention the probably hundredfold greater
number that have existed in the past and are now extinct. Moreover,
this terrestrial diversity is, as it were, only the surface layer of an
underlying diversity of 'fundamental' particles, atoms, molecules
and the various manifestations of energy that are dispersed throughout the universe. Such a visitor could be forgiven, were he/she/it
innocent of terrestrial science, for concluding that there was no
such thing as nature-as-a-whole, that there exists only a multitude of
individual 'natures' according to place and time. Even a denizen of
this planet accustomed to the flora and fauna of a temperate zone
can still be overwhelmed by the sheer fecundity and kaleidoscopic
variety of life in more tropical climes. The briefest view of the
teeming marine life in, say, coral reefs cannot but generate a sense
of wonder at the luxurious and multiform proliferation that has
occurred on this planet alone, let alone elsewhere in the immensity
of space with its 10^9 galaxies each containing 10^8 to 10^{11} stars
(remembering that our Sun with its planetary system qualifies as one
star in these reckonings).

Such a spontaneous sense of wonder is enhanced and heightened
when this great diversity is seen through the lenses of the natural
sciences, for these explicate in increasing detail and comprehensiveness the contemporary interlocking relationships and the mutually
involved histories that characterize this daunting diversity. This
complexity comes increasingly to be seen through the natural sciences as a diversity-in-unity wherein relatively simple laws, principles and relationships weave, through their operation over periods
staggeringly long for the human imagination, the almost extrava-
gantly rich tapestry of the world we now observe. The world has a
simplicity that is sophisticated and subtle in its outworkings and
manifestations through both cosmic and, more locally, terrestrial
space and time. How this rich complexity emanates from simplicity
has been well expounded both on our television screens and in
elegant books by scientific authors of both theistic and non-theistic
persuasions – for the vista of the sciences is capable of evoking a

sense of wonder among scientists whatever their religious convictions or otherwise.[4]

This cornucopian diversity stems from the givenness of certain basic parameters, such as the speed of light, the mass and charge of the electron, certain interaction constants, Planck's constant, etc., combined with the operation of only four fundamental forces. These forces are those of gravity and electromagnetism, the effects of which are comparatively familiar to us in ordinary life in a technological society, and the less obvious, but nevertheless basic, weak and strong nuclear forces which operate within the short ranges characteristic of the atomic nucleus. Physicists have already been able to unify two of these in one mathematical description (the electromagnetic and weak nuclear forces) and there are increasing hopes of uniting with these also the strong nuclear forces in a Grand Unified Theory (GUT) – the ultimate prize being the unification of gravity with these other three forces and the bringing of all this into unity with general relativity and particle theory, into what some call TOE, a 'theory of everything'. This prize may prove to be beyond human reach but the fact that it is even sought is a significant testimony to the underlying unity beneath the complexity of the observed, and to the increasingly warranted convictions of scientists that it is and will be more and more successfully discerned, as it has been over the last few centuries.

This underlying unity has only been wrested from the diversity of visible objects by application of the most abstract powers of thinking of which the human mind is capable, not to mention the extremely sophisticated (and often large and very expensive) equipment required to penetrate the mysteries of the sub-atomic world. From the levels of the atomic through to that of biological populations and ecosystems, the corresponding sciences fortunately afford knowledge of the entities with which they deal that is much more readily picturable, even though the subtleties of what holds these entities together as units and the processes by which they change are still only fully comprehensible with the help of sophisticated mathematical concepts. So it is worth while to take, as it were, a section or slice through space-time at a contemporary instant, confident that the velocities of all observers on the planet Earth relative to each other are sufficiently far from that of light to allow one to speak of 'now' with no need of any relativistic qualifications.

In their accelerating expansion the natural sciences have been giving us a picture of the world as consisting of a complex hierarchy

– a series of levels of organization of matter in which each successive member of the series is a 'whole' constituted of 'parts' preceding it in the series, frequently said (as a convention, with no implication of value judgements) to run from 'lower' to 'higher' as the complexity increases. These 'wholes' are organized systems of parts that are dynamically and spatially interrelated. Such a sequence is particularly well illustrated in the various levels of organization of living systems, namely the sequence (incompletely) represented by: atom – molecule – macromolecule – subcellular organelle – cell – multicellular functioning organ – whole living organism – populations of living organisms – ecosystems – the biosphere. Usually the interactions among subsystems (the 'parts') are relatively weak compared with the interactions within the subsystems themselves, a property which helps to simplify their identification and description. The strength of the additional forces which holds the sub-units together progressively diminishes as one goes up the scale of complexity, while the forces operative at lower levels of complexity also continue to be deployed in holding the more complex structures together. The gravitational forces between the atoms in a molecule are 10^{35} to 10^{39} times smaller than the net electrostatic interactions between them, and the energies of binding of atoms in a molecule are themselves 10 to 100 times smaller than the energies by which electrons are held by the nuclei within atoms, which in turn are 100,000 to a million times smaller than the energies of binding of the 'particles' in the nucleus. It takes much less energy to break a cell wall than it does to atomize a molecule, and to smash atoms needs tens of thousands of 'electron volts' (the energy acquired by an electron in dropping down a potential gradient of one volt per centimetre); to penetrate a nucleus millions of electron volts are deployed – and this increase continues the deeper one goes, for the deeper energy levels are separated by larger energy gaps than the higher, 'surface' ones.

It is tempting to visualize the natural hierarchy of levels as nested in the spatial sense, rather like a series of Russian dolls, with smaller and smaller systems packed inside one another, the smallest being that of the physico-chemical level and the largest being at least that of the biosphere of the planet Earth – which is itself, of course, only a minute speck relative to cosmic scales. However, although this picture would be satisfactory for envisaging the relation between some levels, this kind of spatial inclusion is not adequate for depicting the relation between other kinds of functional complexity, since some of the most elaborate and sophisticated are often relatively small in total physical volume – for example, the human central nervous system. Moreover, each level in the hierarchy is often characterized by a distinctive internal logical structure of its own, its properties describable in terms of a distinctive and logically consistent system of concepts, different from those invoked for adjacent levels 'above' and 'below' or 'inside' or 'outside' of it.

When the hierarchy of complexity is also, in fact, a hierarchy of increasing size (as in the 'biological' sequence described above) then, concomitantly and consistently with this, the larger entities usually also exhibit slower and slower response times to external changes. Furthermore, the sequence of biological evolutionary development in time is, as we shall see in the next section, also a sequence of increased complexity evoked by environmental pressures, and not necessarily following any neat logical prescriptions other than those imposed by the need for one function and structure to precede another as its necessary historical precondition.

3 REDUCTIONISM

Since we are adopting a critical-realist stance, we have to take seriously this picture from the natural sciences of the world as a hierarchy of complexities of the kinds just indicated. Corresponding to the different levels in these hierarchies of the natural world there exist the appropriate sciences which study a particular level – though there are, of course, sciences which cut across a number of disciplines, in the way that, for example, genetics is significant for the whole of biology. Clarification of the relationship between the depictions of reality that the sciences afford at their own distinctive levels of operation is of very great significance in our estimate of the relevance of such knowledge to the wider concerns of humanity and, in particular, with respect to its relation to theology, as mentioned in the previous chapter.

It is a natural transition for a molecular biologist, say, who is accustomed to breaking down complex (biological) entities into units small enough to be examined by the techniques in which they are trained (in this case those of physics, chemistry and biochemistry), to transform this practical, methodological 'philosophy' into a more general, now genuinely philosophical, belief that (in this instance) biological organisms *are* 'nothing but' the bits into which they have analyzed them, 'nothing but molecules and atoms'. Many practising molecular biologists are, because of this transition, implicit 'reductionists'. Some, indeed, are quite explicit; for example, Francis Crick has affirmed that 'the ultimate aim of the modern movement in biology is in fact to explain *all* biology in terms of physics and chemistry.'[5] Whether explicitly or implicitly embraced, such a reductionist interpretation of the relation between the different sciences can limit and determine any understanding of the nature of the levels of the natural world under consideration – in this instance, living organisms including human beings. The issue[6] here is whether or not the theories, experimental laws and theoretical terms and concepts formulated in one science operating at its own level can be shown to be but special cases of, that is 'reduced to', the theories, etc., formulated in some other branch of science operating at a lower level of the natural hierarchies. It is what is often being urged upon us when we are told that 'scientific study X is nothing but scientific study Y' – hence the label 'nothing-but-ery' for this kind of assertion.

There is wide agreement on the need, indeed necessity, to break down unintelligible, complex wholes into their component units and then to see how they fit together, but this does not preclude more holistic methodologies. However, some reductionists, while recognizing this, nevertheless do so only as a kind of concession to the present incompleteness of our knowledge and still believe, however vaguely, that all the sciences will one day be reduced to physics and chemistry. On this view, complex wholes (for example, biological organisms) *are* 'nothing but' their component parts.

There are two forms of this view. The first asserts simply that the laws of physics and chemistry apply to all processes (for instance, biological ones) at the atomic and molecular levels; this excludes, for example, all 'vitalist' views concerning biological organisms. On this there would be wide agreement. A second, and stronger, form of such reductionism asserts that higher complexes *are* 'nothing but' atoms and molecules in the sense that a physico-chemical account of their atomic and molecular processes is all there is to be said about them.

Now it is true that the answer to 'What else is there (other than atoms and molecules) in, say, a living organism?' is 'no-thing at all', but this does not mean that describing its molecular constituents and their properties is all there is to be said, that there is nothing more to be said by way of description of the individuality of a particular living organism, especially if it is a human one.

As we have seen, the expansion of our knowledge of the natural world which has occurred particularly in the twentieth century has shown it to consist of a complex hierarchy of systems, with a science appropriate to each level. At each level distinctive kinds of interlocking relationships occur and these require distinctive concepts to order them and render them coherent. Very often these concepts cannot be envisaged or translated into those appropriate at lower levels of organization; that is, they are not reducible. Because of widely pervasive reductionist pre-suppositions, there has been a tendency to regard the level of atoms and molecules as alone 'real'. However, there are good grounds for not affirming any special priority to the physical and chemical levels of description and for believing that what is real is what the various levels of description actually refer to. There is no sense in which subatomic particles are to be graded as 'more real' than, say, a bacterial cell or a human person or a social fact. Each level has to be regarded as a slice through the totality of reality, in the sense that we have to take account of its mode of operation at that level.

In particular, terms such as 'consciousness', 'person', 'social fact' and, in general, the languages of the humanities, ethics, the arts and theology, to name but a few, are not prematurely to be dismissed from the vocabulary used to describe the human condition, since in all these instances a strong case can be made for the distinctiveness and non-reducibility of the concepts they deploy. The languages, for example, that human beings have developed to articulate and express, as in music and poetry and religion, their states of consciousness and their interactions with each other and with God, many would say, have a genuine *ab initio* claim to be taken as seriously at their own level of reference as the languages of the sciences at theirs.

4 INTERCONNECTEDNESS AND WHOLENESS

The diversity which we, or those extra-terrestrial visitors, see on our planet Earth is real enough, for at the various levels at which particular patterns of organization of matter can be distinguished they certainly exhibit that variety I have been describing. The different structures are presented to us as distinctive and distinct. We have recognized that this variety is the result of the joint operation of surprisingly few forces, basic laws and fundamental constants, and is thereby constitutive of that degree of underlying unity we have already remarked upon. In doing so, we have also recognized the role of the natural sciences in explicating and explaining this diversity-in-unity, both as it is now observed and how it has developed and changed in the course of time, as we shall see in chapter 3.

However, the underlying unity of the world is not only a matter of derivation from common underlying principles, laws and constants, but extends also to a common interrelatedness and interconnectedness. This is manifest at two different levels.

In quantum theory, the amplitude of the wave function that represents the extension in space of any particular 'particle' declines only slowly with distance, and never quite to zero, as the distance from its most probable location increases. Since the square (roughly speaking) of this amplitude at any point in space is proportional to the probability of finding the particle at this point, there is no point in the actual universe at which it is totally impossible to find the particle – no point at which the amplitude of the wave function actually becomes zero. In practice, the values decline so rapidly away from the atom or molecule, or whatever, in which the particle is normally regarded as residing, that for almost all purposes it may be ignored. However, this must not detract from the 'spread-out' character of all matter, so that in a very real sense every fundamental particle, or structure constituted of them (which means every*thing*), is interacting to some extent with everything else in the universe. For example, it has been calculated[7] that, even on the basis of classical physics, the detailed motions (that is, directions and velocities) of a set of billiard balls, colliding with only a negligible loss of energy, would, as we shall discuss in more detail in chapter 3, be affected by an effect as minute as the gravitational attraction of an electron at the edge of the galaxy. Of course, for most practical purposes, and this includes those of science itself, only a very few local interactions amount to anything significant. However, that these minuscule, universal interactions occur at all suggests that we must not take a too excessively fragmented view of the world and its apparently discrete contents. Indeed in certain situations at the subatomic level, it becomes imperative not to consider particles as discrete entities but only conjointly together as total systems (for example, as in the systems that are the concern of J. S. Bell's theorem and its tests[8]).

There is another quite different level at which the interconnectedness and interrelatedness of the diverse, apparently discrete, structures and entities of the world is a dominant feature. All living organisms live in intricate systems consisting of many cross-flows and exchanges of energy and matter that constitute labyrinths of sometimes baffling complexity. These biological ecosystems themselves are incorporated into the much larger inorganic systems of the flows of energy and matter through the seas, in the atmosphere and over the land. This macro-perspective therefore also serves to correct any excessively fragmented understanding of the world, convenient though it often is for clarity of thought and precision in the use of language, which inevitably fragments by naming.

CHAPTER 3

What's Going On?

Up to this point we have deliberately been taking a static view of the world, as if one could take a slice through space-time at a particular time and could then hope to identify meaningfully entities in space at that time which merited analysis and description. Because human observers of the universe are not moving with velocities at all comparable with that of light, relativistic distortions of our perspective of most entities in our observed world are not significant and so in the last section of chapter 2 we were able to give a broad account of the general features of these entities as observed by the natural sciences. However, the world is, almost notoriously, in a state of continuous flux, and it has, not surprisingly, been one of the major preoccupations of science to understand the changes that occur at all levels of the natural world. It has asked 'What is going on?' and 'How did these entities and structures we now observe get here and come to be the way they are?'

Because almost all observable entities and structures are subject to change, though on widely disparate timescales, so that all 'being' is in fact in process of 'becoming', some have argued that the fundamental units of the world are not so much entities or structures constituted of units, as 'events' – trajectories in space-time. There is no such thing, in this perspective, as 'inert stuff'; only, as it were, 'goings on'. But since we can, in fact, discriminate discrete entities and structures, along the lines of the preceding section, it is for the most part not misleading to think that the question of 'What's going on?' can be responded to in terms of accounts of the changes in time of entities and structures observed at particular times, past and present. The object of our curiosity is both causal explanation of past changes in order to understand the present and also prediction of the future course of 'events', of changes in the entities and structures with which we are concerned.

1 Predictability, Causality and 'Top-Down' ('Downward') Causation

The notions of explanation of the past and present and predictability of the future are closely interlocked with the concept of causality. For detection of a causal sequence in which, say, A causes B, which causes C, and so on, is frequently taken to be an explanation of the present in terms of the past (i.e., an historical explanation) and also predictive of the future, insofar that observation of A gives one grounds for inferring that B and C will follow as time elapses, since the original A–B–C ... sequence was itself a succession in time.

There has, of course, been a long and intricate debate over the centuries about the extent to which observation of a 'constant conjunction' of events can be logically predictive of the future – the 'problem of induction'. Common though such inductive reasoning is, however, it has been widely recognized that causality in scientific accounts of natural sequences of events is only reliably attributable when some underlying relationships of an intelligible kind between the successive forms of the entities have been discovered, over and beyond mere conjunction as such. These explanatory relationships often involve an understanding of how the constituent units of any entity give it the form it has and how changes in such 'internal' relationships can manifest themselves in observations on the system as a whole – though such a generalization is far from capturing the enormous variety of explanations of change that the sciences afford across the vast range of their operation. Nevertheless, it serves to emphasize this fundamental concern of the sciences with the explanation of change and so with predictability and causality. It transpires that various degrees of predictability pertain to different kinds of natural systems and that the accounts of causality that are pertinent are correspondingly different. It must be recalled that although absolute simultaneity is lost in the theory of relativity, the succession of events which occur at a given location and which form causal chains is independent of the choice of frame of reference. (The only type of succession whose order depends on the frame of reference is that of causally *un*related events.) Indeed the concept of causality is affected by Einstein's theory of relativity only to the extent that we now have to recognize that causal influences can never be transmitted through the universe at a speed greater than that of light. Let us now examine some natural systems which differ with respect to the predictability of their development in time and with respect to the account we have to give of their causal connectedness.

a Predictability and Causality in Relatively Simple, Dynamic, Law-obeying Systems

Science began to gain its great ascendancy in Western culture through the succession of intellectual pioneers in mathematics, mechanics and astronomy which led to the triumph of the Newtonian system with its explanation not only of many of the relationships in certain terrestrial systems but, more particularly, of the geometrical orbits and periods of planetary motions in the solar system. These orbits and periods obeyed precise mathematical relations and the future states of the systems (with certain notable deviations which were later explained by postulating the existence of previously undetected planets) were predictable from these relationships, which naturally were then regarded as 'laws'. This led, not surprisingly considering the sheer intellectual power and beauty of the Newtonian scheme, to the domination of the criterion of predictability in the perception of what science should, at its best, always aim to provide – even though such single-level systems, we now realize, are comparatively rare. It also reinforced the notion that science proceeded, indeed *should* proceed, by breaking down the world in general, and any investigated system in particular, into their constituent entities. Its procedure was, it was assumed, to determine the relations between these entities, so distinguished, and such modifications with time as they underwent. These relations, if well established, eventually qualified as the laws that, given the initial conditions, determined the future course of events, which were thus predictable. Such procedures naturally gave rise to a view of the world as mechanical and deterministic and the ability to make predictions almost came to be regarded as the necessary criterion of a successful scientific explanation. As we shall see, the dominance of this criterion has had to be qualified but it has, even so, been applicable to a wide variety of other systems less simple than the planetary one.

The concept of causality in such systems can be broadly subsumed into that of intelligible relations with their implication of the existence of something analogous to an underlying mechanism that generates these relationships (the 'generative mechanism').[1]

b Predictability of and Causality in Certain Statistical Properties of Assemblies (In Spite of the Intractability of Micro-prediction)

Certain properties of a total assembly can sometimes be predicted in more complex systems. For example, it was the application of essentially the idea of an assembly of gas molecules as behaving like colliding Newtonian bodies which led to a successful derivation, in broad principle, of the gas laws (e.g., pressure times volume is proportional to temperature) from the collisional behaviour and properties of the individual molecules constituting a gas. This statistical calculation is not vitiated by our lack of knowledge of the direction and velocities of individual molecules. The macroscopic behaviour of the whole gas (e.g., obeying the 'gas laws') can still be attributed to that of the individual molecules and the latter can justifiably be said to be the 'cause' of the former.

As is, of course, notorious, the predictability of events at the atomic and sub-atomic level has been radically modified by the realization that accurate determinations of the values of certain pairs of quantities (momentum/position and energy/time) are mutually exclusive; that is, the uncertainty in the value of one of the pair times the uncertainty in the value of the other is a constant. This constant is very small so that the real uncertainty in the values of these quantities is of numerical significance only for small particles of the sub-atomic order: however, it is not eliminable in practice or, it now seems, in principle and introduces a fundamental uncertainty into the quantitative description of events at this micro-level. This reinforces the unpredictability in all respects, though not in some significant ones (e.g., the gas laws), of such macro-systems. We are here referring, of course, to the famous Uncertainty Principle of Heisenberg, one of the fundamental pillars of quantum theory. Other, related, kinds of unpredictability are now also accepted with reference to other systems at the sub-atomic level. Thus, in a collection of radioactive atoms it is never possible to predict at what instant the nucleus of any particular atom will disintegrate; all that is known is the probability of it breaking up in a given time interval. However, with a given particular kind of atom (e.g., radium) it is perfectly possible to predict with complete accuracy how long it will take for a given fraction, say, one half, to disintegrate, on the basis of earlier observations. Here then is an instance of relative unpredictability (or, better, only probabilistic predictability) at the micro-level in conjunction with statistical predictability at the macro-level. It exemplifies the current state of quantum theory which allows only for the dependence on each other of the *probabilities* of elementary events and so to a looser form of causal coupling at this micro-level than had been taken for granted in classical physics. But note that causality, as such, is not eliminated, for physical situations at this micro-level still depend on each other, if only now in a probabilistic fashion.

c Predictability and Causality in Newtonian Systems Deterministic Yet Not Totally Predictable at the Micro-level of Description

That there are such systems has been a time-bomb ticking away under the edifice of the deterministic/predictable paradigm of what constitutes the world-view of science from at least as long ago as the 1900s. The French mathematician Henri Poincaré then pointed out[2] that, since the ability of the (essentially Newtonian) theory of dynamical systems to make predictions depended not only on knowing the rules for describing how the system will change with time, but also on knowing the initial conditions of the system, such predictability was extremely sensitive to the accuracy of our knowledge of the parameters characterizing those initial conditions. Thus it can be shown that even in assemblies of bodies obeying Newtonian mechanics there is a real limit to the degree of predictability. Indeed, beyond quite restricted limits such systems can become totally unpredictable, in spite of the deterministic character of the laws of Newton, on account of our inability ever to determine sufficiently precisely the values of the initial 'determining' parameters.

For example, in a game of snooker suppose that, after the first shot, the balls are sent in a continuous series of collisions, that there are a very large number of balls (so collisions with any edges can be ignored) and that collisions occur with a negligible loss of energy. One might assume that the ordinary laws of collisions in Newtonian mechanics would allow one to predict indefinitely which balls were moving and with what velocities and in what directions. This was the assumption on which Laplace based his famous assertion that, given knowledge of all the forces controlling nature and of the values of all relevant parameters at any instant, then all future states of the universe would be predictable to a powerful enough intelligence.

However, the results of collisions between convex bodies are exquisitely sensitive to errors in the angle of their impact. If the average distance between the balls is ten times their radius, then it can be shown[3] that an error of one decimal digit at the nth place of decimals in the angle of impact of the first collision leads to the conclusion that after n collisions all certainty in the directions of the balls is lost – it will not be known whether any particular ball is moving in any given direction or one at right angles to it.

For example, an error of one in the 1000th decimal place in the angle of the first impact means that all predictability is lost after 1000 collisions. Clearly infinite accuracy is needed for the total predictability that Laplace assured us was possible. The uncertainty of movement grows with each impact as the originally minute uncertainty becomes amplified and there is an exponential amplification of the uncertainty in the directions of movement after each impact. Even quite small effects quickly reach macroscopic proportions. So, although the system is deterministic at the micro-level – the constituent entities obey Newtonian mechanics – it is never totally predictable in practice at this level.

But it is not predictable for another reason, for even if *per impossibile* the error in our knowledge of the angle of the first impact were zero, unpredictability still enters because no such system can ever be located away from the effects of the gravitational fields exerted by everything else that exists – it cannot be outside the universe. Thus, suppose our ensemble of colliding bodies were actually a gas of billiard-ball-like molecules colliding elastically (the assumption of the quite successful kinetic theory of gases). Then it turns out that the gravitational force exerted by one electron at the observable limit of the universe would render the molecular motion unpredictable (direction uncertain by a right angle, as above) after only 50 collisions, that is, after about only 10^{-10} seconds for such an assembly – or after a minute for a set of actual billiard balls.[4] So, in practice, deterministic 'laws' often still do not allow predictability, even in the mechanistic world of Newtonian mechanics, of all the descriptive parameters of a system, namely the exact description of the velocity and direction of movement of each individual molecule.

Now, attempts to specify more and more finely the initial conditions will eventually come up against the barrier of 'Heisenberg' uncertainty, mentioned above, and this is in principle unsurmountable, according to the most widely agreed interpretation of the Heisenberg Uncertainty Principle, the one that rejects the existence of 'hidden variables'. So even this kind of Newtonian system can be described as unpredictable in principle with respect to any detailed description of its microscopic properties (velocities and positions of individual bodies in such a system). On a critical-realist account of scientific knowledge, this means we can say that such systems *are* indeterminate with respect to these microscopic properties (if not with respect to macroscopic properties of the assembly; see b above).

It should be noted that, as with all smaller entities that are part of larger wholes, the velocity of the whole relative to some frame of reference external to the system is superimposed on that of each molecule relative to the others. To this extent, the movement of the system as a whole (for example, if a box containing gas is dropped) is a causal factor in the movement of the individual molecules – and this constitutes a basic kind of 'top-down' causation, more subtle forms of which will be discussed below.

d Predictability and Causality in Non-linear Dynamical Systems

One of the striking developments in science in recent years has been the increasing recognition that many dynamical systems – physical, chemical, biological and indeed neurological – that are governed by non-linear dynamical equations can become unpredictable in their macroscopically observable behaviour. (In certain cases – in which there is dissipation of free energy in open systems far from equilibrium – they may manifest new levels and kinds of organization and then the non-linearity resides in the relation between certain key variables of the dissipative system, for example the fluxes of material or energy and the 'forces' controlling them.) Examples of such time-dependence include: turbulent flow in liquids; predator-prey patterns; reactor systems that involve autocatalytic relations; yearly variation in insect and other populations in nature; and the weather. The last-mentioned involves what has been called the 'butterfly effect' (Edward Lorenz), whereby a butterfly disturbing the air here today could affect what weather occurs on the other side of the world in a month's time through amplifications cascading through a chain of complex interactions.

It is now realized that the time-sequence of complex dynamical systems can take many forms. Those that have 'closed' solutions to the relevant differential equations can settle down either to one particular state or oscillate, in a 'limit cycle', between a sequence of states that are traversed periodically, such as the solar system (cf.

Section a above) or the pendulum of a grandfather clock. Or, consider chemical reaction systems: normally these are taken to come eventually to the resting state of chemical equilibrium. But there are chemical systems, including some significant biochemical ones, that involve positive and negative feedback and, under particular initial conditions, settle down to regular oscillations in time and space with respect to the concentrations of key constituents. The same applies to biological populations of predators and prey. In both cases the mechanism involves particular values for the parameters that control formation/destruction of the units in question and their rate of movement through space. These are very striking phenomena to observe – startling even – and they are of particular significance in relation to living systems, for they indicate the way patterns can emerge.[5]

What has transpired is that the mathematicians find that when they build up piecemeal, usually with the help of modern computers, the kind of solutions that are given by the non-linear equations governing many natural complex dynamical systems, they find that they do not have such 'closed' solutions and that the following can occur. Variation of a key controlling parameter (or parameters, in some cases) can at first lead to a single unique solution and all seems quite 'normal' and well-behaved from a determinist viewpoint; all is still predictable. But at a certain critical value of this key parameter, the solutions bifurcate into two possibilities, either of which may occur first as this critical point is passed – but *which* one is not predictable. As time proceeds, the system can 'flip' between these two alternative allowed states and, under some circumstances, these interchanges can constitute regular oscillations. As the key parameter increases all kinds of further complexities can occur: successive bifurcations; periods of entirely erratic behaviour, mathematically 'chaotic'; and yet further bifurcations. Finer and finer numerical subdivisions of the key parameters keep on repeating such sequences.[6] It is important to stress that in these cases this unpredictability is, for us, ineradicable since our decimal representation of any initial condition is always finite. There is a genuine unpredictability for us because we will never have a sufficiently accurate knowledge of the parameters prevailing during the fluctuations (especially if it proves necessary to take into account quantum effects) to predict absolutely which way the system will go.

In the real world most systems do not conserve energy: they are usually *dissipative systems* through which energy and matter flow, and so are also 'open' in the thermodynamic sense. Such systems can often give rise to the kind of sequence just mentioned. At one set of values of a controlling parameter the system at first settles down to an equilibrium or near-to-equilibrium steady state in which typical characteristics of the system (e.g., reactant concentrations) do not vary with time. At somewhat higher values of this same system parameter, the solutions bifurcate and seemingly stable behaviour occurs, patterned in space and/or time (e.g., limit cycles). This may be succeeded at still higher values of the controlling parameter by mathematically 'chaotic' behaviour. Many examples of these kinds of system are now known: the formation of vertical hexagonal cells of convecting fluids in liquids heated from below (the Bénard phenomenon); the transition to both irregular and periodic fluctuations in space and time of the concentrations of reactants in chemical systems that exhibit positive and negative feedback with diffusion; pattern formation in developing tissues through which both activators and inhibitors diffuse; the distribution of predators and prey in a particular territory; and so on.

In the change-over to temporal and spatial patterns of system behaviour, we have examples of what Ilya Prigogine and his colleagues at Brussels have called 'order through fluctuations'.[7] For in these systems, at the critical points of bifurcation an arbitrary fluctuation has been amplified to such an extent that its scale becomes comparable in magnitude to that of the whole system and effectively takes it over, as it were, with a consequent transformation of the system's properties. A new regime emerges. In the last two decades, the Brussels school has studied the thermodynamics of such irreversible processes in open, dissipative systems that are a long way from equilibrium and are non-linear (with respect to the relation between controlling fluxes and forces). Thermodynamics, one of the greatest scientific achievements of the last century and a half, embodies its famous Second Law to the effect that, in isolated systems undergoing natural irreversible processes, the entropy and 'disorder' (appropriately defined) always increase. Ilya Prigogine and his colleagues were able to demonstrate that the emergence of new more 'ordered', or rather 'organized', regimes were in fact required by the thermodynamics of such systems.

Explicit awareness of all this is only relatively recent in science and necessitates a reassessment of the potentialities of the stuff of the world, pattern formation in which had previously been thought to be confined only to the macroscopically static, equilibrium state – so that special, somewhat esoteric and conjectural, 'forces' or 'fields' were often (and still sometimes are, even today) postulated to account for the ability of the natural world to engender new patterns and forms of organization. In these far-from-equilibrium, non-linear, open systems, matter displays its potential to be self-organizing and thereby to bring into existence new forms entirely by the operation of forces and the manifestation of properties we already understand – but operating now under the constraints and with the potentialities afforded by their being incorporated into systems the properties of which, as a whole, now have to be taken into account. As Crutchfield *et al.* put it: 'a system can have complicated behaviour that emerges as a consequence of simple, nonlinear interaction of only a few components... Through amplification of small fluctuations it [nature] can provide natural systems with access to novelty.'[8]

e 'Top-down' ('Downward') Causation

Apart from the very simple instance (see section b above) of the effects of the general movement of a whole system on that of its constituent units, the notion of causality, when applied to systems, has usually been assumed to describe 'bottom-up' causation – that is, the effect on the properties and behaviour of the whole system of the properties and behaviour of its constituent units. However, in the case of these dissipative systems which manifest 'order through fluctuations', an influence of the state of the system as a whole on the behaviour of its components units – a constraint exercised by the whole on its parts – has to be recognized. Following D. T. Campbell[9] and R. W. Sperry,[10] we may call this 'top-down' causation For, to take the example of the Bénard phenomenon, beyond the critical point, individual molecules in a hexagonal 'cell', over a wide range in the fluid, move with a common component of velocity in a coordinated way, having previously manifested only entirely random motions with respect to each other. Or, in reaction systems which display rhythmic temporal and spatial patterns in the concentrations of the reactants, thousands of molecules in a particular region at a particular time suddenly all change to another form, whereas previously the probability of change was quite independent of their location. In both these instances,[11] the changes at the micro-level, that of the constituent units, are what they are *because* of their incorporation into the system as a whole, which is exerting specific constraints on its units, making them behave otherwise than they would in isolation.

It is important to emphasize again that recognition of the role of such 'top-down' causation in no way derogates from that of 'bottom-up' causation. But the need for recognition of the former is greater because hardly anyone since the rise of reductionist scientific methodologies doubts the significance of the latter. Indeed, this lack of a proper recognition of the former has unfortunately often inhibited the development of concepts appropriate to the more complex levels of the hierarchy of natural systems. The dual character of the directions in which 'causality' operates in such complex systems is further indicated by the recognition that epistemological analyses of many complex systems and situations also necessitate the distinguishing of a 'top-down' from a 'bottom-up' process. Thus Michael Arbib and Mary Hesse advocate what they call a 'two-way reductionism' as 'a more realistic view of the relation between two sciences, such as those of mind and brain', and go on to expound what they mean by this as follows: 'We use "top-down" and "bottom-up" analysis to refer to the two-way process of modifying and extending, respectively, the lower-level science to explain the higher level, and the higher level in the light of the implication of the lower level.'[12]

Their description of this two-way process as a 'reductionism' is somewhat misleading, since this term has generally been confined to the process whereby 'the theories and experimental laws formulated in one field of science can be shown to be special cases of theories and laws formulated in some other branch of science. If such is the case, the former branch of science is said to have been reduced to the latter.'[13] The direction of this reduction has invariably been that of the putative 'higher' level science to the 'lower', for example of biology to physics and chemistry. But the terminology is less important than what they are referring to, namely the two-way character of the process of epistemological analysis that is required in the natural sciences.

On the critical-realist view of the epistemology of the sciences, this has the further implication that the entities to which the 'theories and experimental laws' refer in our epistemological analyses correspond, however inadequately and provisionally, to realities which must be deemed to exist at the various levels being studied – that is, they also have an ontological reference, however elusive. As

Arbib and Hesse put it, 'there is no question of any of the properties being shown to be unreal', for they, rightly in my view, wish to anchor their epistemology 'in the reality of everyday experience'. There are indeed 'all manner of levels of reality',[14] as we have persistently affirmed in this work. So it is legitimate to describe the realities postulated as existing at the higher levels (the wholes, the 'top' of the 'top-down' terminology) to be causally interactive, in both directions, with the realities postulated as existing at the lower ones (the parts, the 'bottom') – while continuing, of course, to recognize the often provisional nature of our attempted depictions of realities at both levels. For this reason I do not share Arbib's and Hesse's reservations[15] concerning, in particular, R. W. Sperry's emphasis on the causative efficacy of higher level states,[16] since there need be no implication that either 'bottom-up' analyses or the discerning of 'bottom-up' causation is thereby ruled out. For all such 'fundamental and interesting'[17] systems there is indeed, as Arbib and Hesse agree, never likely to be a time when both methods of analysis are not going to be needed and so, I would add, the need to recognize the joint operation of 'causation' in both directions. We shall see that this kind of 'top-down' causation has increasing significance in those kinds of complex systems that are living.

2 THE LIVING WORLD

a The Origin of Life

However else living organisms may be described, there is no doubt that they are, at least, constituted of atoms of kinds widely distributed in the inorganic world. These atoms make up the structures of molecules of a wide range of sizes, almost all of which are engaged in a complex network of reactions also involving molecules entering the organisms from outside – through breathing the atmosphere, or taking in and expelling water (as fishes) and through ingestion of food. Living organisms also have the special characteristic of being able to self-reproduce their whole interlocking structure from one generation to another, and this is a necessary, if not sufficient, requirement for any material system to qualify as 'living'.

The studies on dissipative systems (see pp. 52–3 above) have shown how interlocking systems of reactions involving feedback can, entirely in accord with thermodynamics (and not precluded by its Second Law), undergo transitions to more organized and more complex forms, provided such systems are open, non-linear and far from equilibrium. All these conditions would have been satisfied by many systems of chemical reactions present on the Earth during its first 1,000 million years of existence. Furthermore, with our increasing knowledge of how molecular patterns can be copied in present living systems – the story of the translation of information in nucleic acids to sequences of amino-acids constituting distinctive proteins – it is now possible to make plausible hypotheses concerning the way in which early forms of nucleic acids and proteins might have formed a self-replicating macromolecular system, such as the 'hypercycle' of Eigen and Schuster. Such systems can be shown to multiply at the expense of less efficient rival ones.[18] What these studies indicate is the inevitability of the appearance of more organized, self-replicating systems, the properties of atoms and molecules being what they are; but what form of organization would be adopted is not strictly predictable since it depends on fluctuations.[19] In *retro*spect, the form of molecular organization that is self-reproducing is now intelligible, after three decades of 'molecular biology', but in *pro*spect, even with our present knowledge, it would not have been strictly predictable. So there is an openness and flexibility in the development of life even at this critical juncture which has to be reckoned with as a feature of our world.

b *Evolution*

The forms of living matter, that is, of living organisms, evolve – as we now know – through those changes in the genetic controlling material (DNA) that result in changes in the organism that increase the chance of its having surviving progeny. This is, of course, simply neo-Darwinian evolution which may be summed up in two propositions:[20] all organisms, past, present and future, descend from earlier living systems, the first of which arose spontaneously (according to the principles discussed above); and species are derived from one another by natural selection of the best procreators. The changes in the genetic macromolecule DNA are produced by a variety of agents – for example, the absorption of a quantum of energy from ultraviolet light which thereby changes the chemical structure in one of the units in the DNA chains. This alters or, more often, destroys the genetic information it is conveying at that point in the chain, and thus changes the organism in some respect, however slight, and so the chance, for better or for worse, of its producing progeny in its ecological niche. The significant point for our present purposes is that the changes in the DNA itself are scattered along the read-out sequences of its immensely long chains in a way that is random with respect to the ultimate effects of these changes on the ability of the organism to have progeny. For the effect of any particular DNA change depends on quite other factors, especially the environment of the organism in the widest sense – that is, including not only food resources, but also the nature and number of its predators, the 'social' organization of like organisms, and so on, in an ever-widening network of connections.

The possibility of science being predictive of such a process is vitiated on at least two counts. First, the original molecular event which alters, or destroys, a constituent unit in the DNA comes within the range of unpredictability through the operation of the 'Heisenberg' uncertainty of quantum-scale events. Second, the eventual effect on the ability of the organism to procreate is the result of the intersection of two independent causal chains – that producing changes in the DNA and the interaction between the thus-changed organism (especially in its ability to procreate) and its environment. The requisite knowledge to predict such an intersection is never likely to be forthcoming, as we observe (if only hypothetically) any particular organism in a particular environment; so, on this ground too, the sequence of events is not in practice predictable, though entirely intelligible afterwards. It is this combination of continuous random changes in the genetically controlling material with the 'accidental' filtering out of changes favourable to the production of progeny that gives to the evolutionary process its apparently opportunistic character and its dependence on actual historical situations. Even so, the process does display trends and certain generalizable features which we shall come to.

What concerns us more particularly here is the pattern of 'causal' relationships in this process. We are dealing with a process in which a selective system 'edits', as it were, the products of direct physico-chemical causation over periods of time covering several reproductive generations. Let us take an example from Donald Campbell to illustrate this:[21] the surfaces and muscle attachments of the jaws of a worker termite are mechanically highly efficient, entirely conforming with the best engineering and physical principles, and their operation depends on the combination of properties of the particular proteins of which the jaws are made. Selection has optimized viability at the level of the organism gnawing wood, picking up seeds, etc. So we need the principles operative at this level (laws of

levers, relations between protein structures and mechanical properties of their aggregates, and so on) to explain the structure and
distribution of the proteins in the jaws and hence to account for the
presence in the organism's DNA of the particular sequences it
contains that control the production of these particular proteins. So,
from the perspective of the whole organism's activity and its being
only one in a series of generations of termites, it is the efficacy of the
proteins in constituting jaws, that has been monitored by natural
selection, which is here apparently determining the sequences of the
DNA units – even though when one looks at the development of a
single organism, one observes only, with the molecular biologists,
the biochemical processes whereby protein sequences, and so structures, are 'read out' from the DNA sequences.

Hence there is a sense in which the network of relationships that
constitute the evolutionary development and the behaviour pattern
of the whole organism is determining what particular DNA sequence
is present at the controlling point in its genetic material in the
evolved organism. This consideration becomes even more striking if
one instances those species in which the evolution of division of
labour within it has led to specialization in function and the development of different types of jaws in different sub-groups. Here the laws
of sociological organization are determining the DNA sequences, it
seems. Campbell called this 'downward' or 'top-down' causation,
insofar as specification of the higher levels of organization is necessary for explaining the lower level – in this case, the sequence in a
DNA molecule. Where there is selection of the whole organism at
the higher level, the higher level laws are necessary for a complete
explanation and specification of the lower. The part of the DNA that
controls the jaw protein sequences is constrained to be there and be
what it is by virtue of its presence within the whole system of an
organism-with-an-evolutionary-history.

As Elisabeth Vrba has said, this kind of downward causation is
really a commonsense notion; for instance, 'as natural selection
sorts among organisms it willy-nilly "downward causes" the sorting
of all included lower entities, be they non-coding DNA sequences,
genes, cells, chromosomes, etc.'[22] But, as she also goes on to remark,

There is also a more subtle form of downward causation. The structural or organizational aspects of a particular higher individual may

downward determine the introduction and sorting of variation among lower level entities included in its 'body' ... [for example] the structural group character of group size may downward cause the sorting of variation among included phenotypes (e.g., the spread of altruistic phenotypes by random drift, against the force of natural selection, which requires small population size).[23]

Some biologists have stressed furthermore that what happens, evolutionarily speaking, to organisms are consequences of themselves – that is, of their state at any given moment, with all its dependence on historical accidents – as well as of their genotype and environment.[24] Thus innovative behaviour on the part of a living creature in its environment can be a major factor in subsequent change, and so in its evolution,[25] and this introduces another imponderable limiting predictability in evolutionary change in addition to those already discussed.[26]

Description of such complex interlocking networks of events and changes operating at different levels does not seem adequately to be captured by their description as *causally* connected, with its often hidden assumption that some kind of force is operative in a sequential constant conjunction of events. The word 'causal' is more normally used for the linkage of different events at the same level of explanation (physical, informational, or even psychological). We seem to have here a determination of form through *a flow of information*, rather than through a transmission of energy, where 'information' is conceived of in a broad enough sense to include the input from the environment whereby molecular mechanisms are selected, including, for example, the DNA sequences in the termite jaw example. In this kind of determinative relation, 'causal' explanations are in terms of non-physical categories, like 'information', but real enough, nevertheless – as any computer engineer would testify with respect to the programme controlling the electronic changes in a computer. Such determinative relations may operate between two different kinds of 'level' in nature. One can continue to use the 'top-down' terminology of Campbell, provided one does not thereby assume that such 'causation' can be described only in terms of forces operating to transmit energy or of the movement of matter, as is often true of causality operating at only one level. The determination of form by form requires a flow of information, in this case, between levels.[27]

c The Brain, Mental Events and Consciousness

It is in terms such as those just mentioned that some neuro-scientists and philosophers have come to speak of the relation between mental events and the physico-chemical changes at neur-ones, which are the triggers of observable actions in living organ-isms that possess brains sufficiently developed for it to be appropriate to attribute to them some kind of consciousness. As John Searle has recently put it:

> Consciousness ... is a real property of the brain that can cause things to happen. My conscious attempt to perform an action such as raising my arm causes the movement of the arm. At the higher level of description, the intention to raise my arm causes the movement of the arm. At the lower level of description, a series of neuron firings starts a chain of events that results in the contraction of the muscles ... the same sequence of events has two levels of description. Both of them are causally real, and the higher level causal features are both caused by and realised in the structure of the lower level elements.[28]

This view of consciousness as causal, and as an emergent in evol-ution, has also been espoused by certain neuroscientists, in particu-lar, Roger Sperry, though with a somewhat different terminology concerning causation. (Here, as indicated above, we prefer to follow a usage as clarified by Mackay.)[29] For them, 'mental events' in human beings are the internal descriptions we offer of an actual total state of the brain itself and are not events in some entity called the 'mind' which exists in some other non-physical mode that is ontologically distinct from matter and 'interacts' (mysteriously, one would have to say) with the brain as a physical entity. So this is a monist and not a dualist view of the 'body-mind problem'. The point which has to be emphasized in the present context is that this whole state of the brain (or possibly some parts of it in certain instances) acts as a constraint on what happens at the more specific level of the individual, constituent neurones, so that what occurs at this lower level is what it is because of the prevailing state of the whole. In other words, there is operative here a top-down causation between the level of the brain state as a whole and of the individual neurones. Descriptions of the total brain state in purely neurological terms would be exceedingly complex – and, indeed, considering the com-plexity of the brain, may never be forthcoming in anything other that broad terms. But we do have available the language of ordinary experience to refer accurately, sometimes surprisingly so, to our mental events in a communicable fashion, so that the language of mental events may be taken as genuinely referring to realities that *are* brain states, which are in themselves aspects of the total action that expresses the intention of the agent (cf. the earlier discussion in chapter 2 section 3 of reductionism in relation to the language used to explicate consciousness). The language we use concerning the connections between our mental experiences – the language of reasons, intentions, and so forth – really does, on this view, refer to actual causal linkages between whole brain states. The causal effectiveness of the whole brain state on the actual states of its component nerves and neurones is probably better conceived of in terms of the transfer of information rather than of energy, in the way a programme representing a certain equation, say, controls the chips in a computer – but this whole area of investigation is still very much *sub judice*.

It seems that with the evolution of brains, the significance of this kind of 'top-down' causation has become more and more significant in the evolutionary development as the whole state and behaviour of the individual organism itself plays an increasing role. As we saw, this has introduced a further element of unpredictability into a process which is in principle, at least, intelligible *post hoc*. Furthermore, since the brain-in-the-body is a highly dissipative system, one has to raise the question of whether or not its future states are irreducibly unpredictable and whether this might not, at the level of consciousness, be the physical situation concomitant with the experience of freedom in human beings.

3 THE HISTORY OF NATURE

Our earlier examination of 'what's there' in the natural world led us to emphasize that it contained hierarchies of levels of complexity, often related like a series of nested Chinese boxes – though other forms of hierarchical relation are also manifest in the world, especially within the control mechanisms of living organisms. It is now time for us to take account of the *dynamic* character of these relationships, to recognize that the world in all its aspects, as explicated especially by the natural sciences of the last two centuries (that is, since the 'discovery of time' by the eighteenth-century pioneers of geology), has come to be seen as always in process, a nexus of evolving forms, some changing rapidly, others over immensely long time-scales, but never static. Our accounts of the observed structures of the world ('what's there') can never be separated from our understanding of the way they came to be the way they are, from our accounts of the processes whereby they came into existence. For the 'being' of the world is always also a 'becoming' and there is always a story to be told, especially as matter becomes living and then conscious and, eventually, social too. 'Evolution' in the general sense can be said to occur cosmologically, inorganically, geologically, biologically, socially and culturally. There occurs a continuous, almost kaleidoscopic, recombination of the component units of the universe into an increasing diversity of new forms, which last for a time only to be re-formed out of the same simpler entities into new and different patterns. The process never stops and our accounts of it all are irreducibly narrative.

a Features and Trends

Features and trends in the history of nature which the sciences now bring to our attention include the following.[30] History is a seamless web, a *continuity* which is increasingly *intelligible* as the sciences with more and more success explicate the nature of the transitions between natural forms. The process can be characterized as one of *emergence*, for new forms of matter, and a hierarchy of organization of these forms themselves, appear in the course of time and these new forms have new properties, behaviours and networks of relations which necessitate the development of new epistemologically irreducible concepts in order accurately to describe and refer to them. At each level of analysis, trends can be detected in the history of nature which are significant for eventual theological reflection – though one must always be cautious not to transfer generalizations about trends at one level to other levels without further warrant.

New patterns can only come into existence in a finite universe ('finite' in the sense of the conservation of matter-energy) if old patterns dissolve to make place for them. This is a condition of the creativity of the process – that is, of its ability to produce the new – which at the biological level we observe as new forms of life only through death of the old. For the death of individuals is essential for release of food resources for new arrivals, and species simply die out by being ousted from biological 'niches' by new ones better adapted to survive and reproduce in them. Biological death of the individual is the prerequisite of the creativity of the biological order, that creativity which eventually led to the emergence of human beings. At this biological level we discover the process to be that of 'natural selection', but it is possible to discern cognate processes occurring also at other levels.

Complex living structures can only have a finite chance of coming into existence if they are not assembled *de novo*, as it were, from their basic sub-units, but emerge through the accumulation of changes in a simpler forms, as demonstrated by H. A. Simon in a classic paper (discussed further on p. 67). Having come on to the scene, they can then survive, because of the finitude of their life spans, only by building pre-formed complex chemical structures into their fabric through imbibing the materials of other living organisms. For the chemist and biochemist there is the same kind of difficulty in conceiving how complex material structures, especially those of the intricacy of living organisms, could be assembled otherwise than from less complex units, as there is for the mathematician of conceiving of a universe in which the analytic laws of arithmetic were inapplicable. So there is a kind of 'structural' logic about the inevitability of living organisms dying and of preying on each other – for we cannot conceive, in a lawful, non-magical universe, of any way whereby the immense variety of developing, biological, structural complexity might appear, except by utilizing structures already existing, either by way of modification (as in biological evolution) or of incorporation (as in feeding).[31] The statistical logic is inescapable: *new forms of matter arise only through the dissolution of the old; new life only through death of the old.*

One of the most general and widely agreed trends in nature – indeed, it constitutes one of the pillars of modern physical science – is that there is always an *increase* in the quantity (entropy) which measures *disorderliness* in natural processes in isolated systems, systems across whose boundaries no matter or energy passes. The 'disorderliness', or 'randomness', referred to here is a precisely defined quantity (the entropy) which is related to the number of possible dispositions of matter over the available energy states. It is the converse of the kind of 'order' to be seen in the arrangements of atoms or molecules in a perfect crystal, or in a perfect wallpaper pattern. It is to be distinguished from 'organization', for example that of a biological system, though clearly an increase in 'disorder' is inimical to the presence of biological organization. This trend tow-

ards disorder in individual isolated systems, the famous Second Law
of Thermodynamics, has frequently been generalized and applied to
the universe as a whole, assuming that, almost by definition, it is an
'isolated system' in the sense required by the Second Law. But such
a generalization has always been of dubious validity. Perhaps the
most that may be said is that the Second Law leads one to expect
that over increasingly wide tracts of the universe there will a
tendency to reach thermal equilibrium (the so-called 'heat death').
But how long fluctuations will persist in any given region is extremely difficult to estimate, so that ebbs and flows of matter and
energy may continue long beyond the period of existence of anything like the universe we now observe.

Many regions of the universe will continue to behave as open
systems through which matter and energy are flowing. But in such
regions, if any systems are non-linear and far from equilibrium, then
dissipative structures can arise and new forms of ordering of matter
and energy can occur, in fact *will* do so, as we have already
discussed – 'order through fluctuations'. This is the explanation we
now have of the anomaly that puzzled nineteenth-century scientists
of how, in a universe that was increasingly 'disordered', biological
evolution towards increased 'organization' could occur – the
apparent discrepancy between two of that century's most significant
scientific discoveries, Darwinian evolution and the Second Law of
Thermodynamics.[32]

In our earlier discussion of predictability, it became clear that
although many processes and sequences of events are afterwards
intelligible, there is often an irreducible element of unpredictability
about their future states. That is, there is an *open-endedness* about
the course of many natural events. Indeed, only relatively simple
dynamic lawlike systems, having closed solutions to the equations
that govern their trajectories, could be said to be entirely predictable, and only then in respect to certain well-defined parameters.
But in other systems predictability, although possible at the macro-
level, is impossible at the micro-level; and dissipative systems can
be unpredictable even at the macro-level. This open-endedness of
such natural systems is compounded when they are living.

Furthermore, the course of biological evolution on the surface of
the Earth has a contingent, historical character consequent upon
evolutionary changes being dependent on the crossing of independent causal chains.[33] This open-ended character of biological events

is enhanced as living organisms manifest increasingly individual characters and behaviour patterns. It is a tendency that reaches its apogee in the human experience of freedom, which may itself, as we have hinted, be rooted in a fundamental open-endedness and unpredictability of brain states.

However, this open-endedness is not just a confused jumble, in the usual non-technical sense, for what we call 'chance', whether at the micro- or the macro-level, operates within a law-like framework which constrains and delimits the possible outcomes. As in many games, the consequences of the fall of the dice depend very much on the rules of the game.[34] During the last decade it has become increasingly apparent that it is chance operating within a lawlike framework that is the basis of the inherent creativity of the natural order, its ability to generate new forms, patterns and organizations of matter and energy. If all were governed by rigid law, a repetitive and uncreative order would prevail: if chance alone ruled, no forms, patterns or organizations would persist long enough for them to have any identity or real existence and the universe could never be a cosmos and susceptible to rational inquiry. It is the combination of the two which makes possible an ordered universe capable of developing within itself new modes of existence.[35] *The interplay of chance and law is creative.*

In those parts of the universe where the temperature is low enough for molecules to exist in sufficient proximity to interact, there is a tendency for more and more complex molecular systems to come into existence and this process is actually driven, in the case of reactions that involve association of molecules to more complex forms, by the tendency to greater overall randomization, that is, as a manifestation of the Second Law.[36] Such systems, if open and if they also exhibit feedback properties, can, as we saw, become 'dissipative' and undergo sharp changes of regime with the appearance of new patterns in space and time. In other words, even in these non-living systems, there is an increase in complexity in the entities involved in certain kinds of natural process. This appears to be an example of what Karl Popper has called a 'propensity' in nature.[37] Popper argued that a greater frequency of occurrence of a particular kind of event may be used as a test of whether or not there is inherent in the sequence of events (equivalent to throws of a die) a tendency or propensity to realize the event in question, in this instance an increase in complexity. 'There exist weighted possibilities which are more than *mere possibilities*, but tendencies or propensities to become real: tendencies or propensities to realize themselves.' Such propensities, he argues, 'are not mere possibilities, but are physical realities'.

But this *propensity for increased complexity* is also manifest in the history of living organisms. What significance is to be attributed to this? Is it simply, as W. McCoy has put it,[38] that biological 'evolution is a process of divergence and wandering rather than an inexorable progression towards increasing complexity', so that evolution '*permits* the emergence of new complexity, but does not in any particular case necessitate it'. Certainly, as J. Maynard Smith has pointed out:

> All one can say is that since the first living organisms were presumably very simple, then if any large change in complexity has occurred in any evolutionary lineage, it must have been in the direction of increasing complexity ... 'Nowhere to go but up' ... Intuitively one feels that the answer to this is that life soon became differentiated into various forms, living in different ways, and that within such a complex ecosystem there would always be *some* way of life open which called for a more complex phenotype. This would be a self-perpetuating process. With the evolution of new species, further ecological niches would open up, and the complexity of the most complex species would increase.[39]

But this is, as Maynard Smith goes on to admit, 'intuition, not reason'. Nevertheless, the fact is that there *has* been, taking biological evolution as a whole, an emergence of increasingly complex organisms, even if in some evolutionary lines there has been a loss of complexity and so of organization. So, on Popper's criterion enunciated above, we would be correct in saying that there is a propensity towards increased complexity in the evolution of living organisms.

Saunders and Ho in a (disputed) interpretation[40] identify the basis of this tendency to be the process by which a self-organizing system optimizes its organization with respect to locally defined requirements for fitness. They argue that the random removal of a component from a system which is at or near to a local peak of fitness must tend to make the system less fit than before; whereas the random addition of a component allows the possibility of an increase. So such systems will tend to permit the addition of components more readily than their removal and this, Saunders and Ho suggest, is the chief cause of the observed increase in complexity during biological evolution. This sounds plausible enough but, in the nature of the case, is difficult to substantiate. In any case, the fact is that, even if it cannot be judged as inevitable in any particular evolutionary line, there has over biological evolution as a whole been an overall trend towards and an increase in complexity, so that it is right to speak of a propensity for this to occur.

By 'complexity' in this context we have been meaning simply the number of different types of components that are present in the systems in question. This must be distinguished from the 'organization' which such a system needs in order to survive, with complexity as the necessary but not sufficient condition for organization.[41] The need for organization for survival was beautifully demonstrated by H. A. Simon,[42] who showed that the simplest modular organization of, say, the structure of a watch, so that each module had a limited stability, led to an enormous increase in survivability during manufacture in the face of random destructive events.

So the increases we observe in complexity and organization (subsumed under 'complexity' from now on) in the natural world are entirely intelligible and not at all mysterious in the sense of requiring some non-naturalistic explanation. It is important to emphasize this, since a link has been proposed between this natural increase in complexity and the *increasing levels of consciousness* in biological evolution, for instance by Teilhard de Chardin. Certainly consciousness depends on the coming into existence of certain forms of very complex organizations of matter – nervous systems and brains – but these are particular forms of complexity and it is misleading simply to correlate consciousness with 'complexity' without further qualification.

Indeed, biologists are usually rather cautious about postulating trends in biological evolution and mostly prefer to limit themselves to describing the emergent features of later products of the evolutionary process.[43] These include not only the increase in complexity we have remarked upon already but also an increase in the general energy or maintained level of vital processes, protected reproduction, care of the young, and either an increase in specialization and adaptation or, as in the case of *homo sapiens*, an increase in flexibility and adaptability to an increasing range of environments.

It is from this standpoint that one should appraise the emergence of more and more complex, not necessarily larger, brains in the evolutionary development. The more capable an organism is of recording, analysing and making predictions from information about its environment, the better chance it will have of surviving in a wide variety of habitats. This sensitivity to, this sentience of, its surroundings inevitably involves an increase in its ability to experience pain, which constitutes the necessary biological warning signals of danger and disease, so that it is impossible readily to envisage an *increase of information-processing ability* without an increase in the sensitivity of the signal system of the organism to its environment. In other words, an increase in 'informational' capacity cannot but have as its corollary an increase, not only in the level of consciousness, but also in the experience of pain. Insulation from the surrounding world in the biological equivalent of three-inch nickel steel would be a sure recipe for preventing the development of consciousness.

Each increase in sensitivity, and eventually of consciousness, as evolution proceeds, inevitably heightens and accentuates awareness both of the beneficent, life-enhancing elements and of the inimical, life-diminishing elements in the world in which the organism finds itself. The stakes for joy and pain are, as it were, continuously being raised, and the living organism learns to discriminate between them. So *pain and suffering*, on the one hand, and *consciousness of pleasure and well-being*, on the other, *are emergents* in the world. The presence of the latter never causes any surprise (why not?) and it is the presence of the former which, as is well known, is usually taken to constitute a problem for belief in a creating God. Be that as it may, what it is important to emphasize at this point is that, from a purely naturalistic viewpoint, the emergence of pain and its compounding as suffering as consciousness increases seem to be inevitable aspects of any conceivable developmental process that would be characterized by a continuous increase in ability to process information coming from the environment. For this entails an increase in sensitivity, hence in vulnerability, and consequently in suffering as consciousness ramifies. In the context of natural selection, pain has an energizing effect and suffering is a goad to action: they both have survival value for creatures continually faced with new problematic situations challenging their survival.[44] In relation to our later theological reflections, it must be emphasized that pain, suffering and death are present in biological evolution, as a necessary condition for survival of the individual and transition to new forms long before the appearance of human beings on the scene. So the presence of pain, suffering and death cannot be the result of any particular human actions, though undoubtedly human beings experience them with a heightened sensitivity and, more than any other creatures, inflict them on each other.

b *The Limits of Time*

The foregoing emphasis on the historicity of nature has taken for granted our ordinary, commonsense awareness of time, even if quantified in science and everyday life by measuring devices of various degrees of sophistication. However, as we saw, the nature of time in modern relativistic physics is very different from this commonsense understanding of time as an endless dimension along which entities proceed and change. Modern physics and cosmology have raised again, in a new form, earlier discussions in theology concerning the relation of time and eternity, now more in the form of the question 'Does time have a beginning and end?'.

The concept of time is now seen to be but a component of the more inclusive concept of space-time, the curvature of which is dependent on the distribution of mass, energy and pressure of whatever matter is present. So it is not surprising that, when physicists and cosmologists try to understand that state of the early universe 10–20 thousand million years ago when it was compressed into a space of atomic dimensions, or even less, they find themselves questioning the very nature of 'time' itself. They are able to extrapolate back to a few seconds after the singularity of the 'hot big bang' without having to make any fundamental modifications of the concept of 'time' they have used in relativistic physics, or, for that matter, in ordinary life.

However, recently they have become particularly aware that close to the point from which the history of the universe in classical, ordinary 'time' can be taken forward, and to which it is extrapolated backwards from the present, very surprising events might have occurred in which there was an expansion of the universe by a factor of 10^{50} during the first 10^{-35} to 10^{-30} seconds of the universe's existence. This 'inflationary' period – which, be it noted, is still within classical, ordinary time – allows explanation of certain otherwise baffling features of the universe as it later expands. The state leading to this inflationary period can be understood only by a combination of quantum and relativity theory which involves a radical reformulation of our perception of time in a way not hitherto necessary.

For the concept 'space-time' in general relativity 'only has an unambiguous meaning within the framework of non-quantum physics',[45] whereas the idea of three-dimensional 'space' can be applied in quantum theory, as well as in classical theory. As one goes back in real 'time' (as dimensionally conceived, even in relativity theory) to that original exceedingly small and unimaginably dense early in universe, the distinction between 'space' and 'time' breaks down and they acquire a converging status, according to the recent speculations of J. B. Hartle and S. W. Hawking.[46] C. Isham expounds their ideas as follows:

> it becomes harder to sustain an interpretation of an evolution with respect to a genuine time variable. Basically, as the underlying equality of space and time directions starts to assert itself, the phenomenological time [ordinary, physical dimension time] begins to pick up an imaginary part ['imaginary' in the mathematician's sense of including a factor of i, the square root of -1] with its associated non-physical features. By this means, the problem of the 'beginning of time' is adroitly averted.[47]

In this proposal of Hartle and Hawking (still, be it noted, very much a matter for debate among theoretical physicists) there is no singularity at which phenomenological, physical time 'begins', together with three-dimensional space including matter-energy, and at which the universe could be said to have 'begun'. Rather the universe of space-time-matter-energy appears as the result of a 'quantum tunnelling' effect whereby absolutely nothing (=no space, no time) gives rise to something in (mathematically) imaginary time. From this point on, 'imaginary time' merges more and more into phenomenological, physical time – and the expansion of the universe proceeds in *that* time in the ways the physicists and cosmologists have made familiar.

Many people, like this author, soon find themselves out of their depth in this conceptual abyss – but the significant point is clear enough. Time as we know and record it, in science as in history and ordinary life, is a necessary concept for interpreting all we see in nature and history and life. But we now have to accept that physicists and cosmologists are beginning to question whether time can be naively extrapolated back to the 'beginning' of the universe without a profound modification of the whole concept.

But what about the 'end' of the universe in time? Does it *have* an end? At the moment the evidence is not adequate to decide between two possible fates of the universe as we know it.[48] According to one, the universe will go on expanding, the galaxies moving further and further apart, with a continual drop in temperature, the formation of 'black holes' and the eventual heat death of the universe – though fluctuations and flows of matter and energy might persist for a large proportion of these unimaginably long times, so that dissipative, ordered systems might not be precluded from forming. How long would life persist? Freeman Dyson has suggested that even human life might survive by interstellar migration well beyond the demise of our own solar system.[49] But this is pure speculation; certainly life on planet Earth has a terminus when the energy of the Sun becomes exhausted.

The other possible fate is that, if there is enough matter in the universe, its gravitational attractions will eventually, acting like a long piece of elastic, draw the galaxies back together and the universe will end in a big crunch – from which it may or may not expand again. Nobody knows which of these possible scenarios is the most likely. However, despite Freeman Dyson's speculations, all have the consequence that human life on the planet Earth will disappear, and this is something that any theology must reckon with. Personally I find this no more daunting a problem than facing up to the disappearance from the face of the Earth of that constituent of it with which we are most familiar – our individual selves. For the possible fates of the universe raise the question of whether or not, whatever religious believers may say, its whole history is not, after all, futile.

CHAPTER 4

Who's There?

The most striking feature of the universe is one that is so obvious that we often overlook it – namely the fact that we are here to ask questions about it at all. That the regular laws of nature acting upon and in the entities we have described in chapter 2 should have generated the processes (chapter 3) that in the course of time culminated in an entity, humanity, which can know the route by which it has arrived on the scene, is an astonishing outcome of that highly condensed system of matter-energy enfolded in the tight knot of space-time with which the universe began. What the best explanation is of this well-established feature of the universe must always be a major consideration in any reflection (such as will be undertaken in Part II) upon the meaning and intelligibility of all-that-is. But we need now to be more explicit about what it is that is distinctive about us.

Undoubtedly many of the characteristics of *homo sapiens* which we think are special to us are in fact developments of, extrapolations of, even exaggerations of, features and abilities to be observed in the higher mammals: our ability to expand into a wide variety of environments; our flexibility and adaptability; our long-extended care of our young; our strong individualization; our highly developed and complex brains and the concomitant intelligence which has proved to be such a selective advantage through its ability to monitor and alter our environment for our own purposes; and, dependent on our cerebral capacities, our use of language and the consequent elaborate socialization which we have thus been able to develop.[1] But let us now look a little harder at ourselves and our special peculiarities. For there is no doubt that in humanity there emerge new kinds of behaviour and experiences which demand new non-reducible, autonomous concepts for their description and analysis – as is recognized in calling the human individual a 'person'.[2]

1 HUMAN PERSONHOOD

Evolutionary biology can trace the steps in which a succession of organisms have acquired nervous systems and brains whereby they obtain, store, retrieve and utilize information about their environments in a way that furthers their survival. That this information so successfully utilized must be accurate enough for their survival has led to the notion of 'evolutionary epistemology'. This finds a warrant for the reality of reference of the content of such awareness of living organisms, especially human beings, in their actual successful survival of the naturally selective processes. Awareness and exploration of the external world reach a peak in *homo sapiens* who, through the use of language, primarily, visual imagery and, later, mathematics, is able to formulate concepts interpreting the environment. The role of language is especially apparent in growing children, and observation shows that their abstract concepts and their acquisition of language are developed through their experience and their interactions with adults.

The natural environment, both physical and social, is experienced and becomes a possible object of what we then call 'knowledge' – that which is reliable enough to facilitate prediction and control of the environment, and so survival. Our sense impressions must be broadly trustworthy, and so must the cognitive structures whereby we know the world – otherwise we would not have survived.[3]

The capacity for abstract thought appears to be distinctively human and the acquisition of language is so closely linked with it that many think the latter is necessary for the former. In these parallel processes discrimination occurs within the content of cognitive awareness of the person as 'subject' and the natural environment that is experienced as 'object'. Minimally, and in purely functional terms, 'consciousness' may be defined as that power of the human brain to form internal representations of its physical and social environment (including the body of any particular brain), of its relations to that environment and of itself forming those representations; and this power pertains to both actual and possible (putatively future) representations of the environment, the self and their mutual relations. However clear, though, our awareness of the content of our consciousness is to ourselves, it is obscure and certainly not widely agreed how that same conscious activity may be described in terms of brain activity. Moreover, any such description is itself only articulable, and mutually and reciprocally defined, through its relation to some defensible hypothesis concerning the evolution of consciousness as a facet of brain activity – and there is no agreement on this either.[4]

What also seems to be uniquely characteristic of human beings is their ability as 'subjects' to treat the content of consciousness as putative 'objects', that is, to be self-aware. Human beings develop language that contains concepts of themselves as the subject of experiences and in their use of language they transcend themselves. We may say that human beings are 'self-transcendent'. So self-awareness and self-consciousness, coupled with our intelligence and imagination, generate a capacity for self-transcendence which is the root from which stems the possibility of a sense of the numinous – and so of the divine, we shall be suggesting in due course.

Human beings have a sense of inwardness which is reflected in language in the semantically peculiar ways in which they use 'I' of themselves. This sense is only gradually acquired by the growing child as its self-knowledge, and indeed its self-image, flowers and fructifies, or is withered and stunted, by its interactions with its environment and especially with other persons close to it. For there is considerable evidence that this distinguishing of part of the environment as consisting of persons and the formation of relationships with them is essential to the growing child's sense of personhood. The extent to which these relationships are, or are not, affectionate is, it appears, crucial for the self-image of the child and of the adult it becomes. Thus does the growing child become the centre of a network of relationships which are constitutive of being a person. This has social and, indeed, legal consequences when human beings consider each other as bearers of rights so that, although each is unique, the 'other' is someone with whom the individual self can imagine changing places. This becomes the source both of compassion and of the more legal concept of 'person' continuously transformed, as it has been historically, by changing apprehensions and sensitivities.[5]

As self-awareness, cognition and the conceptual resources for representing other people and the environment develop in the individual, and indeed in the species, human beings become capable of exercising their imaginations and so of choice and intended action. They become agents capable of bringing about one state of affairs rather than another. Since they have, or believe themselves to have, reasons for so acting, human beings may be described as rational agents, making choices for what appear to them to be 'reasons' – even though these are often the complex net sum of other motivations. In any case, the ordinary causal laws operative in the external world are not operative – at least in any obvious way – in making such choices. So human agents have the experience of a sense of freedom, of being able to choose their own thoughts in, for example, making moral choices and aesthetic judgements and in choosing between beliefs. We regard ourselves as having 'free will', so we say, and this enables us to act with creative novelty: it is the basis of that creativity which characterizes our self-awareness and sense of inwardness. Paradoxically, such 'free will' is only possible at all in a milieu in which natural processes follow 'lawlike' regularities so that 'free' choices have broadly predictable outcomes. Choice would be illusory if all were totally unpredictable. Hence a regular environment is the prerequisite for the exercise of freedom and so of moral choices by persons. Furthermore, in making choices persons irreversibly shape their own lives as they bring about their own intentions and thereby transcend the processes of individual development and of the evolution of species which characterize all other living organisms.

A primary characteristic of being a person is a sense of purpose and intentionality and these generate biological and social adaptability. But this thread of intentionality and purpose which runs through a self-conscious human life becomes increasingly coloured by awareness of the inevitable termination of its continuity in death. Human beings – uniquely, it seems, among living organisms – have to come consciously to terms with anticipation of their own demise. *Homo sapiens* has, from the evidence of the earliest traces of its existence on earth, buried its dead with rituals indicative of reflection on this *terminus ad quem*. Such reflections seem to have been linked with the sense of the numinous in relation to the natural world and to the individual's own creative self-transcendence and sense of worth, as evidenced by wall paintings and other artifacts. Here we have to recognize the ancient beginnings of another distinctive feature of human persons – the propensity to worship and prayer to another order of Being conceived as the source of all other lesser being.

The continuities of human beings with their evolutionary predecessors are obvious enough, – in anatomy, biochemistry, physiology, for example, and even, and more clearly perceived than formerly, in activities involved in tool-making, exploring the environment and counting. However, these last-named 'mental' activities occur only partially in other creatures and the features of *homo sapiens* to which attention has been drawn above in fact represent a genuine discontinuity in the evolutionary process.

In human beings a number of cognitive functions, that are also to be found in animals and that individually make their own contribution to survival, are 'integrated into a system of higher order', to use a phrase of Konrad Lorenz.[6] Lorenz has identified these functions as: the perception of form which then constitutes a mechanism of both abstraction and objectivization; the central representation of space, especially through sight; locomotion, following on from visual orientation; memory, storing of information, as the learnt basis of insight-controlled behaviour; voluntary movement in conjunction with the feedback it produces; exploratory behaviour; imitation, the basis for the learning of verbal language; and tradition, the transmission of individually acquired knowledge from one generation to another.

In the integrated unity of the human being, so emerging, there arise the new characteristics of the faculty of language and abstract conceptual thought, the power to foresee the consequences of one's own actions and the ability to accumulate knowledge transmitted non-genetically via a cultural tradition utilizing words and symbols. Human beings in developing language and society create artifacts such as libraries, tapes, music, pictures, sculptures, buildings, diagrams, computer records, etc., which transmit knowledge and experience from one generation to another, thereby outstripping the processes of natural selection through which humanity first emerged and which are still operative in other creatures. Something new has emerged in humanity which requires autonomous concepts for its description and elaboration. In humanity 'biology' has become 'history' and a new kind of interaction – that of humanity with the rest of the natural order – arises in which the organism, *homo sapiens*, shapes its own environment, and so its future evolution, by its own choices through utilizing its acquired knowledge and social organization. The root of human inter-subjectivity manifest in culture is the evolved capacity for self-awareness which arises *pari passu* with that higher-order functioning that integrates all these other functions into one

'distinctive activity, distinctive in being owned, localized, personalized. The unity of personality ... is to be found in an integrating activity, an activity expressed, embodied and scientifically understood in terms of its genetic, biochemical, [etc. . . . .] manifestations. What we call human behaviour is an expression of that effective, integrating activity which is peculiarly and distinctively ourselves.[7]

Yet, oddly enough, there are signs of a kind of misfit between human beings, persons, and their environment which is not apparent in other creatures. We alone in the biological world, it seems, individually commit suicide; we alone by our burial rituals evidence the sense of another dimension to existence; we alone go through our biological lives with that sense of incomplete fulfilment evidenced by the contemporary quests for 'self-realization' and 'personal growth'. We have aspirations and what appear to us as needs which go far beyond basic biological requirements for food, rest, shelter, sex, and an environment in which procreation and care of the young is possible. Human beings seek to come to terms with death, pain and suffering and they need to realize their own potentialities and learn how to steer their paths through life. The natural environment is not capable of satisfying such aspirations – nor can the natural sciences describe, accurately discern or satisfy them. So our presence in the biological world raises questions outside the scope of the natural sciences to answer. For we are capable of happinesses and miseries quite unknown to other creatures, thereby evidencing a dis-ease with our evolved state, a lack of fit which calls for explanation and, if possible, cure. 'Has something gone wrong?' we cannot help asking, as we contemplate human history and the ravaging of this planet by human activity.

2 Conditions for the Emergence of Persons

One of the remarkable features of recent reflections, informed by modern astro-physics, particle physics and cosmology, on the relation of humanity to the rest of the universe has been a reversal of the effect of the Copernican Revolution. This appeared to demote humanity by locating it on a planet which was no longer at the centre of the universe and and whose privileged location was now occupied by the Sun. Subsequently astronomy in the twentieth century accentuated this demotion by relegating the whole solar system to a corner of one among myriads of galaxies. Human life seemed to have only an insignificant role in relation to the vastness of the universe. However in the last two decades we have witnessed amongst scientists an increasingly acute awareness of how finely

tuned the parameters and characteristics of the observed universe
are for us as observers to be present at all. Few would now dispute a
recent formulation, in its weak form, of what has come to be known
as the 'anthropic principle':

> The observed values of all physical and cosmological quantities are
> not equally probable but they take on values restricted by the require-
> ment that there exist sites where carbon-based life can evolve and by
> the requirement that the Universe be old enough for it to have already
> done so . . . It [this principle] expresses only the fact that those proper-
> ties of the Universe we are able to discern are self-selected by the fact
> that they must be consistent with our evolution and present
> existence.'[8]

It appears that this principle places extremely stringent constraints
on the values of many fundamental constants if life is to have
anything like the form we know (hence the 'carbon-based' in Barrow
and Tipler's formulation) and is to evolve at all in any conceivable
universe. These constants include the actual strengths of all the
forces that operate in the universe (gravitational, strong and weak
nuclear, electromagnetic), the electronic charge, the velocity of
light, Planck's constant and various particle masses – and even then
the list is not complete. It is this universe that is cognizable, which
can generate in itself life and so, eventually, that form of life,
ourselves, that can observe it. Far from our presence in the universe
being an inexplicable 'surd', our presence is tightly locked into the
universe actually having the properties we now observe it to possess. There are, it can now be confidently affirmed, the closest
possible links between many quantitative features of the universe
being precisely what they are and the possibility of life, and so of us,
being here at all.

The anthropic principle in its most widely agreed, 'weak' form,
refers to the links between 'carbon-based life' and many universal
parameters having particular values. We have already seen that,
once life started, there would be an inbuilt tendency for it to
increase in complexity of organization in its various manifestations.
It is also becoming clear that the acquisition of cognitive skills
confers a very great advantage in natural selection. Such skills are
dependent on having an increasingly sensitive apparatus for receiving signals from the environment and a highly efficient apparatus for
both processing that information and transmitting appropriate signals to the motor system of the organism. More precisely, the four

parts of the perceptual apparatus that are needed are input analysers, motivational and behavioural controllers and an energy regulator.[9] All these have to develop together in a process of mutual reinforcement and stimulation and the very process of relating perception, analysis and action is of the essence of cognitive activity, so that the 'mind' becomes the 'cognitive organ of the body'.[10] The systems that have survived this evolutionary process, which is facilitated by social cooperation and the development of language, must *prima facie* be presumed to be giving sufficiently reliable knowledge of the environment to make that survival possible. Hence the evolutionary scientist's approach to a theory of 'knowledge' is one of 'hypothetical realism', affirmed by Konrad Lorenz in the following terms:

> The scientist sees man as a creature who owes his qualities and functions, including his highly developed powers of cognition, to evolution, that age-long process of genesis in the course of which all organisms have come to terms with external reality and, as we say, 'adapt' to it. This process is one of knowledge, for any adaptation to a particular circumstance of external reality presupposes that a measure of information about that circumstance has already been absorbed.'[11]

The advances in cognitive powers must have compensated in natural selection for the increase in vulnerability that must inevitably accompany an increasingly sensitive apparatus for monitoring and sensing the world external to the organism. Indeed, human beings have manifestly only survived their weakness, slowness and general vulnerability by the exercise of cognitive powers which in them reach a unique peak of development. The combination of vulnerability and increased sensitivity to signals from the environment has, as its concomitant, a heightened ability to suffer pain and it is not at all easy to conceive how one could have the former without the latter. Moreover, pain is a necessary danger signal which warns off the organism from courses of action, or feeding habits, or actions in relation to predators, and so on, which would otherwise threaten its survival. We cannot avoid concluding that the pain and suffering consequent upon vulnerability are the inherently necessary price that has to be paid for consciousness to emerge with its associated cognitive powers.

The self-awareness of human individuals is so closely linked to their linguistic and conceptual powers that it is difficult to attribute any distinctive causal advantage it might have had in the processes of natural selection. These same powers clearly facilitated analysis of the environment, of predators and of food resources and the execution through foresight of planned, cooperative action so that the physically relatively weak *homo sapiens* began to establish itself in every conceivable habitat. The subsequent emergence of culture, based on those resources for transmitting knowledge across the generations that we have already referred to, have now led to the domination of the earth by humanity. This domination is undoubtedly the consequence, if only indirectly, of human self-awareness and self-consciousness, as expressed through its cultural systems held together by communication through language and symbol. But this very self-awareness and self-consciousness is the stage on which is enacted the human drama of pain, suffering and the sense of finitude and anticipation of death and all that flows from them – the whole tragedy of the human condition. So that our inner awareness and sense of selfhood both enhance our ability to survive as individuals and as a species and, at one and the same time, snatch from us the fruits of a happiness that is available to a merely animal consciousness. Individuality, and awareness of it, reach a new peak on *homo sapiens* comcomitantly with an increased reliance on socialization for the survival of the species.

CHAPTER 5

What Does It All Mean?

It seems that the human being is alone among living organisms in asking questions about the content and meaning of the world in which it has evolved. Over the course particularly of recent centuries it has acquired a vast new body of information about that world and how human beings have come to exist in it. To that world so understood it reacts in a variety of ways, not all mutually consistent. How does the world appear to human beings in the light of their new knowledge? How does it seem to be? What are the human reactions to the features of the world we have been relating?

To the scientist it is a continuous wonder that the world turns out to be so intelligible and so amenable to rational inquiry based on observation. As Fred Hoyle once said, 'When by patient enquiry we learn the answer to any problem, we always find, both as a whole and in detail, that the answer thus revealed is finer in concept and design than anything we could ever have arrived at by a random guess.'[1] Mathematics, a construction of the human mind – pure deductions from postulated axioms – turns out to be the necessary means for understanding the fundamental structure and relational networks of the physical world and, increasingly, of being able to articulate the basis of biological complexity.[2] In Einstein's words: 'The eternal mystery of the world is its comprehensibility.... The fact that it is comprehensible is a miracle.'[3] Our earlier consideration of 'evolutionary epistemology', that is, of the evolutionary role of cognitive processes, may serve to diminish our wonder a little – but not overmuch, for penetration of the secrets of the nature of, say, the sub-atomic world and of quantum field theory can hardly be postulated as necessary for biological survival. The powers of human ratiocination and conceptual imagination far exceed the demands for survival. Their extraordinary ability to represent aspects of the world inaccessible to the ordinary senses and incapable of depiction by any extrapolations from ordinary experience is still a striking feature of our relation to the world and of our reactions to that relation.

Because of the witness of the sciences we see the world as an unbroken, even if tangled, web of causal order in which multiple, but discernible, chains of causality interlock and intersect, constituting patterns of intelligible relationships. Sometimes the track of causality becomes too ill-defined to trace and intelligibility is obscured, but it has been the continuously validated experience of three centuries of natural science that gradually the network of relations and interactions becomes clearer and light is cast over a wider swath. So, in this sense, our understanding of the world becomes more and more complete, for the gaps in our ignorance and in our comprehension continue to narrow and often disappear.

Yet, oddly enough, there is always a certain baffling incompleteness to our understanding as evidenced by the limitations on predictability already mentioned in chapter 3. For, although we find the emergence of new properties and behaviours of entities in the natural world intelligible after the event, we would often be incapable of predicting them in advance and, indeed, find them entirely surprising on reflection after the event. As our knowledge of the natural world stretches out in both directions – to the basic constituents of physical reality on the one hand, and to the higher levels of biological complexity on the other – we cannot but be more and more impressed by the way the operation of a few simple principles on a finite number of basic entities produces the vast richness and fecundity of this planet and of the universe of which it forms such a small part. Only the dullest could fail to react with awe at the immense inbuilt and inventive creativity of the world in which we have evolved. The elusive and unpicturable basic sub-atomic entities out of which all else is made, including ourselves, have potentialities unknown and undescribable in terms of the physics that discovers and the mathematics that symbolizes them. Hence at both of the extremities of our comprehension – the sub-atomic and the personal – we face baffling depths in the actual nature of reality that make many scientific writers refer to the sense of 'mystery' that is stirred in them as they contemplate the universe through the lenses of the natural sciences.

This sense of mystery engendered through science has been particularly stressed by Harold Schilling.[4] He traces it firstly to the sense of wonder at the infinity and unfathomability of the unknown, quoting Victor Weisskopf: 'Our knowledge is an island in the infinite ocean of the unknown'[5], – and the larger this island grows, the more extended are its boundaries toward the unknown. Secondly, he encounters it among scientists as they reflect on the infinity and unfathomability of the known, the mysteries at the two extremities of the sub-atomic and biological that we have referred to already. Every apparent answer confronts us with even more numerous unanswered questions.

So there is an ambiguity in our knowledge of the natural world – increasingly rich and exciting to the intelligence, but increasingly eliciting intellectual vertigo as, viewing from the dizzy heights of the new perspectives, we try to plumb challengingly new conceptual depths. But there is another, more ancient, ambiguity that human beings experience in regard to the natural order. This is the awareness that the natural order is essential to our existence and nurtures us through its resources but that it can, nevertheless, also be tragically destructive of human existence and aspirations. The root of this is to be found in our inherent ambiguity as parts of nature that, in our self-consciousness, also transcend it as subjects. Again, our distinctively human characteristics emerge as the source of the possibility of enhanced fulfilment concomitant with a sensibility readily offended and pained.

For, finally, as we contemplate the future of our planet in the solar system in its galaxy, we have to reckon with its certain disappearance. The energy of our Sun which sustains life on Earth is finite: the Sun is about half-way through its life and the time left for the existence of the Earth is about the same as the length of time it has already existed. So the demise of all life, including human, on earth is quite certain. Since it is entirely problematic whether human beings will be able to 'colonize' any other planets, we have to ask: Is the whole experiment of life, which has such significance for us in interpreting the universe, after all going to prove futile and abortive? What is the *meaning* of this universe and of our presence in it? Thus we come to ultimate questions and find them not answerable through the resources of science itself.

PART II

Divine Being and Becoming

CHAPTER 6

Asking 'Why?': The Search for Intelligibility and Meaning

At the end of Part I, we recognized that there was a somewhat mixed response on the part of human beings to the hard-won scientific perspective on the being and becoming to be discerned in the natural world. The scientists, we noted, respond with a mixture of wonder, even awe, and intellectual excitement tinged with a sense of mystery concerning the ultimate nature of the world and awareness at the essential incompleteness of our real understanding and comprehension of it all. Such ambiguity in our response to this new perspective on the world is compounded when we reflect on humanity's place and destiny in it, as we contemplate and experience the pain, suffering and evil that it evidences – and finally as we face the enigma of death both of the individual and of the whole human species when the Earth eventually ceases to exist, as surely it will. Are all our thoughts and strivings doomed to ultimate futility? We find we cannot escape the question of the meaning of it all and this inevitably takes us beyond the end of the tether of the natural sciences.

The scientific and theological enterprises are, like many other human endeavours, characterized by their search for intelligibility, for what makes the most coherent sense of the experimental and experiential data with which each are concerned. We cannot help pressing 'why?' questions to their intelligible limits. Science directs such questions to the nexus of events in the natural world: it seeks to provide answers to the question 'why?' by depicting the realities of the natural world in metaphorical language.[1] But there are other broader 'why?' questions than those directed to what is in and going on in the natural world. 'Why is there a universe at all?' 'Why should it be of this particular kind?' 'Why is it open to rational inquiry?' 'Why is it beautiful?' 'Why does it generate a creature that can discern values?'

The religious quest, or rather, its intellectual aspect in the form of the theological enterprise, presses such 'why?' questions to their attainable limits – until to press them further 'becomes plain silly'.[2] The problem is that there is no agreement concerning the point at which this limit is reached, for the point at which one stops is controlled by one's willingness to allow the quest to enter that area of discernment which has a wider, essentially religious, import. This has certainly been the case with respect to what is often regarded as the paradigm of religious questions, namely the mystery-of-existence question 'Why does the world exist?'. Fewer philosophers today than a decade or so ago are willing to dismiss such questions as meaningless by, for instance, asserting that to argue for them is already to assume the existence of (a) necessary being. For example, we find Munitz in 1965 arguing minimally that questions in the form 'Is-there-a-reason-for-the-existence-of-the-world?' are meaningful – even if possibly unanswerable.[3] The philosophical suspicion of such questions is not unfounded if the answer to them is sought as an 'explanation' conceived of as operating in the same way as explanations of events do within the natural causal nexus. There is a genuine difficulty in postulating one ultimate explanation *of* the universe in the same way as we 'explain' individual events *within* the universe. But 'explanation' does not have to be restricted only to causal explanations and the acceptance of this and other developments in philosophy, principally the demise of the Verification Principle in its strong form, has rendered theism as an attempt to respond to such questions a much more lively option than would have been thought philosophically respectable even a decade ago – as was brought out very clearly in the radio interviews with leading philosophers conducted by Keith Ward in 1986.[4] As Ward himself has written elsewhere, 'explanation' might, more usefully, be equated with 'that which renders intelligible' and, in this sense: 'For the Christian, God, as the power making for intelligibility, beauty and righteousness, may be said to explain the universe in that he gives it meaning and intelligibility, provides purpose and significance, and so sets all things within an overall context'.[5] But this is to rush our fences, for at this stage of our inquiry we simply wish to identify some of what we might call these 'limit-questions', recognizing that it is not intellectually and philosophically disreputable to ask them.

I suggested earlier[6] that there are two kinds of search in which we are engaged in relation to the world in which we live. One – primarily intellectual, though not without existential urgency – is the search for intelligibility, inference to the best explanation, where 'explanation' is now to be construed in the qualified sense of the preceding paragraph. This search, involving as it does the mystery-of-existence question in its various forms, adds impetus to that other search – the search for personal meaning in human existence, in general, and our own, in particular. The twentieth-century scientific perspective of a developing cosmos which generated persons now ties together in a stronger bond than ever before these two quests. For it now appears (the 'anthropic principle') that the universe is such that it is characterized by values of the fundamental constants that are precisely those necessary for our existence[7] and that we are generated within it out of its own constituents by its own natural processes: then, having arrived, we seek intelligibility and meaning in that universe and in those processes. Indeed we cannot avoid, in the light of the scientific perspective, merging these two searches into one by urging our questions about the cosmos in forms that include ourselves: 'What is the intelligible meaning of a cosmos in which the primeval assembly of fundamental particles has eventually manifested the potentiality of becoming organized in forms that are conscious and self-conscious, human and personal, namely ourselves, and whose thinking transcends that out of which they have emerged?'; or, 'If we continue to press for 'explanation' and to search for 'meaning', does not the very continuity of the universe, with its gradual elaboration of its potentialities, imply that any categories of 'explanation' and 'meaning' must at least include the personal?'; or, 'What is the 'explanation' and 'meaning' of a cosmos that generates from within itself entities, *homo sapiens*, who, in knowing and knowing that they know, creatively seek truth; respond to, and themselves create, beauty; strive after goodness, have moral purposes, and create community – and can also ambiguously counter and confound these values?'; or, more darkly, ' What is the 'explanation' and 'meaning' of a cosmos in which pain, suffering and death of sentient creatures is inbuilt as a transformative principle whereby new forms of increasingly conscious life become possible?'; or, darker still, 'Why does the universe generate from within itself by its own inherent, inbuilt processes a creature, *homo sapiens*, which is such a misfit with its environment that, at best, a general sense of incompleteness and lack of fulfilment pervades and colours their consciousness, and, at worst, they are overwhelmed by *angst*, suffering and tragedy?'; or, perhaps not surprisingly in view of all these questions, 'Why do these human beings, the product of the cosmos and its forces, experience a sense often of *sacred* mystery hidden within and veiled by their experience of that same cosmos, both in its particular and general features?'

If we pursue the quest of science to its limits we cannot avoid coming to questions such as these which, while they go beyond the remit and power of the natural sciences to answer, nevertheless demand a response. Difficult though such a response may be, it would be intellectually irresponsible, indeed a twentieth-century *trahison des clercs*, not to ask and seek to answer these questions. To decline to do so is to be less than human and to leave ourselves with no map, however sketchy, by which to steer our lives from birth to and through death.

It is in responding to challenging questions like these, referred to the cosmologies of their own day, that from time immemorial men and women have postulated the existence of an ultimate Reality that is the source of all being as both the meaning and explanation of all that is – that Reality which, in English, we call 'God'. But the postulate of 'God' is inseparable from the question of 'What sort of God?'. Both the postulate and the associated question have been the perennial concern of philosophers and to some of their more recent reflections we must now turn.

CHAPTER 7

'God' as Response to the Search for Intelligibility and Meaning

1 'GOD' IN THE PHILOSOPHY OF RELIGION

Since the demise of positivism, traditional metaphysical questions have increasingly during the last two decades come to be recognized as again worthy of the attention of philosophers. Paramount in such traditional metaphysical questions evoking renewed philosophical consideration is, of course, the question of 'God', both with respect to the epistemological questions concerning what sort of arguments should properly be deployed and the arguments as such. Indeed, Keith Ward affirms that 'Theism . . . has gone onto the attack; and we can see very clearly how it joins hands with science in proposing the possibility of making God the best explanation of how the world actually is.'[1] I have already advocated[2] that theology, like any other human inquiry into the nature of reality, must use the same general criteria of reasonableness as, say, science itself. So that inference to the best explanation is assessed[3] by its fit with the data ('existential relevance'[4]), internal coherence, comprehensiveness and general cogency ('adequacy'[5]), simplicity ('economy'[6]) and fruitfulness in producing new ideas and, in the case of theology, in giving meaning for personal existence. As suggested in the comment of Keith Ward, applying these criteria and coming to the conclusion that the existence of 'God' in the Judeo-Christian sense is probable, has become more frequent in recent years.[7] Needless to say, this conclusion has not gone uncontested.[8] There can be no doubt that the 'question of God' is no longer regarded as simply meaningless, as in the earlier days of 'logical positivism'.

What we can usefully mean by 'God' and how we might depict God's relation to the world and to humanity will only gradually unfold later. For the moment, we would do well in seeking to obtain an insight into the philosophical debate to turn to Richard Swinburne's significant book on *The Existence of God* and the reply he made to J. L. Mackie's criticism of it.[9] There, Swinburne claims that

> most of the well-known *a posteriori* arguments for the existence of God could be construed as inductive arguments in which the observable phenomena cited in the premises (the existence of the universe, its orderliness, the existence of consciousness, various opportunities available for men, reports of miracles, and religious experiences) provided evidence for (in the sense of raising the probability of) the existence of God and that overall they rendered the existence of God more probable than not.[10]

By 'God exists' (= 'There is a God'), Swinburne means that 'there exists a person without a body (i.e. a spirit) who is eternal, is perfectly free, omnipotent, omniscient, perfectly good, and the creator of all things.'[11] He uses 'God' as the name of the person picked out by this description. These descriptions he elaborates thus:[12]

> *person*, used 'in the modern sense', more specifically, not in the sense of *persona* or *hypostasis* of Christian trinitarian doctrine;[13]
> *eternal*, God 'always has existed and always will exist' (not in the sense of 'timeless' or 'outside time');
> *perfectly free*, 'no object or event or state (including past states of himself) in any way causally influences God to do the actions which he does – his own choice at the moment of action alone determines what he does';
> *omnipotent*, God 'is able to do whatever it is logically possible (i.e. coherent to suppose) that he can do';
> *omniscient*, God 'knows whatever it is logically possible that he know';
> *perfectly good*, God 'does no morally bad actions', and does any morally obligatory action;
> *creator of all things*, 'everything which exists at each moment of time (apart from himself) exists because, at that moment of time, he makes it exist, or permits it to exist'.

Swinburne argues that the theist holds that God possesses these properties necessarily in the sense that 'having those properties is essential to being the kind of being which God is ... He could not lose any of the properties analysed [as set out above] without ceasing to be God.'[14] But is 'God exists' necessary too? This is a subtle question to which Swinburne's response is 'that God's essence is an eternal essence; that there is a being who is essentially a personal ground of being (which includes being eternal) is the inexplicable brute fact, a terminus of explanation, how things are.'[15] He terms this a 'factually necessary existence', as distinct from a 'logically necessary existence'.

The contested issues between Mackie and Swinburne concerned *inter alia* Swinburne's claim that 'God is the simplest kind of person there can be because a person is a being with power (to do intentional actions), knowledge, and freedom (to choose, uncaused, which actions to do).'[16] Linked with this claim is Swinburne's insistence that to postulate God as agent in bringing about all-that-is is a *personal* explanation, whereby the occurrence of a phenomenon is explained as brought about by a rational agent doing some action intentionally.[17] Mackie disputed the simplicity of personal explanation, since human personal agents act through a complex causal chain to implement their intentions. His undermining of this claimed simplicity, Mackie argued, reduces the support Swinburne says it gives to the *a priori* improbability of the evidence for regularity in the world of our observations. Swinburne rejects these criticisms as inadequate, finally affirming

> It is very unlikely indeed *a priori* that there should be a Universe made of matter behaving in totally regular ways, giving rise to conscious beings capable of changing themselves and others, making themselves fit for the Heaven of which they have a glimpse in religious experience. Hence the reason which we use about science and history demands that we postulate a simple explanation of these phenomena in terms of a creator and sustainer God.[18]

I have dwelt on Swinburne's account and arguments for theism not because I wish to support their every nuance but because they seem to me broadly to represent the position of many Christian theists and because his has been one of the most ably expounded and philosophically defended expositions of theism of recent years. Many others, of course, have contributed to the revival of the philosophy of religion in the last twenty years, as demonstrated in the representative collection compiled by Thomas Morris on *The Concept of God*.[19] While recognizing that this effort has yielded a better understanding of the arguments for the existence of God, the problem of evil and the nature of claims based on religious experience, he is concerned, in his introduction to this volume, to point out the considerable attention that has been devoted to examining the *concept* of God. He claims that

Beneath the many deep differences that divide philosophers on the nature of God, a single unifying consideration seems to have been operative ... most recent contributors to the literature on divine attributes have worked in the broad tradition of perfect being theology. That is to say, their overall conception of God has been that of a maximally perfect or greatest possible being.[20]

He urges that such a 'perfect being' theology is rationally the method most suited to governing our thinking about God. God as such a 'perfect being' will then be conceived as having some unsurpassable array of properties that make for greatness and which can be possessed together without contradiction. Relying, as this does, on our intuitions concerning what properties make for greatness, this clearly goes beyond the constructing of a concept of God as the result of inference to the best explanation of the existence of the world and of its actual features and characteristics in the style of Swinburne, for example. Such empirically based constructions of the concept of God are more likely to be pertinent to our purpose, in this book, of discerning the extent to which the scientific perspective of the world might or should affect Christian concepts of God. Naturally, we have to recognize that, in the end, no sharp, classificatory lines can be drawn between the concepts of God that the different approaches yield, for there is much overlap and common ground. However, before we can undertake that study of the impact of science on the concept of God, which is the principle theme of Part II of this book, we must examine more closely what the addition of the adjective 'Christian' to 'theism' purports and implies.

2 'GOD' IN CHRISTIAN BELIEF

The foregoing sketch of some philosophical analyses of the concept of God may well have left the reader feeling that what philosophy can deliver is only an arid and desiccated version of the rich depths of the God whom individual Christians trust and worship and whom the Christian church affirms and proclaims. The faith of the Christian church derives from its experience, the principal resource and source for which are those archetypal and seminal experiences and encounters with God recorded in its scriptures. Such belief is a shared possession which cannot be acquired simply by an individual effort divorced from the entry of the individual into the well-winnowed common inheritance of a community continuous through many generations.[21] Hence in pressing our inquiries into the possible impact of the scientific perspective on the Christian understanding of God, we need first to try to expound the content of this understanding as it has been shared by Christians down the ages, even into our own pluralistic socieites. To ascertain this content of Christian belief in God is a subtle and complex task, but we are fortunate in having available a recent concerted effort by theologians of the Church of England, which, in this respect (as in others), stands within the scope of both catholic and reformed belief concerning God – for fortunately the unhappy divisions between the churches have not been in this basic area. I refer to the 1987 report of the Doctrine Commission of the Church of England, *We Believe in God*,[22] the main ideas of which I will attempt to summarize in the following paragraphs (giving page numbers as references in the text and using its general phrasing), for it represents the most recent attempt by a church to expound the content of belief in God in at least one Christian community. It is the more valuable for our purpose in that it does not attempt to argue for the 'God of the philosophers', surmising, quite rightly, that the God who is believed in and trusted by Christians is thought of in more personal and less abstract terms than are properly appropriate to philosophical discourse.

The Christian Bible, that marriage of the already sacred writings of the people of Israel with focal written sources of the early Christians, is *par excellence* the product not simply of individual authors but also of communities. In the communities that generated and possessed this literature, God was spoken about by means of narrative, so that, to this extent at least, God is personal. The biblical stories express a faith which tried to see a coherent divine purpose in events (pp. 54–6). The God of the Bible who features in these narratives is described in many, often apparently inconsistent, ways – both as severe judge and as loving father, with both what we would regard as 'masculine' and 'feminine' images (in spite of the blinkers with which subsequent believers have seen the texts), as characterized by both 'wrath' and mercy. The relation of the biblical narratives to history is subtle, varied and complex, and the fact that it is impossible to define exactly where sacred history ends and secular history begins is in itself a significant pointer to the nature of God himself – namely that God's action in history is both real and elusive of definitive de-limitation (pp. 58–61). This is notoriously true of attempts to determine what is the 'end' of its principal narratives, most notably that about Jesus himself (pp. 61–3). This fluidity of interpretation should not surprise us for, as the Report puts it,

> Like the hypotheses used by scientists to describe the physical universe, the models used in the Bible to describe God are valid up to a certain point of experience and understanding, but (in theory, at least) they are corrigible in the light of new challenges to faith and further moments of revelation. (p. 64)

This process is to be seen at work within the Bible, or more strictly, the biblical experience, itself – most significantly, as we shall see in a moment, in the way Jesus himself revised and amplified the tradition of the 'Old Testament' he received. In doing this he was, in one sense, being true to those very traditions, for the story of Israel can be seen both as a voyage of discovery of God on the part of the people of Israel and as a story of the activity of God (p. 70). God was discovered and revealed himself as a personal being who is intimately involved both in human life, as provider, healer and friend, and in the natural world as the source of the world's stability and life (pp. 72–4).

Nevertheless, the God of the Old Testament is not just a human person writ large; there is a mysterious otherness about him. He is the Holy One, demanding awe in worship with a holiness inseparable from his righteousness and love. In Israel's religious consciousness the concept of the holiness is bound up with ethical qualities, with sheer goodness. Holiness and love are inseparably linked. God is supremely one in the unity of his love and justice and his attributes are not split between a multiplicity of minor deities, though God's power within persons is often objectified, as 'Spirit' or, later, 'Wisdom', so as not to compromise God's essential otherness from humanity (pp. 75–6). God's goodness could be fully displayed only in the salvation of his people, a salvation which a few prophetic souls saw, because of God's oneness as Creator of all, must be extended to all humanity in God's good time (pp. 76–7).

For Christians, Jesus the Christ constituted a radical revision, *the* most radical revision, of human ideas about God, that is of the understandings of God of the people of Israel, in Jesus's historical setting. He does not invalidate this tradition, nor even that of other religions –

> But by his suffering, death and resurrection he significantly enlarges the range of human experience which can be 'read' as a testimony to

the love and power of God; and in his teaching he offers new 'models' of understanding which go far beyond what was available before. (p. 66)

This authority to reveal the nature of God stems, historically, from a uniquely intimate relation between himself and God that involved an exceptional degree of personal knowledge (p. 67). Jesus addressed God as 'Abba', the family word for 'father' and the title used by disciples for a rabbi: it suggests attitudes both of dependence, security and confidence, on the one hand, and of humility, obedience and reverence, on the other. A new richness of content came to the fore in Jesus' teaching about the activity of God in the world and especially in human life. 'God is one who loves, cares, gives, listens, welcomes, seeks, accepts, forgives, provides' (p. 81). The character and attributes predicated of God that generate such features in his action are focused by affirming a divine fatherhood. This is worked out in parable and prayer (the Lord's Prayer and that in Gethsemane) in terms of both authority and caring, with hardly a hint of 'wrath'.

Jesus was uncompromising in his prophetic message of the immanent confrontation of his contemporaries with God in 'all his holiness, purity, goodness, mercy and love' (p. 84). A response was called for that was, in the end, evoked by his making his death a sacrifice, thereby affirming his teaching about the God whose power extends beyond the grave and whose good will for mankind cannot in the end be thwarted. Because of Jesus' life, suffering, death and resurrection he became for them, as they assimilated this experience, the 'Christ', 'Son of God', the 'Word and Wisdom of God'. What is important to us at this stage of our inquiry is that the God who was made known in his self-disclosure through Jesus was supremely and essentially total self-giving love. God is revealed in Jesus the Christ as the 'Father of a crucified Son' (p. 97) who is 'deeply involved in the total act of redemptive suffering' (p. 98), that is in the life, suffering and death of the historical Jesus. Indeed, the unity between Jesus and God the Father, the Creator (all that Jesus affirmed he was), was so profound that in St John's Gospel the death of Jesus, in spite of all its bitterness and exemplification of the sordid corruption of humanity, could be called Jesus's 'glorification'. Here the evangelist is pointing to a new kind of relation which all might have with God on account of these events.

In the experience of the disciples and the early Church this new

kind of relation was sustained in the human community by what
they came to call 'God the Holy Spirit', the counterpart of 'the spirit
of Yahweh' of the Old Testament. This experience and its interpretation constituted a significant development of the understanding of
God, for it denoted a recognition of the personal presence of God
the Spirit as 'abiding in the life of the Christian community and of
the individual believer, inspiring both, and transforming them into
the likeness of Christ' (p. 101). So it moved beyond the Old Testament view of the Spirit as the transcendent God intervening from
time to time in his creation. It is the foundation for a specifically
Christian and strong emphasis on the immanence of God in his
world as a personal presence, awareness of whom is particularly
and powerfully vouchsafed to the believing community. This presence of God, strong as was the awareness of it in the Church and in
individuals in particular seminal historical experiences, could not, in
the end, be confined to the Christian, or even the human, community
alone.

The *Christian* doctrine of God is not a philosophical and metaphysical theory; it is, rather, an attempt to understand and to
come to terms with a profound religious experience centred on the
life, death, resurrection and teaching of Jesus. This had 'brought a
new realization of God's accessibility, a recognition of his entrance
into human suffering and of his relationship to his people, and
at the same time a new estimate of the persons of Christ and of the
Spirit in relation to God himself' (p. 101). But, because it was believed that the love of *God's own self* that had been demonstrated in Jesus and which had become accessible through him, this
could never lead to the conclusion that Jesus was a 'second god'.

Already we see here the beginnings of the understanding of the
one God as triune in his character, as personally transcendent,
personally incarnate and personally immanent[23] – 'Father, Son
and Holy Spirit', in the classical formularies. 'God, the God of
Israel, is also known as the Father of his crucified and redeeming
Son, and in the distinguishable person of his sanctifying Spirit. But
precisely because these are, theologically speaking, also functions
or attributes of the one God, the unity of God is not impaired' (p.
102).

CHAPTER 8

The Concept of God: Implications of Scientific Perspectives

We come now to the crucial stage of this enterprise, to inquire into the extent to which these concepts, models and images of God that have been winnowed and refined in religious experience, in particular the Christian, and have been supported by philosophical reflection, might need to be modified and enriched by the impressive new perspectives on the world that the natural sciences now give us. Of course, the philosophical concepts of God have already attempted to take into account many of the broad features of the world that the natural sciences have unveiled. I refer *inter alia* not only to the existence of the world but also to it being an intelligible nexus of relations exhibiting regularities without which personal existence would be impossible. Inference to God as the best explanation – what I take to be the perennial task of 'natural theology' – has always looked closely at what the sciences have been saying about the world, sometimes too closely in the sense that God's finger has been too readily discerned in details of the world's phenomena. However, the undoubted fact that the philosophers of religion have often been concerned to take account of their contemporary scientific world view serves only to encourage us in the task. For their efforts to do so have tended to be only partial and intermittent.

The panorama of the sciences has so widened in the present century that philosophers of religion and theologians have scarcely been able to adjust to the sweeping conceptual changes that they entail. The study of the philosophy of religion and of theology have become such demanding disciplines that these remarks are not intended as criticism but, rather, as a recognition of the magnitude of the task facing all thinkers about God in this century. That is why before setting out on our more particularly theological task it has been necessary to try to set out as coherently and succinctly as possible the perspective on the world that the sciences today actually give, and not that of the mechanistic accounts which have dominated theological exposition for well over three centuries.

It was found necessary in Part I to express our scientific knowledge of the world in terms both of its being – what is there – and of its becoming – what is going on. That account had, moreover, to take seriously the advent of the personal in and through the natural and the loose ends, and indeed mysteries, that this introduced into an otherwise coherent perspective. So we must expect that scientific perspective on the world to affect our understanding of both the 'being' of God and of God's 'becoming', and for it to raise questions about the significance of the personal in relation to God.

The philosophers of religion and the religious believer have now to reckon with their one God's relation to a continuously developing world – and this implies at least a continuously changing relation of God to the world, including persons, and so the further possibility that God is not unchanging in certain respects. So the question of the nature and attributes of God cannot in the end be separated neatly and clearly from the vital question of how God's interaction with a world described by the natural sciences is to be conceived. Traditionally, at least in Eastern Orthodox theology, there has been a distinction made between God's 'essence', what he is in himself, his 'being', on the one hand; and God's 'energies', what he does, his 'becoming', on the other.[1] This can be a useful distinction, provided we recognize that it can never be absolute, for what we are prepared to affirm about God's 'essence' nearly always depends on what we discern of his 'energies', what we believe or infer to be his activity in the world. So in the following our account of the implications of various aspects of the world view of the sciences for our understanding of God will inevitably move between these two poles of our questioning, between asking who or what God is, or is like, and asking how this God interacts with the world.

This latter will be the more explicit concern of chapter 9, but our concern now is certainly with *both* divine being and becoming – with both static and dynamic metaphors. For convenience of exposition in this chapter we attempt to separate them, but it has to be admitted that these two aspects of divinity are inextricably and mutually interwoven. In pursuing this inquiry we shall inevitably be partly traversing again ground already covered in many of the classical philosophical treatments of the nature and attributes of God. However, the same territory of the world of nature has a way of being perceived very differently in the context of the wider landscape of late twentieth-century science. A shift of context can alter our judgement of the nature of, the weight to be given to, and the consequences of arguments that have already been well aired in the long tradition of philosophical theology.

1 DIVINE BEING

a Ground of Being

As we saw in chapter 6, the postulate of the existence of *God as the Ground of Being* has become a respectable, though disputed response to the mystery-of-existence question, 'Why is there anything at all?'. Substantiation of this response has been the aim of the philosophical work already referred to above.[2] The scientific perspective outlined in Part I does not substantially alter the nature of the philosophical debate or the status of the theistic claim, it seems to me, but it does highlight with greater intensity some of the issues at stake. Thus, what one might call the sheer apparent 'givenness' of the world, with its cosmological, biological and social history – its contingency – is not abated by our newfound awareness of the regular lawfulness of its interconnectedness through space and time. We have good reason for thinking that this goes back to the first fluctuations in the quantum 'vacuum', or whatever it was that led to the setting off of the expansion of the universe. Let us suppose for the moment that these speculations do refer to what 'actually happened'. Even so, such a quantum field that undergoes these fluctuations (the quantum 'vacuum') is not, strictly speaking, simply 'nothing at all'. *Its* existence still calls for explanation of some kind – in the sense that it need not have existed at all with its particular properties, namely those represented by quantum theory. There is a need too to explain the existence of the mathematical laws by which the properties and transformations of this quantum field can be elucidated and made intelligible and coherent. There is also a need to explain the existence of the entities, structures and processes that stem from those primordial events and of the laws and relationships that govern their unfolding and evolution. So the mystery-of-existence question becomes even more pressing in the light of the cosmic panorama disclosed by the natural sciences.

But those same sciences now lead us to recognize that the 'mystery' is not confined simply to the fact of experience as such.

For the deepest scientific studies of the very nature of *what* exists run out, in particle physics and cosmology, towards boundaries where the ontological status of the entities, structures and processes propounded have a character that raises profound questions about what it is that science *can* actually affirm about 'reality' at these levels.[3] This has engendered, as we saw in chapter 5, a new sense of mystery about the nature of physical existence and has raised important epistemological questions concerning the deductions made from the results of the interactions of our measuring instruments with this deepest level of the physical world. Furthermore, a sense of genuine mystery is also generated by the other extreme of biological complexity with its experienced properties of consciousness, self-consciousness and personhood. All of which is a good antidote for that peculiarly scientific *hubris* which has too often characterized the accounts of the world in much so-called 'popular science' – the 'scientism' that believes that natural science alone gives clear, direct knowledge of all that is in the world. For if we can run up against such barriers to scientific comprehension in relation to both the physical and personal worlds, then the traditional reticence of theists concerning the nature of God as the Ground of all Being thereby becomes the more acceptable. This recognition of an ultimate ineffability in the nature of the divine parallels that of our ultimate inability to say what even things and persons *are* in themselves.

b *One*

We saw in our consideration of the scientific perspective that the world exhibits beneath its remarkable diversity, fecundity and complexity an underlying unity.[4] This unity is manifest in both the multiple, intricate interconnectedness[5] of the natural world at many levels and also in the ultimate and beautiful, though abstract, unity of at least some of the fundamental forces and principles that govern the properties of matter and the forms into which it evolves. The natural sciences have demonstrated a remarkable unity underlying the often overwhelming diversity we encounter in the world. This unity refers both to origins and to the principles that govern its development. The 'best explanation' of such a world's existence and character, if any is to be found at all, cannot but be grounded in *one* unifying source of creativity, multiple though its outreach may be. Thus it is that the scientific perspective on the world continues to reinforce the long-held intuition and inference of theists that *God is One* and is the underlying ground not only of the being of all-that-is but also of its deep unity, interconnectedness and wholeness – whatever differentiations within this unity may eventually be required from other, theological considerations (for example, any revelation by this one God of a threefoldness within this unity).

c Of Unfathomable Richness

We saw indeed that this underlying unity was capable of giving rise to immense diversity in the natural world, culminating in the enormously varied richness of human experience and societies. The world is characterized both in its development and in its present state by a hierarchy, or rather hierarchies, of complexity wherein entirely new kinds of properties and modes of existence emerge at new levels that are only understandable in terms of new nonreducible concepts.[6] As the creative source of all that is, *God must be a Being of unfathomable richness* to be able to conceive of and to bring into existence a cosmos with such fecund potentialities.

d Supremely Rational

It has been a perennial feature of their experience over the last three centuries that scientists have been impressed by the intelligibility and comprehensibility of the natural world. This has often generated a sense of wonder and even awe in twentieth-century scientists of many kinds of theistic belief or non-belief, as witnessed by the remarks of Einstein and Hoyle quoted earlier.[7] Often this awareness of a profounder rationality in the nature of things than had previously been imagined enters the general consciousness of the scientific community through encountering an impasse in their inquiries (as it often does in the case of scientific discovery by individuals). One could instance the profounder rationality of quantum field theory which made intelligible, though no longer picturable, the apparently contradictory behaviour, as particles and waves according to the experimental context, of electrons and other subatomic particles. Or one could cite the now intelligible way in which the interplay between chance-governed, random events and the lawlike framework constraining them are productive of irreducibly unpredictable new regimes of structures and processes in complex dynamical systems, including those that are living.[8] This has only relatively recently been recognized and resolves a number of puzzles generated by what had been thought of as anomalous or idiosyncratic observations. So twentieth-century science reinforces this experience of the inherent, yet always challenging, intelligibility and putative comprehensibility of the world's entities, structures and processes. This cannot but render more probable than ever before inference to the existence of a supra-rational Being as Creator as the 'best explanation' of such a world's existence and character. In other words, the affirmation of the existence of *God as the supremely rational Creator* is strengthened and its truth rendered more, rather than less, probable by the increasing success of science in discovering the inherent, but in content ever-surprising, rationality of the cosmos.

e Sustainer and Faithful Preserver

Relativity theory in its special form, as we saw earlier,[9] does not vitiate the concept of causality, the idea of sequences of causes and effects succeeding each other in time. It modifies the concept only to the extent that it is now realized that causal effects cannot be transmitted at speeds greater than that of light. However, scientific knowledge of the entities, structures and processes of the world, especially of complex living organisms, has shifted the focus of interest of much of the sciences away from the search for 'causes', as such, to seeking to understand networks of intelligible relationships both static, in structures and entities, and dynamic, in processes. So the classical argument of the 'Second Way' of St Thomas Aquinas,[10] which, finding intolerable an infinite chain of alternating causes and effects, goes on to infer the existence of a First Cause (to which everyone gives the name 'God') loses its cogency through this diminished interest in cause-and-effect sequences – even though the whole idea of an infinite series is itself more acceptable now that it is so commonplace in quite elementary mathematics. In any case the concept of God as 'First Cause' is not satisfactory theologically, for it makes God an element, admittedly a limiting boundary one, within the sequence of natural events and so not ultimately different in kind, however much greater in magnitude, from the natural world, thereby lacking the transcendence which is demanded by the primary experience of the divine.

Although for these reasons the concept of God as 'First Cause' terminating a *temporal* sequence has lost its cogency today, the natural sciences have nevertheless led to such a revision of our concept of the nature of time that the relation of God to time needs itself to be reconsidered. This is one of the concerns of the following section, but let us here note two aspects of this relation. First, we are aware that time is an aspect of the natural order, being closely integrated with space, matter and energy,[11] and so, for theists, must be regarded as being a real relation within the created order. Second, the realization that time has a direction,[12] in which there emerge new entities, structures and processes reinforces the idea that God is, as Creator, both its *Sustainer and faithful Preserver* through time. If 'God' is still to be the 'best explanation' of all-that-is, then as Creator he[13] must be regarded as holding all in existence and maintaining the validity of all laws and relations throughout time. It should be noted that there is implied, if God is personal, a moral quality in the divine sustaining and preserving – that of faithfulness or 'steadfast love', as the Old Testament calls it. However, this classical concept of sustaining and preserving as a characteristic of the divine Creator, valid as it as as far as it goes, appears to be singularly static in its impact, words such as 'sustaining' evoking pictures of a somewhat Atlas-like figure holding up the world.

f Continuous Creator

What the scientific perspective of the world inexorably impresses upon us is a dynamic picture of the world of entities and structures involved in continuous and incessant change and in process without ceasing. As we have seen,[14] new modes of existence come into being, and old ones often pass away. In the world new entities, structures and processes appear in the course of time, so that God's action as Creator is both past and present: it is continuous. Any notion of God as Creator must now take into account, more than ever before in the history of theology, that *God is continuously creating*, that God is *semper Creator*. In this respect, God has to be regarded as related to created time as the continuously creating Creator. Thus it is that the scientific perspective obliges us to take more seriously and concretely than hitherto in theology the notion of the immanence of God as Creator – that *God is the Immanent Creator creating in and through the processes of the natural order*. The implications of this will need working out further in our consideration of the divine becoming.[15]

g Personal – Creator of An Anthropic Universe

We have noted[16] that philosophical inferences to the best explanation of all-that-is lead to the conclusion that the postulate of a creator and sustainer God as the agent bringing about all-that-is is a *personal* explanation, whereby the occurrence of a phenomenon is explained as brought about by a rational agent doing some action intentionally. There are, as we shall shortly argue, grounds for believing that God might be 'personal', or 'at least personal', or even, if one is more robust, 'a person'.[17] This belief, indeed experience, is basic and fundamental to the Judeo-Christian religious tradition – one could hardly worship and pray to the 'Ground of Being', and even less to the 'Best Explanation of all-that-is'. We saw, too, that the distinctive contribution of Jesus's teaching to our understanding of God was to heighten and stress this personal relation of God to his people by his referring to God as 'Father' in a particularly intimate way and in the verbs with which he described the actions of this God his Father.[18] So the understanding and experience of God as personal is deeply embedded in the philosophical, theological and religious traditions. What bearing does the scientific perspective have on this conviction?

In our account[19] of the conditions required for the emergence of human persons – our discussion of the so-called 'anthropic principle' – we came to the conclusion that the world does seem to be finely tuned with respect to many physical features in a way conducive to the emergence of living organisms and so of human beings. We also gave reasons why living organisms might develop, through basically intelligible natural processes, cognitive powers and consciousness as they increased in complexity and flexibility – and how the development of self-consciousness would involve awareness of pain, suffering and death. None of this, we have argued, need imply a reductive account of the content of human consciousness or diminish our awareness of the deep mystery of human personhood. It does indeed seem to be the case that the universe is of such a unique kind that it can generate through its own inherent properties living organisms, including *homo sapiens*. Our presence in the universe is closely interlocked with the universe being of the kind it actually is, down to some very precise physical details. The presence of humanity in this universe, far from being an unintelligible surd, represents an inherent inbuilt potentiality of that physical universe in the sense that intelligent, self-conscious life was bound eventually to appear although its form was not prescribed by those same fundamental parameters and relationships that made it all possible.

This now well-established 'anthropic' feature of our universe has been interpreted in various and mutually inconsistent ways. Thus for some[20] it renders any talk of a creator God more than ever unnecessary since we would not be likely, would we, to be able to observe a universe that did *not* have the right conditions for producing us? D. J. Bartholomew, himself a theist, has argued[21] that the 'weak' anthropic principle ('what we can expect to observe is constrained by the conditions which are necessary for our existence as observers') is irrelevant to any argument for the initial state of the universe being divinely determined. For the probability of the initial conditions and laws of physics being as we now know them to be (which is the probability relevant to whether or not the initial state was divinely determined) hardly affects the value of what that probability would be *given that we exist*. This latter is certainly close to one in the light of the (non-controversial) 'weak' anthropic principle. Others[22] have seen in it a new and more defensible 'argument for design', or, rather, an 'argument from design' for the existence of a creator God. The whole debate is philosophically a very subtle and puzzling one,[23] depending as it clearly does on the presuppositions and interpretative framework that one brings to bear on any assessment of the *a priori* probability of all the constants, etc. – all the 'fine tuning' – coming out just to have the values that could lead to life and so to us.

Much of the current argumentation in favour of a theistic interpretation[24] has been concerned to base itself on a demonstration that this is indeed the only universe with which we have to deal. It is certainly the only one of which we have any knowledge and the one in which we seek meaning and intelligibility. Those arguing in favour of a theistic conclusion from anthropic considerations frequently reject any notion of the existence of (to us) unobservable, multiple universes. These have been postulated as existing simultaneously with us now as a result of a multiple splitting occurring at the beginning of this universe; or existing successively, as a result of a cycle of expansions and contractions ('hot big bangs' alternating with 'hot big crunches'); or as forming at every instant of time through a quantum splitting effect (the not-widely-held 'many worlds hypothesis' of some theoretical physicists). Those in favour of a theistic inference from anthropic relationships take this line, it would seem, because they believe that only if the 'fine tuning' to which the anthropic principle draws attention is operative in *one* universe can a theistic argument get off the ground. 'Look at these extraordinary coincidences that have made us possible in this one-off universe' is what we seem to be invited to do. So provoked, we are then asked to conclude that the remarkable emergence of persons (and it *is* remarkable, as we shall later have cause to stress) in this one universe is evidence for its origin in a creative personal God.

I myself do not want to dissent from the broad conclusions of this argument, but I urge that it does not depend on our universe being the *only* existing one and in there being no other universes, in any of the three possible senses already mentioned. Some years ago I made a theological appraisal[25] of the anthropic principle in the light of an acceptance of the mutual interplay of chance and law as the basis of the evolving forms in this universe (in the context particularly of biological evolution). I saw, as we shall again discuss below, this interplay as entirely consistent with how a creator God would act. If this is so, and we take seriously the possibility of there being an 'ensemble' of universes, in one of the three senses stated above, then, as I wrote:

> ... if we are [also] to look upon the role of 'chance' as the means whereby all the potentialities of the universe are explored, then we have to extend the time-scale and the ontological range over which 'chance' is thought to operate. Chance must now be regarded as, not only operating ... to elicit the potentialities of matter-energy-space-time over the spatial and temporal scale of our present universe, but also over the ensemble of possible universes, in most of which matter-energy-space-time might be replaced by new entities consistent with other values of the physical constants and possibly acting, presumably, according to quite different physical laws than those we can ascertain in principle in this universe. Even so, the point is that over the extension of space-time (or whatever replaces it) the potentialities of the ensemble of universes, as well as of this particular universe, are being or have been run through, or 'explored' ... For however long it may have taken on the time-scale of our universe, or however many universes may have preceded (and might follow) it [or might exist along with it], the fact is that matter-energy-space-time, in *this* universe, acquired the ability to adopt self-replicating structures which have acquired self-consciousness and the ability to know that they exist and have even now found ways of discovering how they have come to be.

So it is that we come to stress the particularity of our universe. For in this universe there are certain basic given features ... which limit what can eventually be realized through its dynamic, evolutionary processes.... Man's existence is non-necessary, that is, is contingent, in the sense of his not being present in all possible actual worlds, whose existence he can infer [on the 'ensemble of universes' assumption], and the same could also be affirmed of any other self-conscious being composed of particles of the kind that make up this universe.[26]

Whatever the constraints and framework of meta-laws and supervening relations that operate in bringing about the range constituting any postulated ensemble of universes, they must be of such a kind as to enable in one of the universes (*this* one) the combination of parameters, fundamental constants, etc., to be such that living organisms, including ourselves, could come into existence in some corner of it. So, on this argument, it is as significant that the ensemble of universes should be of such a kind that persons have emerged as it would be if ours were the only universe. Whether our purview is that of the present cosmos (broad enough on any account) or of the whole range of a hypothetical ensemble of universes, it is still a fact that the conditions were such on this planet Earth, in this galaxy, in this universe, for living organisms and self-conscious persons to come into existence. The fact is that it has happened at least once, here, and was thus among the range of potentialities of the whole natural order, whether this extends over many universes or only this one. Hence any argument for theism based on 'anthropic' considerations may be conducted independently of the question of whether or not this is the only universe.

Thus we return, after this digression, to the tricky question of how one should interpret these recent discoveries that the universe we observe is so 'finely tuned' to the existence of living organisms, including ourselves, whose presence therefore makes this a cognizable universe. The universe appears to be such that it has generated through its own processes, following their own inherent principles of unfolding new forms, a part of the universe (us) that knows that it exists in such a universe and moreover, knows that it knows. We have stressed that the emergence of cognizing living organisms, *homo sapiens*, is intelligible, with hindsight, through our increasing understanding of the evolutionary processes and of human biology, coupled with the anthropological sciences. However, this should not lead us to underplay just how unexpected our arrival on the scene is from the point of view of the natural sciences. Because of their inevitably reductionist methodology, which constitutes no criticism of them, the sciences are acutely limited in their explanatory power of precisely what new kinds of organized modes of being can emerge at levels of complexity above that at which the science in question operates. *Post hoc*, such developments can seem intelligible while not being strictly predictable. Most of all is this the case with the emergence of humanity and the experience of being persons.

We have earlier[27] given some account of the singularity and distinctiveness of personhood, even within a purely biological context. But now is the point at which the truly astonishing character of this emergence of personhood can be properly emphasized. For, we may well ask, why did the world, before the emergence of living organisms, and *a fortiori* of humanity, not just go on being an insentient, uncomprehending mechanism – 'merely the hurrying of material, endlessly, meaninglessly'.[28] The fact is, it didn't; and it is indeed significant, as John Durant has remarked,[29] that, with all its impressive knowledge of the physical and biological worlds and of our human physical nature, science can tell us nothing about why we have the experience of subjectivity. It is this that generates all the language of personal experience and personal interaction that constitutes for most people the bulk of their waking lives, and is reflected in our literature, art and music, indeed in our general culture. Although biology helps us to understand how our cognitive processes help survival and the neuro-sciences are beginning to help us see how our brains might be effective cognitively, this is light-years away from describing the actual experience of cognition, let alone the myriad other facets of subjectively experienced human personhood. We do not seem to be much nearer bridging this gap than the early pioneers of the scientific method 300 years ago.

We are certainly nearer, as outlined in Part I, to explaining how matter can become self-reproducing, and so living, and thereafter to become more and more complex with acquisition of cognitive powers conducive to survival, but this in no way describes how we think, feel, etc., in ourselves the way we do – that is, what our lives are actually like to ourselves. If we only had the sciences to go on, we would have no reason to predict or expect the arrival of personhood on the scene in *homo sapiens*, to suppose that the world could have persons in it at all. The subjectivity of our self-conscious personhood is quite unpredictable from even our present state of sophisticated science. With hindsight we see it emerging little by little, but once persons have arrived something qualitatively new has appeared. A real boundary is encountered by the natural sciences at the threshold of personality. In saying this I am not intending to introduce any note of mystification into the discussion, but I do mean that we should recognize frankly our actual incomprehension of the nature of the 'person'. There is a huge gap between what mechanism, and even organicism, can predict and any plausible explanation of the presence of persons in the universe eludes science as such. To use our earlier terms, the concept, and so actual instantiation, of personhood is the most intrinsically irreducible of all emerging entities that we know.

It seems, therefore, that the universe has through its own inherent processes – and there is no need to depart from this well-warranted assumption – generated a part of itself which, as persons, introduces a distinctively new kind of causality into itself, namely that of personal agency. The 'anthropic principle', the fine-tuning that allows the emergence of life and humanity, emphasizes the deep connection between the presence of life and of ourselves, on the one hand, and the intrinsic properties of the physical universe, on the other. Yet this very connectedness itself poses a problem because of those unique features of personhood already emphasized[30] which not only render the nature of persons irreducible to other scientific levels (a common feature of the relation between different levels[31]) but also introduces the possibility of a new kind of explanation, namely *personal* explanation.

So we cannot help asking what kind of universe is it, if it can generate such entities as persons? As I have put it elsewhere,[32] if the stuff of the world, the primeval concourse of protons, neutrinos, photons, etc. has, as a matter of fact and not conjecture, become persons – human beings who possess 'inner' self-conscious lives in relation to other human beings – then how are we properly to interpret the cosmological development (or the development of the ensemble of universes) if, after aeons of time, these fundamental particles and energy have evidenced that quality of existence we call 'personal', with its distinctive self-awareness and new kind of agency in the world? Does not the very intimacy of our relation to the fundamental features of the physical world, the 'anthropic' features, together with the distinctiveness of personhood, point us in the direction of looking for a 'best explanation' of all-that-is (both non-personal and personal) in terms of some kind of causality that could *include* the personal in its consequences? That is to say, the single 'best explanation' of all-that-is, this 'X', would have to be of a quite different essence, over and beyond the order of created beings. In other words 'X' must transcend the personal in such a way that 'X' could be the ground of that distinctive mode of actual being we call personal, as well as of the non-personal being we have already considered. Since the personal is, for the reasons given above, the highest category of entity we can name in the order of created beings, and since 'God' is the name we give to this 'X', we therefore have good reason for saying that *God is (at least) 'personal'*, or 'supra-personal' and for predicating personal qualities of God as less misleading and more appropriate than impersonal ones – even while recognizing, as always, that such predications must remain ultimately inadequate to that to which they refer, namely, God.

h Purposive

It is of the nature of human persons to have purposes particularly in their seeking to embody their values in individual and social life. Of our innate 'values' – those goal-seeking patterns of behaviour that are built in by evolution and cannot be altered by human beings – some, what G. E. Pugh[33] has called the 'selfish' ones, we share with the higher primates, but others, the 'social' ones, only partly so; and yet others, the 'intellectual' ones, are distinctively human. For, as persons, we are also characterized by continually endeavouring to do what we 'ought' do, to respond in action to more than what simply 'is'. These distinctively human values cannot, it seems to me, be reduced to the purely biological, as the programme of some sociobiologists claims, and are distinctive of the emergence of personhood in human beings.[34] If that is so, then human beings have arrived on the scene as potential carriers of values, so the God who created such personal existences must in his own inherent self be an ultimate source of values, for by their very nature values transcend the physical and biological and partake of the nature of the personally purposive. Any relationship of such a creator God to created persons would *ipso facto* be personal in character and it becomes eminently reasonable to affirm that such a personal, creator *God has purposes* that are manifest in the existence and destiny of persons embodying values.

It is at this point that the inadequacy of our talk only of the 'being' of God, of God as the one Ground of Being, becomes increasingly apparent. For it is of the nature of the personal not only to be capable of bearing static predicates, referring to stabler settled characteristics, but also of predicates of a dynamic kind, since the flow of experience is quintessential to being a person. So the 'static' predicates, such as 'supremely rational', 'omniscient', 'omnipotent', 'sustaining', 'preserving', 'faithful', and so on, with which we have hitherto been largely concerned to talk of God, must be enriched by other and more 'dynamic' predicates appropriate to the personal – as we saw was also implied by our earlier inference that God must be an immanent, continuously creating Creator. To put it another way, for our models of God to be personal they must be dynamic as well as static. So it is more appropriate to develop our consideration of the creative actions and activity of a personal God under the heading of 'Divine Becoming'.

2 DIVINE BECOMING

It is distinctive of free persons that they possess intentions and purposes and act so as to implement them. If, then, we accept the clue to the nature of the Creator afforded by the existence of such free-willing purposive persons in the universe it becomes proper to ask: can we infer from what is going on in the natural world[35] anything about what might properly be called the 'purposes' of God as personal Creator acting in the created world? That is, can we discern the purposes of this personal God in any ways that are consistent with what we now know of the universe through the sciences? The monotheistic religious traditions, especially Christianity, make strong claims to know aspects of God's purposes. We do not want to derogate from these claimed revelations but does the scientific perspective on the natural world, including humanity, enhance and add to or diminish and subtract from our notions of the purposes of God in creation that the Judeo-Christian tradition in particular has affirmed? More broadly, is our understanding of God the personal Creator as the 'best explanation' of all-that-is enriched by what science shows us concerning the being and becoming of the natural world, including humanity?

a Joy and Delight in Creation

We have seen[36] that the natural world is immensely variegated in its hierarchies of levels of entities, structures and processes, in its 'being'; and abundantly diversifies with a cornucopian fecundity in its 'becoming' in time. From the unity in this diversity and the richness of the diversity itself, we earlier adduced,[37] respectively, both the essential oneness of its source of being, namely the one God the Creator, and the unfathomable richness of the unitive Being of that creator God. But now we must reckon more directly with the diversity itself. The forms even of non-living matter throughout the cosmos as it appears to us is even more diverse than what we can observe immediately on the Earth. Furthermore the multiply branching tree of terrestrial biological evolution appears to be primarily opportunist in the direction it follows and, in so doing, produces the enormous variety of biological life on this planet. As Charles Darwin himself put it in a famous passage,

> It is interesting to contemplate a tangled bank, clothed with many plants of many kinds, with birds singing on the bushes, with various insects flitting about, and with worms crawling through the damp earth, and to reflect that these elaborately constructed forms, so different from each other, and dependent upon each other in so complex a manner, have all been produced by laws acting around us ... There is grandeur in this view of life, with its several powers, having been originally breathed by the Creator into a few forms or into one; and that, whilst this planet has gone cycling on according to the fixed law of gravity, from so simple a beginning endless forms most beautiful and most wonderful have been, and are being evolved.[38]

We can only conclude that, if there is a personal Creator, then that Creator intended this rich multiformity of entities, structures, and processes in the natural world and, if so, that such a Creator God takes what, in the personal world of human experience, could only be called 'delight' in this multiformity of what he has created – and not only in what Darwin, in that same passage, called 'the most exalted object which we are capable of conceiving, namely the production of the higher animals'. The existence of the *whole* tapestry of the created order, in its warp and woof, and in the very heterogeneity and multiplicity of its forms, must be taken to be the Creator's intention. We can only make sense of that, utilizing our resources of personal language, if we say that *God has joy and delight in creation*. We have a hint of this in the satisfaction attributed to God as Creator in the first chapter of *Genesis*: 'And God saw everything he had made, and behold, it was very good.'[39] This naturally leads to the idea of the 'play' of God in creation on which I have expounded elsewhere,[40] in relation to Hindu thought as well as to that of Judaism and Christianity. That this 'play' of God in creation is, in certain respects, akin to a game of chance is something that has become increasingly apparent from a number of developments in the sciences and it is to this aspect of the sciences and our perception of the world that we must now turn.

b Ground and Source of Law ('Necessity') and 'Chance'

Our games obey given rules but, because of the involvement of an element of chance, there is a certain unpredictability and open-endedness in their outcome which, indeed, constitutes their attraction and fascination. Interestingly, these same features are also aspects of the natural world that the sciences have now discerned.[41] We saw in Part I[42] that there are various kinds of system in the natural world which may be differentiated with respect to their predictability or otherwise. In particular, we noted that there are non-linear complex dynamical systems that can undergo transitions at the observable macro-level that are unpredictable, even though all of their subsidiary processes are governed by deterministic laws. Their existence has only gradually and recently become increasingly clear to scientists in a number of diverse fields. In the form of 'dissipative systems'[43] they are particularly relevant to our understanding of biological systems. For, as we saw,[44] they gave us a clue as to how the interplay of random, chance-like events at the micro-level could lead to a form of self-organization that is also self-reproducing and so living – that is, the transition from non-living to living matter was rendered intelligible by its consistency with the properties of these kinds of physico-chemical system. Such transitions in such systems would be unpredictable before the event but intelligible afterwards as being within the range of possibilities available to the system as a whole, for they are the results of the lawlike amplification of the effects of a single or of a few micro-events. This creative interplay of 'chance' and law is even more obviously apparent in the evolution of living matter by natural selection, but what we mean by 'chance' in this context first needs closer examination.

Micro-events are unpredictable by us in two ways:

1 They can be unpredictable because we can never possess the necessary detailed knowledge with the requisite accuracy at this micro-level of description. In such cases talk of the role of 'chance' can mean either (a) we cannot determine accurately

the micro-parameters of the initial conditions determining the macro-events (e.g., the forces on a tossed coin), while often knowing the overall constraints that must operate on the system as a whole (e.g., the symmetry constraints making for equal probabilities of heads and tails); or (b) the observed events are the outcome of the crossing of two independent causal chains, accurate knowledge of which is unattainable both with respect to the chains themselves and to their point of intersection.

2 Micro-events can also be unpredictable because of the operation of the Heisenberg Uncertainty Principle[45] at the sub-atomic level and this unpredictability is inherent and ineradicable.

Both of these two categories of micro-events unpredictable as they are, produce effects at the macroscopic level which operate in a lawlike framework that constrains their possible consequences. These 'lawlike' constraints may be viewed as delimiting the scope of the consequent events or as providing them with new and unexpected outcomes. Both ways of viewing the matter are pertinent to one of the most significant arenas in which there is an interplay of 'chance' events in a lawlike framework, that of biological evolution.

We saw earlier[46] that biological evolution depends on a process in which changes occur in the genetic information carrying material (DNA) that are random with respect to the biological needs of the organisms possessing the DNA; and in particular, are random with respect to its need to produce progeny for the species to survive. What we call 'chance' is involved both at the level of the mutational event in the DNA itself (1(a) and/or 2, above), and in the intersecting of two causally unrelated chains of events (1(b), above) – those that give rise to the change in the DNA and the consequences of such changes for those features of the organism that affect its survival in its particular biological and ecological niche.

The original mutational events are random with respect to the future of the biological organism, even its future survival, but these changes have their consequences in a milieu that has regular and lawlike features. For the biological niche in which the organism exists then filters out, by the processes of natural selection, those changes in the DNA that enable the organisms possessing them to produce more progeny. The details of how such 'selection' operates in any given case are, of course, individual to that species but the statistics of the process are amenable to mathematical description in an entirely lawlike fashion. This interplay between 'chance', at the molecular level of the DNA, and 'law' or 'necessity' at the statistical level of the population of organisms tempted Jacques Monod, in his influential book *Chance and Necessity*,[47] to elevate 'chance' to the level almost of a metaphysical principle whereby the universe might be interpreted. As is well known, he concluded that the 'stupendous edifice of evolution' is, in this sense, rooted in 'pure chance' and that *therefore* all inferences of direction or purpose in the development of the biological world, in particular, and of the universe, in general, must be false. In so arguing, he thereby mounted, in the name of science, one of the strongest and most influential attacks of the century on theism. For, as Monod saw it, it was the purest accident that any particular creature came into being, in particular *homo sapiens*, and no direction or purpose or meaning could ever be expected to be discerned in biological evolution. Even if there were a creator God, for all practical purposes he might just as well not exist, since everything in evolution went on in an entirely uncontrolled and fortuitous manner.

The responses to this thesis and attack on theism – mainly, it is interesting to note, from theologically informed scientists, and some philosophers, rather than from theologians – have been well surveyed by D. J. Bartholomew[48] and their relative strengths and weaknesses analyzed. I shall here follow what I consider to be the most fruitful line of theological reflection on the processes that Monod so effectively brought to the attention of the twentieth century – a direction that I began[49] to pursue in response to Monod and which has been further developed by the statistically informed treatment of Bartholomew.

There is no reason why the randomness of molecular event in relation to biological consequence has to be given the significant metaphysical status that Monod attributed to it. The involvement of what we call 'chance' at the level of mutation in the DNA does not, of itself, preclude these events from displaying regular trends and manifesting inbuilt propensities at the higher levels of organisms, populations and ecosystems. To call the mutation of the DNA a 'chance' event serves simply to stress its randomness with respect to biological consequence. As I have put it elsewhere:

> Instead of being daunted by the role of chance in genetic mutations as being the manifestation of irrationality in the universe, it would be more consistent with the observations to assert that the full gamut of the potentialities of living matter could be explored only through the agency of the rapid and frequent randomization which is possible at the molecular level of the DNA.[50]

This role of 'chance', or rather randomness (or 'free experiment') at the micro-level is what one would expect if the universe were so constituted that all the potential forms of organizations of matter (both living and non-living) which it contains might be thoroughly explored. Indeed, since Monod first published his book in French in 1970, there have been those developments in theoretical and molecular biology and physical biochemistry that cast new light on the interrelation of what we call chance and law (or necessity, to use Monod's term) in the origin and development of life – namely the investigations of the Brussels school led by Ilya Prigogine[51] and of the Göttingen school led by Manfred Eigen.[52] They demonstrated that it is the interplay of chance and law which is in fact creative within time, for it is the combination of the two which allows new forms to emerge and evolve; so that natural selection appears to be opportunistic.

This has been superbly illustrated by Richard Dawkins[53] with his computer programme for what he calls 'biomorphs', two-dimensional patterns of branching lines generated by random changes in a defined number of features combined with a reproduction and selection procedure. It was striking how subtle, varied and complex were the 'biomorph' patterns after surprisingly few 'generations', that is, reiterations of the procedure. Such computer simulations go a long way towards making it clear how it is that the complexity and diversity of biological organisms could arise through the operation of the apparently simple principles of natural selection. For these involve only the interplay and consequences of random processes (in relation to biological outcome) in the lawlike framework of the rules governing change in biological populations in complex environments. These rules are what they are because of the 'givenness' of the properties of the physical environment and of the already evolved other living organisms with which the organism in question interacts. All these constraints themselves arise from the inherent properties of the world in which the organism is developing and so go back to that basic contingency of the universe itself having the particular laws, relationships, entities, structures and processes it in fact has.

This givenness, for a theist, can only be regarded as an aspect of the God-endowed features of the world. The way in which what we call 'chance' operates within this 'given' framework to produce new structures, entities and processes can then properly be seen as an eliciting of the potentialities that the physical cosmos possessed *ab initio*. Such potentialities a theist must regard as written into creation by the Creator's intention and purpose and must conceive as gradually being actualized by the operation of 'chance' stimulating their coming into existence. One might say that the potential of the 'being' of the world is made manifest in the 'becoming' that the operation of chance makes actual. Hence we infer *God is the ultimate ground and source of both law ('necessity') and 'chance'.*

I have elsewhere[54] attempted to express this characteristic of the Creator's mode of action – a characteristic of which we have only in this century really become aware – by means of a musical analogy, a model of God as composer, and to this we shall revert in chapter 9. To a theist, it is now clear that God creates in the world *through* what we call 'chance' operating within the created order, each stage of which constitutes the launching pad for the next. The Creator, it now seems, is unfolding the potentialities of the universe, which he himself has given it, in and through a process in which these creative possibilities and propensities, inherent by his own intention within the fundamental entities of that universe and their inter-relations, become actualized within a created temporal development shaped and determined by those selfsame God-given potentialities.

However, the actual course of this unfolding of the hidden potentialities of the world is not a predetermined path, for there are the irreducible unpredictabilities in the actual systems and processes of the world to which we have already referred (micro-events at the Heisenberg level and non-linear dynamical complex systems). So there is an open-endedness in the course of the world's 'natural' history. In other words, we now have to conceive of God as involved in explorations of the many kinds of unfulfilled potentialities of the universe he has created – and we must recognize that the transition from 'causal' to anthropomorphic-narrative language cannot be avoided at this juncture. It thus transpires that the creativity of God is to be seen as genuinely innovative and adaptive, but not inchoate and without purpose. For there are, as we saw, inbuilt propensities – a theist would say 'built in by God' – in the natural, creating processes which, as it were, 'load the dice' in favour of life and, once living organisms have appeared, also of increased complexity, awareness, consciousness and sensitivity, with all their consequences. New though such a conception may be for theists, especially Judeo-Christian believers in God with their sense of creation as the expression of divine will and purpose (perhaps less so for Hindus with their sense of the play, *lila*, of God in creation[55]), nevertheless this proposal, far from being inherently inimical to belief in God actually enriches our understanding of divine creation. For the original quantum vacuum, or whatever current theory postulates as the origin of our universe, must have had the potentiality of being able to develop so as to display those qualities of complexity, awareness, consciousness and sensitivity that characterize the higher forms of life. It is this which is significant about the emergence of life in the universe and the role of chance is simply what is required if all the potentialities of the universe, especially for life, are going to be elicited effectively. As I have expressed it elsewhere:

> if we propose that the world owes its being to a Creator God then I see no reason why God should not allow the potentialities of his universe to be developed in all their ramifications through the operation of random ['chance'] events; indeed, in principle, this is the only way in which all potentialities might eventually, given enough time and space, be actualized. Or, to change the metaphor, it is as if chance is the search radar of God, sweeping through all the possible targets available to its probing.[56]

D. J. Bartholomew has urged that God and chance are not only logically compatible, as the foregoing has argued, but that there are 'positive reasons for supposing that an element of pure chance would play a constructive role in creating a richer environment than would otherwise be possible'.[57] He argues that 'chance offers the potential Creator many advantages which it is difficult to envisage being obtained in any other way.'[58] Since in many natural processes, often utilized by human beings, chance processes can in fact lead to determinate ends, for many of the laws of nature are statistical, 'there is every reason to suppose that a Creator wishing to achieve certain ends might choose to reach them by introducing random processes whose macro-behaviour would have the desired character.'[59] Thus the determinate ends to which chance processes could lead might well be 'to produce intelligent beings capable of interaction with their Creator'.[60] For this it would be necessary, Bartholomew suggests, to have an environment in which chance provides the stimulus and testing to promote intellectual and spiritual evolution. Indeed, he goes further and asserts that

> a world of chance is not merely consistent with a theistic view of nature but, almost, required by it ... It is more congenial to both faith

and reason to suppose that God generates the requisite degree of randomness much as we do, by deterministic means. We emphasize again that this does not imply or require fore-knowledge of the consequences at the micro-level on God's part. He is concerned with macro-effects.[61]

Such a 'strong' view on the part of Bartholomew of the role of chance in the divine purposes has repercussions for how we might conceive of God's interaction with the world. What is clear at this juncture is that, in a world in which chance plays the role both Bartholomew and I have depicted, God is taking risks in his creation and, as we shall see, most of all with created humanity.

It seems that we now have to take account of: (1) this new perspective of God the Creator as acting through chance operating within the constraints of law, that is, of the God-given properties and propensities of the natural world; (2) a renewed emphasis[62] on the immanence of God in the processes of the creative and creating world; and (3) our earlier recognition of the irreducible unpredictability of much of what goes on in the world.[63] These considerations steer us towards new models of God's creative action that stress that the rationality that is evidenced in the creation is one that is exploratory of new possibilities, generating them through the conjunction of chance and law. They lead us to see that *God the Creator explores in creation*.

c Self-limited Omnipotence and Omniscience

Considerations such as these on the role of 'chance' in creation impel us also to recognize more emphatically than ever before the constraints which we must regard God as imposing upon himself in creation and to suggest that *God has a 'self-limited' omnipotence and omniscience*. For, in order to achieve his purposes, he has allowed his inherent omnipotence and omniscience to be modified, restricted and curtailed by the very open-endedness that he has bestowed upon creation. This open-endedness and unpredictability of the world's processes increases with the complexity of organization of the entities and structures undergoing them, particularly when these are living and most notably in the human experience of that freedom possessed by the human-brain-in-the-human-body.

The attribution of 'self-limitation' to God with respect to his omnipotence is meant to indicate that God has so made the world that there are certain areas over which he has chosen not to have power (for example, human free will, as generally recognized by theologians). Similarly, the attribution of 'self-limitation' to God in regard to his omniscience is meant to denote that God may also have so made the world that, at any given time, there are certain systems whose future states cannot be known even to him since they are in principle not knowable (for example, those in the 'Heisenberg' range). If there is no particular point in time of which it could truly be said of those systems 'this will be its future state', then it could not be known at any instant, by God or by us, what the future state of such systems will be. It seems that God has made the world so that, in these systems, he himself does not know their future states of affairs, since they cannot be known.

As we saw in chapter 7,[64] God's 'omniscience' has to be construed as God knowing at any time whatever it is *possible* that he know at that time. This excludes such incoherences as God possibly knowing that $2+3=6$ etc., and also knowing in advance what human beings would freely actually choose, since it would be logically incoherent if God did know this *and* human beings were genuinely free. The unpredictability for us of events in the sub-atomic ('Heisenberg') range and in non-linear, dynamic macroscopic systems is not 'logical' in this sense but, I would suggest, they are also unpredictable for God. For in these situations it transpires that the unpredictability is inherent in the nature of the systems themselves: there are no 'hidden variables' in the 'Heisenberg' case; and, in the non-linear case, there may not only be no closed solutions, but the same Heisenberg Uncertainty Principle also sets a limit to the accuracy with which the determining initial conditions *can* be known. This is, then, a limitation on God's omniscience. But in these cases not a purely logical one (as in the arithmetical example above): it is a *self*-limitation, because God as Creator 'chose' (that is what is implied by God being Creator) to create a world in which these subatomic constituents and non-linear systems had such an unpredictable character. Their unpredictability, their inherent indeterminacy, is not logically necessary but contingent – the contingency of the way God made these particular kinds of systems with these properties. If this expansion of what is 'impossible' is allowed, then God is still omniscient in the sense of Swinburne's definition but, in respect of these particular kinds of events and systems, only contingently so – a contingency of God's own choosing by creating them thus. It is this aspect of God's knowledge of the world he has created to which I refer as the 'self-limitation' of God's omniscience.

These considerations do not, of course, preclude God from knowing the probabilities of the sequence of events in such systems and so of knowing, and – we shall later suggest – of influencing, the general direction of the history of these natural events, in particular, and of nature, in general.

d Vulnerable, Self-emptying and Self-giving Love

Thus it is that we come to a recognition that in creating the world continuously God has allowed himself not to have overriding power over all that happens in it nor complete knowledge of the direction events will take. This self-limitation is the precondition for the coming into existence of free self-conscious human beings, that is, of human experience as such. This act of self-limitation on behalf of the good and well-being, indeed the existence, of another being can properly be designated as being consistent with, and so exemplifying the ultimate character of *God as 'Love'*. For in human life – and it can only be a human analogy – love is supremely manifest in self-limiting, costly action on behalf of the good and existence of another. The designation of God *as* 'Love' is, of course, a specifically Christian insight and I am not suggesting that without the revelation of God in Jesus the Christ we could have known this explicitly simply by reflecting on the world. But such reflections leading to the notion of God's self-limitation of his omnipotence and omniscience at least render it meaningful to speak of the *vulnerability of God*, indeed of the *self-emptying* (kenosis) *and self-giving of God* in creation. This is an insight that has been recovered for the church in recent years especially by the writings of J. Moltmann, C. Hartshorne and W. H. Vanstone.[65]

It appears that not only does God remain faithful and reliable in his giving being to the world but he has also concomitantly made himself vulnerable to its costly becoming. He has put his ultimate purposes at risk by incorporating open-endedness, and so eventually human freedom, into the created world. Yet this expresses a transcendent rationality of a subtle kind for, as Bartholomew argues, it seems to be the only way of bringing into existence intelligent, self-conscious, sensitive, free beings who can relate personally to God who 'chose to make a world of chance because it would have the properties necessary for producing beings fit for fellowship with himself'.[66] There were many branching lines in biological evolution but, in fact, one did lead to human beings who are distinctive in knowing the world (including, now, their own evolutionary origins), who know that they know, can relate as persons and can act freely with intention and purpose. We are beginning to recognize, as was pointed out earlier in this chapter,[67] in what respects the arrival of human persons on the biological scene is intelligible in the light of their precursors and in what respects the leap that constituted the transition to humanity is conceptually baffling. Any theistic account of the existence of *this* kind of natural order and process must therefore incorporate into its understanding of God the Creator the notion that God had a purpose in creating such distinctive beings capable of inferring his existence and seeking to come into relation to him through prayer and worship, as has always characterized humanity from its first glimmerings of self-consciousness.

As we have just seen, the conditions for the emergence of open-endedness in natural systems – and so, in due course, the experience of freedom of the human-brain-in-the-human-body – involve a subtle interweaving of chance and law, with consequences that are often not readily predictable in principle (and, indeed, are often inimical to too narrowly-conceived human interests). If God willed the existence of self-conscious, intelligent, freely-willing creatures as an end, he must, to be self-consistent, logically be presumed to have willed the means to achieving that end. This divine purpose must be taken to have been an overriding one, for it involves as a corollary an element of risk to his purposes whereby he renders himself vulnerable in a way that is only now becoming perceivable by us. This idea that *God took a risk in creation* is not new – as evidenced by the traditional theology implicit in the 'narratives' of creation in the Old Testament – but is now, I am suggesting, reinforced and given a wider context by these biological considerations.

To instantiate truth, beauty and goodness, that is value, in the created order, the possibility of generating a *free* being had to be incorporated as a potential outcome of the cosmic processes. The cost to God, if we may dare so to speak, was in that act of self-limitation, of *kenosis*, which constitutes God's creative action – a self-inflicted vulnerability to the very processes God had himself created in order to achieve an overriding purpose, the emergence of free persons.

e Natural Evil

God's act of creation is not, as we saw, something done once for all – creation still proceeds and God is immanently present in and to the whole process. These processes that the natural sciences now unveil for us include the operation of chance in a law-like framework as the origin of life; the emergence of new forms of life only through the costly processes of natural selection with death of the old forms; and the emergence of sensitive, free, intelligent persons through a development that inevitably involves increasing sensitivity to pain and the concomitant experience of suffering *pari passu* with a growing consciousness and self-consciousness. Death, pain and suffering constitute the sting of what has often been called 'natural evil', those events, involving apparently pointless suffering and tragedy, which are inimical to human health, welfare and happiness, and indeed life. 'Natural evil' refers to those events that stem from the non-human, natural world – including *inter alia* earthquakes, floods, 'accidents' (the crossing of two independent causal chains), as well as the breakdown of the biological organization of the human physical/mental organism.[68] Pre-eminently it is such disruption of human bodily and mental organization, whether arising spontaneously (as in the malformation of a growing human embryo or in cancer) or as the result of the invasion of other organisms (disease), that are for us at the same time the most tragic of human experiences and the most directly experienced manifestation of how delicately and subtly balanced – and so vulnerable – is the intricate, dynamically balanced, network of the human living organism.

We have seen how it is that 'chance', or randomness, together with 'law' (the regularities resulting from the lawlike framework within which 'chance' operates) through their mutual interplay are necessary in any universe that is to be the matrix for the emergence of free-willing, responsible, conscious and self-conscious persons. So that in willing this end, instantiated in *homo sapiens*, God inevitably wills also the means – and these cannot but involve those random effects of 'chance' that are inimical to humanity and other living organisms and constitute the 'natural evil' to which all life is heir. It is this incidence of random processes within the regularities of a biological system, this combination of 'chance' and 'law', that, while it can be the root of individual tragedies, is also the fundamental basis for there being any life at all and any particular form of biological life, especially free-willing, self-conscious life such as our own. The chance disorganization of the growing human embryo that leads to the birth of a defective human being and the chance loss of control of cellular multiplication that appears as a cancerous tumour are individual and particular results of that same interplay of 'chance' and 'law' that enabled and enables life to exist at all. Hence such interpretations based on the understanding that the sciences have afforded us now mitigate and diminish greatly the problem of the existence of 'natural evil' and its widely assumed undermining of theistic belief.

Nothing, however, can diminish our sense of loss and tragedy as we experience or witness particular natural evils, especially in individuals known to us. But, at least, we can now better understand how it is that God wills into existence the kinds of living creatures that depend on the operation of the same factors that produce those particular 'natural' evils. The interplay of 'chance' and 'law' is the necessary condition for the existence of certain good eventualities and the 'natural evil' consequences need not be regarded as either avoidable or as intended in themselves by God. Even God cannot have one without the other.

God has created a universe in which, it transpires, certain situations have unpredictable outcomes and in which it is the existence of such situations that enables propensities towards complexity, consciousness and freedom to become actualized in the universe on the surface of the Earth, at least. God, we suggested, has thereby, and for those ends, in his acts of creation implicitly limited himself from knowing the particular outcomes of certain processes and also, as a consequence, his power over them. So we come to regard God's omniscience and omnipotence as 'self-limited' in these senses in order that the universe should be of a certain kind – namely, capable through its open-endedness and flexibility of generating complexity, consciousness and freedom. Again, in this wider context, the new perspectives of the sciences help to draw the sting of the problem of 'natural evil' and so contribute to a more defensible theodicy.

f A Suffering God

If God is immanently present in and to natural processes, in particular those that generate conscious and self-conscious life, then we cannot but infer that *God suffers in, with and under the creative processes of the world* with their costly, open-ended unfolding in time.[69]

Rejection of the notion of the impassibility of God has, in fact, been a feature of the theology of recent decades. There has been an increasing assent to the idea that it is possible 'to speak consistently of *a God who suffers eminently and yet is still God, and a God who suffers universally and yet is still present uniquely and decisively in the sufferings of Christ.*'[70] As Paul Fiddes points out in his survey and analysis of this change in theological perspective, the factors that have promoted the view that God suffers are new assessments of 'the meaning of love [especially, the love of God], the implications of the cross of Jesus, the problem of [human] suffering, and the structure of the world'.[71] It is this last-mentioned – the 'structure of the world' – on which the new perspectives of the sciences bear by revealing the world processes to be of such a character, described above, that involvement in them by the immanent Creator has to be regarded as involving suffering on the Creator's part. God, we find ourselves having to affirm, suffers the 'natural' evils of the world along with ourselves because – we can but tentatively suggest at this stage – he purposes to bring about a greater good thereby, the domain of free-willing, loving persons in communion with himself and with each other.[72]

The magnitude and scope of the divine loving vulnerability that puts itself at risk in creation only becomes fully apparent with the arrival on the scene of *homo sapiens*. For human beings can not only constitute the highest fulfilment of the Creator's purposes but, through their freedom, they are also that part of the created order most capable of frustrating the divine will and purpose and of sinking to depths of degradation and denial of values in ways not open to, or actualized in, any other creature. They are also capable of experiencing to a unique degree pain, suffering and the loss which is death. With the arrival of human beings on the earth the free creation of value – of truth, beauty and goodness, to use for brevity the classical trio – first became possible, along with their deliberate and wilful rejection. This paradox of the creation of a humanity capable of alienating itself from the source of its own being merits deeper inquiry but, at this point, I wish to draw attention principally to the support for the notion of divine passibility which comes from the scientific perception of the role and inherent inevitability of pain, suffering and death in a universe capable of evolving free, intelligent persons.

g God and Time

The revived insight that God suffers in the processes of creation and, supremely, with suffering humanity, raises again[73] the question of God's relation to time. For if God 'suffers' with creation in some sense analogous to that of human suffering, God must be conceived as being changed through this interaction with the world. Indeed, this is precisely how the narratives of the biblical tradition depict God – the story of God's dealings with his people and God's reactions to their response, or lack of it. They depict God as somehow 'in time' in unashamedly anthropomorphic language, while acknowledging the impossibility of doing justice to what God is in himself.

Analyses of the relation of the question of the relation of God to time show that a number of important traditional attributes of God (for example, his personhood, his ability to act in the world,[74] his ability to know the world as temporal and changing[75]) lose coherence and meaning if God is regarded as 'timeless' in the sense of being 'outside' time altogether in a way which means time cannot be said to enter into his nature at all, so that he possesses no succession in his experience – that is, nothing akin to temporality. To affirm, as we have done, that God is, in some sense, 'personal' can only have any meaning if God experiences something like the succession of conscious states that being a person involves in ourselves. To be a person with consciousness *is* to be aware of a succession of states of mind (and in our case, though not God's, of body too).

Yet, we have suggested,[76] that physical time and space may be regarded as created by God in the sense of them being real relations within the created world of matter-energy that physics now describes – while recognizing that temporal relations (that is, in physical time) nevertheless have distinct differences from spatial ones.[77] If God thus *creates* time, does he not 'transcend' it in the sense of viewing the whole course of 'our' time from the mountain top, as it were, of another dimension – 'above' or 'outside' time so that our 'before', 'now' and 'after' are all spread out for him to see? In which case, does not God see ahead in time so that all is 'actually' predetermined – and our talk of unpredictability has to be taken to refer only to human and not divine foreknowledge? But we had to recognize that events at the sub-atomic ('Heisenberg'), quantum micro-level, and often also the development of non-linear dynamical systems, are unpredictable. At best only the *range* of possible outcomes of certain events (e.g., of a quantum measurement, or in a complex, non-linear dynamical system) is predictable and the actual event itself is not predictable. The future of the quantum or complex system is genuinely open and genuinely new states of the system occur. On these grounds we argued also that the outcome of such events must also be inherently unpredictable to God, if God is to be self-consistent and faithful to his own laws and constrained by the laws of logic and mathematics, as he must be for the concept of God to have any coherence at all. *A fortiori*, if human free will is to be genuine and not illusory, even if more constrained than we think as we experience it, then God cannot so 'transcend' the time in which we act that he can know precisely and definitively what our future free actions will be. As Keith Ward puts it:

> If genuinely free creatures are admitted, there is an overwhelmingly strong argument against Divine immutability and for Divine temporality. For the free acts of creatures will partially determine the initial conditions of the next temporal segment of the world. Before he creates that next segment, God must therefore know what choices have been made. The creation is consequent upon God's knowledge, which depends in turn upon free creaturely acts; so God must be conceived as responding to free acts moment by moment, as they are decided.... The combination of non-temporal knowledge, non-temporal creation and free creaturely action is contradictory.[78]

However, as was pointed out in relation to 'Heisenberg' micro-events and non-linear dynamical systems that are irreducibly unpredictable, this does not mean that God cannot have the most complete knowledge that is possible of the probabilities of the outcomes of the operations of our free will – rather as a parent might in relation to a child's decisions, or a wife in relation to her husband's. That is, God will have full knowledge of all possible outcomes of our decisions and because of this comprehensive knowledge of us and of all the circumstances, he will know their relative probability of occurrence -- but he cannot know certainly what *will* happen if our wills are to be genuinely free.

How then are we, in the light of these various considerations, best to conceive of God's relation to time? These and related questions have, for centuries, been central to the philosophical and theological discussions of major issues such as free will, predestination, the purported changelessness and impassibility of God and the relation of time to eternity, to name but a few. We are primarily concerned here with the impact of the perspectives of twentieth-century science on traditional debates, the percipience of which must-still command respect.

Special relativity raises a particular difficulty in all talk of God's relation to 'time'. For that theory replaces the one, universal flowing time assumed by Newton and by common sense, by many different 'times' specific to different observers, each with their own positions and velocities, that is, their own frames of reference. To which of these 'times' does God relate? Could he relate to all of them? However, as John Polkinghorne points out:

> We can picture each observer's 'instant' as being a three-dimensional slice through four-dimensional spacetime... An *omnipresent* observer, whose direct contact with the way things are is not located at a point within the slice but spread out all over it, would in due course experience everywhere and everywhen. That would be true whatever his choice of time axis... The omnipresent God has no need to use signalling to tell him what is happening and so he has instant access to every event as and when it occurs.[79]

Moreover since the succession of any particular created, causal sequences is independent of the reference frame of any and all observers, there is no incoherence in conceiving of God as having experience of, and so relating to, them all successively in his own self-awareness.

There is no reason why succession in God should not relate to each and every such framework, just as God relates to many other multiple aspects of the created order. This is indeed one sense in which God might be said to 'transcend' all created times. As John Polkinghorne also points out,[80] there is a natural frame of reference that cosmologists use when speaking of the age of the universe; 'cosmic time' provided by certain changing features of the whole universe. Hence there is no incoherence stemming from relativity in our continuing to speak of God's experience of 'time' in the created order rather than of 'times', meaning by the use of the singular this 'cosmic time'.

Also of general significance is the renewed support that the theory of general relativity now gives to the idea, already noted, in accord with St Augustine's famous assertion,[81] of physical ('clock') time being an aspect of the created order, for in that theory time is closely interlocked conceptually with space, matter and energy. Our own sense of psychological time, the sense of succession of our conscious states, with which our own sense of personhood is so bound up, is closely related to this physical time. For we move freely from one sense of time to the other even though they seem, often, to proceed at different rates while sharing many interactions and running in parallel. This relationship can perhaps at least make intelligible to us how God's own inherent self-awareness of successive states (which must be attributed to God if God is to be 'personal' in any meaningful sense) might be closely linked to physical, created time, while yet remaining distinct from it. On such a model, God would not be 'timeless' and could be thought of as the Creator of every instant of physical time. Creation by God would be regarded as that activity whereby God gives existence to each instant of physical time, the 'now' of the hand of the clock, and each instant has no existence prior to its being so created with all the entities, structures and processes that fill it. Keith Ward's suggestion that 'One might say that God timelessly generates, by the necessity of his own nature the infinite series of temporal states in which he freely acts'[82] is in accord with this, though couched in language derived more from theological than scientific discourse. This idea of God eternally giving existence to each successive moment of time, expressed in either of these two ways, illuminates the concept of God the Creator as sustaining and preserving the world.

On this interpretation, then, the future does not yet exist in any sense, not even for God; God creates each instant of physical time with its open, as yet undetermined, outcomes, fecund with possibilities not yet actualized. If the future does not yet exist for God, any more than it does for us, there is no question of God seeing ahead what the future is going to be, even though he can still have purposes to implement in that forthcoming future. That does not preclude God in his omniscience (qualified in the ways we have already suggested[83]) from knowing comprehensively, in a way not open to us, not only what these possibilities might be but also their relative probabilities of occurrence. This created time is, in Schilling's striking phrase, 'the carrier or locus of innovative change',[84] and it has a direction in which new systems emerge through the cosmic, inorganic, chemical and biological evolutionary processes. According to this proposal, God is conceived as holding in being in physical time all-that-is at each instant and relating his own succession of divine states (the divine 'temporality') to the succession of created instants without himself being subject to created physical time. Moreover, God transcends *past* time in the traditional sense of having total knowledge of it all stored in the perfect, permanent memory of God. But even God cannot know the future with absolute certainty when he has not yet given existence to those systems between whose constituent entities time is a real relation and which are irreducibly unpredictable with respect to their temporal histories.

Our own psychological time, of course, does not transcend physical time, indeed it is the captive of it, but our experience of our own succession of conscious states is sufficiently distinct from physical ('clock') time to make it at least intelligible and conceivable how temporality within God, God's own awareness of succession within the divine life, could be relatable to created physical time. God transcends created time as its Creator (we shall have to affirm, in accord with some later considerations, that created time is 'in God'), but is himself immanent in created time, being present to every moment of it as he creates it. There is no created time to which God is not present as he gives it existence, just as he is present to all space.[85]

To summarize, we can affirm that: *God is not 'timeless'; God is temporal in the sense that the Divine life is successive in its relation to us – God is temporally related to us; God creates and is present to each instant of the (physical and, derivatively, psychological) time of the created world; God transcends past and present created time: God is eternal*, in the sense[86] that there is no time at which he did not exist nor will there be a future time at which he does not exist.[87]

A consequence of this understanding of God as transcendent yet personal, and so possessing succession – that is, some kind of temporality – in conjunction with the acceptance that God is passible, is that God can no longer be thought of as immutable in the strong, classical sense of not changing at all. But the relation of the passible God to time is entirely consistent with a weaker, though more intelligible and relevant, sense of immutability, namely that God cannot change in character (and so in purpose, intent and disposition).[88] This is, indeed, precisely the sense in which we attribute 'consistency, faithfulness and reliability' to persons.[89] As the Report *We Believe in God* puts it:

> we meet in the Old Testament an insistence that 'the Living God' is to be recognized by his capacity to react and respond and adapt his actions to changing circumstances, and to find a way round each new frustration. Such a God, by virtue of creating in Space and Time a

universe with some degree of inbuilt freedom, exposes himself to being acted upon and, in that sense, being compelled to change.[90]

h God and 'Imaginary' Time

The foregoing exposition has spoken of time as if it were meaningful to think of time as extrapolatable backwards at least as far as the 'point' in time, the singularity, from which the expansion of our known universe began (the 'hot, big bang'). This is indeed the presumption of the most generally held picture of the cosmic development, whether or not the phase of expansion we now observe was preceded by an 'inflationary' stage – which has also been conceived of as occurring on the same time scale. However, we must also consider now that speculative proposal in which, as we saw earlier,[91] Hartle and Hawking in their attempt to combine quantum with gravitational theory were led to the idea that the further one goes back along the ordinary 'real' timescale the more it has to be replaced by a new parameter which includes also a mathematically 'imaginary' component (i.e., one involving i, the square root of -1). According to Hawking,[92] using this 'time', involving an imaginary component, leads to the disappearance of the distinction between time and space. Furthermore, space-'time' (this imaginary time) proved to be finite in extent and yet 'have no singularities that formed a boundary or edge'.[93] This conceptualization, it must be remembered, is still highly controversial, is not widely accepted by physicists and still does not have a basis in a properly formulated quantum theory of gravity. According to this speculation:

> There would be no singularities at which the laws of science broke down and no edge of space-time at which one would have to appeal to God or some new law to set the boundary conditions for space-time. One could say: 'The boundary condition of the universe is that it has no boundary'. The universe would be completely self-contained and not affected by anything outside itself. It would neither be created or destroyed. It would just BE.[94]

By the point at which biological organisms appeared on the Earth, the postulated imaginary component in Hartle and Hawking's physical time would have diminished to insignificance in their theory. So, with this cosmology, we are still free to employ the concept of the personal to interpret God's relation to the universe, which goes on being created by God. Moreover, the mystery-of-existence question still has to be pressed for, as Hawking himself has put it,

> The usual approach of science of constructing a mathematical model cannot answer the questions of why there should be a universe for the model to describe. Why does the universe go to all the bother of existing? Is the unified theory so compelling that it brings about its own existence? Or does it need a creator, and, if so, does he have any other effect on the universe? And who created him?[95]

To Hawking's question 'Does it [the universe] need a creator?', we have been urging the answer 'yes' on the grounds that, from the existence of the kind of universe we actually have, considered in the light of the natural sciences, we do infer the existence of a creator God as the best explanation of all-that-is. We have, so far, been attempting to discern more accurately the character and attributes of this creator God. But his further question 'Does he [a creator God] have any other effect [other than creating it] on the universe?' calls for more deliberation. For it is to the inability of twentieth-century, scientifically educated, human beings even to conceive of how such a creator God could plausibly interact with, act in or through, the regular lawlike world, which they believe the sciences to have established as fact, that disbelief in even the existence of a creator God is widely attributed. So we turn, in the next chapter, to the question of God's interaction with the world.

CHAPTER 9

God's Interaction with the World

1 THE CONTEMPORARY DISCUSSION

a 'The God Who Acts'

Various modes of interaction of God with the world have engaged the faith and attention of believers in God down the ages and some of these have already been part of our concerns. They may, following M. J. Langford,[1] conveniently be classified into:

1 The creative activity of God.
2 The sustaining activity of God.
3 God's action as final cause.
4 'General providence'.
5 'Special providence'.
6 Miracles.

Langford illustrates the distinctions involved in this classification by instancing three ways in which a leader and guide of a climbing party can control events. There is, he suggests, the initial planning of the expedition, corresponding to 1 and 2. Then there is the actual leading of the party up the rock face, the control that involves the smooth and predictable running of the climb, corresponding to 3 and 4. Finally, there is the exercise of leadership in the *ad hoc* actions and decisions in emergencies which, though perhaps predictable in general, are not so in detail, corresponding to 5 and 6.

Insofar as God may be conceived of in personal terms and may be regarded as having purposes which he is working out in the world, category 3 can be subsumed into the others, for they all imply purposive action on the part of God. Reasons for affirming the creative and sustaining activities (1 and 2) of God in the natural, evolving world have already been given in chapter 8, and there are those who regard these as an adequate representation of all of God's activity in the world and doubt the need for the other categories at all. Thus John Macquarrie affirms that the doctrine of general providence (4) in the form that 'asserts that the same God who gave the world being continues to govern its affairs' is 'just another way of asserting his constant creating and sustaining energy', for creation is not to be thought of as a past event with God as 'a kind of absentee landlord who set things going long ago and now leaves the world to its own devices'.[2] This latter has also been the contention of chapter 8 above, with its emphasis on God's immanent creative presence in the natural world; but, we have to ask, does it follow that assertion of the reality of God's creative and sustaining energy exonerates us from any further decision about or analysis of God's interaction with world?

Christoph Schwöbel has urged that 'talk about divine providence does not add anything to our understanding of divine agency as the work of God, Father, Son and Holy Spirit' – that is, apart from, as he argues, God's 'creative and sustaining activity, apart from God's agency in Christ and apart from God's agency in the inspiration of the Holy Spirit'.[3] In this context by divine providence Schwöbel means, along the same lines as Macquarrie,

(1) Apart from what can be said about creation, redemption and salvation, there is a divine ordering of events in the ordination of all things to an end and this applies generally to the way things go in the world, as well as specifically to the way things go in my own life. (2) This divine ordering can (at least to some extent) be discerned in the course of worldly events ... what we mean by 'providence' concerns the correlation of our understanding of divine agency with our experience of the way things go in the world.[4]

Such a belief in divine providence is founded existentially on Christian experience, indeed on religious experience in general, and forms the presupposition of prayer, worship and the daily lives of believers in God. It is not therefore to be summarily dismissed and subsumed under the more abstract categories of the creative and sustaining activity of God. In any case the problems it raises concerning *how* God can actually interact with a world that is increasingly describable in scientific, psychological, sociological and historical terms also underlie any notion of God's immanent creative and sustaining activity in the world, as well as God's activity in those more individual and personal contexts.

But the discernment ((2) in the above quotation from Schwöbel) of both the 'divine ordering of events in the ordination of all things to an end' in 'the way things go in the world' and of 'the way things go in my own life' are notoriously obscure and incapable of clear verification, in this life, at least. God's act of *creatio ex nihilo*, of giving being to all-that-is, must in principle remain ultimately ineffable and mysterious, so that tendering possible models of and analogies for this act, as we shall, is all that is possible. However, this prescinding of God's ultimate act of creation from the requirement to explain *how* God creates does not apply so obviously to the other postulated kinds of divine action. Now the affirmations that God is continuously acting creatively in the world through its natural processes, that he acts to redeem and save in history and that he shapes the course of individual lives are all central to Christian belief. Their very plausibility and intelligibility is widely questioned today in the light of, it is often claimed, that scientific perspective which we have been elaborating. The examination of this issue is more central to our concerns here than whether or not the traditional term 'providence' has any continuing usefulness. Only if we think it plausible that events in nature, society, history and individuals might be intelligibly and plausibly regarded as in any sense the results of *God's* interaction with them would it become worthwhile to speak of 'providence' in the general course of events (4 above) or in special, particular clusters of events (5 and possibly 6 above). Even then we would still have to admit our difficulty in unambiguously discerning what God was doing.

There can be little doubt of the centrality of this question for the plausibility of belief in the God of the Judeo-Christian tradition. For the worship of both Jews and Christians affords a prominent place for the reading of their scriptures, much of which consists of narrative interpreted as the actions of God in history to which the worshipper is invited to attend as exemplifying the nature and character of the God active in those events and still active today. Vernon White has, somewhat uncompromisingly, described as the 'demands of revelation regarding the nature, scope and efficacy of God's activity in the world' that we do not ignore the biblical account of God as one who 'acts personally, universally, with priority and sovereign efficacy; he acts in relation to particular events in which he finds ends as well as means.'[5] In a somewhat more detached vein, Langford summarizes the Old Testament as giving 'continual testimony to belief in an intensely active and personal God, one who both provides for and governs the world',[6] and he concludes also that the New Testament presents a portrait of an intensely personal and active God, which is the foundation of the Christian doctrine of special providence... the actual words and actions of Jesus are the most important examples. Apart from the allegedly miraculous episodes, these are manifestly 'natural', in the sense that they illustrate the use of nature rather than its suspension, but on a Christian interpretation they are all particular manifestations of the love of God himself.[7]

The biblical themes have constituted one of the principal formative strands in Christian theology – though, it must be stressed, not the only ones. Nevertheless their continued influence is obvious even in a post-Christian country such as modern Britain, when a lightning strike on an ancient cathedral is seriously interpreted by certain Christian ministers as an act of God in which he is showing his disapproval of the beliefs of a theologian recently consecrated therein as a bishop! More seriously, with both greater sophistication and immensely more scholarship, for a decade or so after the end of the Second World War, there was dominant in Western Protestant Christianity a 'biblical theology' which, while certainly not fundamentalist, held to 'a doctrine of unique historical revelation through God's self-declaring actions.... God is known through the particular acts in which he shapes the history of Israel and redeems all of humankind.'[8] Their emphasis is apparent even in the titles of the books of major exponents of this biblical theology, such as *God Who Acts: Biblical Theology as Recital* (G. Ernest Wright, 1952) and *The Book of the Acts of God* (Reginald H. Fuller, 1957). However, as Thomas Tracy has put it, 'Biblical theology has crumbled under a number of pressures.'[9] For, when pressed to say what God has actually done in the supposed 'mighty acts' that biblical theologians find in the Scriptures, the answers turn out to be accounts of what the ancient Hebrews, or the early Christians, *believed* God to have done. The biblical theologians accepted that nothing outside the usual laws of nature or the processes of history would have been recorded from the viewpoint of one without faith – they would have been, as Langdon Gilkey put it in a key article deflating the claims of biblical theology, 'epistemologically indistinguishable from other events for those without faith'. But, as he continues,

for those of faith it must be objectively or ontologically different from other events. Otherwise, there is no mighty act, but only our belief in it... Only an ontology of events specifying what God's relation to ordinary events is like, and thus what his relation to special events might be, could fill the now empty analogy of mighty acts, *void since the denial of the miraculous.*[10]

The italicized phrase reminds us that the biblical theologians adopted that scepticism concerning the occurrence of 'miracles', in the sense of events 'breaking the laws of nature', which is characteristic of our scientific age. The point now is not whether or not they were right to do this, but that the whole exercise of 'biblical theology' as an exposition of God's acts in history was based on theological and philosophical presuppositions which had not been adequately examined. As Gilkey puts it,

> When we use the analogies 'mighty act', 'unique revelatory event', or 'God speaks to his people', therefore, we must understand what we might mean in systematic theology by the general activity of God. Unless we have some conception of how God acts in ordinary events, we can hardly know what our analogical words mean when we say: 'He acts uniquely in this event' or 'this event is a special divine deed.'[11]

So the question now is: 'What kind of conception of how God acts in or, more generally, interacts with, the world can we possibly have in the light of scientific perspectives on that world – the presuppositions of which also underlie our scientific, psychological, sociological and historical explanations of events in human experience?' We are concerned with human experience as well as events in the natural, non-human world, for if God is presumed to interact with human beings, then these interactions eventually have to take the form of changes in ourselves (including our brains) as we initiate actions that would have been otherwise but for God's influence. To some recent attempts to answer this question and to a re-examination of the implications of scientific perspectives we must now turn.

b Presuppositions

Consideration of how God might plausibly be conceived of as interacting with the world has for over three centuries been largely coloured by two presuppositions which were taken to be either as validated by the world-view of the natural sciences or, at least, as being implications of it. It would not be too strong to aver that these were two ghosts that still haunt some theological thinking even of recent decades. I refer to (1) the understanding of the natural world basically as a mechanism, controlled by inviolable 'laws of nature', deterministic and therefore, 'in principle' at least, predictable; and (2) the dualist assumption that human beings consist of two entities – mind and body – and that these represent two different orders of reality, sometimes denoted respectively as 'matter' and 'spirit', whose relationship, admittedly problematical, mysterious even, is regarded as exemplified in the human experience of being an agent.

With presupposition (1), it is not possible to conceive of God's interaction with the world, other than his general and perpetual sustaining of it in existence, except in terms of God 'intervening' in the natural course of events. That is, God is regarded as bringing about results which would have been otherwise in the absence of such 'interventions' by God, namely exemplifications of the law-determined processes which the sciences reveal. I have inserted the single inverted commas here, and occasionally later around the verb to 'intervene' and its derivatives when applied to God's action in the world, because I believe there is some ambiguity about its meaning. For example, David Brown[12] is very concerned to defend theism against a 'deism' characterized as 'belief in a non-interventionist God', for he believes that 'for certain types of religious experience such a ['interventionist'] framework is essential' and argues, for example, that 'the argument [for belief in God] from religious experience is only effective when appeal is made to the type of experiences for which such a framework is essential'. However, I have considerable reservations about the use of 'intervention' on the part of God as that which distinguishes deism from theism, as if 'theism', on the contrary, necessarily involves God 'intervening' in his created world as a kind of *deus ex machina* interrupting otherwise orderly created processes.

It seems to me that what Brown wishes to argue for (*inter alia* the validity of religious experience as above, and later on in his extensive work, the doctrines of the Incarnation and the Trinity) depends on God being conceived of as in continuous *interaction* with and a continual influence on the created order, in general, and human experience, in particular – rather than on God 'intervening' in any way disruptive of the natural and human processes he has created. As I hope will become clear, it is possible to think of this continual, and effective, interaction of God with the world in ways that are not crudely 'interventionist' in the manner I have just depicted, yet can still serve to underpin the doctrines Brown is rightly, in my view, concerned to defend.

This is also the view of William P. Alston who, in a very clarifying article,[13] reflects that:

> Many people think, and I myself at one time thought, that the belief that God enters into active interaction with his creatures, a belief crucial to the Judeo-Christian tradition, requires us to suppose that God directly intervenes in the world, acting outside the course of nature ... Just by virtue of creating and sustaining the natural order God is in as active contact with his creatures as one would wish ... If God speaks to me, or guides me, or enlightens me by the use of natural causes, he is as surely in active contact with me as if he had produced the relevant effects by direct fiat ... After all, when one human being directly interacts with another ... the agent is making use of aspects of the natural order ... And surely this does not imply that we are not in active contact with each other in such transactions. However necessary direct intervention may be for the authentication of messengers, it is not required for genuine divine-human interaction.[14]

For Alston (it is interesting to note in relation to our subsequent discussion), 'when we speak of 'special' acts of God, the specialness attaches to our talking rather than to the action itself ... Our account is rather in terms of how the subject is thinking about the matter, what the subject believes about it ... it is only the demarcation of 'special' acts of God that is made to rest on human reactions. Members of this class share with innumerable other happenings the objective feature of being acts of God, a feature that attaches to them however we think, feel, or experience!'[15]

Those who share 'interventionist' views seem to be assuming that if God is 'omnipotent', then he has the power to achieve particular purposes, to 'set aside' his own laws operative in the world he has created. So, what can be said to constitute God's knowledge and power is pertinent to this issue.

c Objections to Divine 'Intervention'

There have been weighty objections to such a picture of God as *deus ex machina*; some of the relevant considerations[16] are as follows.

1 The idea of an 'intervening' God appears to presuppose that God is in some sense 'outside' the created world and has in some way, not specified, to come back into it to achieve his purposes. Yet we

have already found good reason why the presence and immanence of God within the created order needs to be re-emphasized. A mechanistic view of the world inevitably engenders, as it did in the eighteenth century, a deistic view of God and of his relation to it.

2 The very notion of God as the faithful source of rationality and regularity in the created order appears to be undermined if one simultaneously wishes to depict his action as *both* sustaining the 'laws of nature' that express his divine will for creation *and* at the same time intervening to act in ways abrogating these very laws – almost as if he had second thoughts about whether he can achieve his purposes in what he has created. Even if one conceives of these 'interventions' as rare, as made only for significant purposes such as, say, the education of humanity in God's ways or for the revelation of his purposes, one still faces the question of whether it is a coherent way to think of God's action in the world in the light of other insights into the nature of God of the kind we were formulating in the last chapter.

This theological unease about the concept of an intervening God has been very well expressed by David Jenkins in his Hensley Henson Lectures:

> it ... becomes clear that the God who is held to be in some decisive sense the author of the whole [human] story, in some real sense the basic presence in and animateur of the whole story, and in some truly imposing sense the purpose and possibility of the entire story, when and if it reaches its end – that this God cannot and ought not to be thought of ... as if he were the supreme *controller* of the universe who *manages* its affairs by a series of direct interventions for which he alone is responsible and to which response is inevitable in a cause-and-effect way.[17]

3 Furthermore, one has to recognize, with Hume, that adequate historical evidence for such a contravention of the originally divinely established laws of nature could never, in practice, be forthcoming. *Ex hypothesi* the 'laws' are themselves statements of both regularities in sequences of events (as Hume saw them) and also expressions of underlying fundamental relationships and realities (as modern science more frequently sees them). So one would need vastly *more* evidence for the occurrence of any event supposed to have contravened such 'laws of nature' than for one not thought to be doing so – and it is of the nature of our fragmentary historical (even contemporary) evidence that this cannot be forthcoming. Any

favourable assessment that the historical evidence could indeed be interpreted as evidence for a divine 'intervention' would clearly be sensitively dependent on the degree to which the assessor believed *a priori* in the possibility of such 'intervention' ever occurring. Scientists who are theists still find it difficult to conceive of such 'interventions' except as very rare occurrences indeed – and, even then, often prefer to regard such supposed interventions of God in the world's processes and events as manifesting the existence of 'higher laws' or a 'profounder rationality' than have yet become clear to us.

4 There are, of course, also well-known moral objections to simplistic ideas concerning God's intervening in events, both in the natural world and in human affairs, that have to be regarded in retrospect as inimical to human life and welfare. If God *can* intervene consistently with his own being and purposes, why did he not do so to avert disasters in the world of nature or human history, floods in Bangladesh or concentration camps in Auschwitz? Some, like David Jenkins, feel very strongly about this:

> A God who uses the openness of his created universe, the openness and freedom of men and women created in his image and the mystery of his own risky and creative love to insert additional causal events from time to time into that universe to produce particular events or trends by that eventuality alone would be a meddling demigod, a moral monster and a contradiction of himself.... God is not an arbitrary meddler nor an occasional fixer. This is morally intolerable, and no appeal to the mysteriousness of particularity or its scandal can overcome this... However he [God] interacts or transacts he cannot intervene as an additional and inserted and occasional historical cause.[18]

Not all (many did not) agree with such a forthright position, but Jenkins' remarks do serve to highlight the difficulty which many theists feel and which also leads many, if not to atheism, to wistful agnosticism.

To what extent are considerations such as those listed above dependent on presupposition 1 concerning a mechanistic, predictable lawlike universe as the world-view authenticated by the sciences, and indeed also by the commonsense interpretation of events in human affairs? It will emerge that this is not the world-view licensed by the sciences, at least, and to this extent the whole debate takes on a new slant.

d *The Analogy to Personal Agency and Dualism*

Meanwhile we need also to look briefly at presupposition 2 in the 'intervening' model for God's action in the world, that of a dualistic interpretation of human nature and, specifically, of mental experience. That God is not to be conceived of as a 'God of the gaps' in our knowledge of the natural, including the human, world is widely agreed – for such a 'god' has the habit of shrinking to nothingness as our knowledge increases. A parallel set of considerations has deterred many theologians from thinking of God as First Cause if 'cause' in this attribution means a cause within the natural nexus of linked events. It has been generally thought that, insofar as God may be said to be causally related to all-that-is, it is in the way that a personal agent may be regarded as causing things to happen by realizing intentions in action. So it is that the affirmation of the notion that God can and does act in the world has been modelled on the relation of human intentionality, will and purposes to human action in our bodies and through them to the world at large, the world of entities and processes described by the sciences. A dualistic view of human nature qualifies neatly, it has seemed traditionally, as a su .able model for the relation of God to the world. The ultimate ineffability, mysteriousness and transcendence of God appears to be properly analogous to that parallel mystery concerning the nature of human consciousness, a property of that purported distinct entity, the 'mind'.

Two of the distinguished attempts in recent years – those of Schubert Ogden[19] and Gordon Kaufman[20] – to resolve the problem of how God acts in the world have relied on this analogy of divine to personal agency. However, both are vulnerable to the criticism[21] of resting too heavily on an implicitly dualist, Cartesian even, account of human nature and so of human agency. As Thomas Tracy puts it,

> The disconcerting thrust of such criticism is that the person concepts at work in these proposals are philosophically problematic at just those points where they appear to be most useful theologically.... Both Ogden and Kaufman seem to trade on a strong distinction (though not necessarily the same distinction) between the agent and his body as the basis for talk of a God who can be distinguished from the world but who acts upon or through it.[22]

Whether or not these criticisms of these particular authors are justified to the extent these remarks of Tracy suggest is less important for us at this stage than that we recognize the critical sensitivity of talk about God's action in the world to the wider philosophical discussion concerning the nature of human action[23] and the mind/body problem.[24] But those wider discussions have been strongly influenced by scientific developments which thereby alter greatly not only the context of theological discussion but the very plausibility even of some of these relatively recent offerings.

e How?

A major problem created for belief in God is generated by this scientific milieu which, quite properly, presses on the theist the question 'How can one conceive of God acting in the world?' The contemporary sceptic expects, again quite reasonably, that any analogies the theist may wish to make between God's action(s) in the world and human agency should, for them to be intelligible and plausible, be consistent with our best knowledge of that agency. As we shall see later in this chapter, there are grounds for thinking that presuppositions 1 and 2 are no longer warranted by science, so that the whole question of God's action in the world is ripe for reassessment – not least because we now have to ask how God might act in a lawful universe in which 'much of the order arises from the aggregate properties of random events.'[25]

But to ask 'How does God act in the world?' is a more complex question than first appears. Owen Thomas[26] has usefully distinguished the following senses of 'how?' relevant to this question:

A By what means?
B In what way or manner?
C To what effect?
D With what meaning or for what reason or purpose?
E To what extent or degree?
F On analogy with what?

The different positions adopted with respect to how God acts in the world address different combinations, or only one, of these various senses of 'How?'. They also differ, as Thomas points out,[27] in the extent to which they are analogies or theories (metaphysical analyses of the relation of divine activity to processes and events in the created order), or combinations of both – or neither, for example the 'two perspectives and languages' approach.[28]

Thomas further provides[29] a succinct and helpful analysis of the various approaches to this question which have been offered classically and in recent theological studies.[30] The reader is referred to his analysis, for it is not our aim here to provide an overview of the whole discussion but to highlight any repercussions upon it of the twentieth-century scientific perspective. Nevertheless it will be helpful, for clarity, to set the scene by reproducing his classification and some of his comments (quotations are from his chapter 14, see n. 10).

f Views on Divine Action

Apart from the two-languages approach, the following distinct positions need to be considered.

Personal action (addressing 'how?', F above)　'based on the analogy of human personal action in the world as elaborated in the philosophy of action', already discussed in relation to the views of Ogden and Kaufman.[31] This approach is not really offering any explanation, or theory, of God's action. It is indeed an analogy employed in all of the other approaches (including that of 'biblical theology'), though in ways that differ with regard to the aspect of human action that is stressed. The possibility of particular divine actions occurring is given credibility by this analogy, but it can help in addressing the 'how?' questions A to E only if it spells out far more than most authors have attempted *how* human intentions and purposes, as described in mentalistic language, can take effect in the physical system of the human brain and body, and thereby in the world at large. In other words, the analogy can reduce to mere assertion of the claimed similarity between human and divine action unless there is further clarification of the position assumed on such matters as the nature of the human person, the mind-body problem and the philosophy of human action.

Primary cause (addressing 'how?', A and E above)　'God as primary cause acts in and through all other secondary causes in nature and history. . . . In its traditional form this view is a complex theory with the occasional use of the artisan-instrument analogy [of human action]. In its liberal form [e.g., Kaufman[32]] it is neither a theory nor an analogy but simply an affirmation'. Particular divine actions do occur, according to this view.

Process theology (addressing 'how?', A, B, E and F above)[33] 'holds that God acts in all events by influence or persuasion. By being prehended or experienced God offers an initial aim to each emerging event, which aim may be accepted in varying degrees... The analogies offered are those of self-body, mind-brain, and self-constitution.' Particular divine actions do occur, according to this view.

Uniform action (certainly addressing 'how?', E and, less clearly, B above) 'God's action in the world is understood as uniform and universal, and [in the form proposed by M. Wiles[34]] the appearance of particular divine activity is given by the variety of human response.' No *particular* divine actions can be said to occur on this view. This approach merits fuller discussion for it has been specifically propounded to meet the considerations of section c (1 to 4) which tell so heavily against any model of God's action in the world whereby God is said to 'intervene' in some explicit sense in the course of ordinary events. It is supported as a currently defensible view in the light of these considerations which otherwise would seem fatal to traditional views, and certainly to those of 'biblical theology' (which, it must be admitted, is the assumption of most expository sermons!).

The authors who propose various nuanced versions of this 'uniform action' approach seem to hold the presuppositions to which we earlier referred – namely those of a law-governed, determinist world (1) and an implicitly dualist account of human nature (2).[35] This is an assumption which they share with the proponents of other views such as the postulate of a primary cause and process theology. Consequently, with intervention by God in the events of the deterministic world of presupposition 1 becoming implausible, the analogy for God's action provided by the dualistic human model of presupposition 2 involves such a sharp dichotomy between God and the world that no *continuing* interaction of God with, or action of God in, the world becomes at all intelligible. So it is not surprising that authors sharing these presuppositions tend to gravitate in their conclusions towards affirming, as the *only* action of God, his 'one' act of creation and sustaining of all-that-is, his giving of being and keeping in being of the universe.

Thus for Kaufman the 'whole complicated and intricate teleological movement of all nature and history should be regarded as a single all-encompassing act of God.'[36] Maurice Wiles in his Bampton Lectures for 1986[37] affirms, in agreement with these authors, that the idea of divine action should be in relation to the world as a whole rather than particular occurrences in it . . .

For the theist, who is necessarily committed to a unitary view of the world, the whole process of the bringing into being of the world, which is still going on, needs to be seen as one action of God . . .

. . . we can make best sense of this whole complex of experience and of ideas if we think of the whole continuing creation of the world as God's one act, an act in which he allows radical freedom to his human creation. The nature of such a creation . . . is incompatible with the assertion of further particular divinely initiated acts within the developing history of the world.

g An 'Ontological Gap' at the 'Causal Joint'?

The trouble with this conclusion of these authors, explicitly and frankly spelt out above by Wiles, is not only the bleak prospect it holds out for the life of the individual in his or her relation to God in their lives, but its close dependence on presuppositions 1 and 2 which are themselves questionable and, as I shall argue, have lost support in the natural sciences. It is indeed difficult to imagine *how* God might be an agent in a world conceived of as ruled by deterministic laws at all levels when the only analogy for such agency has itself been formulated in dualistic terms that involve a gap dividing action in the 'body', and so in the natural world, from intentions and other acts of the 'mind'. This is an *ontological* gap between two kinds of entities across which it is difficult to see how in principle a bridge could be constructed. Use of the analogy of human action does not exonerate the theologian from entering into the very fraught issue of how mental acts might be conceived of as issuing in, indeed even *being*, processes in the human body and thereby in the natural world. This is a somewhat daunting task, it must be admitted. But it does seem to be the case that, just at this crucial point, theologians expounding apparently very different understandings of how God acts in the world, or of whether he does so or does not do so, tend to resort to just assertion that there *is* such a link in the case of human action and that the link in God's action is analogically similar. They make such assertions usually without saying anything about human action itself, which illuminates *how* God might be conceived of exercising his influence on events in the world.

This omission is not confined to those holding the 'uniform action' position. For example, Austin Farrer's treatment[38] of the notion of God as agent – his use of the concept of 'double agency' – has been regarded[39] as one of the best attempts to say what talk of God's action might be understood to mean. The notion of double agency asserts that events in the world (natural events and human actions) can be regarded as both acts of God and those of finite agencies:

> two agencies of different level taking effect in the same finite action, the finite agency which lives in it, the infinite agency which founds it ... On the theistic hypothesis everything that is done in this world by intelligent creatures is done with two meanings: the meaning of the creature in acting, the meaning of the Creator in founding or support-ing that action ... Where the creature concerned is non-intelligent there are not two meanings, for only the Creator has a meaning or intention. But there are still two doings; it is the act of the Creator that the creature should either act or be there to act.[40]

However, advocacy of this paradox[41] comes perilously close to that mere assertion of its truth already criticized, since Farrer on his own admission can give no account of the 'causal joint' between the agency of the Creator and even human action:

> The causal joint (could there be said to be one) between God's action and ours is of no concern in the activity of religion. ... Both the divine and the human actions remain real and therefore free in the union between them; not knowing the modality of the divine action we cannot pose the problem of their mutual relation.[42]

The problem is, as Wiles stresses, that 'We do not understand the modality of the divine action in a way which enables us to define its relation to our finite human acting.'[43] But if this is the case for the interaction of the divine with the human, which is at least intuitively intelligible by analogy with personal interaction, it is *a fortiori* harder to conceive of the 'causal joint' between the divine and natural non-human events. The hiatus in his exposition frankly admitted by Farrer in the above quotation is also to be found in other recent authors.

For example, Michael Langford[44] works with the idea of God, in his 'general providence', intelligently planning and governing events in a continuing way. The divine 'steering' of nature to fulfil God's purposes he sees as also applying to 'specific events rather than to general movements'. This 'special providence shares with general providence the idea of intelligent control'.[45] But Langford chooses to be 'agnostic about the methods by which God acts, assuming that he does so'.[46] He is properly 'wary of the request for an account of the "mechanism" of his [God's] action, since this may suggest that whatever the manner may be, it must be akin to the way in which one part of a machine works on another part'.[47] He then employs the 'fruitful image'[48] of God as creative artist.[49] However, although he considers that this analogy does 'bring out some of the meaning of the idea of [God as] 'steering' nature',[50] yet it still does not, and is not meant to, 'indicate how God initiates change'.[51]

This is also the position of Vernon White, who asserts that 'if we can and must accept in human experience the hidden causal efficacy of human intention in physical action, without knowing its precise causal modality, then we can surely affirm by analogy the hidden causal efficacy of divine intention on creaturely activity without knowing its modality.'[52] This is true as far as it goes, the analogy does help us to conceive *that* God might act in the world, but does not render the notion at all plausible without more spelling out of the analogy. This requires supplementary conceptual resources that explicate human action to make the idea of God's acting in the physical world at all clear. For without some plausible (certainly not mechanistic) account of *how* God might interact with the causal nexus of individual events in the world, including human-brains-in-human-bodies, we cannot with integrity assert that God does, or might, do so.[53]

This absence of explication of the causal joint is also the weak point of Vincent Brummer's otherwise admirable treatment of *What Are We Doing When We Pray?*[54] In the course of an analysis of divine agency and natural law, Brummer has to resort to a rhetorical question at the crucial point:

> By our actions we cause contingent events by bringing about conditions necessary for them which would otherwise be subject to chance. But if human persons can intervene in the course of nature in this way, why cannot God do so as well? Divine action in the world need therefore not take the form of miraculous intervention in violation of the natural order, any more than human action need do so.[55]

The analogy referred to in the question in this quotation has, as we have seen, often been used as the basis for arguing that God, supposedly like us, on presuppositions 1 and 2, *does* 'intervene' in the world. The mere assertion of the analogy to human action without any further explication of it, and so also analogically of divine action, leaves us still sceptical of the mere possibility of the latter. For we experience our intentions becoming actions in the physical world as a basic feature of our existence, but in the case of all events in the world other than those we initiate we observe only the events themselves and not God as such intending or acting in them. So we cannot use *our* experience as such for saying that God does actually act in these other, vastly more numerous, non-human natural events – whatever other good grounds there might be for supposing that there is such a continuously creating Reality which we name as God. We need further grounds for the plausibility of such an assertion.

For all these authors the notion of God as personal agent remains central to the whole concept of God, as we have also seen already in chapters 7 and 8, and to the widespread human experience of relationship to God being *personal*. These concepts and convictions therefore remain vulnerable to the criticism that the analogy from human agency to divine action cannot do the work it is intended to do – namely render the idea of God acting in the world intelligible – in the absence of any spelling out of the 'causal joint' in *both* human *and* divine action in the world. It is to the absence of this explication of the 'causal joint' that we must attribute the fact that so many contemporary theologians have to resort simply to the assertion that God *does* act in the world with no further attempt to make the idea intelligible other that drawing the analogy to human agency.

It is therefore important to examine if new scientific perspectives throw any light on the deterministic and dualist presuppositions 1 and 2 relevant to the question of the 'causal joint'.

2 How God Might Interact with the World in the Perspectives of Science

In chapter 8 we recognized a number of significant ways in which our scientific understanding of what is in the world and of what has been and is going on in it has modified, indeed enriched, our reasons for believing in God as Creator of that world, and what we are to mean by 'God' – that is, our understanding of various aspects of such a God's relation to the created world and what that relation implies about the nature of God. We saw *inter alia* that the intelligibility of the natural world pointed to the basic rationality of God as Creator; the regularity of its processes to the divine faithfulness to the created order; and the continuity of these processes and their emergent character to the continuing immanence of the divine creative activity. We saw also how the omnipotence and omniscience of God had to be understood with important qualifications of the way they have been interpreted both by many philosophers of religion and by traditional piety. The way of regarding these essential attributes of God that most commended itself was seeing God as having a self-appointed vulnerability towards the events and processes of the world in the creation of which there had been a self-emptying (*kenosis*) by God's own self. If, as we argued, the source of the being of the world is other than itself, then we inferred that the 'best explanation' of that world is a creator God who must be at least personal and who possesses a mode of rationality creative of and exploratory in new possibilities in the world. But now we have to inquire if scientific perspectives on the world can make any contribution to our conceiving of how God so described might interact with that world.

a Unpredictability, Open-endedness, Flexibility and Propensities

Although the natural sciences have traditionally concerned themselves with the regular, predictable, law-governed phenomena of the natural world, they have had to recognize in the twentieth century that there are systems, at every level of complexity, whose future development is unpredictable. These were:[56] subatomic systems, at the ('Heisenberg') micro-level; many-bodied Newtonian systems at the micro-level of description; and non-linear dynamical systems at the macroscopic level.[57] Awareness of the existence of this last-mentioned category is relatively recent in spite of the wide range of situations that are unpredictable in this way – for example, turbulent liquids, some networks of chemical reactions or of neurones and the weather. It must be stressed that the non-linear, macroscopic, open systems in question are as deterministic at the micro-level as any 'classical' system. Their unpredictability at the macro-level results from the nature of the solutions to the mathematical equations that govern the behaviour of these systems as a whole, and from their sensitivity to initial conditions.

Thus the world looks less and less like the deterministic mechanism that has been the presupposition ((1) above) of much theological reflection on God's action in the world since Newton. It is now seen to possess a degree of openness and flexibility within a lawlike framework so that certain developments are irreducibly unpredictable and we have good reasons for saying, from the relevant science and mathematics, that this unpredictability will remain.

We also saw that the historical course of natural development manifested a kind of rising curve of such unpredictability at the macroscopic level, especially in the open-endedness of the biological evolutionary development and ultimately in the increasing freedom of conscious organisms. The most immediate and notable instance of the latter is, of course, the experience of human freedom which one is strongly inclined to associate with the non-linear far-from-equilibrium dynamical complexity of the neuronal network constituting the human brain.

The history of the relation between the natural sciences and the Christian religion affords many instances of the gap in human ability to give causal explanations, that is, instances of unpredictability, being exploited by theists as evidence of the presence and activity of God who thereby filled the explanatory gap. But the advance of the natural sciences showed just how vulnerable was such a 'God of the gaps', as science gradually filled these supposed opportunities in which such a 'god' could flex his 'omnipotent' muscles. But we now have to reckon with a new irreducible kind of unpredictability in systems such as those mentioned above and so with a new flexibility in the events occurring in such systems – *rigid* determinism no more universally rules at the macroscopic level than it does, as recognized since the 1920s, at the subatomic level.

We therefore have to take account of, as it were, permanent gaps in our ability to predict events in the natural world. Should we propose a 'God of the *unpredictable* gaps'? There would then be no fear of such a God being squeezed out by increases in scientific knowledge. But this raises two further theological questions: (1) 'Does *God* know the outcome of these situations that are unpredictable to us?', and (2) 'Does God act within the flexibility of these situations to effect his will?' As regards question 1, his omniscience might be such that he would know and be able to track the minutiae of the fluctuations, unpredictable and unobservable by us, whose amplification leads at the macroscopic level to one outcome rather that another, also unpredictable by us. Only if we answered question 1 affirmatively (i.e., if we thought of God, even if not we ourselves, as being able to predict the outcome of any initial conditions) could we then go on to postulate that God could act to change the initiating, subsequently amplified, fluctuation event so as to bring about a macroscopic consequence conforming to his will and purposes – that is, also to answer question 2 affirmatively. God would then be conceived of as acting, as it were, 'within' the flexibility of these unpredictable situations in a way that, in principle, could never be detectable by us. Such a mode of divine action would always be consistent with our scientific knowledge of the situation, which itself includes our recognition of only a limited ability to predict on our part, and sometimes of a total inability to do so. If this were the case, God would be conceived of as actually manipulating micro-events within these initiating fluctuations in the natural world in order to produce the results that he wills. This appeared to be the implication of John Polkinghorne's treatment in *Science and Providence*, where he, rightly in my view, stressed that 'the concept of divine immanence helps us to understand something of the scope of God's activity'[58] and quoted approvingly John V. Taylor's statement in *The Go-between God*: 'the hand of God . . . must be found not in isolated intrusions, not in any gaps, but in the process itself.'[59] Polkinghorne then urges that the 'notion of flexible process helps us to see where there might be room for divine manoeuvre, within the limits of divine faithfulness'.[60] His subsequent contention that God's immanent action 'will always lie hidden in those complexes whose precarious balance makes them unsusceptible to prediction'[61] seems to me to be susceptible to the (I gather, unintended) interpretation that that would simply be God putting what could only be called an 'intervening' finger into those (to us) uncloseable gaps in the predictability of the natural world which are manifest particularly in the form of complex non-linear systems. If this *were* so, God would both have to be able to predict the outcome of God's actions within the 'flexible process' and also actually to make some micro-event, subsequently amplified, to be other than it would have been if left to itself to follow its own natural course, without the involvement of divine action. This is the dilemma if God is conceived of as acting in some way *within* the processes at their micro-level, that is by the 'isolated intrusions' that Taylor precludes.[62]

Such a conception of God's action in these, to us, unpredictable situations would then be no different in principle from the idea of God intervening in a deterministic, rigidly law-controlled, mechanistic order of nature of the kind thought to be the consequence of Newtonian dynamics. The only difference, on this view, would seem to be that, given our irreducible incapacity to predict the histories of many natural systems, God's intervention (for that is what it would properly have to be called) would always be hidden from us, whereas previously, God's intervention in a mechanistic, rigidly law-controlled, world could always have been regarded as open to verification by us provided we could ascertain the natural laws usually operative. For then we would know what regularities were not being conformed to, what laws were, so to speak, being set aside.

Thus, although at first sight this introduction of an unpredictability, open-endedness and flexibility into our picture of the natural world seems to help us to suggest in new terminology how God might act in the world in its unclosable 'gaps', the above considerations indicate that such divine action would be just as much 'intervention' as it was when postulated in relation to a mechanistic world view. This analysis has, it must be stressed, been grounded on the assumption that God *does* know the outcome of natural situations that are unpredictable by us (i.e., on an affirmative answer to question 1). It assumes total divine omniscience and prescience about all natural events.

However, we have already[63] given reasons for regarding God's omniscience, at least in some respects, as 'self-limited'. This means that God does *not* know which of a million radium atoms will be the next to disintegrate in, say, the next 10^{-3} seconds and only (like ourselves) what the average number will be that will break up in a given time interval. The proposal of self-limiting omniscience means that God has so made the natural order that it is, in principle, impossible, for him and for us, to predict the outcomes of certain classes of events – which is what I take 'in principle' to mean in this context.[64] In other words if, in the above example, it is genuinely indeterminate which particular radium atom will break up in a particular given time interval, there would then be no question of God's being able to intervene in the micro-events at this level to influence the natural order. Not only these events at the subatomic level but a wide range of macroscopic events are also unpredictable in principle.[65] It must be concluded that the outcomes of these kinds of macroscopic event cannot be known to God and their manipulation by God would then be impossible (in this universe with its actual created characteristics). There just does not exist any future, predictable state of such systems *for* God to know.

For such reasons, we earlier[66] propounded that God's omniscience and omnipotence must be regarded, in some respects, as 'self-limited'. This, we hinted, is the origin of the natural order possessing that genuine degree of open-endedness and unpredictability required for the interplay of chance and law in its creative processes and, eventually, for real human freedom to emerge. On this view God bestows a certain autonomy not only on human beings, as Christian theology has long recognized, but also on the natural order as such to develop in ways that God chooses not to control in detail. That natural order he allows a degree of open-endedness and flexibility which becomes the natural, structural basis for the flexibility of conscious organisms and, in due course, of the freedom of the human-brain-in-the-human-body, that is, of persons.

We concluded above that this new awareness of the unpredictability, open-endedness and flexibility inherent in many natural processes and systems does not, of itself, help directly to illuminate the 'causal joint' of how God acts in the world. But it does help us to perceive the natural world as a matrix within which openness and flexibility and, in humanity, freedom might naturally emerge. It also provides an apt context within which free persons can fruitfully act – namely one where there is regularity enough on which to base decisions and action but also one which provides unexpected challenges to conscious organisms and which is not so rigid that the exercise of creativity and spontaneity is impossible.

We saw in Part I[67] that the processes of the natural world displayed certain tendencies, some of them strong enough to be called *propensities* in the sense that Karl Popper has again recently brought to our notice.[68] These include propensities for an increase in complexity which is the basis for an increase in organization in living organisms, itself the basis for the emergence of consciousness and so of self-consciousness. These propensities must be regarded on any theistic interpretation of the universe as built-in and intended by God their Creator. So that, although we have had to infer that God cannot predict in detail the outcome of in-principle unpredictable situations, this does not derogate from his having purposes which are being implemented through the inbuilt propensities that load, as it were, the dice the throws of which shape the course of natural events. The world has, it seems, been so constituted, a theist would say 'created', that there is a kind of ratchet effect such that once a certain level of complexity, and then organization, and then consciousness and then self-consciousness has been attained, these form the 'launching pad', as it were, for the next exploration of new possibilities. And this movement continues even though retrogressions are still possible and, from time to time, actually occur. As D. J. Bartholomew puts it, 'God chose to make a world of chance because it would have the properties necessary for producing beings fit for fellowship with himself.'[69]

In summary, it would seem that the new scientific awareness of unpredictability, open-endedness and flexibility and of the inbuilt propensities of natural processes to have particular kinds of outcomes show that the world we have is the kind that could be the matrix in which free agents could develop; and that in itself it has such a degree of open-endedness and flexibility that we are justified[70] in attributing an exploratory character to God's continuing creative action. However, we also found that these features of the world did not, in the end, help us very much in unravelling the problem of how best to conceive of and articulate God's action in the world, the question of the 'causal joint', much as they altered our interpretation of the meaning of what is actually going on in that world. Defining the problem as that of the 'causal joint' between God and the world is inappropriate, however, for it does not do justice to the many levels in which causality operates in a world of complex systems multiply interlocking at many levels and in many modes. It is to this major feature of the world as perceived by the sciences that we must now turn.

b Top-down (or Downward) Causation

We saw in Part I[71] that, in a number of natural situations, causality in complex systems constituted of complex subsystems at various levels of interlocking organization could best be understood as a two-way process. Not only did events at the 'lower' levels in the hierarchy of complexity in the long run (however slightly) influence how the total inclusive system-as-a-whole behaved, but also the state of the system-as-a-whole could itself properly be regarded as a causal factor influencing events in the 'lower' subsystems, constraining them to follow one course rather than another. Now the events at each particular level, or in each particular subsystem (whichever way of speaking is appropriate to the particular situation, and sometimes it could be both) are explicated and described in language that makes use, on the critical-realist view adopted here, of the concepts which refer to the realities operative at those levels. This is true also of the system-as-a-whole, so that real features of the total system-as-a-whole may well be properly regarded as causative factors in, constraints upon, events happening within the subsystems at lower levels – events, which, it must be stressed, in themselves are describable in terms of the sciences pertinent to that lower level. Thus we drew attention to the examples[72] of the seemingly coordinated movement, or chemical transformation, of individual molecules in, respectively, the hexagonal flowing 'cells' of Bénard convection in a liquid and the spatial organization of a previously homogeneous reaction system. In biological systems, especially, we noted[73] how such 'top-down' causation happens in evolution so that selective evolutionary processes may properly be regarded as the cause of changes that are established in the DNA of living organisms. We noted particularly[74] that such considerations were providing significant clues to how conscious brain states could be 'top-down' causes at the 'lower' level of neurones – and so conceivably of human actions stemming from brain states. This constitutes a new insight into the nature of human agency very pertinent to our central problem.

In the light of these features of the natural world, might we not properly regard the world-as-a-whole as a total system so that its general state can be a 'top-down' causative factor in, or constraint upon, what goes on at the myriad levels that comprise it? I suggest that these new perceptions of the way in which causality actually operates in our hierarchically complex world provides a new resource for thinking about how God could interact with that world. For it points to a way in which we could think of divine action making a difference in the world, yet not in any way contrary to those regularities and laws operative within the observed universe which are explicated by the sciences applicable to the level of complexity and organization in question. It also provides an appropriate and helpful model of how natural events, including the unpredictable ones and the outcome of freely-willed human decisions, could work their way up through the hierarchy of systems and contribute to the state of the whole. It therefore helps us to model more convincingly that interaction, dialogue even, between human decisions and actions, on the one hand, and divine intentions and purposes, on the other. It is in such a context that the significance of prayer, worship and the sacraments are rooted.

Attempts to hold together the notions of God's transcendence over the world, his ultimate otherness, with that of his immanent Presence in, with and under the world often find it helpful to deploy models of the world as being, in some sense, 'in God', but of God as being 'more than' the world, and so as the circumambient Reality in which the world persists and exists ('pan-en-theism').[75] God is the one in whom 'we live, and move, and have our being.'[76] This is the model that St Augustine has depicted so memorably and in such graphic terms, addressing God thus:

> I set before the sight of my spirit the whole creation, whatsoever we can see therein (as sea, earth, air, stars, trees, mortal creatures); yea and whatever in it we do not see . . . and I made one great mass of Thy creation . . . And this mass I made huge, not as it was (which I could not know), but as I thought convenient, yet every way finite. But Thee, O Lord, I imagined on every part environing and penetrating it, though every way infinite: as if there were a sea, everywhere and on every side, through unmeasured space, one only boundless sea, and it contained within it some sponge, huge, but bounded; that sponge must needs, in all its parts, be filled with that unmeasurable sea: so conceived I Thy creation, itself finite, full of Thee, the Infinite; and I said, Behold God, and behold what God hath created; and God is good, yea, most mightily and incomparably better than all these . . .'[77]

On this model of God's relation to the world-as-a-whole, the total world system is seen as 'in God' who (uniquely) is present to it *as a whole*, as well as to its individual component entities. If God interacts with the 'world' at this supervenient level of totality, then he could be causatively effective in a 'top-down' manner without abrogating the laws and regularities (and the unpredictabilities we have noted) that operate at the myriad sub-levels of existence that constitute that 'world'. Particular events could occur in the world and be what they are because God intends them to be so, without at any point any contravention of the laws of physics, biology, psychology, sociology, or whatever is the pertinent science for the level of description in question. Furthermore, we should expect the irreducible unpredictability, open-endedness and flexibility that characterize lesser complex dynamical systems within the world also to be a feature of the world-as-a-whole, rather in the same way that the succession of human brain states has an unpredictability (from outside) that may be related to human freedom. Might not this be the correlate of divine freedom in relation to the world?

In thus speaking of God, it has not been possible to avoid talk of God 'intending', of God's 'freedom', that is, to avoid using the language of personal agency. For these ideas of 'top-down' causation by God cannot be expounded without relating them to the concept of God as, in some sense, an agent, least misleadingly described as personal. We cannot examine further the usefulness, or otherwise, of this notion of 'top-down' causation by God without looking again at the dualistic assumptions about human nature which, as we saw, have so frequently been presupposed in attempts to use the model of human agency for God's action in the world.

c Personal Agents As Psychosomatic Unities

Over recent decades the pressure from the relevant sciences[78] – studies of the evolution of brains, pharmacology, brain biochemistry, neurophysiology, neuropsychology, psychology, the brain sciences, and the cognitive sciences in general, to name only a selection – has been inexorably towards viewing the processes that occur in the human brain and nervous system, on the one hand, and the content of consciousness, our personal, mental experience, on the other, as two facets or functions of one total unitive process and activity.[79] One could instance the well-known effects of hormone balance, of brain lesions, and of drugs on both personality and the content of mental experience and the research on the unity, or rather disunity, of the experience of patients with 'split' brains. I have argued elsewhere[80] that the mind-body identitist view which most readily accords with such observations is in fact quite acceptable to Christian theology – and is indeed also consistent with Biblical presuppositions concerning human nature – provided it is qualified by being held with the proviso that the language of mental events is not reducible to that of the physical and neurological sciences which are also attempting to describe the one unitive process that is going on when we think. The description of an event in the mind/brain in non-reducible mentalist language is regarded, and this is the force of the qualification, as referring to a *real* feature of the unitive mind/brain event. This is indeed a widely held view amongst philosophers on the mind-body problem, sometimes denoted as 'soft materialism', though what is then to be meant by 'materialism' needs considerable qualification,[81] since matter is thereby recognized as capable of thought when it is in the form of the human brain in the human body.

We have already seen[82] that combining a non-dualist account of the human person and of the mind-body relation with the idea of top-down causation illuminates the way in which states of the brain-as-a-whole (a) could be causally effective at the level of neurones, and so of action; and (b) could actually also be mental states to which non-reducible mentalist, including first person, language could legitimately refer as a real modality of that total unitive event which is the activity of thinking accomplished by the human-brain-in-the-human-body. A total brain state, experienced as '*I* intend to do x as I do x', has a causal relation to, is a constraint upon, a series of subsystems (down to muscles and their coordinated actions), which just *is* the intended action and which is fully explicable in terms of the sciences appropriate to those levels (muscle biochemistry, physiology, anatomy, etc.).

My suggestion is that a combination of the notion of top-down causation from the integrated, unitive mind/brain state to human bodily action ((a) above) with the recognition of the unity of the human mind/brain/body event ((b) above) *together* provide a fruitful clue or model for illuminating how we might think of God's interaction with the world. According to this suggestion the in-principle cognizable aspects of the state of the world as a whole (all-that-is) would be known only to God and would be the field of the exercise of God's influence at God's own level of comprehension. Just as our human personal subjectivity (the sense of being an 'I') is a unitive, unifying, centred influence on the conscious, willed activity of our bodies, and this is what characterizes personal agency, so God is here conceived as a unifying, unitive source and centred influence on the world's activity. We are exploring here the notion that the succession of the states of the system of the world-as-a-whole is also a succession in the thought of God, who is present to it all; and that this is a model for, is analogous to, the way, it has to be presumed, a succession of brain states constitutes the succession of our thoughts. In this model, God would be regarded as exerting continuously top-down causative influences on the world-as-a-whole in a way analogous to that whereby we in our thinking can exert effects on our bodies in a 'top-down' manner.

Earlier[83] we surmised that 'the causal effectiveness of the whole brain state on the actual states of its component nerves and neurones is probably better conceived of in terms of the transfer of information rather than of energy.' This now affords a further clue to how the continuing action of God with the world-as-a-whole might best be envisaged – namely as analogous to an input of information, rather than of energy. But since God is personal, this flow of 'information' is more appropriately described as a 'communication' by God to the world of his purposes and intentions through those levels of the hierarchy of complexity capable of receiving it. The implications of this will have to be considered later.[84]

This holistic mode of action and influence is God's alone and distinctive of God. God's continuous interaction with the whole and the never-ending constraints he exerts upon it could thereby shape and direct all events at lesser levels so that his purposes were not ultimately frustrated and were attained. Such interaction could occur without ever abrogating at any point any of the natural relationships and inbuilt flexibilities and freedoms operative at all the lower levels, and discerned by the sciences and ordinary human experience – any more than the 'program' of the software used in a computer overrides the laws of solid state physics operating in the processes going on in the hardware.

Only God in his transcendence is present to the totality of all-that-is as well as, in his immanence, also to the individual entities that comprise created existence. Accordingly, God's experience is of the world-as-a-whole as well as of individual entities and events within it. By analogy with the relation of our private awareness and the corresponding descriptions of our own mental states to scientific accounts of our brain states and our bodily actions, I suggest that only God could be aware of the distinctiveness of any state of that totality and what states might or might not succeed it in time (or whatever is the appropriate dimension for referring to 'succession in God'). So this divine knowledge would always be hidden from and eternally opaque to us, existing as we do at levels at which the conceptual language will never be available for apprehending God's own 'inner' life. The best we can do, as we have already urged, is to stretch the language of personal experience as the least misleading option available to us. According to this approach, we are free to describe any events at our own level of existence in the natural terms available to us (e.g., those of the sciences) and at the same time to regard those same events, whether private and internal to us or public and external to all, as manifesting God's overall intentions, that is, his general providence. For God could have brought it about that they are what they are and not something else by an overall comprehensive influence which God exerts, in a top-down causative way, upon all the constituting events in the totality of existence. God is thus to be conceived of as the continuing, supra-personal, unifying and unitive influence upon all-that-is. We must go on recognizing – and this is essential to the whole proposal – that, in the light of our earlier discussion, God himself has chosen to allow a degree of unpredictability, open-endedness and flexibility in the world he continues to create.

What does this imply about the 'causal joint' between God and his action on the world? I would emphasize, with Kaufman and Wiles,[85] that God's action is on the world-as-a-whole, but to stress more strongly than they do that this maintaining and supporting interaction is a continuing as well as an initial one; and can be general or particular in its effects. The freedom of God to affect the world is indeed reinforced and protected in this model. The idea of God's continuous interaction with the world as being best conceived of in terms of 'top-down' causation also helps to bridge what some, for example Hugh Montefiore,[86] have viewed as a tendency towards postulating the 'God of the deists' in the kind of immanence that I have urged here and elsewhere.[87] I attempted to meet this criticism by stressing[88] that the creative processes of the natural order, involving chance operating in a lawlike framework, are themselves the immanent creative activity of God – and a musical analogy can, I think, help us to imagine this (see below, chapter 9, section 3b).[89]

The notion of top-down causation has the merit of allowing us to understand how initiating divine action on the state of the world-as-a-whole can itself have a causative effect upon individual events and entities within that world. Any change in God's interaction with the world-as-a-whole can on this top-down causative model thereby influence particular events in the world, within those limitations of unpredictability, open-endedness, and flexibility in nature (including humanity) that God himself has created. Moreover, such divine causative influence would never be observed by us as a divine 'intervention', that is, as an interference with the course of nature and as a setting aside of its observed relationships.

d How?

It might be helpful in clarifying this way of looking at the interaction of God with the world to revert to Owen Thomas's classification[90] of 'how?' in the question, 'How does God act in the world?':

A *By what means?* This question amounts to an earlier one, namely, 'What is the "causal joint" in this postulated holistic interaction?' Any description of the world-as-a-whole pertinent to an answer is available only to God, who alone has that relevant and requisite experience of the world-as-a-whole. This is analogous to our description of our own brain states being privately accessible only to us and then only in mentalistic language. There is therefore still a lacuna in our explication of the God/world 'causal joint', but it has reached an inevitable boundary, namely that between the world-as-a-whole and the inner life of God within which God represents the world to himself in such a way that he can alter its overall state. I have suggested that the influence of God on the world-as-a-whole might be appropriately conceived of in terms of a flow, an 'input', of information rather than of energy. Now, as pointed out elsewhere,[91] at all levels observable by us any input of information requires *some* input of matter/energy, however minimal. So we still have a problem of the 'causal joint', now in the form of: How can God exert his influence on, make an input of information into, the world-as-a-whole without an input of matter/energy? This seems to me to be the ultimate level of the 'causal joint' conundrum, for it involves the very nature of the divine being in relation to that of matter/energy and seems to me to be the right place in which to locate the problem, rather than at some lower levels in the created order at which divine 'intervention' would then have to be postulated, with all of its difficulties.

B   *In what way or manner?* – by continuously interacting, as a top-down agency, with the world-as-a-whole but without infringing any of its natural relationships, so that no 'interventions', in the sense of rupturing previously observed regular relationships, occur to our observation.

C   *To what effect?* – primarily on the world-as-a-whole, but thereby on any constituent entity or event in the world that God wishes to influence, within the God-imposed limits of the creation's inbuilt unpredictability, open-endedness and flexibility which include the exercise of human freedom. These effects operate in a top-down manner through the boundary conditions and constraints that the state of the whole exerts upon all subsidiary, constituent entities and processes.

D   *With what meaning or for what reason or purpose?* – the question of theodicy still remains open for discussion, though certain guidelines can already be discerned from the character of those self-imposed limits (see C above).

E   *To what extent or degree?* – on the world-as-a-whole and thereby and selectively, according to God's working out of his purposes, on individual entities and events as he purposes.

F   *On analogy with what?* – on analogy with the personal agency of the psychosomatic unity of the human mind-brain acting in a top-down causative manner on the human body and so affecting events at lower levels, as described by the relevant sciences, and so also effecting action in the world. This process is analogous to an input of 'information' and so to the kind of patterning and redisposition of the material world that our brains-in-our-bodies continuously perform.

This treatment of the God–world interaction is, of course, but a variation on the widely adopted analogy of personal agency for God's action in the world. But I would suggest it renders this analogy more apt and convincing by its taking account both of the psychosomatic unity of the 'personal' and of top-down causality by the human 'agent'. It is offered as an enrichment of what Galilee and Hebblethwaite[92] interpret as the general thrust of Farrer's account, including his agnosticism over the modality of divine action, which is 'not to be confused with agnosticism over the meaning of the basic analogy of action with which Farrer operates or over the necessity of its use'.[93] Their description of Farrer's approach, albeit in terms of 'Spirit' (which, in this context, is a term for God's outreach into the world-as-a-whole) and going further theologically than the stage we are at present at, nevertheless coheres with the kind of understanding of God's interaction with the world developed above:

> In his treatment of divine providence, Farrer invites us to think much more holistically of the web of creaturely interaction as the field of divine action than the analogy of one agent among others might suggest. Although each created energy-system is given the power to 'run itself its own way' neither the natural world nor the human world is a closed system, impervious to the divine Spirit. On the contrary, the divine Spirit 'radiates' upon his creation, superimposing higher levels of organization and drawing the various threads of evolution, history and individual life-stories into the providential patterns we observe. The modality of the divine Spirit's operation may be unknown, the hand of God perfectly hidden, but the effects of divine agency in the emergence of man, in salvation-history, and in the lives of Christ and the saints are not hidden at all.[94]

In conclusion, it would seem that new perspectives afforded by the natural sciences on the processes of the world, including especially those on top-down causation and on the human-brain-in-the-human-body, have provided not only a new context for the theological debate about how God might be conceived to interact with the world but have also afforded new conceptual resources for modelling it. There have been a number of ways in which this interaction of God with the world has in fact been modelled by different authors and we now need to consider some of these.

3 MODELS OF GOD'S INTERACTION WITH THE WORLD

These have to be reconsidered in the light of the understanding of divine being and becoming that we developed[95] in response to the new perspectives on the world which the natural sciences have stimulated. The past few decades have witnessed attempts by various authors to meet this challenge by proposing new models, or older models revised, in response to various pressures, including those from the sciences. In doing so they have participated in that rebirth of images of God's relation to the world which is the general and perennial task of theology. Not, of course, that a plethora of models (we shall employ this word, rather then 'images' in accordance with our earlier usage) were at all lacking in the Judeo-Christian tradition to represent this relation.

a *Models of the God–world Relation*

John Macquarrie[96] has usefully and perceptively classified these models as being broadly either 'monarchical' or 'organic'. The former stress 'God's transcendence over and priority to the world'[97] and the relation between God and the world is asymmetric: the world is dependent on God, but not God on the world; God affects the world but not *vice versa*; and so on. The latter, 'organic', approach 'envisages . . . a much more intimate relation between God and the world than the monarchical model. It does not abolish the ideas of transcendence and priority of God, it qualifies them . . . I should prefer myself to regard it as a variety of theism, differing from classical theism in the stress which it lays on elements of intimacy and reciprocity in the God-world relation.'[98]

The monarchical models include *inter alia* God as Maker, Father (conceived in patriarchal terms[99]), Lord, King and Sovereign of the universe. Even within such models of kingship, two different pictures may be distinguished,[100] namely, those of the 'philosopher-king' and the 'saviour-king'. The former is the model of a king 'by whose wisdom and power everything is so controlled that nothing can be present in the kingdom which is alien to his will'.[101] In the latter model, which predominates in the Bible, what happens in the realm of the 'saviour-king' is often not as he wishes and he is 'constantly meeting, redressing and redeeming that which is alien to his will'.[102]

The organic models with their stress on intimacy and reciprocity between God and the world are less prominent in the Bible, though certainly not absent – for example, the notion of God as closer to human beings than their own breath; Hosea's picture of God as the faithful husband; God as the Shepherd of Israel; the image of creation as the garment worn by God; in the Wisdom literature, the idea of *Sophia* going out from God as the personal agent and expression of God's own being in creation; and, in the New Testament, the doctrine of the incarnation according to which God embodies himself in creation in a created human being.

There have been a number of proposals in contemporary theology to soften the distinction between these two limiting models both of which, it must be noted, are used by biblical authors with no apparent sense of disparity. Thus Sallie McFague,[103] *inter alia*,[104] has urged the model of God as Mother along with that of God as Father, and the Doctrine Commission of the Church of England (not expected to be ultra-radical theologically) has stressed in its 1987 Report that the model of God's relation to the world as that of *parent*-child 'is of great importance in both Judaism and Christianity'.[105] Sallie McFague also goes on to explore the models of God as Lover and God as Friend in a very interesting and fruitful way. In such exercises it is important to remember that, as we indicated in the Introduction,[106] such models utilize metaphors, with the concomitant and simultaneous 'is' and 'is not' character of their affirmations. Hence different models can be employed together without contradiction and with mutual enrichment of our perception.

As we saw earlier in this chapter, personal agency has traditionally been used as an analogy for God's interaction with the world and has recently been subject to much reassessment. Although traditionally the soul/body relation has not been widely used in Christian theology for the God/world relation, except in certain limited ways, in recent years process theologians have extensively used the analogy in the form self:body::God:world. As we saw, holistic conceptions of the human person which have arisen in response to scientific knowledge and which conceive the 'self' and the 'body' as two aspects of one total unity, then serve in combination with this analogy to facilitate a non-interventionist way of thinking of God's agency in the world and a more intimate and internal form for God's knowledge of the world. The metaphor of the world *as* God's body has been explored particularly by Sallie McFague and by Grace Jantzen.[107] The former assesses this model sympathetically, especially for its world-affirming and ecological implications and for its ability to stress God's genuine involvement in the suffering and joys of the world, but she does not lose sight of the metaphorical character of such language.

Grace Jantzen goes further and regards the world as God's body in a much stronger ontological sense – God is no longer 'incorporeal', for God is embodied in the world as the medium of God's life and action. Her exposition of this concept is stimulating for its illuminating qualifications of much that is now inconsistent with our scientific understanding of the world in many more monarchical and near-deistic ways of speaking of God's relation to the world. However, in the end, one cannot but think that her position steers too near to a pantheism in which all-that-is becomes identified so closely with God that God's role as Creator is compromised. Furthermore, the world, all-that-is, is not an integrated organism in anything like the sense that *our* bodies are a single organism – it is, rather, a nexus of intricately interacting living organisms interlocked within various assemblies of inorganic systems, the vast majority of which have no direct interaction with living organisms. Moreover, the problem of the existence of evil becomes particularly intransigent if the world *is* God's body, for then evil becomes a part of God's own being. Yet, in its very indiscretions, if one may, not disrespectfully, so put it, this attempt to depict the world *as* God's body serves to remind[108] us how few have been models adequate to expressing God's intimate contact with and presence to and in the world which God is deemed to have created. The notion of God as Creator is fundamental to the Judeo-Christian concept of God and various ways of conceiving this creative activity of God lie behind these models for God's relation to the world. Indeed, the difficulties hinted at in the idea of the world as God's body and the plethora of alternative models for God's relation to the world suggest that it should be fruitful to examine more closely what we might mean by saying that God 'creates' all-that-is.

b Models of God's Activity as Creator[109]

There are two ways, broadly speaking, in which the activity of divine creation has been modelled in the Judeo-Christian tradition, according to another analysis of John Macquarrie[110] – the models of 'making' and of 'emanation'. The basic analogy in the former is that of a craftsman making something for use – for example, a potter making a pot, something that did not exist before in that form. This model points to the dependence of what is created on the creator for both its form and existence; to the intention and purpose in the mind of the creator that is implemented; and to the relatively independent existence that is accorded to what is created by the act of creation. Such models for divine creation are defective insofar as they imply that the 'matter' on which the act of creation operated was already in existence – that is they do not express the idea of *creatio ex nihilo* which is so essential to the doctrine of God as Creator, as the *one* source of being of all-that-is. Nevertheless they do serve to stress the transcendence of God and that the act of creation entirely stems from the free, divine initiative. However, they also inevitably tend to establish a distinct gap between the Creator and what is created.

The other model – that of emanation – is less biblical but early entered Christian theology and has served historically[111] to supplement, and even correct, the other model. The classical example of 'emanation' is that of the Sun emitting from within itself its rays which permeate the Earth, where they stimulate warmth and life. Thus it is, the model suggests, God from within God's own being goes out to be actively involved in giving and sustaining the being of all-that-is. An 'admirable statement of what may be called the Christian form of creative emanation', as Stephen Hobhouse puts it,[112] is afforded by William Law in regard to the human condition:

> The creation, therefore, of a soul is not the creation of thinking and willing, or the making that to be and to think, which before had nothing of being or thought; but it is the bringing the powers of thinking and willing out of their eternal state in the one God into a beginning state of a self-conscious life, distinct from God.

And earlier in the same work:

> Here, O man, behold the great original and the high state of thy birth.... Thou beginnest as time began, but as time was in eternity before it became days and years, so thou wast in God before thou wast brought into the creation; and as time is neither a part of eternity, nor broken off from it, yet come out of it; so thou art not part of God, nor broken off from him, yet born out of Him.[113]

This model of emanation certainly places a proper stress on the immanence of God in the created order and the continued closeness of God to that which is created. Yet it avoids the danger of identifying God's presence in the created world too much with the world – the danger of regarding that world almost as an extension of the divine being and of the same 'substance', or mode of being, as God. Furthermore it entails a sense in which creation goes on all the time and is not just a one-off event. However, it can sometimes also convey the impression that the process of emanation is inevitable in the sense that God's nature is of such a kind that emanative creating is constitutive of God's own being in such a way that no deliberate, free act of will and love on God's part is involved in the process. It is then being pressed too far, for the notion of creation being a freely-willed expression and act of God's love must be retained.

Too often attempts to combine the insights of both of these kinds of traditional model, as Macquarrie advocates,[114] result only in an uneasy juxtaposition with no sense of a really unified picture emerging. Moreover, the second model of emanation, in particular, does not, as we had hoped these models would, illuminate very much the actual notion of 'creating', the act of creation. It is at this point that the aesthetic activity of artistic creation, in its widest sense, has recently been much canvassed as a suitable model for creation by God.[115] For a work of any kind of art is given being by the artist's own spontaneous activity. Its form is chosen by the artist and, once decided upon, this form exercises a constraint on the artistic activity. The proposal of artistic creation as a model of divine creation was interestingly expounded by Dorothy Sayers in *The Mind of the Maker*.

> The components of the material world are fixed; those of the world of imagination increase by a continuous and irreversible process, without any destruction or rearrangement of what went before. This represents the nearest approach we experience to 'creation out of nothing', and we conceive of the act of absolute creation as being analogous to that of the creative artist... This experience of the creative imagination in the common man or woman and in the artist is the only thing we have to go upon in entertaining and formulating the concept of creation.[116]

This suggestive model takes somewhat different forms according to the human creative process that is being referred to.

Dorothy Sayers herself, as might be expected for a distinguished novelist, took as her prime example that of creative writing. She discerned a threefoldness in the response of a reader's mind to a written work which 'corresponds to the threefoldness of the work (Book-as-Thought, Book-as-Written, Book-as-Read), and that again to the original threefoldness in the mind of the writer (Idea, Energy,

Power)';[117] and this threefoldness she saw as inevitable because of the structure of the creative mind. She had expounded this earlier in the concluding speech of St Michael in her play *The Zeal of Thy House*, which she quotes thus in her later book:

> For every work (or act) of creation is threefold, an earthly trinity to match the heavenly.
>
> First, (not in time, but merely in order of enumeration) there is the Creative Idea, passionless, timeless, beholding the whole work complete at once, the end in the beginning; and this the image of the Father.
>
> Second, there is the Creative Energy (or Activity) begotten of that idea, working in time from the beginning to the end, with sweat and passion, being incarnate in the bonds of matter: and this is the image of the Word.
>
> Third, there is the Creative Power, the meaning of the work and its response in the lively soul: and this is the image of the indwelling Spirit.
>
> And these three are one, each equally in itself the whole work, whereof none can exist without the other: and this is the image of the Trinity.[118]

The explicitly trinitarian interpretation is not our immediate concern; rather it is the percipient analysis she provides of the act of creative imagination, for this passage comes closer to what is being postulated of *divine* creation than any of the other analogies we have looked at hitherto. It possesses the essential feature of bringing into existence that which exists up to this point only as an idea in the mind of the maker. The novelist's freely willed initiative in the process is unambiguous, so his or her 'transcendence' over the novel is quite clear. But, the model also involves the writer's 'immanence' in the created work since 'if ... he is to perform an act of power in creation, [the writer] must allow his Energy to enter with equal fullness into all his creatures, whatever portions of his personality they emphasize and embody.'[119] The model also has the further advantage that it incorporates a certain freewheeling independence from the creator of that which is created. For, as Dorothy Sayers pointed out, the characters created by the author in a novel begin, in her experience, to take on a certain life of their own which reacts upon their author as a constraint upon his development of the plot. This is certainly a feature of God's relation to a world that God is going on creating but which contains free-willing self-conscious creatures that God has endowed with a degree of autonomy. As Austin Farrer later expressed it:

The Creator of the world is not to be compared with those bad novelists who make up the plot of their story first, and force the characters to carry it out, all against the grain of their natures. He is like the good novelist who has the wit to get a satisfying story out of the natural behaviour of the characters he conceives.[120]

To that extent, any scheme that the author originally had is perpetually at risk, vulnerable to a natural development of the action consistent with the personal development of the characters as they interact. All of this is analogous to what we wish to affirm about God's relation to human action, but one wonders if the model is really adequate, for human agents possess an autonomy far greater than that of any character in a novel vis-à-vis its author.

It would seem, from Dorothy Sayers's account of her own experience, that the playwright has to be concerned, even more that the novelist, with the internal coherence and consistency of the created characters, for they have to come to life on the stage and be performed by actors and actresses who need to enter into their parts if they are to be convincing. So the writing of a play perhaps provides a better model for divine creating. In order to strengthen this model of the playwright, Maurice Wiles has proposed that we should think rather of an improvised drama 'in which the actors are each given the basic character of the person he or she is to represent and the general setting in which their interaction is to be worked out but in which they are left free to determine experimentally how the drama is to develop'.[121] Then the drama might well develop in principle, though not in detail, in the way the playwright always intended and would be, in a sense, both the playwright's and the actors'. This seems to be as far as one can go in elaborating this particular model without it becoming too cumbersome.

Taking account of this possibility that the interaction between the creator of a work of art and what is being created determine the eventual outcome is also a feature of other artistic models of divine creating: 'In artistic activity a certain struggle or adventure is involved – the endeavour to contain or express spontaneity within form. . . . Having freely chosen to create something in a particular 'medium', God may no longer be free to escape the constraints which that medium imposes.'[122] Such constraints, for a sculptor, may be imperfections, such as a sudden change of grain in the stone or a knot in the wood which is being worked, so that to continue with the creative work the artist has now to exploit this impediment so as to fulfil his creative intentions – a crucial test of inventive skill. This model thereby affords a hint of how the divine creating could become also a divine redeeming.

There comes a point at which the work of any author is regarded as 'finished', such is the limitation of our finitude: even the extemporizing play in Wiles's model presumably comes to point when the players and spectators leave. But, as Dorothy Sayers says, we have to consider

God as a living author, whose span of activity extends infinitely beyond our racial memory in both directions. We never see His great work finished ... We are thus considering the temporal universe as one of those great serial works of which instalments appear from time to time, all related to a central idea whose completeness is not yet manifest to the reader. Within the framework of its diversity are many minor and partial unities – of plot, of episode, and of character.[123]

But the art form *par excellence* into which time enters as an inherent, essential and constitutive element is music. There is, of course, a long tradition, going back to Pythagoras and Plato, of using the experience of music to model one's understanding of the universe. Many, too, in the Christian tradition have resorted to music for this purpose, notably Kepler:

Thus the heavenly motions are nothing but a kind of perennial concert, rational rather than audible or vocal ... Thus there is no marvel greater or more sublime than the rules of singing in harmony together in several parts, unknown to the ancients but at last discovered by man, the ape of his Creator; so that, through the skilful symphony of many voices, he should actually conjure up in a short part of an hour the vision of the world's total perpetuity in time; and that, in the sweetest sense of bliss enjoyed through Music, the echo of God, he should almost reach the contentment which God the Maker has in His Own works.[124]

Karl Popper, from whom this splendid quotation was obtained, himself remarks that 'a great work of music (like a great scientific theory) is a cosmos imposed upon a chaos – in its tensions and harmonies inexhaustible even for its creator',[125] here echoing a common theme both in classical (Greek and Roman) and the biblical literature[126] of creation by God being the formation of order, a 'cosmos', out of 'chaos'.

Music is especially appropriate as a source of models for divine creativity for a number of reasons. In music there is an unfolding in time of the composer's intentions and the significance of any given moment is constituted by both what precedes it and by the way it forms a growth point for what follows. Particular notes, rhythms, harmonies and dissonances – all that constitutes the music – have a different impact on the listener according to what has gone before. And this instantaneously experienced effect itself is the initiating point of and gives a distinctive meaning to its sequel. This is analogous to the way in which any meaning and significance we might wish to attribute to any given stage of the world's history are dependent both on what precedes and follows the point in question. In music new melodies and developments emerge intelligibly, yet inventively, out of earlier themes and fragments; and similarly in the processes of the world new forms develop, often surprisingly, though *post hoc* intelligibly in the light of the sciences, from what precedes them.

We saw earlier[127] that in the ongoing processes of the world new, and increasingly complex, forms of both inorganic and living matter emerge by a combination of what we briefly designated as 'chance' and 'law' and that to their mutual interplay is to be attributed the inherent creativity of the natural processes of the world. The question for any theistic doctrine of creation is then: how is the assertion of God as Creator to be interpreted, indeed rendered intelligible, in the light of this interplay between random chance at various levels and 'necessity'? This necessity arises from the stuff of the world having its particular 'given' properties and lawlike behaviour, which can be regarded as possessing potentialities that are, as it were, written into creation by the Creator's intention and purpose and are gradually actualized by the wide-ranging exploration that the operation of 'chance' makes possible. It is here that musical creativity appears to be especially helpful as a model of God's creative activity. For in music there is an elaboration of simpler units according to, often conventional, rules intermingled with much spontaneity, surprise even. God as Creator we might now see[128] as a composer who, beginning with an arrangement of notes in an apparently simple subject, elaborates and expands it into a fugue by a variety of devices of fragmentation, augmentation and reassociation; by turning it upside down and back to front; by overlapping these and other variations of it in a range of tonalities; by a profusion of patterns of sequences in time, with always the consequent interplay of sound flowing in an orderly way from the chosen initiating ploy.... Thus does a J. S. Bach create a complex and interlocking harmonious fusion of his seminal material, both through time and at any particular instant, which beautiful in its elaboration, only reaches is consummation when all the threads have been drawn into the return to the home key of the last few bars – the key of the initial melody whose potential elaboration was conceived from the moment it was first expounded.

The listener to such a fugue experiences,[129] with the luxuriant and profuse growth that emanates from the original simple structure, whole new worlds of emotional experience which are the result of the interplay between an expectation based on past experience ('law') and an openness to the new ('chance' in the sense that the listener cannot predict or control it). Thus might the Creator be imagined to enable to be unfolded the potentialities of the universe which he himself has given it, nurturing by his redemptive and providential actions those that are to come to fruition in the community of free beings – an Improvisor of unsurpassed ingenuity. He appears to do so by a process in which the creative possibilities, inherent (by his own intention) within the fundamental entities of that universe and their inter-relations, become actualized within a temporal development shaped and determined by those selfsame potentialities.

This model could be further refined if it referred to a composer extemporizing a fugue on a given theme – as on the famous May evening in 1747 at Frederick the Great's court in Potsdam when Johann Sebastian Bach, visiting his son Carl Philipp Emmanuel, was called upon by the king to improvise, playing on one of the king's prized new Silbermann 'piano-fortes', a three-part fugue on a theme supplied by the king himself. Not every subject is fit for such full development, so next day Bach chose a theme of his own and proceeded to improvise on the organ a *six*-part fugue – an extraordinary feat. Or perhaps a more modern model for those of other tastes might be the extemporization of a jazz virtuoso, say, in Preservation Hall in New Orleans. Introduction of improvisation into this model of God as composer incorporates that element of open adaptability which any model of God's relation to a partly non-deterministic world should, however inadequately, represent.

This model of the world process as the unfolding music of the divine Creator-Composer also illuminates his relation to the human listener to that 'music'. Although a given human work of musical composition attains a kind of consummation in its closing cadence, it would be nonsense to suggest that the 'meaning' of a musical work was to be found only there. Each instant, with its concurrent stored memory of the past as the ambience of the present and its ability already to be forming the reaction to the music yet to be heard, has a significance which is *sui generis* and takes its meaning from its relation to the whole that is being gradually unfolded.

The model also helps us to imagine a little better what we might mean by God's immanence in the world.[130] There is no doubt of the 'transcendence' of the composer in relation to the music he creates – he gives it existence and without the composer it would not be at all. So the model properly reflects, as do all those of artistic creativity, that transcendence of God as Creator of all-that-is which we, as 'listeners' to the music of creation, wish to aver. Yet, when we are actually listening to a musical work, say, a Beethoven piano sonata, then there are times when we are so deeply absorbed in it that for a moment we are thinking Beethoven's musical thoughts with him. In such moments we experience

> music heard so deeply
> That it is not heard at all, but you are the music
> While the music lasts.[131]

Yet if anyone were to ask at that moment, '*Where* is Beethoven now?', we could only reply that Beethoven-*qua*-composer was to be found only in the music itself. The music would in some sense be Beethoven's inner musical thought kindled in us and we would genuinely be encountering Beethoven-*qua*-composer. The whole experience is one of profound communication from composer to listener. This very closely models, I am suggesting, God's immanence in creation and God's self-communication in and through what he is creating. The processes revealed by the sciences are in themselves God acting as Creator and God is not to be found as some kind of *additional* factor added on to the processes of the world. God, to use language usually applied in sacramental theology, is 'in, with and under' all-that-is and all-that-goes-on.

The necessity for music to be performed for it actually to communicate to the listener, for it to *become* music, also gives rise to some suggestive analogies to divine creation. For what the composer writes down is only a kind of blueprint, an outline sketch, of his intentions which only come to fruition at the hands of the performers, his interpreters. Humanity is called upon to be a sensitive co-creator with God of the music of creation, for only human beings in the created world are capable both of discerning what God is doing in the natural world through the sciences; and of having an insight into God's intentions, through reflection upon their direct and mediated experiences of God. God's creative intentions are reflected in and also come to fruition in and through human creativity.[132] Now the performance of a musical composition depends very much on the perception of the individual composer's intentions at a later period by musicologists and by the performers they influence. These perceptions change, so that one can, perhaps, draw suggestive parallels between those who insist that the playing of Bach, for example, on period instruments is the only authentic style and those who wish to express their own insights into Bach on modern instruments. I leave it to the reader to elaborate this possible extension of the analogy.[133]

Clearly the model of God-the-Composer creating the music of creation is a rich and fruitful one, for it gives insights both into the relation of God as Creator to the creation and into our human apprehension of and participation in the creative process. Together with the other artistic models of divine creativity, it points to an aspect of the divine interaction with the world that we have not yet sufficiently taken into account and to which we must now turn. This is the notion that, if God is a *personal* Creator who has been acting in and through a created order that has a created inbuilt propensity to develop into self-conscious persons who are characterized by their uniquely developed ability to communicate with each other, then it would be consistent with such ideas to expect that the creator God would, in ways to be examined, seek to communicate with created persons. There would be little point in the divine artist-playwright-composer creating, never to have his/her works appreciated or responded to, their Creator unidentified and undiscerned. It is in the context of this possibility of the self-communication of the divine in the natural order that we can then consider more fully, in the light of the interpretations already given of the divine interaction with the world, both what has conventionally been called 'special' providence and 'miracles'.

4 GOD'S SELF-COMMUNICATION: SPECIAL PROVIDENCE AND MIRACLES[134]

Consideration of how we might today conceive of God's continuing interaction with the world has led, not surprisingly, to the perennial model of God as a personal agent interacting with and acting on the world – a model modified and enriched by recent insights into the unity of the mental and physical in the human-brain-in-the-human-body and into top-down causation. Now the meaning of an action by a human agent is not to be found by scientific analysis of the physiological, chemical, and mechanical processes going on in the agent's body, but by discovering the person's reasons and intentions, that is, the mental events which are involved in the action in question. That meaning is expressed in terms of its own language (of reason, intention, etc.) even if the meaning has to be conveyed through physical signs, on paper, or as sound vibrations, or whatever. The model of personal agency therefore suggests that if God is to be regarded as, in some sense, an agent interacting with and acting on the world, then we should look for the meaning of those events in God's reasons and intentions, i.e., God's own purposes. For the affirmation of God as Creator is an answer to the questions we ask about the meaning of the existence of the world and of the processes that occur in it. Such an attribution of meaning is at least rendered intelligible by the analogous attribution of meaning in mental terms which we give to the physical actions of human agents, even if we cannot absolutely prove its applicability. It is therefore appropriate to inquire into the reasons and intentions, that is, the purposes, that God is implementing in the world – or, rather, those that God *aims* to implement, since the world actually contains created autonomous agents who can frustrate his purposes.

The model of personal agency for God's interaction with and action on the world has a further implication. For developmental psychology and studies on the acquisition of language skills make it abundantly clear that the sense of being a self, of being a particular person, arises only in so far as we interact and communicate with *other* persons. Our selfhood seems only to be able to be constituted if we are in personal contact with others – and this is a deep-seated need that continues throughout our lives. Thus any model based on ourselves as agents of our bodies and God as in some sense a personal agent interacting with and acting on the world implicitly involves the notion that God must be a *communicating* selfhood. Now we express our meanings – our intentions, reasons and purposes – through our bodies, especially, though not only, through our speech organs. *Our* meanings are discerned, with varying degrees of accuracy, by other personal agents, but – we may well ask – who discerns *God*'s purposes that constitute, as it was suggested in the previous paragraph, the meaning of the world and its processes?

It appears that human beings are *par excellence* those created entities who uniquely seek to discern, even to create, meaning in the structures of their existence – natural, personal and social. We have had to stress that God's meanings are to be found within the very texture of the network of the processes that constitute the world. But within those processes, there have emerged those intricately ramified and interlaced structures we call human brains, the very processes of which so operate that they can discern meanings in the natural world and in their own processes. It is as if the Creator has endowed matter-energy-space-time, the stuff of the universe, with a propensity now actualized in humanity to discern the meaning in the cosmic process which its Creator has written into it. For in humanity, the stuff of the world has acquired a form and functionality that makes it capable of reading those meanings in existence which are the immanence of the transcendent God of the whole cosmic process. The way in which God has made himself heard and understood is by endowing the stuff of the world with the ability in *homo sapiens* to acquire discernment of his meanings and to listen to his self-communication, his word, in creation. 'By the *word* of God were the heavens made.'[135] If indeed the world is created, then that creation is the expression of the purpose and intention of God its Creator, and these purposes have apparently expressed themselves in and through a cosmic evolutionary process which has generated within its own fabric beings (ourselves) who can listen to and discern God's meanings. God as the personal agent of creation has created human beings capable of receiving his self-communication. His meanings, those communications which he addresses to the human beings who emerge with this capacity, cannot but be patterns of meaning within the world of nature. We recall[136] that top-down causation in complex systems (and notably in the brain–body relation) is frequently characterized by an input and consequent flow down to lower levels of 'information'. That is, God can quite properly be conceived of as sending signals to humanity through particular events and through special clusters or patterns of events that God himself has initiated through his general ('top-down') interaction with the world.

John Macquarrie has usefully elaborated what talk of God's 'meaning' indicates in this context.[137] He freely interprets the opening of St John's Gospel, 'In the beginning was the Word ...', as 'Fundamental to everything is meaning ...', and that 'God is to the world as meaning is to a process or series of events', presumably the interpretation of ' . . . and the Word was God' of John 1:1. When he speaks of God as meaning he has in mind

> a unity that gives order to the world-process and confers significance on its constituent parts; and also the idea that the process has direction and moves towards some goal. . . . The theist claims by contrast [to the atheist] that he discovers and participates in a context of meaning that is prior to himself and has a ground independent of him.[138]

Since God is worshipful, talk of God as a context of meaning, he continues, implies that 'this context [of meaning] is to be discovered on the personal and historical level as well as on the physical'. However, 'there is no simple pantheistic identification of God with the world-process. He is the partly hidden, partly revealed meaning coming to expression in the process.'[139]

As we have seen,[140] the events and entities of the world consist of natural hierarchies of complexity so that the aspects of God's meaning(s) expressable by any one level in these hierarchies cannot but be limited to that for which it has the capacity. Hence the 'meanings' of God so unveiled, the 'revelation' of God so afforded, by the various and distinctive levels of the natural order can only be complementary and individually incomplete without the others. What is expressed in the different orders of creation and in the pattern of events involving these multiform levels of complexity will not all have the same pertinence to human beings in their search for meaning and intelligibility. They would be expected to vary in what they communicate to us of God's meaning(s), in their ability to unveil God's purposes, according to the level at which they operate in the natural hierarchies of complexity, levels of which we have distinctive kinds of knowledge. As Charles Raven put it over thirty years ago, in the creative process 'from atom and molecule to mammal and man each by its appropriate order and function expresses the design inherent in it and contributes, so far as it can by failure or success, to the fulfilment of the common purpose.'[141] So we might expect that God, the transcendent Creator, immanent in the created world which is his self-expression, should make his meanings known most fully not only to but in and through those creatures, human persons, that mirror and reflect God's own nature of transcendence-in-immanence by themselves possessing a subjective transcendence over their objective physical embodiment.

Moreover, although God is not more present at one time or place

than at others (he is not a substance present at various concentrations) – all is of God at all times – human beings find that in some
sequences of events in created nature and human history, God
unveils his meaning more than in others. God is equally and totally
present to all times and places but human awareness of that Presence is uniform neither in intensity or content. God may well
communicate meaning which is neither comprehended nor apprehended. There are meanings of God waiting to be unveiled but
not all are read: some events will be more revealing than others. In
such a notion of the varied degrees of unveiling of the meaning(s)
that God has written in his creation, of different degrees of what we
can now properly call 'revelation', we are simply elaborating further
the model of human agency for the relation of God and the world.
For our bodies are a causal nexus of events and we are the agents of
many of its activities – yet some of our actions, gestures and
responses are more characteristic and revelatory of our distinctive
selves than others. Thus it is not improper to seek in the world for
those events and entities, or patterns of them, which reveal God's
meaning(s) most overtly, effectively and distinctively. Some events
will be more revelatory, more indicative of God's presence and
purposes, than others – while they all continue to be intelligible in
terms of the accounts given of them by the science(s) appropriate to
their level in the hierarchies of natural complexity.[142] Yet, as Grace
Jantzen has pointed out,

> there is a disanalogy between God's revelatory presence and the
> presence of a person revealed through his activities. Part of the reason
> that some activities of a person are more revelatory of him than others
> is that persons have only limited freedom ... Thus one of the grounds
> for differentiating the degrees of revelatoriness of a person's behaviour
> is removed in the case of God: we cannot think that any of God's
> actions are less deliberate or less free than others.[143]

God is free to act without any constraints other that those he
imposes on himself to implement his overall purposes, for his
omnipotence to do anything logically possible is, we have suggested,
self-limited.[144] The restriction on God–human communication
comes from our side, our limited ability to discern and listen. So the
point about degrees of revelation of God in the events of the world
remains and it is in the light of this, and of the whole understanding
of God's interaction with the world, that we are now in a position to
consider those items in Langford's classification[145] that we have not
yet discussed, namely 'special providence and miracles'.

These terms have been used with a variety of nuances and I can but refer the reader to the useful discussions *inter alia* of Langford and of Macquarrie.[146] Our present reflections bear on these discussions as follows. We have argued above that *particular* events or clusters of events, whether natural, individual and personal, or social and historical, (a) can be specially and significantly revelatory of the presence of God and of the nature of his purposes to human beings; and (b) can be intentionally and specifically brought about by the interaction of God with the world in a top-down causative way that does not abrogate the scientifically observed relationships operating at the level of the events in question. The combination of (a) and (b) renders the concept of God's special providential action intelligible and believable within the context of the perspective of the sciences, always with the proviso, as Langford puts it, that 'the presence of special providence is never guaranteed by events; it is an interpretation of events that depends on faith. It may be compatible with reason, but it can never be absolutely demanded by it.'[147]

The situation as regards 'miracle' is more complex. We are free, of course, to use the word 'miracle' in whatever new way suits us in the present intellectual climate and it has, in fact, undergone much redefinition in the course of time. As Langford points out,[148] the English word 'miracle' in a *biblical* concordance translates words standing for 'wonder', 'an act of power' or 'a sign'. Nevertheless, since the general establishment of the non-biblical idea of an 'order' of nature, ordinary usage of the word 'miracle', and not only by Christians, implies 'some contrast with the natural order' and an event 'not fully explicable by naturalistic means',[149] where the 'natural order' here referred to can in our age mean only that established by the sciences. This is a much stronger claim than in the case of 'special providence', for events falling under that description do not demand some necessarily extra, non-natural causal factor at their own level of operation. Whether or not one considers that events have occurred that fulfil these criteria of the miraculous depends ultimately on one's judgement of the historical evidence. This latter will itself be influenced both by one's *a priori* attitudes towards the very possibility of such events occurring in principle; and additionally, for the theist, by whether or not the claimed miracle is generally consistent with one's understanding of the nature of God and of his purposes for the world and for humanity – understandings themselves at least partly dependent on revelation of a kind entirely consistent with one's knowledge of the natural world through the sciences.

Given that ultimately God *is* the Creator of the world and that God is free to set aside the self-chosen limitations (other than those which are logically necessitated) of his own omnipotence which we have been detecting through our consideration of the nature of the created world, can we rule out the possibility that God might 'intervene', in the popular sense of that word, to bring about events for which there can never be a naturalistic interpretation? We have given cogent reasons[150] for questioning whether such direct 'intervention' is compatible with and coherent with other well-founded affirmations concerning the nature of God and of God's relation to the world. Even if we are mistaken in this view of God's nature and relation to the world, then the historical evidence that such an intervention *had* happened would need to be especially strong. We may well conclude from the historical record, given the growing ability of the sciences to give intelligible naturalistic explanations of an increasingly wide range of phenomena, that there are in the end no events that pass through this sieve, but consideration of this possibility can never be entirely precluded. Meanwhile, under pressure from the scientific perspective on the way the world goes, a more holistic and coherent model of God's continuing interaction with and on the world has emerged – one consistent with our new understandings of the natural order. Because our brains-in-our-bodies are part of the natural order, God's continuing interaction with and action on the world can include human persons – but can the traditional language of the Christian religion which sees the relation of God to humanity in personal terms and as a real interaction, be maintained and preserved as intelligible and consistent with our scientific perspectives? This will be the initial concern of Part III.

CHAPTER 10

Conclusion to Part II

In Part II of this volume I have been trying to express how we might refer both more accurately and more adequately to that ultimate Reality that is God in the light of what we know of natural being and becoming, as expounded in Part I. The notion of 'being' and 'becoming' as applied to the natural world that the sciences depict have distinguishable meanings. For it is intelligible to see the natural world as containing entities and structures undergoing processes, even though quantum physics has to speak more circumspectly with respect to such easily visualizable distinctions. In doing so, these developments in physics reinforce philosophical reflections such as those of John Macquarrie:

> The fact that whatever becomes both is and is not shows that the distinction between being and becoming is of a peculiar kind. In so far as what becomes is, then becoming must be included in being as well as distinct from it. Two consequences seem to follow. The first is that being cannot be identified with a static, changeless, undifferentiated ultimate.... the fundamental contrast between being and nothing would seem to be made possible only in so far as being includes becoming and gets differentiated, otherwise being and nothing would be indistinguishable.... we talk about being and distinguish it from nothing only in so far as it includes becoming ... The second consequence is that becoming is unintelligible apart from some conception of being, in which the becoming is included. A mere flux would be a chaos, and so would a sheer pluralism.[1]

But what of *divine* 'being' and 'becoming'? God, we have suggested, is the ultimate Reality, Being-itself, who 'all the time' (we have to say, meaning *our* time) gives being to[2] all other, dependent realities that constitute the world, all-that-is. In giving being to entities, structures and processes *in* time, God cannot have a *static* relation to that time which is created with them. Hence we have to speak of a dynamic divine 'becoming' as well as of the divine 'being'.[3]

God as ultimate Being gives ordered being to ('lets-be') a world that has sufficient order to be constituted of continuing entities and structures; but God as ultimate Becoming also gives the world an existence of a kind that exhibits an unfolding and opening up, an actualization of created potentialities, that leads to a fruition and a flourishing in and to which God is present. Now the divine Being is not one being, that is one existent, among other existents. God is not *a* 'being' in that sense or even the sum of all beings, for God's being is the source of all the other existents. God is Being itself. God is the one who 'lets-be' and who is totally distinct from, over against, all-that-is: God is 'wholly other'. We encapsulate this in affirming that God is 'transcendent'.

But God creates and dynamically 'lets-be' in created time and so God as the divine Becoming continually interacts with that which becomes in the created order. For God would not be Creator unless the divine Being and the divine Becoming were facets of the same ultimate divine Reality. God so conceived is deeply involved with time and natural becoming. God is present at all times and spaces and to all created entities, structures and processes. We encapsulate this in affirming that God is 'immanent' – and this in no way subsidiary to our affirmation of his transcendence.

God is the Transcendent One who is immanent in the created world; God is the Immanent One who is transcendent over the created world; and only if God is both could God be continuing Creator. The predication of creativity to God is rooted in this conjunction. Thus 'creativity' is a basic attribute[4] of God and is closely linked with other more fundamental aspects of the divine nature, namely God's transcendence and immanence, that God is ultimate Being and Becoming. *Both* transcendence and immanence have, paradoxically, to be affirmed of God. A famous attempt by Gregory of Nyssa to resolve this paradox involved asserting another, believed to be more acceptable: namely, that God is both knowable and unknowable. God, it was suggested, is unknown in his essence (*ousia*) yet makes himself known in his energies (*energeiai*) – in his works, the results of his creative activity. But the usefulness of this idea turns on what knowing God 'in his acts' might mean.[5] It is doubtful[6] whether this distinction of Gregory of Nyssa should indeed be the basis of the later, more metaphysical, one made by St Gregory Palamas, according to which: 'to know God is to know and participate in his "acts", flowing from the three divine persons, but the divine substance remains entirely transcendent and incommunicable, the totally mysterious, indescribable reality shared by the persons.'[7] It turns out not to be helpful simply to equate the transcendent with the unknowable in God and immanence with the knowable: for we need to affirm, as true to religious experience as well as for reasons of coherence, that God is revealed *and* hidden both in his transcendence and in his immanence.

We have made much use of personal predicates of God as being the least misleading available and preferable to saying nothing at all about God. However, we must not be misled by this into so emphasizing the personal that the concept of *a* 'person' as an individual centre of consciousness serves to weaken the collateral emphasis on the divine immanence. The nature of the human person itself provides us with a corrective to any such tendency, for it affords a clue, a sign pointing to a clearing in the mist, of the direction in which, as created human beings, we might look for illumination concerning this conjunction of transcendence and immanence in God. For we have seen that the human-brain-in-the-human-body, the only instance of the personal we know directly, displays a transcendence and an immanence – both created, in this case. We survey our bodies as subjects, as we do the world with which our bodies interact. Yet the 'I' who is thus transcendent over our bodies expresses its selfhood and identity only by acting in, through, and with the processes of those bodies at all levels. The transcendent, personal 'I' can only be a particular 'I' through its immanent activity in the body.[8] In the human person there is a kind fusion, without loss of distinction, between the transcendent 'I', the self-conscious personhood, and the immanent 'I' expressed in and through the body.

Now we have had to recognize that the meanings that God wishes to unveil in the created order, his self-communications to and for man, cannot but be the more partial, broken and incomplete the more the level of creation under consideration departs from the human, and so the personal, in which the transcendence of the 'I' is experienced as immanent in our bodies. Thus, although God is, in some sense, supra-personal, we may well expect[9] in the personal – that is, in persons, in history, in personal experience, in personal encounter – to find meanings of God unveiled in a way not possibly communicated by the meanings God has written into non-human, impersonal levels of existence. The level of the personal (with all its uniqueness, new language, non-reducible concepts, new modes of experiencing, etc.) allows expression of new aspects of the meaning and purpose God is expressing in creation which could only be incompletely expressed, if at all, through the non-personal, and historically earlier, levels. The more personal and self-conscious is the entity in which God is immanent, the more capable is it of expressing God's supra-personal characteristics and the more God can be immanent personally in that entity.

In humanity, the processes within creation become aware of themselves and seek their own meaning – that is, the processes (expressing the immanence of the Creator God) acquire a dimension of self-transcendence, that of the 'I', which we have just been considering. This raises the possibility (and so hope) that the immanence of God in the world might display, in humanity at least, a hint of, some kind of reflection of, the transcendence/immanence of God. The transcendence-in-immanence of human experience raises the hope and conjecture that in humanity immanence might be able to display a transcendent dimension to a degree which would unveil, without distortion, the transcendent-Creator-who-is-immanent in a uniquely new emergent manner – that is, that in humanity (in a human being, or in human beings), the presence of God the Creator might be unveiled with a clarity, in a glory, not hitherto perceived. Might it not be possible for a human being so to reflect God, to be so wholly open to God, that God's presence was clearly unveiled to the rest of humanity in a new, emergent and unexpected manner? If that were to be so, would it not then be accurate to say that, in such a person, the immanence of God had displayed a transcendent dimension to such a degree that the presence of God in and to the actual psychosomatic unity of that person required and requires new non-reducible concepts and language to express its character and uniqueness? The mere posing of such a question cannot but raise our hope for the lifting of at least the corner of the veil that shrouds the mystery of God in an act or process initiated by God within the nexus of the history of persons. Whether or not we have been given this is a matter for further inquiry in Part III.

Human Being and Becoming

'Verbum Dei, Jesum Christum Dominum nostrum:
qui propter immensam suam dilectionem
factus est quod sumus nos,
uti nos perficeret esse quod et ipse.'

'The Word of God, our Lord Jesus Christ
Who of his boundless love
became what we are
to make us what even he himself is.'

Irenaeus (*Adv. Haer.*, V praef.)

CHAPTER 11

God's Communication with Humanity

1 GOD'S INTERACTION WITH A WORLD THAT INCLUDES HUMANITY

In the preceding Part II, we were concerned with God's interaction with the world as a whole, but have nevertheless had to take note of the distinctiveness of the 'personal' as manifest in human beings. Furthermore we adduced considerations that led us to regard God as 'at least personal' and we used the traditional model of personal agency for God's interaction with the world as whole – qualifying[1] it with an emphasis on the role of top-down causation and of body-mind unity in any contemporary account of human action, and finding it to be akin to a flow of 'information' in the sense of alteration of patterns of events in the world. In that discussion[2] the main objective was to think through how God might interact with the world, that is, influence the occurrence of certain events and sequences of events rather than some others. Our recognition that God is 'at least personal', that is, in some sense 'supra-personal', also led us to recognize that such a God would be self-communicating. In making this suggestion – which is the main concern of this chapter – we were in fact recognizing the validity of a distinction made explicitly over seventy years ago by O. C. Quick in connection with his study of the Christian sacraments.[3]

He pointed out that in human experience we make the distinction, while recognizing its frequent arbitrariness, between those 'outward' things or realities 'which occupy space and time and are in principle, though possibly not in fact, perceptible by bodily senses'[4] and those 'inward' things or realities which do not satisfy those conditions. He went on to point out that the material objects which constitute part of our 'outward' reality can have two different relations to our 'inward' mental life: they can be instruments that take their character from what is *done* with them; or they can be symbols that take their character from what is *known* by them.[5]

This useful working distinction in human experience has a parallel, he pointed out,[6] in two ways in which God may be regarded as related to the world. The world may be viewed as the instrument whereby God is effecting some cosmic purpose by acting on, or doing something with, it. Or the world may be viewed as the symbol in and through which God is signifying and expressing his eternal nature to those who have eyes to see, that is, revealing Godself within it. Our earlier exposition[7] of how God interacts with the world was chiefly concerned with devising a model for the former 'instrumental' kind of relation that was consonant with scientific perspectives on the world. Now we have to think through the implications of this model for explicating God's 'symbolic' relation to the world. In doing so, we shall have to clarify both the context and the means of any possible revelation to humanity of God in the world ((2) below) and how it is actually experienced by humanity in that world ((3) below). We have already recognized that one feature of the world – its multi-layered levels of complexity – suggests that different 'levels' in the natural hierarchy of complexity would be expected to differ in the extent to which they can communicate to us God's meanings and purposes, that is of being 'symbols', in the sense of Quick. We also suggested[8] that the transcendence-in-immanence that character-izes human persons could well be the basis for a special role in this 'symbolic', communicating relation of God in and to the world. For human beings seem to be uniquely capable of a personal relation to God and so of being sensitive to any *self*-communication of the divine.

In order to examine what the nature of this communication to humanity might be and how it could be conveyed we need to recall first our earlier discussion of God's interaction with the world. This is summarized in Figure 1 in a necessarily inadequate but what I hope is a helpful way.

Figure 1 attempts to express on a two-dimensional surface the relation between different modes of being – it is an ontological representation (rather like a Venn diagram representing the logic of the relation between different classes). The two distinct relations of God to everything else ('all-that-is' or 'the world', including humanity) are distinguished by God being denoted by the (imagined) infinite planar surface of the page on which the representations of everything else are printed. This may be regarded as a two-dimensional representation of the world being 'in God'[9] and of God as (ontologically) 'more than' the world – in the spirit of the earlier quotation from St Augustine.[10] For the representations of the world and humanity and their inter-relations are printed on the page and are distinct from the paper of the page, which is itself present 'under' and 'to' those shapes as God is to all that God has created. For God is the circumambient and underlying and ultimate Reality from whom all else derives its dependent being. In Figure 1, humanity is placed inside the circle denoting the world to indicate that humanity is an evolved part of nature. No time scale has been represented – one could denote this by thinking of a series of pages each with a figure, like that shown, stacked on top of each other increasing in height as time proceeds. So diagrams representing some earlier epochs would show a world without humanity and the Being of God would have a three-dimensional representation in such a stack of diagrams. Clearly the limitations of this kind of representation must be borne in mind! But I hope it can nevertheless help to clarify our present discussion.

It is of interest to relate this representation to another one – that of Karl Popper.[11] He has usefully distinguished three kinds of constituents[12] of the 'world': (1) physical objects and states, including human artefacts (what we have earlier summarily called the entities, structures and processes of the world); (2) states of consciousness (chiefly human consciousness); and (3) knowledge in an objective sense (the cultural heritage coded on material substrates).[13] Although characterized by its special information-carrying capacity, (3) as understood here[14] is a subset of (1).

It is clear that all mutual interactions between human beings and the world (the solid and dashed single-shafted, double-headed arrows of Fig. 1) are through the mediation of entities, structures and processes in (1), for human beings are part of (1) and human actions occur within it. Furthermore all interactions between human beings (the pairs of solid single-headed arrows in Fig. 1) occur through the mediation of the contents of (1) and (3) and this includes communication between human beings, that is, between their states of consciousness. On the non-dualist account of the human person adopted here,[15] states of consciousness (2) are also,

Legend to fig. 1

 is represented by the whole surface of the page, imagined to extend to infinity (∞) in all directions

 the WORLD, all-that-is: created and other than God and including -

HUMANITY

⟹   God's interaction with and influence on the world and its events - both general and particular (see Ch.9)

---->   effects of the non-human world on humanity

⟶   human agency in the non-human world

⇌   personal interactions, both individual and social, between human beings

..?..>   direct communication from God to humanity? (see p.208)

(See main text, pp.192-3, 196 for fuller explanation)

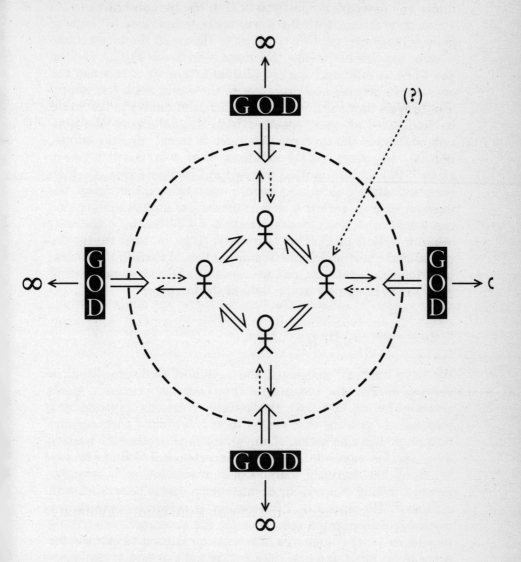

Figure 1. Diagram representing spatially the interaction
between God and the world, including humanity.

under one description, patterns within the human brains in (1) whose interactions with the world are best described in terms of personal agency, still fully within (1). Hence all the interactions within the world (inside the dotted circle of Fig. 1) can be described as relationships and mutual interactions between the entities, structures and processes of the world, with the important proviso that the many-layered levels of reality in the world be recognized as such, together with the autonomy (the non-reducibility) of the concepts that refer to them[16] and the subtle, mutual, two-way, causal relations that can occur between them.[17] Since these mutual interactions include those in which communication[18] occurs between human beings, this raises the question of how, within such a framework of understanding, one can conceive of God's communication with humanity, the self-communication of *God* to humanity. This in turn raises the traditional question of how God might reveal Godself to humanity – how, in what way, can we conceive of God communicating with and to humanity in the light of the foregoing?

2 Revelation and Human Experience

We have earlier[19] suggested the notion of God 'unveiling' in varying degrees the meaning(s) that God has written in God's creation, by analogy with the variety of actions, gestures and responses of persons that reveal their intentions, purposes and meanings. But this notion of 'unveiling' is altogether too passive a concept for representing human experience of God. As Rowan Williams has warned; 'the model of revelation as a straightforward "lifting of a veil" by divine agency has to be treated with caution.'[20] He continues, '"Revelation" is certainly more than a mythologically-slanted metaphor for the emergence of striking new ideas ... the language of revelation is used to express the sense of an initiative that does not lie with us and to challenge the myth of the self-constitution of consciousness.'[21] That is, in revelation God is *active*.[22]

Let us now examine the ways in which such a putative revealing activity of God might occur in the different ranges and contexts of human experience, graded according to the increasing extent to which God is experienced as taking the initiative in making Godself explicitly known.

a General Revelation

If the world is created by God then it cannot but reflect God's creative intentions and thus, however ambiguously, God's character and purposes; and it must go on doing so if God continuously interacts with the world in the way we have proposed.[23] The *locus classicus* of this concept of a 'general revelation'[24] to all humanity is, of course, St Paul: 'For all that can be known of God lies plain before their [men's and women's] eyes; indeed God himself has disclosed it to them. Ever since the world began his invisible attributes, that is to say his everlasting power and deity, have been visible to the eye of reason, in the things he has made.'[25]

This expresses the belief that there is a knowledge of God, however diffuse, that is available to all humanity through reflection on the character of the created world, its entities, structures and processes, and through the processes of personal and social experience. That there should be such a knowledge of the divine nature and purposes which is mediated through the world, including humanity, is entirely coherent with the understanding of God's interaction with the world we have been proposing, as represented in Figure 1. The double arrows denote an input into the world from God that is both influential in the top-down causative manner already discussed, and also in input of 'information' in the sense of altering patterns of events in the world.[26] Human brains can properly be considered to be amongst these patterns, so that it is entirely intelligible how God might implant the means for knowledge of Godself within the world and consequently in human experience. Hence, in the model we are deploying, there can be a general revelation to humanity of God's character and purposes in and through human knowledge and experience of the world.

b Revelation to Members of a Religious Tradition

Belonging to a religious tradition provides one with the language and symbols to articulate one's awareness of God at any instant and as a continuing experience. Immersion in a tradition through ritual, liturgy and its devotional activities provides an ever-renewed opportunity of making real in the present (*anamnesis*) those significant past experiences of individuals and groups in that community which are regarded as especially revelatory of

God (see *c* below). The tradition helps the individual both to have and to enrich the means of identifying his or her own experience of God. Thus there is a general experience of the ordinary members of a continuing religious community which may properly be regarded as a mode of revelation that is an enhancement of, and is more explicit than, that general revelation to humanity already discussed. As Grace Jantzen has remarked, with respect to Christianity (though no doubt it would also be applicable to adherents of the other monotheistic faiths):

> A great many Christians would say that they continue in their faith in God because, in spite of all the problems (intellectual and otherwise) which attend on religious belief, they would be fundamentally untrue to their own experience if they abandoned their faith . . . they are indicating the sense of the presence of God in their daily, ordinary lives, giving purpose to routine, providing courage, comfort, and hope, strengthening and deepening their moral commitment and sensitivity, leading them to worship and praise.[27]

This kind of what one might call 'religiously general' revelation arises when there is a confluence between: the streams of general human experience and revelation (*a* above); and the recollected and re-lived particular and special revelations of God (*c* below) that a tradition keeps alive by its intellectual, aesthetic, liturgical, symbolic and devotional resources. These all nurture the unconscious experience of the adherent to that tradition (possibly in the form of Jungian archetypes, postulated as common to all human beings) and so shape their conscious awareness of God.

c Special Revelation

Some experiences of God by individuals, or groups of individuals, are so intense and subsequently so influential that they constitute initiating, 'dubbing' experiences[28] which serve in the community to anchor later references to God and God's relation to humanity, even through changes in the metaphorical language used to depict that ultimately ineffable Reality. So, we earlier argued 'it is not improper to seek in the world for those events and entities, or patterns of them, which reveal God's meaning(s) most overtly, effectively and distinctively.'[29] The Judeo-Christian tradition has, more than other religious traditions, placed a particular emphasis on God's revelation in the experienced events of the history of Israel and Christians have furthermore located a unique revelation in the life, teaching, death and resurrection-exaltation of Jesus of Nazareth, viewed as the consummation of the preceding revelation to Israel. This is what is usually called 'special' revelation and involves 'the sense of an initiative that does not lie with us',[30] indeed a sense of being initiated by *God*. Such special revelation has been regarded by Christians as recorded particularly in the Bible – but how we are to receive this record today in the light of critical and historical study is a major issue in contemporary Christianity. This is not our immediate concern except to note that this issue is but a contemporary manifestation of the dialogue which originates in the need for all generations subsequent to the initiating, putatively revelatory, events to sift and winnow them in the light of their own experience and knowledge – and so transmit them to their successors. As indeed in the Bible itself, each generation in a religious tradition is involved in a dialogue with its own past and often re-writes and recasts it, even sometimes consciously controverting it from a new perspective.[31]

In involving itself with such a dialogue with its past, a community is also *ipso facto* engaged in a dialogue with God in its own times. David Brown[32] has developed a strong case for using this model of divine dialogue for (special) revelation as being one that preserves both the divine initiative and divine freedom together with human freedom:

> ... revelation is a process whereby God progressively unveils the truth about himself and his purposes to a community of believers, but always in such a manner that their freedom of response is respected ... the notion of dialogue fully acknowledges that God's communication with man takes place in very specific contexts with certain things already assumed at each stage, an already existing canon of assumptions ... that has shaped the community's conception of God, and thus inevitably shapes both the present experient's response to a particular experience and also what it is possible for God to put into that particular experience by way of content.[33]

To postulate such a model of dialogue rests on an interactionist understanding of God's relation to the world, along the lines we have developed above.[34] It must be pointed out, too, that this dialogue, as Brown has cogently argued, is not confined only to the exchange of words and ideas but, even more profoundly, consists in the creative transformation of natural symbols in our unconscious.[35]

d Revelation and 'Religious Experience'

This attempt to discriminate between modes of revelation according to the degree to which God is experienced as taking the initiative in making Godself explicitly known is helpful up to a point. But we must avoid the not uncommon tendency to press the distinctions too sharply and to ignore the smooth gradations between the different categories of revelation (*a*, *b* and *c*, above). For example, it has been shown that between a third and a half of the population of certain 'Western' countries (the USA, Great Britain, and Australia) respond positively to questions such as 'Have you ever been aware of or influenced by a presence or power, whether you call it God or not, which is different from your everyday self?'[36] or 'Have you ever felt as though you were very close to a powerful spiritual force that seemed to lift you out of yourself?'[37] According to one survey in Great Britain carried out in 1986 'if one includes responses claiming some sort of premonition as a religious experience, the total rises to two-thirds of the population',[38] which far exceeds active membership of religious institutions. As might be expected, the proportion reporting religious experience is greater amongst those claiming an institutional religious adherence,[39] but the significant point for our present purposes is how widespread such experience is, even in the secularized West, and that it is continuous in its distribution over those who are members of a religious community and those who are not. The evidence is that the boundary between 'general' revelation and revelation to members of a religious tradition (*a* and *b*, above) is very blurred. But so also is that between the second and third categories (*b* and *c*, above). For there are well-documented accounts over the centuries of devotional and mystical experiences among those who do belong to a religious tradition. These are regarded by them as experiences, and so revelations, of God. Such experiences of God partake of the character of many of those that are usually included within the category of 'special' revelation. Indeed the believers having these experiences recognize their adherence to the tradition which enshrines the 'special' revelations and through whose resources of language, symbol and imagery these experiences are expressed.

It is also widely recognized that the classical distinction between 'natural' and 'revealed' theology has proved difficult to maintain in modern times. For as David Pailin has pointed out:

> ... it can be held that all theological understanding is a matter of gaining insights into the ultimate nature of reality and that the only significant difference between supposedly 'natural' and supposedly 'revealed' insights is that the former are derived from considering a broader (though still selected) range of situations than the latter.[40]

The same could also be said of the subsequently more widely favoured distinction between 'general' and 'special' revelation, for the range of, and overlap between, the means whereby insights are gained into the divine reality has had to be recognized. For in the end, as Pailin himself puts it in accord with the critical-realist stance adopted here: 'the ultimate justification is by showing that the resulting understanding is a coherent, comprehensive, fruitful and convincing view of the fundamental character of reality.'[41]

There is, in fact, a very real danger of bracketing off 'religious' experiences from the rich variety of human experience – in all its complex physical, atheistic, intellectual, personal and social forms – forgetting that 'it is not the case that all experience of God is necessarily religious in form or content, and . . . that not everything which it would be appropriate to characterize . . . as "religious" experience would thereby necessarily constitute experience of God.'[42] It is true that for the religious believer the whole of life can be revelatory of God. Nevertheless, 'special' revelations (c) can occur and be identified. When they do so, it is usually among members of a religious tradition (itself preserving earlier special revelations) who themselves experience God in their own way (b) and, as human beings, also in the way common to the rest of humanity (a).

There is then a genuine gradation but there are also real differences in intensity and the degree of explicitness with which these experiences are received as revelations of *God* as its initiator – rather as a variegated and rough terrain may be accentuated to give rise to distinctive hills and even sharp peaks without loss of continuity. It is useful to have a word to denote the more prominent of these knolls and eminences among the human experiences of God[43] which will include all experiences in the range *a-b-c* that have become sufficiently articulated to the one experiencing to be significant for them – and for others if adequately communicated to them. The only available adjective appears to be 'religious', in spite of its unfortunate connotations for many (e.g., its association with less than attractive 'religious institutions' and with the baneful history of 'religion' at many times and places – as well as its frequent confusion with 'religiosity'). Provided the caveats of the preceding paragraph are always borne in mind, there is a more positive reason for continuing to use the term 'religious' experience'.[44] For religious experience, in the sense elaborated here, has played an important role in recent years in inductive, cumulative arguments which claim to warrant belief in God – or, rather, to render the existence of God more probable than not and so being, to that extent, rational arguments.[45]

This significance assigned to religious experience in philosophical theology renders even more urgent the need to address questions that are implicit in the foregoing considerations, namely: 'How does our understanding[46] of God's interaction with the world including humanity relate to revelatory human experiences of God?', 'How can the notion of religious experiences be accommodated by, be rendered intelligible in, be coherent with the understanding[47] of God's interaction with the world that we have developed in the light of the perspectives of science?' That is, in view of the general position we have reached, we now have to ask

3 How Does God Communicate with Humanity?

To attempt to answer this question we need to differentiate between the different kinds of religious experience that have been reported (*a* below). We shall go on to ask if the way in which human persons communicate with each other can give us any clues about how God might communicate with humanity (*b* below). We shall then be in a better position to investigate (in *c* below) the relation between religious experience and the way in which we have been conceiving that God interacts with the world, including humanity – that is the question of *how* God might be thought of as communicating with humanity, given what we know of the world, particularly from the sciences.

a Varieties of Religious Experiences

Figure 2 reproduces in outline, with one minor modification,[48] the classification of religious experience given by Swinburne,[49] which he says is both exclusive and exhaustive,[50] and that given by Brown.[51] Swinburne defines a 'religious experience' as 'an experience which seems (epistemically) to the subject to be an experience of God (either of his just being there, or doing or bringing about something) or of some other supernatural thing'.[52] This corresponds closely to the way we have been using the term above.[53] The distinction in Figure 2 between religious experiences that are 'mediated' and 'unmediated' by something sensory is based on whether or not, respectively, there is an answer by the subject to the question, 'What was it about your experience which made it seem to you that you were having an experience of God?'.[54] Figure 2 classifies the phenomenology of religious experience and is concerned with the *means* whereby God is known.[55] It is with such modalities (the question 'how?' of the sub-title of this section), rather than with the actual content of the experience of God that we are at the moment concerned.

b Communication between Persons

We have been maintaining that personal language, with all its recognized limitations in this context, is the least misleading language to use of God, so it is appropriate to examine the means and nature of intercommunication between persons as a possible clue to understanding that between God and humanity. How do human beings communicate with each other and get to know each other, not only by description, but also by acquaintance – that is get to know what is, as we say, 'in each other's minds'?

All communication at its most basic level is mediated through the senses – hearing, sight, touch, taste, smell. The physical intermediaries are thus, respectively, vibrations in pressure in the air, electromagnetic waves, physical pressure, molecules, all members of the class of constituents 1 of the world, in Popper's scheme. Our genes, culture, nurture and education have all enabled human beings to decode patterns of these physical intermediaries that convey information about the content of the consciousness of the one attempting to communicate. These patterns can be immensely complex, associated with long

Figure 2

VARIETIES of RELIGIOUS EXPERIENCE

	MEDIATED by something sensory				UNMEDIATED by something sensory
	PUBLIC		PRIVATE		
Swinburne	(1) Common, well-known phenomena Perceiving ordinary non-religious objects	(2) Perceiving very unusual public objects (may or may not involve violation of a natural law)	(3) Sensations describable by the normal vocabulary used for sensations of the five senses	(4) Sensations not describable by the normal vocabulary used for sensations of the five senses (these 'religious' sensations only analogous to the latter)	(5) No sensations Subject aware of God, or of a timeless reality . . . – 'just so seems to' the subject, but not through having sensations
Brown	I Thematic experiences – where the theme or interpretative framework is believed to have been set by the divine. No unusual features.	II Sensory experiences. Unusual sensory perceptions, irrespective of whether or not the object so perceived is conceived of as existing in the external world (e.g. vision, dreams, auditions, etc.).		III Mystical experiences, of intimacy with the divine	IV Numinous experiences in which awe of the divine is the central feature

histories (as is language and Popper's constituents 3, the objective carriers of a cultural heritage)[56] and can weave subtle patterns in time, as in music and language and as we now know from research into 'body language' and communication through 'eye-to-eye' contact. In all these ways individual persons communicate with each other and also with the human community, both past and present.

The receptor of this 'information' in the individual person is the individual human brain which stores this variegated 'information' that constitutes knowledge of the inner state of other brains (and so of their states of consciousness, under another description) at different levels and integrates it into a perception of the other person in his/her totality.[57] Such knowledge of the other person can be recalled, with varying degrees of rapidity and accuracy, into consciousness, constituent 2 of Popper.[58] On a non-dualist view, this process can be regarded as a re-activation of the brain to reproduce the original patterns that previously constituted this conscious awareness of the other person – as long as it continues to be recognized that these conscious 'mental' events are a non-reducible reality that is distinctive of the human-brain-in-the-human body.

It seems that all the processes involved in inter-communication between human persons can be investigated and described at different levels by the methods and concepts appropriate to the level in question without invoking any special 'psychic' medium, unknown to the natural sciences, as the means of communication. This is not to say that the meaning of what is communicated can be reduced simply to physical patterns in the media in question, for the interpretation of these necessitates a recognition of their distinctive kind of reality.[59] But it is to stress that all communication between human beings, even at the most intimate and personal level, is mediated by the entities, structures and processes (constituents, for brevity) of the world.[60] The subtly integrated patterns of these means of communication do in fact allow mutual comprehension between two human individuals of each other's distinctive personhood. This knowledge of two persons of each other, this knowledge by acquaintance, is notoriously not fully expressible in any of the frameworks of interpretation appropriate to the various modalities of the interaction process. There remains an inalienable uniqueness and indeed mystery concerning the nature of the individual person[61] and of the nature of the interaction between two persons. Not only the sense of personhood, of being a person, but also awareness of inter-personal relations are unique, irreducible emergents in humanity.[62]

Recognition of the rootedness of the means of inter-personal communication in the constituents of the world[63] does not diminish or derogate from the special kind of reality that constitutes persons and their mutual interactions. For in such communication between persons there occurs a subtle and complex integration of the received sense-data with previous memories of that person under the shaping influence of a long-learnt cultural framework of interpretation that provides the language and imagery with which to articulate the relation in consciousness. So recognition of the physical nature of the means of communication between persons (Popper's[64] constituents 1 and 3) in no way diminishes the uniqueness and 'in depth' character that can pertain to personal relationships at their most profound level for the individuals concerned – indeed often the most 'real' and significant experiences of people's lives.[65]

c *Relation of Religious Experience to God's Interaction with the World*

If God interacts with the world in the way already proposed,[66] through a kind of top-down influence on the whole world system, how do we think God could communicate with humanity in the varieties of religious experience (Figure 2)? The previous section argued that all the inter-personal relationships that we know of occur through the mediation of the constituents of the world. This suggests that all religious experience, as defined in section *a*, that is mediated through sensory experience (left of the double line in Figure 2) is intelligible in the same terms as the inter-personal experience of human beings. We can therefore, in the light of this, readily conceive of God communicating with human persons through the constituents of the world, namely, all that lies inside the dashed circle representing the world in Figure 1. God is then to be conceived of as communicating through such mediated religious experiences by imparting meaning and significance to constituents or patterns of events among these constituents. This may properly be thought of as a 'flow of information' from God to humanity, so long as the reductive associations of such terms are

not deemed to preclude, as they need and should not, inter-
personal communication from its reference.[67] In such ways
insights into God's character and purposes for individuals or for
groups of individuals can be generated. Thereby God reveals
God's own self in a range of contexts from the most general to the
special (section 2, (*a*)-(*b*)-(*c*), above). So conceived, God's means of
revealing himself would then be entirely of the same character as
the mediation by the constituents and patterns of events in the
world of the interpretations evoked by the organized study of
nature and humanity in, for example, the natural and human
sciences and history. However the concepts, language and means
of investigating and appraising these 'signals' from God would
operate at their own level and not be reducible to those of the
natural and human sciences. The interpretation of mediated
religious experience would have its own autonomy in human
inquiry – theology cannot be reduced without remainder to
sociology or psychology, or *a fortiori* to the biological and physical
sciences.

What about the 'unmediated', private forms of religious experience (on the right of the double line in Figure 2)? These are
differently classified by Brown and Swinburne. Brown[68] subdivides them into: the mystical 'where the primary import of the
experience is a feeling of intimacy with the divine, whether this is
taken to involve a union with the divine, where distinctness is
retained or total absorption'; and the numinous, 'those
experiences where awe of the divine is the central feature'.
Swinburne divides these religious experiences not mediated by
'something sensory' into: 'the case where the subject has a
religious experience in having certain sensations private to
himself, yet these are not of a kind describable by normal
vocabulary'[69] (these 'sensations' are only 'analagous' to normal
ones); and also 'religious experiences which the subject does not
have by having sensations . . . he is aware of God or of a timeless
reality . . . it just so seems to him, but not through having
sensations'.[70]

These attempts to sub-divide the broad category of religious
experience serve at least to indicate the kinds of experience of God
(or of the 'divine', or of a 'timeless reality') which are not mediated
by something sensory. These finer discriminations matter less for
our present purpose than that these analyses of Brown and
Swinburne explicate such 'unmediated' experiences of God. Do

we, in such instances, have to postulate some action of God whereby there is a direct communication from God to the human consciousness that is not mediated by any known natural means,[71] that is, by any known constituents of the world? Is there, as it were, a distinctive layer or level within the totality of human personhood that has a unique way of coming into direct contact with God? This was certainly the assumption when the human person was divided into ontologically distinct parts, one of which (often called the 'spirit' or the 'soul') had this particular capacity. If we assume that, then there would have to be added to Figure 1 arrows (dotted) going *directly* from God to wherever we located this entity ('spirit' or 'soul') in the human person – and not mediated at all through anything else in the world.

In our brief discussion of miracle[72] we had to consider the possibility that ultimately God, being the *Creator* of the world, might be free to set aside any limitations by which God has allowed his interaction with that created order to be restricted. However, we had to recognize that those very self-limitations which God is conceived of as having imposed on Godself are postulated precisely because they render coherent the whole notion of God as Creator with purposes that are being implemented in the natural and human world we actually have. Such considerations also make one very reluctant, as in the case of arbitrary law-breaking miracles, to postulate God as communicating to humanity through what would have to be seen as arbitrary means totally different in kind from any other communications to human consciousness. These latter include the most intensely personal inter-communication but even this, as we saw above, is intelligibly comprehensible as mediated subtly and entirely through the biological senses and the constituents of the world.

Furthermore we have been assuming hitherto[73] the psychosomatic unity of the human persons, both on scientific and biblical grounds. Hence, to be consistent, we cannot but regard even this particular kind of apparent 'unmediated' capacity for experiencing God as somehow a mode of functioning of the total integrated unity of whole persons – persons who communicate with other persons in the world through the world's own constituents. This communicating nexus of natural events includes, for human beings, not only human 'sense data' and the human use of knowledge in the objective sense (Popper's[74] constituent 3), but also all states of consciousness (his constituent 2), as we earlier argued.[75] So *within* the world, there has to be included all the states of the human brain that are, under another description, the contents of the unconscious as well as of consciousness. This will include all that the individual has stored in his or her lifetime in the form of symbols and possibly those archetypes which Jung has claimed to have shown to operate at these deep levels of the person. This process of storage and accumulating both conscious and unconscious resources is mediated by all the varied ways in which communication to humanity can occur – and all these ways of communication we have seen to be effected through the natural constituents of the world and the patterns of events which occur in them.

In those states in which they have experience of God 'unmediated' by something obviously sensory,[76] human subjects can receive a communication from God by means of their recollected memories and through the workings of the unconscious – and everything that has gone into their *Bildung*, everything that has made them the persons they are. All of which is mediated through patterns in the constituents of the world, including brain patterns. This is entirely consistent with such experiences of God being the fruit of much self-discipline and quietly allowing God so to communicate. 'Be still and know that I am God'.[77] Experiences of God are indeed often ineffable, incapable of description in terms of any other known experiences or by means of any accessible metaphors or analogies. This characteristic they share with others, such as aesthetic and inter-personal experience which are unquestionably mediated through patterns in the events of this world. In relationships with other persons, we only get to know them if they choose to reveal to us their 'innermost selves', as we say. In such a mutual relation an initiative is taken so that the revealing of one to the other can occur, again through natural means. There is no reason why God's communicating to us through the undoubtedly subtle means we have been trying to discern should not also be the result of an initiative from God – in other words, a revelation. Such revelations could take the variety of forms that we have already described and could all be mediated by the constituents of the world and through patterns of natural events, yet would nonetheless be definitive and normative as revelations. Moreover, even those revelations from God which are experienced purely 'mentally', and as apparently 'unmediated', fall within this description. For if, as we have argued, God can influence patterns of events in the world to be other than they otherwise would have been but for the divine initiative – and still be consistent with scientific descriptions at the appropriate level – then it must be possible for God to influence those patterns of events in human brains which constitute human thoughts, including thoughts *of* God and a sense of personal interaction *with* God.

On examination, therefore, it transpires that the distinction between 'mediated' and 'unmediated' religious experiences breaks down because the 'unmediated', in fact involve the constituents of the world, and patterns of events in them, just as much as the 'mediated' ones. The distinction is less between the means of communication by God than in the nature of the content of the experience – just as our sense of harmony and communion with a person far transcends any description we can give of it in terms of sense data, even though they are the media of communication. We simply *know* we are at one with the other person; in contemplation similarly the mystic can simply be 'aware of God . . . it just seems so to him';[78] and both experiences can be entirely mediated through the constituents of the world. The involvement of the constituents of the world in the so-called 'unmediated' experiences of God is less overt and obvious because in them God is communicating through subtle and less obvious patterns in the constituents of the world and the events in which they participate. These latter include the patterns of memory storage and activity of the human brain, especially all those operative in communication at all levels between human persons (including *inter alia* sounds, symbols and possibly Jungian archetypes), and the artefacts that facilitate this communication (Popper's constituents 3). God speaks to us through memories which involve symbols, words, images and sounds and much else stored in our brains and through the stimulus of recent events and of the moment. Such address from God can come unexpectedly and uncontrived by us by the use of any apparently external means, thus it seems to us to be *un*mediated, even though it depends on a long history of mediation through the constituents of the world.

This account of the way in which God communicates to humanity through the constituents of the world and through the patterns of events in which they are involved assumes that God is able to shape these events and these patterns to convey God's meanings, intentions and purposes, to humanity. This implies that some events and patterns of events in the constituents of the world are what they are and not something else because God has willed them so to be in order to communicate with humanity. In other words, this understanding of how God communicates with humanity rests on an interpretation of God's interaction with the world, such as that given earlier[79] in terms of a top-down holistic influence expressing God's intentions and purposes, which renders particular actions of God in the world feasible and consistent with scientific accounts of natural events. What the treatment in this chapter has been indicating is that it is also intelligible how God can communicate *personally* to human beings within a world coherently and consistently with the descriptions of that world given at other levels by the natural and human sciences.

However, we have to revert to the same ambiguity as we encountered in our discussion of miracles.[80] The foregoing can be held to describe how God according to all the evidence communicates with humanity consistently with the way he has made the world. But because God is *God*, does God allow himself occasionally to be free to set aside, as it were, the self-limitations of his relation to his creation to communicate with humanity in some unique way for a special purpose? Whether or not God has done so is a question of the evidence,[81] which we recognize would have to be exceptionally strong historically to be convincing.

The way in which God communicates with humanity that has been elaborated in the foregoing depends, as does the previously developed model of God's interaction with the world, on a strong doctrine of God's immanence in the world – of God's presence in, with, under and through the many levels of the fabric of the natural and human world woven by its entities, structures and processes – and most distinctively and fully at the level of the personal. At the level of the human, and so of the personal, there might be anticipated an outreach of God's own ultimate Being into the becoming of the world and of God thereby communicating God's own self: in the classical Christian terminology, God as Holy Spirit comes to us and is the presence of God in and to us. God as Spirit *dwells* in us, if we will allow that refining fire within. And the One who so indwells can at the same time be encountered as the ultimately Other who transcends all and is immanent in all – and yet remains ineffable. On the inner throne of the interior castle of our personhood it might be possible for there to sit the One whose true being and becoming are beyond all talk of 'transcendence' and 'immanence'. That is the hope and possibility opened up by the recognition that God both can and wills to communicate with us.

Part II was concerned with the general revelation of God in the natural being and becoming of the world described in Part I. In Part III, *Human* Being and Becoming, we are concerned not only with *how* but *what* God has communicated to humanity, that is, with 'special revelation' and its incorporation into the 'ordinary' religious experience of the believer. The existence and significance of this claimed self-communication of God to humanity can be judged only if we undertake a further appraisal of what distinctively constitutes human being and becoming in the light of the sciences and of human experience. We need to amplify what was said in Part I about human nature in order to identify what human beings are and what they might need to have communicated from God that is appropriate for their flourishing – that is, for the becoming that human being needs for its fruition.

CHAPTER 12

Natural Human Being:
The Perspectives of the Sciences and
Their Implications for Theology

We are exploring if there can be a Christian theology which is consonant with the best-established perspectives on the natural world that the sciences can provide. A significant element in these perspectives – in chemistry, biochemistry and biology *inter alia* – is that human beings are inherently part of nature, evolved out of the very stuff of the world. Not surprisingly, in view of the perennial interest of humanity to itself, many of the sciences have been concerned with human beings as such, though other studies not so directed have sometimes generated results pertinent to this inevitable concern (e.g., the anthropic principle from physics and cosmology). Scientific perceptions of what we are continually change in content and focus of interest and our understanding of the relation of nature-humanity-God itself cannot remain impervious to these new perceptions. One could instance how, in the wider society outside scientific circles, the widespread use of computers leads to their being regarded as a model for human thinking and this influences the very language which is beginning to be used about persons – and possibly also how they are valued. What are the consequences of thinking of the relation between human beings, and between humanity and God, in terms of 'interfaces' and 'information input and output', for example?

At this point in our inquiry, we are chiefly concerned with what the sciences can tell us about human *being*, about what human beings *are*, what the theological textbooks have traditionally called 'the doctrine of man' – the distinctive nature of humanity, the *humanum*. As any rapid perusal of such sources would soon indicate, there is a distinctively normative tone to these traditional theological expositions, for they are as much concerned with

what human beings should be *becoming* as with what they are.
Since the sciences, as such, aim to be descriptive in depicting
natural realities rather than prescriptive, the whole theme of
human 'becoming' will not be the principal concern of this chapter
– even though some individual scientists do arrogate to themselves a prescriptive role based not on science as such but on their
own personal philosophical and ethical presuppositions. It is
indeed difficult for all of us, and not just scientists, to separate our
appraisal of the nature of humanity from the voices of our culture,
both traditional and contemporary. Our first and primary concern
here, however, is with the sciences, with their possible effects on
our understanding of humanity and hence on their implications
for theology.

1 Levels: Foci of Interest and Hierarchies of Complexity

We have already discussed some of the distinctive features of
evolved human personhood[1] and have stressed the irreducibility
of many of the concepts that refer to these features.[2] This was
relevant especially to the body-mind relations[3] which was
illuminated by the notion of 'top-down' (or 'downward')
causation.[4] But these distinctive holistic qualities of human
personhood depend on the operation of many lower levels in the
hierarchy of complexity each of which is the focus of interest of a
particular scientific discipline. In order to obtain a broad but
reasonably accurate impression of what the sciences are telling us
about human nature,[5] we must now look more closely at these
various 'levels' (see Figure 3,[6] to be explained below). This is
imperative because 'Far from man's presence in the universe
being a curious and inexplicable surd, we find we are remarkably
and intimately related to it on the basis of the contemporary
scientific evidence'[7] (e.g., the anthropic principle; the evolution of
life and of *homo sapiens*; comparative biochemistry). This 'far
greater degree of man's total involvement with the universe'[8]
implies that many of the levels of analysis, description and study
of human beings will be the same levels as those that pertain to
the rest of the world. To this extent the relation of humanity to the
universe is somewhat similar in the light of modern science to the
traditional image of humanity as a 'microcosm' – a model or
epitome – of the 'macrocosm', the world as a whole.[9]

  However, as John Macquarrie points out,

The human being is not a surd in the universe, but it is not necessary either to claim that he is the clue to everything. The most inherently plausible view is that humanity, more than any other form of existence known to us on this planet, does bring to light something of the creative forces at work in the world, and to that extent man is indeed a microcosm, a becoming that bears the stamp of being.[10]

Such an approach encourages us to look more closely at the various focal 'levels' of interest and of analysis pertinent to human beings. There is a multiplicity of such levels and the way these may be classified depends on the criteria used for characterizing the different kinds of complexity.

In view of the justifiably *methodologically* reductionist techniques of the sciences – the breaking down of complex wholes into smaller units for investigation – it is not surprising that one of the commonest ways of organizing the systems observed in the natural world, and the scientific disciplines relevant to them, is in terms of 'part-whole' relations.[11] Such 'part-whole' hierarchies are defined in terms of their systems and sub-systems which themselves may be described in terms of their constituent structures and/or their functions. (An outstanding example of such systemization is the *tour de force* of J. G. Miller in *Living Systems*[12] which at least serves to show the complexity of living organisms.) However, the structure/function relation is relative, for 'an entity that is viewed as a structure from the point of view of one discipline might itself be viewed as a functional product of other structures in another discipline'.[13] Furthermore, although part-whole hierarchies[14] make much sense from a biological viewpoint as they range from the components of cells to complex eco-systems, there are also part-whole hierarchies that remain entirely within the physical, non-biological domain (e.g., atoms, molecules, rocks, plants, galaxies . . .).[15] Abrahamsen[16] has differentiated scientific disciplines by means of another criterion, namely, by virtue of their specialization of focus, which varies as they deal with the different phenomena of special interest to the human beings who investigate nature. The following four 'levels' of focus are distinguished:

(1) *the physical world*, whose domain can be construed, from one aspect, as that of all phenomena since everything is constituted of matter-energy in space-time, the focus of the physical sciences; (2) *living organisms*, the focus of the biological sciences; (3) *the behaviour of living organisms*, the focus of the

Legend to Fig. 3

A 'hierarchy of disciplines' (an elaboration of Figure 8.1 of Bechtel and Abrahamsen).[17] 'Levels' correspond to foci of interest (see text). Level 4 is meant to give only an indication of the content of human culture (cf. Popper's 'World 3').

Solid horizontal arrows represent part-to-whole hierarchies of structural and/or functional organization. (N.B. Molecules and macro-molecules in level 1 are 'parts' of the 'wholes' in level 2). Dashed boxes represent sub-disciplines in particular levels that can be coordinated with studies at the next higher level (the connections are indicated by vertical, dashed, double-headed arrows). In each of the levels 1–3, examples are given of the *systems* studied which can be classified as being within these levels and also of their corresponding scientific disciplines. Level 2 elaborates additionally the part-whole hierarchy of levels of organization in the nervous system (after Fig. 1 of Churchland and Sejnowski).[18]

In level 2, the science of genetics has relevance to the whole range of the part-whole hierarchy of living systems and so, if included, would have to be written so as to extend across its entire width. CNS = central nervous system including the brain.

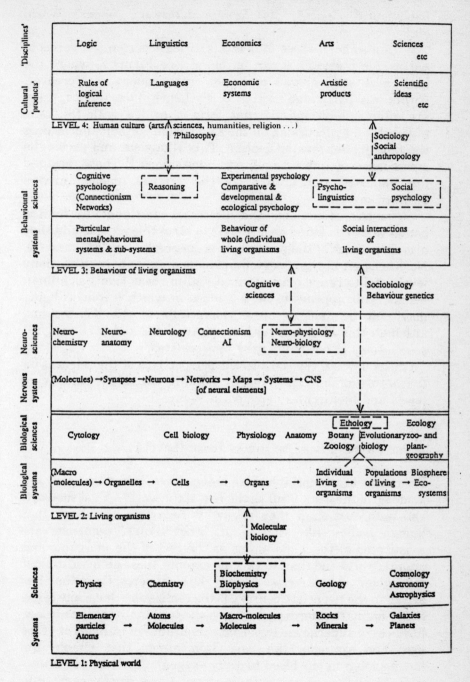

behavioural sciences;   (4) *human culture* (cf. Popper's 'World 3').[19]

Within some of these four levels at least portions of series of part-whole hierarchies can be found (see Figure 3, where the horizontal, solid arrows represent such sequences). Moreover, within any particular level of this scheme of disciplines, there are often sub-disciplines that form a bridge with the next higher level by focussing on the same events or domains as does the next higher-level discipline. This allows for and shows the significance of interdisciplinary interactions.[20] These 'bridges' are indicated in Figure 3 by the vertical, dashed arrows between levels.[21]

Structures, functions and processes pertinent to human beings are to be found at levels (1) to (3) of this scheme and they also span much of the part-whole sequences in levels (1) and (2). No other part of the observed universe appears to span so many levels and to range over so much within these levels as human beings. This appears to be the sense in which a human being may now be said to be a 'microcosm' of the 'macrocosm', although this language with its pan-psychic and even magical associations is not today very appropriate.[22]

Let us now survey the current perspectives of the sciences on the nature of human being by making use of the schema of levels and hierarchies depicted in Figure 3.

2 THE PHYSICAL BASIS OF HUMAN BEING (Level 1)

From time immemorial human beings have known that they are made up of the same stuff as the rest of the world – 'dust thou art, and unto dust shalt thou return'.[23] Today we would say that human bodies, like that of all other living organisms, are constituted of the same atoms as the rest of the inorganic and organic world and that, to varying extents, these atoms also exist throughout the universe. One of the new perceptions that has arisen in the twentieth century is the realization that some of the heavy atoms that form part of our bodies originated in the nuclear furnaces of supernovae explosions thousands of millions of years ago. For example, the very iron atoms that enable the haemoglobin in our blood to carry oxygen to activate our brains (say, to enable us to write and read these words) came into existence long before the Earth was formed and biological evolution began, and so before humanity appeared Such is our affinity with the actual physical fabric of the universe.

Another feature of the physical (atomic-molecular) level of natural reality pertinent to our existence is its capacity to form structures that can undergo replication in self-perpetuating processes and patterns. This is the focus of 'molecular biology' which grew explosively from the discovery of the structure of DNA in 1953 and now forms the *bridge between levels 1 and 2*, that is, between the studies of the chemistry and physics of the components and processes of biological systems (biochemistry and biophysics) and the study of reproducing, living organisms as such. These scientific disciplines have entirely exorcised any ghostly remnants of the 'vitalism' that was mooted in the earlier half of the twentieth century to account for the distinctive characteristics of living organisms and so of 'living matter'. There is now no need to *add* some unknown entity ('elan vitale', 'entelechy', 'life force') to matter to understand why it has self-replicative and self-organizing abilities, remarkable though these are.[24]

It is this conviction which has made it increasingly implausible to think of the qualities that emerge in evolution, not least in *homo sapiens*, as due to the *addition* of some entity to the very stuff of which living organisms and human beings are constituted, rather than as the emergence of new functions and capabilities consequent upon that growth in complexity which characterizes the evolution of biological systems. However, the remarkable growth of *molecular* biology does not compel us to go along the road of some of its practitioners by claiming that biology is 'nothing but' physics and chemistry. Such epistemological reductionism is not a necessary conclusion from the success of molecular biology, as we argued earlier.[25] To find what does emerge we need to consider

3 HUMAN BEINGS AS LIVING ORGANISMS (Level 2)

All the biological sciences depicted in this level in Figure 3 can, in one way or other, include within their scope some aspects of human beings. Indeed, most of the advances in medical science depend on research into human beings conducted on the same pre-suppositions as pertain to the study of other living organisms.

This is not surprising in view of the evolutionary origins of humanity, as manifested particularly in the fact that 97.5% of human DNA is the same as that of the DNA of chimpanzees (close cousins evolutionarily), with respect to the sequences of base-pairs that carry the genetic information defining the whole organism. We also share, for example, common biochemical pathways not only with the higher primates but with many other organisms, even including bacteria. All are part of the same branching tree of life.

Earlier[26] I argued that there are propensities in evolution towards the possession of certain characteristics, propensities that are inherently built into an evolutionary process based on natural selection of the best procreators. These properties enhance survival for procreation in a wide range of environments. Thus it is that the evolutionary process is characterized by propensities towards increase in complexity, information-processing and -storage, consciousness, sensitivity to pain, and even self-consciousness (a necessary prerequisite for social and development and the cultural transmission of knowledge down the generations). Successive forms are likely to manifest more and more of these characteristics. However, the actual physical forms of the organisms in which these propensities are actualized and instantiated is contingent on the history of the confluence of disparate chains of events. So it is not surprising that recent re-interpretation of the fossils of very early (c.530 million years ago) soft-bodied fauna found in the Burgess shale of Canada show that, had any a larger proportion of these survived and prevailed, the actual forms of contemporary, evolved creatures would have been very much more disparate in anatomical *plans* than those now observed to exist – albeit with a very great diversity in the few surviving designs.[27] But even had these particular organisms, unique to the Burgess shale, been the progenitors of subsequent living organisms, the same propensities towards complexity, etc., would also have been manifest in their subsequent evolution, for these 'propensities' simply reflect the advantages conferred in natural selection by these features. So that, providing there had been enough time, a complex organism with consciousness, self-consciousness, social and cultural organization would have been likely eventually to have evolved, that is, 'persons' would have appeared on the Earth (or on some other planet amenable to the emergence of living organisms), though no doubt with a physical form very different from *homo sapiens*. There can, it seems to me (*pace* Stephen Gould[28]) be overall direction and implementation of purpose through the interplay of chance and law,[29] without a deterministic plan fixing all the details of the structure(s) of that which emerges possessing personal qualities. Hence the emergence of self-conscious persons capable of relating personally to God can still be regarded as an intention of God continuously creating through the processes of that to which he has given an existence of this kind and not some other. (It certainly must have been 'on the cards' since it actually happened – with us!)

Remarkable and significant as is the emergence of self-conscious persons by natural processes from the original 'hot big bang' from which the universe has expanded over the last 10–20 thousand million years, this must not be allowed to obscure another fact about humanity, namely its relatively recent arrival in the universe, even on a time-scale of the history of the Earth. Although modern *homo sapiens* had humanoid, tool-making ancestors (e.g., *homo habilis* of the Oldovan culture of about 1.5–2 million years ago), our species only appeared in its present form some 30,000 years ago.[30] How recent our arrival is can be realized if one takes the age of the Earth as two days of 48 'hours' (1 such 'hour' = 100 million years): then *homo sapiens* appears only at the last stroke of midnight of the second day.[31] However, living organisms had existed for some 2000 million or more years (= over 20 'hours' on the above scale) before this, our relatively late arrival. The evidence is that biological evolution has proceeded continuously since that distant time by evolution of populations of living organisms through natural selection of the best procreators.[32] Great as is the signficance of the emergence of self-conscious persons within the very fabric of the universe for any reflection on its possible meaning and purpose, this must not lead us to underplay the significance also of the rest of the universe and of all other living organisms to God as Creator – even though we are able to depict only in imagination the kind of delight that God may be conceived to have in the fecund multiplicity and variety of created forms.[33]

Evolution can operate only through the death of individuals – 'new forms of matter arise only through the dissolution of the old; new life only through death of the old'.[34] We as individuals would not be here at all, as members of the species *homo sapiens* if our forerunners in the evolutionary process had not died. Biological death was present on the Earth long before human beings arrived on the scene and is the pre-requisite of our coming into existence through the processes of biological evolution whereby God, we have argued, creates new species, including *homo sapiens.* So when St Paul says that 'sin pays a wage, and the wage is death'[35] that cannot possibly mean for us now *biological* death and can only mean 'death' in some other sense. Biological death can no longer be regarded as in any way the *consequence* of anything human beings might have been supposed to have done in the past, for evolutionary history shows it to be the very *means* whereby they appear and so, for the theist, are created by God. The traditional interpretation of the third chapter of *Genesis* that there was a historical 'Fall', an action by our human progenitors that is the explanation of biological death, has to be rejected. This means that those classical formulations of the theology of the 'redemptive' work of Christ that assume a causal connection between biological death and sin must also be recast.

Those traditional interpretations concerning a historical 'Fall' of humanity from a paradisiacal state have been undermined in another respect, quite apart from the general realization that the stories are mythological. For the biological-historical evidence is that human nature has emerged only gradually by a continuous process from earlier 'hominids' and that there are no sudden breaks of any substantial kind in the sequences noted by palaeontologists and anthropologists. This is not to say that the history of human culture is simply a smooth rising curve. There must have been, for example, key turning points or periods in the development of speech and so of social cooperation; and of rituals for burying the dead, with provision of food and implements, testifying to a belief in some form of life after death. These apparently occurred among the Neanderthals of the middle Palaeolithic even before the emergence of *homo sapiens* some 30,000 years ago, when some further striking developments occurred.[36] However, there is *no* past period for which there is reason to affirm that human beings possessed moral perfection existing in a paradisiacal situation from which there has been only a subsequent decline. All the evidence points to a creature slowly emerging into awareness, with an increasing capacity for consciousness and sensitivity and the possibility of moral responsibility and, the religions would affirm, of response to God (especially after the 'axial period' around 500 BC[37]). So there is no sense in which we can talk of a 'Fall' from a past perfection. There was no golden age, no perfect past, no individuals, 'Adam' or 'Eve', from whom all human beings have now descended and declined and who were perfect in their relationships and behaviour. Mention of human behaviour brings us within the scope of level 3 but, before this is examined, we need to look at:

4 HUMAN BEINGS IN THE PERSPECTIVES OF SCIENCES BRIDGING THE BIOLOGICAL AND THE BEHAVIOURAL (between levels 2 and 3)

Sciences which bridge levels 2 and 3 include, on the one hand, cognitive science (or, 'cognitive neuroscience'[38]) and, on the other hand, sociobiology (called by some 'behavioural ecology') together with behaviour genetics.

Within level 2 one can identify a collection of subdisciplines (neuro-chemistry, neuro-anatomy, neurophysiology, together with neurology, concerned with pathological conditions in human beings) which are collectively known as the neurosciences. The focus of interest of these subdisciplines (see the upper box of Level 2 of Figure 3[39]) spans the range of the structural levels of *organization* from the molecular to that of the central nervous system (CNS) of human beings, the concern of neurophysiology. These levels of organization are more easily separable conceptually than detachable physically.[40] Furthermore they also represent, in various combinations of 'hardware' and mechanisms, the multiplicity of that level of analysis in this field which has been identified (in terms originating in computer science) as the *level of implementation*.[41] For it is at this level that there is implemented, embodied and expressed the next higher one, namely, the *level of the algorithm(s)* specifying a formal procedure to bring about a particular output from a given input; this last is itself subject to the *computational level* of abstract problem analysis, the decomposing of a task into its main constituents.[42]

Cognitive science is concerned with relating meaningfully to behaviour all these three different levels of analysis of information-processing (roughly, 'cognition').[43] It thereby forms a bridge between the purely biological neurosciences and the sciences of behaviour, and it is especially concerned with trying to understand how the mind-brain works, particularly in human beings. The detailed ways in which the various levels of analysis are being applied and shaping investigations concerns us less here than the now wide-spread realization by cognitive scientists that, in order to understand the relation between the behavioural, at one pole, and the molecular, at the other, knowledge and understanding of all levels of analysis, organization and processing are necessary.

In this field of cognitive science, investigators have had to acknowledge that

> The research strategy developing in cognitive neuroscience is neither exclusively from the top down, nor exclusively from the bottom up. Rather, it is a coevolutionary strategy, typified by interaction among research domains, where research at one level provides constraints, corrections, and inspiration for research at other levels.[44]

We recall that the vertical arrows in Figure 3 represent some inter-disciplinary relations and serve to remind us that such relations are 'often fruitful, and suggest it is advantageous to retain multiple levels of analysis rather than engage in a reductionist program'.[45]

The pressure to integrate the study of different levels is, it seems, generated by the nature of the problems themselves which cognitive scientists address.[46] Moreover, what applies to the operation of the nervous system also applies to the operation of the brain as a whole.[47] Nor is this simply now a methodological recommendation for even an in-principle materialist such as Patricia Churchland, in her article with T. Sejnowski, significantly entitled '*Perspectives* in Cognitive Neuroscience', can recognize that

> The ultimate goal of a unified account does not require that it be a single model that spans all the levels of organization. Instead the integration will probably consist of a chain of models linking adjacent levels. When one level is explained in terms of a lower level this does not mean that the higher level theory is useless or that the high-level phenomena no longer exist. On the contrary, explanation will coexist at all levels, as they do in chemistry and physics, genetics and embryology.[48]

I have quoted here, and in the endnotes, from these cognitive scientists themselves because it is important to realize that it is because of the nature of the complexity of all biological systems, in general, including nervous systems and *a fortiori* the human-brain-in-the-human-body, that no one description at any one level can ever be adequate and that therefore no one level has ontological priority.[49] The emergent properties and functions at the more complex levels of analysis, organization and processing are emergent *realities*.

The recognition of the relation between different levels of investigation, analysis and description both within cognitive science and with respect to its relation to levels 2 and 3 is important for understanding the context of disputes within cognitive science itself. These concern for example, the question of whether or not the human brain operates as a digital computer (broadly, the programme of 'Artificial Intelligence' (AI)[50]) or by 'parallel distributed processing (PDP)' (the programme of 'Connectionism'[51]). Such questions can only be settled by the ordinary processes of scientific research (experiment and theoretical analysis) conducted, in this sensitive case, with philosophical acumen. Whatever the conclusions emerging from such research, the recognition of their many-levelled character means that there is no necessary conflict either with those arising from the investigations and analyses of human mental activity by the behavioural sciences (level 3) or *a fortiori* with those arising from the study of human culture. The ultimate aim is a description that takes account of all levels of investigation, analysis and description and integrates them into a unified perspective. In particular, we now know from the study of non-linear dynamic systems[52] that even systems which are deterministic at the micro-level can be unpredictable in their succession of overall states at the macro-level. If the human brain turns out to be a system of this kind, as seems increasingly likely, we may well have here the physical correlate of the experience of consciousness, and so the warrant for giving a 'causal' account in *mentalistic* terms of successions of what we experience as mental states, including the operations of 'free will'. As Crutchfield *et al.* conclude in their survey of determinative chaos:

Even the process of intellectual progress relies on the injection of new ideas and new ways of connecting old ideas. Innate creativity may have an underlying chaotic process that selectively amplifies small fluctuations and molds them into macroscopic coherent mental states that are experienced as thoughts. In some cases the thoughts may be decisions, or what are perceived to be the exercise of will. In this light, chaos provides a mechanism that allows for free will within a world governed by deterministic laws.[53]

None of this is inconsistent with that Christian anthropology, stemming from that of the Bible, which regards human beings as psychosomatic unities[54] displaying a many-faceted personhood uniting many properties, abilities and potential relationships – and rooted in materiality.[55] Indeed Margaret Boden has argued that, in attributing 'subjectivity, purpose, freedom and choice'[56] to a material system (a computer), AI (and the same would also be true of connectionism) reinforces the validity of these concepts when applied to the psychology of human beings that are also material systems.[57].

It will be necessary to revert to the implications of cognitive science for our understanding of human nature when we examine the 'cognitive turn' in the behavioural sciences (section 5, below), but we must now consider those other sciences which bridge the biological and the behavioural.

Sociobiology[58] may be broadly defined as the systematic study of the biological, especially the genetic, basis of social behaviour and, in relation to human beings, aims at exploring the relations between biological constraints and cultural change. It thereby encroaches, in the ambitions of at least some sociobiologists, on to level 4. It is indeed attempts to extend these ideas to particular forms of human behaviour and to the development of human culture that have generated controversy, especially with sociologists and anthropologists, not to mention philosophers (theologians seem to have been less exercised on these matters, perhaps because of insulation from the discussion). In an earlier survey[59] of the discussion, I quoted the conclusion of J. H. Crook as one of the fairest, and it still seems to me valid a decade later:

> The tentative explanation of human conduct that stems from the sociobiological paradigm . . . for the first time anchors the study of society in evolutionary biology through a fundamental theory. None the less the enormous variety of cultural processes cannot be interpreted solely by sociobiological explanation. Cultures express the attempts of individuals to find meaning in their lives and to produce collectively systems of meaning that make life comprehensible and legitimize action . . . Cultural evolution comprises the historical process which provides the sociobiological environment within which the basic biological strategies of the species find varied expression.[60]

Clearly this whole development is of theological concern.[61] For, by thus encompassing in one theory human culture and the non-human biological world (especially in its genetic aspects), sociobiology must inevitably influence our thinking about what human beings are. The debate is not entirely a replay of the old nature-nurture dichotomy for the subtlety and complexity of the strategies of gene perpetuation have undergone much revision and, as is transpiring in the treatment here, the many-levelled character of humanity is becoming more and more apparent. The emphatically evolutionary outlook of sociobiology raises no new questions for Christian theology that have not been raised by the general idea of evolution, both cosmic and biological, in relation to the affirmation of God as Creator, as already discussed.[62] However, because of the predominantly reductionist tone in the writings of many sociobiologists,[63] there has been a tendency to interpret human behaviour functionally only as a strategy for the survival of genes. So the theological response to such suggestions must, in its general thrust, be that which is made to any purely deterministic and reductionistic accounts of human behaviour.[64] But in making such a riposte, theologians should nevertheless recognize, far more explicitly than they have done in the past, that human nature is exceedingly complex and that its basic foundational level is biological and genetic, however much it is overlaid by nurture and culture.

However, it must also be recognized by all concerned in the debate that sociobiology is based on the presupposition that any particular behaviour of an organism is, at least partly and to an extent to be ascertained by research, under the control of a gene or, rather, of a system of concomitantly acting, linked genes. This is often in fact asking more than the relevant sciences can at present deliver for, as some of the scientists involved in this area have put it, 'It seems premature to build exotic sociobiological theories to account for certain kinds of genetic polymorphism, developmental process or social interaction until we have understood the basic parameters within which such effects operate.'[65] This is true *a fortiori* in the case of the study of human beings.

It has been the purpose of general *behaviour genetics* since 1960,[66] when it first came to be recognized as a distinct discipline, to examine 'the inheritance of many different behaviours in organisms ranging from bacteria to man'.[67] Sociobiology focusses mainly on differences in social systems and patterns of behaviour between species in an evolutionary context, whereas behaviour genetics is 'predominantly concerned with explaining individual differences within species'.[68] As a discipline it represents a fusion of the interests of genetics and psychology and moves between the two poles of a genetics of behaviour and a genetically-aware psychology.[69] This new subdiscipline is currently being vigorously applied to human beings.[70]

A prerequisite of such human studies, which it has proved difficult to satisfy, is agreement upon a measure of behaviour.[71] It is claimed[72] that there does exist a paradigm correlating human personality traits which is agreed upon between most investigators with human subjects taken from a wide range of cultures. If this is the case, then there exists the basis for the examination of the genetic basis of differences in human personality, though doubts of a more philosophical character have been expressed about the reliability of the self-reporting relied upon in many personality studies hitherto.[73] The research proceeds and, like all scientific research, as it does so it both clarifies and generates new problems. Eaves, Eyseneck and Martin conclude their survey confident that:

> There are consistent patterns in the causes of variation in personality and attitudes. The consistencies occur in the different effects of genes and environment on different attitude and personality measures, and in the similarities that we find between studies of different populations.[74]

Yet they also recognize that the causes of variation in personality and attitudes are more complex than previously thought. Even in their present form such studies are producing evidence of the genetic underpinning of much in personal behaviour and traits previously considered as entirely environmental and cultural.

Some accounts of these 'bridge' sciences of sociobiology and behaviour genetics tend to give an excessively mechanistic impression of the relation between evolutionary development and the behaviour of living organisms, including *homo sapiens*. Evolution is conceived as an 'unfolding' of the basic internal programme of an organism, regarded as already encoded in its genes, and the behaviour of an organism is seen as a consequence of this 'unfolding'. I have already drawn attention[75] to the stress of a number of leading biologists[76] on the controlling and often decisive role of behaviour in evolution, especially innovative behaviour. As Gunter Altner puts it:

In its dual capacity as a product of evolution and as a controlling principle . . . behaviour constitutes a system of feedback with regard to the evolution process as a whole . . . The function of modelling the variable genetic substratum is now no longer performed by selection alone, but is to an increasingly great extent subject also to the control exercised by behaviour – whether the behaviour of lower organisms or the civilised behaviour of man . . .[77]

It is this role of behaviour that gives a uniqueness to each step in evolution from lower to higher stages of organization – and also causes the evolution of *homo sapiens* to become 'psychosocial',[78] for humanity shapes its own evolution by shaping its own environment.[79] The feedback effect of behaviour on evolution moves it on to a new plane, as it were, in humanity. Thus Altner draws attention to 'the special characteristics of man, to the multiple achievement of his civilization, to his enhanced freedom from the bondage of instincts, to his high level of self-consciousness which allows him an entirely new degree of controlling influence'.[80]

Sociobiology and behaviour genetics cannot but influence our general assessment of human nature and, in particular, the degree of responsibility assigned to societies and individuals for their actions. The genetic constraints upon our nature and behaviour are, from a theistic viewpoint, what God has purposed shall provide the matrix within which freedom shall operate. Furthermore, theologians should acknowledge that it is this kind of genetically-based creature that God has actually created as a human being through the evolutionary process. This process, through its naturally selective and genetic mechanisms, has evolved the human brain with its powers of thinking and reasoning. The limits and scope, and perhaps even the procedures, of these thinking and reasoning abilities are – and here the implications of the biological 'turn' of twentieth-century perceptions on humanity are inescapable – clearly dependent on the genetic heritage of human beings. However, that heritage cannot in advance itself determine the *content* of thinking and reasoning – even if it is the prerequisite of the possession of these capacities.

This general view of the relation between the content of human thought and genetic endowment, which seems warranted by the creativity of human thought and reasoning, has been challenged in the case of moral reasoning. I am not here referring to the long debate about 'evolutionary ethics', the notion that ethical norms could, or at least should, be derived from our knowledge of the evolutionary process itself. This, as is well known, foundered on the rock of its vulnerability to perpetrating the 'naturalistic fallacy' of deriving what *ought* to be the case from what *is* the case.[81] So the evolutionary process came to be regarded simply as a factor, admittedly a relatively new and significant one, that ethical decisions, particularly on social matters, now needed to take into account.

The debate about the contribution of evolutionary ideas and of genetics to ethics has now, however, been re-opened by some scientists and philosophers who base their arguments on sociobiological ideas.[82] My conclusion concerning such 'sociobiological ethics' was, and still is, that:

> this new twist to 'evolutionary ethics' is still guilty of the well-known, and in the circumstances ironically and ambiguously designated, 'genetic fallacy', whereby the ultimate form of a human cultural development is thought to be reductively entirely explained in terms of its biological or cultural origins. Just as science is not magic, so ethics, on the same grounds, is not genetics.[83]

Even so, the Christian theologian does not have to enter this debate with destructive ambitions. For, if God, as a scientifically-sensitive theology affirms,[84] creates immanently through the evolutionary processes, it would not be inconsistent with such a theology for human moral awareness to have originated in the way the foregoing sociobiological hypothesis affirms. Hence to unravel the origins of moral awareness is not to preempt its ultimate maturation in the moral sensitivity of self-aware, reasoning persons whose emergence in the created order God can properly be posited as intending. Christian theology then goes on to stress that, through the freedom God has allowed to evolve in such created persons, God has also opened up new possibilities of self-fulfilment, creativity and openness to the future which require a language other than that of biology and genetics to elaborate and express.

Hence, the vital question becomes: what do we human beings make of these possibilities? I earlier drew attention to 'signs of a kind of misfit between human beings, persons, and their environment which is not apparent in other creatures'[85] and described some of the indications of this. The biological endowment of human beings does not appear to be able to guarantee their contented adaptation to an environment which is, for them, inherently dynamic. For they have ever-changing and expanding horizons within which they live individually and socially, physically and culturally, emotionally and intellectually. In particular, when one reflects on the balanced adaptation of other living organisms to their biological niches, the alienation of human beings from non-human nature and from each other appears as a kind of *biological* anomaly within the organic world. Thus it is not surprising to find Eaves and Gross, pointing out the 'possible gulf between the ecosystem in which human evolution occurred and the global environment into which humanity is now projected'; and going on to suggest that human favouring of genetic kin is a sign, at best, of tribal self-interest and that this 'gives a new slant to the problem of original sin because it truly implies that humans bring into the world by virtue of their ancestry biological baggage which is ill adapted to the present world'.[86]

As human beings widen their environmental horizons, so they experience this 'gulf' between their biological past environment out of which they have evolved and that in which they conceive themselves as existing or, rather, that in which they wish they existed. Some of the features of experience with which we human beings have to come to terms in trying to answer the famous question of Tolstoy, 'What do men live by?' I have elsewhere[87] identified as: our own death, our sense of finitude, suffering, the realization of our potentialities, steering our path from life to death. Others[88] can amplify and enrich such an account of this experienced 'gulf', but its mere existence certainly raises a problem for any purely biological account of human development. We may well ask, 'Why has, how has, the process whereby there have so successfully evolved living organisms finely tuned to and adapted to their environments failed in the case of *homo sapiens* to ensure this fit between lived experience and the environing conditions of their lives?'. It appears that the human brain has capacities which were originally evolved in response to an earlier environmental challenge but the exercise of which now engenders a whole range of needs, desires, ambitions and aspirations which cannot all be harmoniously fulfilled.

Such considerations raise the further question of whether or not human beings have really identified what their true 'environment' really is – that 'environment' in which human flourishing is possible. Such is the depth of human *angst* and tragedy that it would clearly be unwise to expect to be able to answer such questions from within the scope of biology – even though modern biology is digging deeply into our origins and has uncovered genetic foundations for more of the superstructure of our personal and social behaviour than had been anticipated.

The complexity and character of the human predicament clearly involves more subtle levels of human nature than are the focus of level 2 or of the 'bridge' sciences to the next level. Human feelings as well as our more rational endeavours are engaged in our assessment of our relation to our 'environment' and of our interactions with each other. So we turn to those sciences concerned with human behaviour.

5 THE SCIENCES AND HUMAN BEHAVIOUR (Level 3)

Some of the principal behavioural sciences and the systems on which they focus are indicated in level 3 of Fig. 3. Again a part-whole hierarchy can be discerned, though this subdivides into fewer categories than do the systems in levels 1 and 2. Level 3 includes various forms of psychology which is, etymologically, 'discourse on the mind (*psyche*)' and, in its usage since the eighteenth century, the 'study of the phenomena of mental life'.[89] At first, this naturally included the (largely introspective) study of such human activities as perceiving, remembering, thinking and reasoning, but in the twentieth century until the mid-60s psychology was dominated by behaviourism and psychoanalysis. Behaviourist psychology excluded the study of conscious subjective states as being too elusive and confined itself to aspects of behaviour that could be observed systematically and, it was hoped, objectively. Although entirely different in approach, psychoanalysis, originating with Freud,[90] moved the focus of psychology towards unconscious states and forces which, it was claimed, strongly influenced human behaviour. Although there was some continued interest in cognitive and other mental processes (e.g., the 'Gestalt' school and Piaget and his successors), they were not in the forefront or in the public image of psychology. This has now changed and mental processes have begun to be taken much more seriously. As the brain scientist R. W. Sperry has perhaps overstated it:

By the mid-1970s, mainstream psychology had also revised its earlier views concerning consciousness and the subjective, replacing long dominant behaviorist theory with a new mentalist or cognitive paradigm. This changeover, impelled by a large complex of cognitive, linguistic, computer, and related theoretic and sociologic developments . . . has now legitimised the contents of inner experience, such as sensations, percepts, mental images, thoughts, feelings, and the like, as ineliminable causal constructs in the scientific explanation of brain function and behaviour.[91]

This 'cognitive', 'consciousness' or 'mentalist' shift of emphasis in psychology moves its focus of interest towards the content and activities of ordinary consciousness (sometimes neutrally denoted as 'self-modification'). Consciousness is now much more frequently regarded as a theoretical term that refers to realities whose existence is inferred from observation.[92]

These shifts of emphasis have spread to a number of disciplines such as cognitive and developmental psychology, linguistics, some aspects of anthropology and even (on one side) philosophy and (on the other) the neurosciences – and were indeed a factor in the rise of the cognitive science we have already discussed. How it is to be a thinking and feeling human being have again come on to the agenda of many of the behavioural sciences (level 3), although, it has still to be admitted, none as yet can encapsulate and describe the content of human consciousness with the directness of many of the activities in level 4, with all their admitted inadequacies.[93] Sperry asserts[94] that there is a new openness in the behavioural sciences, not only in a 'downwards' direction via cognitive science[95] to the neurosciences, but also 'upwards' to all those studies and activities that regard human consciousness and its content as real and worthy of examination and interpretation. There appears to be occurring a re-habilitation from a scientific perspective of the reality of reference of humanistic studies – in which theology should be included, if only because of its concern with religious experience. It also gives scientific credibility to what had never been doubted in theology – the pre-eminence of the concept of the personal in the hierarchy of our interpretation of the many-levelled structure of humanity and of the world of which humanity is an evolved constituent.

In view of the history of the awareness of the multiplicity of these levels, it would be unwise to think that by using the words 'person' and its cognates we now possessed the talisman for understanding humanity. We should, rather, accept it as a kind of

boundary-marker to designate the uppermost level in the hierarchy of complexity of natural entities. With this must go the
recognition of our inability to know what persons *are* in themselves, in spite of our being able to identify many of their
characteristics.[96] This impasse arises because experience of
ourselves and of others makes us only too aware of the mystery of
the nature of human personhood.[97] In particular, our sense of our
own freedom and our awareness of its corollary, that we are
responsible for our actions (however constrained by genetics and
other factors), remain obstinately raw data that neither science
nor philosophy can ignore.[98]

In all of this, the many-levelled approach that was seen to be
necessitated by the exigencies of research in the cognitive
sciences, bridging the neurosciences and studies of behaviour, has
to be extended *a fortiori* when the relationships between brain
activity, mental experience and individual and social behaviour
are under scrutiny. As the experimental psychologist M. A.
Jeeves says,

> What is evident is that opportunities exist now, as never before, for a
> concerted and interdisciplinary approach investigating links between
> brain and behaviour. What is also clear is that the advances in anatomy,
> neurophysiology and molecular neuroscience will be fully understood only
> in the context of the awake, behaving animal, whether human or non-
> human.[99]

and

> . . . we need a hierarchy of levels and their corresponding categories of
> explanation in order to do justice to the complexity and richness of what
> we find when we study man . . . we are trying to discover how the stories at
> different levels correlate.[100]

The replacement of behaviourist and psychoanalytical psychologies with a new 'mentalist' or 'cognitive' paradigm has important implications for the relation of science and religion. For
instead of a dichotomy between, on the one hand, a dualism of
'body' and 'mind' (a common misapprehension of the Christian
view of humanity[101]) and, on the other, a reductive materialism, a
new integrated 'view of reality' could emerge which, so Sperry
hopes, 'accepts mental and spiritual qualities as causal realities,
but at the same time denies they can exist separately in an

unembodied state apart from the functioning brain'.[102] This denial will have to be considered again when we are concerned with the Christian understanding of resurrection,[103] but for the moment the situation looks more encouraging for a fruitful dialogue between religion and the sciences of human behaviour than it has been for many decades.[104]

Psychology, of course, figures prominently in the sciences of behaviour (Level 3 of Fig. 3), but it is beyond the scope of what is being attempted here to give any adequate account of the relation of the plethora of theories of human psychology to theology. The very multiplicity of these theories reminds us that in level 3 the theories of the psychological sciences are 'underdetermined by the facts', a characteristic they, in fact, share with the theories of the sciences of levels 1 and 2, though it is often less obvious with them. This marked underdetermination by the facts must be the explanation of the existence, at least in the past, of so many rival, and even contradictory, schools of human psychology, each with its own leading figure, its own theoretical framework and its only group of therapists implementing its principles. Nowadays psychology is often more modestly concerned with problem-oriented theories of smaller scope than these former 'schools'. The 'cognitive turn' in psychology at least renders its variety intelligible by stressing that any psychological theory is never entirely an objective theory about other people, considered as 'objects of study' like those of other sciences: it is also a theory about 'subjects', that is, about one's own subjectivity as well as that of other people.[105]

In displaying this variety and the difficulty of obtaining purely objective criteria, psychology is being paradigmatically illustrative of what is true more generally of the human sciences. for, as Holmes Rolston observes:

> . . . when we come to the human sciences . . . unity [of the sciences] seems entirely out of sight . . . The phenomena are too complex, perhaps in part beyond the limits of science, and any major theory is going to be crude. We must rest content with a piecemeal science, a multiple-paradigm science, full of minitheories . . . the human sciences will inevitably be softer than the hard natural sciences.[106]

We therefore have to tolerate the variety of theories in psychology as an inevitable consequence of the nature of their 'subject-matter' (*mot juste* in this instance!). However, this variety renders difficult any attempt to discern their implications for and possible effects on a Christian theology of humanity, a theology which can properly claim, like all the major religious traditions, to have its own distinctive insights into human nature, namely, that of the Judeo-Christian tradition enriched by the experience of many generations for more than two thousand years.

In any such inquiry it will be essential to recognize, even more explicitly than usual, the inevitably metaphorical character of the language of psychological, as of all scientific, theories and how their models are systematically developed metaphors.[107] Otherwise, the transitions from purely scientific hypotheses to metaphysical systems that they all make[108] will be obscured, with consequent obfuscation of their implications for Christian, or any other, theology. D. Browning has been particularly concerned to stress, in the case of the psychotherapeutic psychologies he has studied,[109] that

> all of them have given birth to scientific myths which have in turn implied cosmologies or metaphysical systems. If this is true, *then these scientific myths (and their metaphysical implications) and the myths, metaphors, and stories of the Judeo-Christian tradition are at this point on equal logical footing.* In view of this, two fundamental questions need to be addressed: (1) Are these metaphysical models truly required by the particular scientific tradition from which they come? and (2) are these metaphysical models adequate to experience in the broad sense of the term?[110]

Browning's answer to the first question, with respect to the psychologies in question, was an emphatic 'No!' and he consequently argues that

> psychology – especially the psychotherapeutic and developmental psychologies – needs to be part of a wider critical and normative theory of person and society. Hence, society needs two models of psychology – one more properly scientific, descriptive, and predictive and one more self-consciously critical and normative.[111]

Of these two models of psychology, the former, insofar as it remains a rigorous science, could possibly, with its metaphysical overload reduced to a minimum, provide important data for consideration by a Christian anthropology. However, the latter model inevitably involves a strongly controlling metaphysics and/or a critical theory of society not warranted by the science of the first model. So it is problematic to what extent it could help theology in its task 'to orient the believer to the broadest ranges of human experience, to describe and represent what experience testifies to be its ultimate context and to induce the appropriate existential and ethical response'.[112]

Clinical psychologies, which is what most non-professionals usually encounter, stand somewhere between, on the one hand, experimental psychology (Browning's first model) and, on the other, his second model and theology. They 'often proceed by correlating internally perceived introspective knowledge with externally observed patterns, themes and modalities'.[113] Browning includes amongst these broadly clinical psychologists S. Freud, C. Jung, E. Erikson, H. Kohut and the humanistic psychologists C. Rogers, A. Maslow and F. Perls.[114] These clinical psychologies have had great cultural influence in the twentieth century for 'People are desperate to find workable technologies to organize the new vacuums in their interior psychological lives that . . . social changes have inflicted upon them'.[115] So the content of these psychologies will always be of immense *pastoral* concern to the Christian church. Our problem here is to determine their theological significance for a theology of human nature, especially as each carries its own self-generated metaphysical 'overload'.[116]

The insights into human personality of the various psychologies have been surveyed by P. Morea[117] and, with special reference to religion, by H. Rolston,[118] as well as by D. Browning.[119] The reader is referred to these sources. However, the unavoidable omission here of a detailed examination of the various psychologies is not detrimental to the pursuing of our main theme for, because of the under-determination of all psychological theories by the facts, no one of them may claim to be so definitive and so established that theology must come to terms uniquely with it. All, especially Jungian psychology[120] which is so sensitive to religious experience, can throw light on human personality and need to be considered by theology especially in those various particular contexts which are usually the foci of attention of applied psychologists. Rolston Holmes considers psychology in an evolutionary perspective and raises in that context, the possibility mooted earlier[121] that humanity needs some other, as yet only dimly apprehended, 'environment' for its true flourishing and consummation: 'religious minds wonder if these [wider, evolutionary] phenomenal developments do not signal a supernatural environment, some larger prime movement under which the cosmic drama takes place ... Every religion wants to place the self in a much larger environment.'[122]

In such reflections based on a study of psychology we are reminded of the sense of 'mystery' about the nature of human personhood that is also our common experience.[123] The psychologist Morea entitles the concluding chapter to his study of the theories of psychology 'The Mystery' for, he says: '... in our attempt to grasp personality scientifically, we experience something strange. As we reach out and are confronted by boundaries, we are filled with wonder at human personality, and we seem to touch mystery.'[124]

An inherent aspect of this mystery of human personality which is of particular concern to us in relation to theology is the incomplete and unfinished quality we find reflected in our experience and our alienation from nature, humanity and God (indeed 'sin'). There is nothing static about this condition; again Morea: 'We are not so much human beings as human becomings'.[125] He, too, points out the biological paradox of our lack of 'fit' with our environment as we perceive it.[126] Human beings are a problem to themselves and for themselves and the character of this problem is closely linked with the apparent paradox of God creating a mis-fit, or so it seems, in a world in which other living creatures are finely and appositely adapted to their environments.[127] In the end the clinical psychological, humanistic problem becomes a theological one. Theists could well ask 'What did God think he was doing in creating such a misfit?' Or, 'Why did God create this human part of nature, so uniquely *not* at home on Earth, apparently its only home?'[128] We are beings who comprehend and understand through the sciences vast tracts of the obscurities of the universe in which we find ourselves – only to be confronted with the most intransigent and unfathomable mystery when we face ourselves.

Does the very existence of this barrier to our total comprehension itself provide a clue to the fundamental nature of humanity? We have earlier seen that when we speak of God as the ground of being and becoming of all-that-is we have been impelled towards the use of personal terms, drawn from human experience. We talked of God as being 'at least personal', even if we drew back from saying God is 'a person', sensing *that* would be a reduction and limitation of the inevitably ineffable nature of the Divine Being and Becoming. However, this conditional, legitimate use of personal terms for God reflects back, as so often, on what we can, or could, or might, mean by the very term 'person' itself. There is a two-way traffic, as it were, between the use of the word as applied to humanity and as applied to God and a concomitant enrichment of its meaning. In his study of six theories of human personality, Morea[129], for example, finds that attempts on the grounds of psychology to explain, or explain away, a moral element in personality proved to be inadequate and that what we hear in moral conscience is 'a voice, a voice in relationship. What we hear is not something but Someone. There is a moral element in personality because a Moral Being is at the origin of the universe from which personality emerged.' If God is the ultimately free and the ultimately good and has created us uniquely with a limited, but real, freedom and capacity for goodness, then we are to this extent potentially *imago dei*, created 'in the image of God'.[130] If that is so – and the biblical tradition certainly affirms it[131] – then it is not surprising that we also encounter mystery when we contemplate the inherent and inner nature of human personhood, as an, admittedly distorted, image of the mystery of the divine. This inference has been finely expressed by Morea at the conclusion of his study of personality in the light of theories of psychology:

> 'Thrown into the world I become a puzzle to myself'; scientific theory has failed to find a solution to St Augustine's puzzle. But in examining and analysing personality scientifically, we confront boundaries and encounter a mystery. Religion has traditionally taught that human beings are made in the image of God. This would explain why we have difficulty in understanding personality. It would explain why, in our attempt to understand personality, we often experience wonder and awe. If human beings are made in God's image it would explain why – at the boundaries of our scientific knowing of human personality – we sometimes sense beyond the mystery of human personality a much greater Mystery.[132]

6 THE SOCIAL SCIENCES (Between levels 3 and 4)

The sciences variously designated as 'social' form a bridge between the behavioural sciences and culture. The more the sciences are concerned with the mental life and behaviour of human beings, the more they will impinge on the concern of the Christian community with the nature and destiny of humanity. For example, religious education has to take account of discoveries in developmental psychology with respect both to its method and to the content of what it presents as Christianity to the young at different stages of development. Moreover, corporate religious bodies such as the Christian churches need to take account in their actions of the social psychology of religion. These are not our direct concerns here, though it is worth noting that the social conditioning of religious beliefs which the social sciences disentangle and reveal does not, of itself, settle any questions as to the truth of these beliefs – the general criteria for which we have already discussed.[133]

The evolutionary process, however, introduces another dimension into this complex relation between religious belief and social setting, namely that of evolutionary epistemology – the realization that cognition of its environment by a living organism has to be sufficiently trustworthy in its content to allow it to be viable under the pressures of natural selection.[134] We have already referred to the way that sociobiologists have identified an 'altruism'[135] that is exerted by individual organisms on behalf of the survival of other members of the species that share their genes. Although this helps to explain how human behaviour has, and still is, often directed towards the survival and welfare of genetic kin, it fails to explain how humanity has been able to go beyond this by generating loyalty on the part of individuals to groupings of wider and wider scope, far transcending the limits of genetic relationship. Of course, the ability of human beings to transmit knowledge from one generation to another by its linguistic and cultural resources is vital to the existence of these wider human 'groupings', but is itself the means rather than the cause of their occurrence. Social anthropologists seek to understand what could have brought into existence the necessary wider loyalties and increasingly many of them converge on the emergence of 'religiously' warranted imperatives as the explanation. The cumulative wisdom of the religious traditions has, by setting up norms related to the existence of a 'transcendental reality' other than human authority, contributed crucially, in the view of such investigators, to the process of human social organization, wider and more complex than that of any other living organism.

For example, Donald Campbell, well known for his advocacy of an 'evolutionary epistemology' on the lines already indicated, made a significant move away from the traditionally anti-religious stance of psychologists in his ice-breaking address[136] to the American Psychological Association in 1975 when he stressed the crucial role of religion in the cultural history of humanity. Speaking, as he put it, as a 'hard-line neo-Darwinian' he analysed social evolution in terms, such as 'natural selection', analogous to those of biological evolution. Human urban social complexity, he argued, has been made possible by *social* evolution which, in optimizing social system functioning, has to counter individual selfish tendencies for which *biological* evolution continued to select ('selfish' here in the sense of the 'selfish' gene, protecting one's genetic kin) – and religion, he urged, has been the principal countering agency.

> Committing oneself to living for a transcendent God's purposes, not one's own [or those of one's genetic kin], is a commitment to optimize the social system rather than the individual system. Social groups effectively indoctrinating such individual ['transcendent'] commitments might well have had a social-evolutionary advantage and thus have discovered a functional, adaptive truth. It seems from cross-cultural surveys that belief in transcendent deities that are concerned with morality of human behavior toward other human beings occurs more frequently in more complex societies.[137]

In other words, humanity could only survive and flourish if it took account of social and personal values that transcended the urges of the individual, embodying 'selfish' genes. But does not this imply that these social and personal values, enshrined in moral codes and imprinted in ethical attitudes, are part of the realities with which we humans have to deal and of which we have to take account or otherwise die out? Have we not learnt, in this twentieth century above all else, how the failure to recognize the objectivity and reality of social and personal values can be as destructive of society as the failure to recognize the physical and biological parameters within which life is set? This increasingly accepted role of the religions of humanity in socio-cultural evolution points to the existence of values as constituting a reality-system that human beings neglect to their actual peril.

Since the subtle relation between religion and the social sciences has a strongly cultural component, any analysis of this relation will itself be strongly dependent on the social philosophy that is deployed. As such it is beyond our scope here and I can but refer the reader to the recent survey of Holmes Rolston.[138] His conclusion is:

> There is . . . no particular warrant for thinking that either human minds or their communities are the exhaustive paradigms with which we must interpret culture, set as this is in natural history. Nothing learned in social science forbids asking whether there is something transcendent to the human world, something sacred exerting its pull over society, and out of which the human natural worlds may be derived. What if there are some challenges and conflicts that a society can solve only religiously? . . . The fact is not so much that religion calls for an explanation outside itself in society. It is rather society that calls for an explanation outside itself in those realities to which religion points. Society, not just religion, is the effect.[139]

7 HUMAN CULTURE AND ITS PRODUCTS (Level 4)

Such perceptions bring us clearly to the domain of human culture, that of level 4 (Fig. 3 – of *'cultural products arts and sciences* . . . products of the behavior of organisms, especially humans (e.g., rules of logical inference, languages, economic systems, and physical products such as buildings', as Bechtel and Abrahamsen, somewhat over-selectively, describe it.[140] Their schema (basically that of Fig. 3) illuminates the way in which 'the distinctive constructs of each of the four different levels can be applied to the same events or domains and that interdisciplinary interactions can be helpful, if not essential, in doing so'.[141] However, while showing how each of the four focal levels might be relevant to the same events or domains, the schema also serves to emphasize that vast tracts of what constitutes level 4 are not at present, or in the foreseeable future, capable of being so integrated with other levels.

For the 'cultural products' of level 4 are embodiments of human creativity in the arts and sciences and in human relations (including, I would add, relations to God) which are best, and in most cases only, discernible and transmissable by their own distinctive means through meaningful patterns created in what is received initially through our senses. These patterns, which are the means of communication between human beings[142] and, we suggested, between God and humanity,[143] are *sui generis*. They are generated through historical formation in continuous cultures which invest them with meaning for such communication. They thereby have the unique power of inducting humanity into an encounter with the transcendence in the 'other', whether in the form of another human person or of God, the Beyond within our midst. George Steiner in his penetrating *Real Presences* has called all such encounters a 'wager on transcendence':

> . . . the wager on the meaning of meaning, on the potential of insight and response when one human voice addresses another, when we come face to face with the text and work of art or music, which is to say when we encounter the *other* in its condition of freedom, is a wager on transcendence.[144]

He does not hesitate to point to its theological import:

> The wager – it is that of Descartes, of Kant and of every poet, artist, composer of whom we have explicit record – predicates the presence of a realness, of a 'substantiation' (the theological reach of this word is obvious) within language and form. It supposes a passage, beyond the fictive or the purely pragmatic, from meaning to meaningfulness. The conjecture is that 'God' *is*, not because our grammar is outworn; but that grammar lives and generates worlds because there is the wager on God.[145]

To ask what it is we 'know' in explicit, linguistically communicable terms about human nature from the immense inheritance of human culture, which is still being enriched, is to ask a question which is unanswerable not only because of its scope but also because it is inappropriate. For in any significant creative encounter (and *a fortiori* in our encounter with God) what we experience is experienced only *ambulando* – as we look at the picture, listen to the music, attend the opera, immerse ourselves in the liturgy, or open ourselves to God in prayer. We can expect all such encounters with 'cultural products',[146] all such 'wagers on transcendence', to communicate only in their own way, in their own 'language,' with immediacy at their own level – and not to be reducible to the languages of others. Some 'cultural products' will be concerned with events or domains to which knowledge at other levels has been shown to be relevant.[147] But modest successes at interrelating levels in some instances should not be allowed to detract from the perceived autonomy of the wider range of aesthetic, humanistic and religious experiences that are significant for human insights and flourishing.

Such a robust assertion of the conceptual and experienced autonomy of what is communicated in human culture is reinforced by the re-habilitation of the subjective, of inner experience, in cognitive science and in psychology[148] – in fact, in the recovery of the personal, the recognition of the reality of personhood. This seems to me, and in this I concur with R. W. Sperry,[149] to constitute a major shift in our cultural and intellectual landscape which opens up the dialogue between the human spiritual enterprise (broadly, 'religion') and that of science in a way long barred by the dominance of a mechanistic, materialist[150] naturalism, thought erroneously to have been warranted by science itself. The human is, for example, biological, but what is distinctively human transcends that out of which and in which it has emerged. As apparently a Chinese proverb has it:[151] 'All that is animal is present in man, but not all that is human is present in the animal; all that is human is present in God, but not all that is divine is present in man.'

It must be stressed again that this pressure for a wider perspective on humanity is being generated from within the sciences themselves (if not by all scientists, as such) in attempting to cope with the many levels of reality represented in the structure, functions and behaviour of *homo sapiens*. It is not too much to hope that we see here the first glimmerings for some time of a genuine integration between the humanities, including theology, and the sciences; and a breakdown of that dichotomy between the 'two cultures' which was engendered by the absence of any epistemological map on which their respective endeavours could be meaningfully located. Furthermore, this strengthens the claims of a *Christian* humanism not only within the domain of humanism as such, but also within that of theology[152] – for, as will transpire later, Christian theology is (or should be) concerned above all else with the consummation of the human and with human flourishing both in this life and *sub specie aeternitatis*.

Since all of human culture is a source for discerning the nature of humanity no one volume – indeed all the volumes that ever were – can hope to distil the essence of our humanity.[153] But we can note this new legitimization, from within the perspectives of the sciences themselves, of that 'proper study'[154] of humanity which is that of ourselves in the *whole* range of our experiences, including those of God.

8 THE THEOLOGY OF HUMAN BEING IN THE LIGHT OF THE SCIENCES

The re-habilitation of the distinctively human and so of at least
the possibility of theological interpretation of human nature
encourages us to draw together now some of the threads of
theological import that can be extracted from of the subtly woven
and ever elaborating fabric of the sciences which are today
shaping our understanding of the nature of human being. Some of
these strands of thought are congenial to traditional Christian
theology. For example, that human beings have a contingent
existence as part of a contingent world is part of classical Thomist
and earlier theology. That this contingency extends to the very
physical form that personhood[155] actually takes, namely *homo
sapiens*, should therefore evoke no surprise, especially in the light
of the evidence that there are inherent propensities in the very
processes of natural selection towards complexity, consciousness
and self-consciousness.[156] The contingency of *human* being is
consistent with the working out of a divine purpose in creation,
that of eliciting the emergence of self-conscious persons, whatever physical form these may eventually possess as a result of
the creative interplay of chance and law.[157] Even if 'Life is a
copiously branching bush, continually pruned by the grim reaper
of extinction, not a ladder of predictable progress'[158] and even if
'humanity arose just yesterday as a small twig on one branch of a
flourishing tree',[159] this 'twig' of humanity would still be unique
as the one evolved organism that is a person and capable of a
personal, conscious relation to the Creator of the evolutionary
process.

Furthermore, that human beings are part of nature, of the
very stuff of the world[160] is not only consistent with biblical
perspectives but also demonstrates that 'matter' has potentialities unrecognized and unheeded by a reductionist 'materialism'[161] and that consequently a Christian anthropology has no
vested interest in any form of vitalism. Nevertheless, we need to
know in a wide range of contexts what kind of unity that
'psychosomatic' one might be that we earlier recognized[162] as
both implied by the sciences concerned with *homo sapiens* and as
the biblical anthropology. Light has been thrown on this by our
examination of these sciences in this chapter. We found[163] that
there is now a widespread recognition among scientists themselves that, in order even to pursue their investigations, it is

necessary to hold together in as unified a perspective as possible the knowledge that is appropriated at the many different 'levels' upon which the various sciences focus (as in Fig. 3). All living organisms operate simultaneously at levels 1 to 3 and human beings are exceptional only in that we know they also incorporate levels (some of 3, all of 4 in Fig. 3) which involve activities that affect and communicate states of consciousness, many of which are self-referring. In other words, human beings are *persons*.

Our earlier analysis of communication between human persons[164] sufficed to show that – profound, mysterious even, though it can be – such communication nevertheless has to be conceived of as mediated by the actual contents of the world as delineated in the sciences. We were also able, I suggested, to interpret in basically similar terms possible communications from God to human beings in 'religious' (which were more often than not quite ordinary) experiences. The more thorough account in this chapter of the multiple focal levels which constitute a human being may be regarded, in this context, as an elaboration of the multiple levels at which God can communicate with that humanity which God has thus constituted through the complexification of the creative evolutionary process. I argued[165] that communications of God to humanity could be subsumed within the general mode of God's top-down, holistic influence on patterns of events within the world in general and that such an effective interaction would not abrogate scientific perceptions. What we now see with the more detailed examination of the various sciences in this chapter, is the sheer *multiplicity* of levels that must be affected in God's interaction with humanity (at least all those of Fig. 3). Now this multiply-levelled character of humanity is actually what constitutes the very essence of *being* a *person*, as we have just noted in the preceding paragraph. Hence the multi-levelled interaction of God with humanity is best described, as with interactions between human beings themselves, as being essentially *personal*,[166] or, rather, since God is one of the participants in the relation, as 'at least personal'; or even, 'more than personal'. For we need to convey the awareness, in such experiences of God, of the transcendent – of the intimate yet paradoxically distant presence of the Other that is God.

Recognition of the various focal levels in human beings has

another obvious but significant implication. It prevents any over-ready dichotomization of human beings into, on the one hand, a body and, on the other, mind/spirit/soul. It reinforces what biblical scholarship has long affirmed, namely, that in St Paul's epistles, for example, there must be no naive identification of, for example, *sarx* (traditionally translated 'flesh') with the former and of *pneuma* ('spirit') with the latter.[167] It transpires that much human behaviour, both what has been designated 'altruistic' and 'aggressive', or even 'sinful', may turn out to be much more genetically imprinted in humanity than previously thought – as well as behaviour patterns in non-ethical contexts. Theologians will have to come to accept that this as the way God has creatively evolved humanity into existence[168] and that our genetic constitution embodies and preserves the results of this process of creating by God. There is therefore now a need to consider whether or not this 'gives a new slant to the problem of original sin', as we noted Eaves and Gross have suggested.[169]

This impels us towards those other implications of the perspectives of the sciences on the nature of humanity which do not fit in well with 'traditional' theology. The designation 'traditional' here, as the inverted commas indicate, depends for its meaning very much on where one draws a datum line. It would be true to say, nevertheless, that for some eighteen centuries out of the nineteen and a half of its existence – that is, until the 'discovery of time' by the eighteenth century geologists and then Darwin – the Christian church had with everyone else, at least in western culture, assumed the fixity of species, all of which had been taken as arriving on Earth within a relatively short time by direct, divine *fiat*.

Recognition of how very recent is the arrival of *homo sapiens* on planet Earth (only for about one thousandth of one percent of its total age) has already[170] evoked the question of God's relation to non-human created nature, especially other living organisms which existed long before human beings appeared. Even though personhood as instantiated in *homo sapiens* can properly be regarded as an ultimate purpose of God in creation, the existence of the rest of creation must also be regarded as having its own *raison d'être* in God's purposes – that is, other than simply providing the random, zig-zag, bifurcating course that would yield humanity as its branch most capable of personal relationship with God. We earlier concluded from this that God is a 'Being of unfathomable richness' and that God may properly be said to have 'joy and delight in creation'.[171] Now we have to recognize that these are not only positive enrichments of our concept of God but that they also relativize the significance of humanity as such in the purpose and providence of God. For although humanity may still be held to be unique and to have a distinct place in the purposes of God, this status now has to be seen as a position of responsibility for the rest of all that is created. For humanity is that part of creation which alone is aware of its origin and its power over the rest of the created order. In other words, the beneficent purposes of God for humanity can only be properly formulated if they include a concomitant flourishing of the rest of creation. This introduces the need for an ecological dimension into Christian ethics so that a widening even of 'Christian humanism'[172] will have to be a component in any concept of 'human becoming' that we might wish to develop.

Another consequence of the evolutionary history of living organisms including *homo sapiens*, which the sciences now entail is the need for a re-appraisal of biological death.[173] This we now know did not enter human existence as a result of the action of any one (or two) human individuals, however primeval – as in the literalistic interpretation of the Adam and Eve myth – but is actually the means whereby God has enabled new forms of life to be created through evolution, long before human beings appeared.[174] Moreover, we also saw that there was no 'golden age' of a state of human perfection from which the humanity known to palaeontology, archaeology and history could honestly be said to have 'fallen'.[175] These two consequences of scientific discoveries have profound repercussions on the way in which it is possible to conceive of what has traditionally been called the 'work of Christ' in his life, death and resurrection-exaltation. Any account of this 'work of Christ' that is to be credible today must surely take these new perspectives on human origins and history into its system at a very fundamental level.[176]

9 THE PARADOX OF HUMAN BECOMING

These perspectives raise more acutely than ever the paradox of a humanity that is a kind of misfit in its biological environment[177] – 'evolution seems to have played a nasty trick, bringing into existence human beings vast in their desire and potential, but minute in their fulfilment and satisfaction'.[178] Such judgments still represent the dis-ease of humanity in terms drawn from biology and psychology. Profounder and more extensive insights have been and still are forthcoming from novelists, poets, dramatists, as well as from historians and social philosophers – indeed all who have reflected on the enormities and degradations that mar our twentieth-century history. They have used more personal and starker terms to describe the perennial human predicament still manifest today, terms such as: 'angst', 'alienated', 'false self-consciousness', 'one-dimensional', 'unintegrated', etc.

These terms of modern authors, generated by the modern predicament, reflect the perennial insights of the Judeo-Christian tradition into the significance of the Adam-and-Eve myth, of the 'Fall' and of 'original sin'.[179] The general thrust of modern theological interpretations is well represented by the biblical scholar, Alan Richardson:

> The doctrine of Original Sin is not so much an *a priori* theory as an empirical description of human nature; we all of us tend at every moment to put ourselves in the place of God by setting ourselves in the centre of the universe . . . The time element in the myths of the Creation and Fall (as in all biblical myths) must be discounted; it is not that *once* . . . God created man perfect and then he fell from grace. God is eternally Creator; he is eternally making man and holding him in being and seeing his handiwork is good (*Gen.* 1, v. 31). And just as creation is an eternal activity, so the 'Fall' is an ingredient of every moment of human life; man is at every moment 'falling', putting himself in the centre, rebelling against the will of God. Adam is Everyman.[180]

So interpreted this ancient myth becomes for us a shrewd analysis of the condition of human beings as the possessors of a self- consciousness, which by enabling them to be a 'subject' over against 'objects' *ipso facto* renders them out of harmony with themselves, with each other and with God – and so capable of, and actually, thwarting the divine purposes. The religious and moral experience of humanity is that this self-consciousness, by its very character as *self*-consciousness, has made human beings aware of what they might become – and of their failure to fulfil their potentialities and to satisfy their highest aspirations. It has also made them aware of their failure to come to terms with death and finitude and of their need to bear suffering in others as well as for themselves.[181] Moreover, according to the theological tradition and its contemporary interpretation, this characteristic of the *individual* is activated by and perpetuates itself by a transmission, within the *culture* into which individuals are born, of a social bias that thwarts the divine purposes. Thus 'sin' is not only individual but also cultural and corporate and, in this sense, it may be said to be 'original', i.e., consequent upon origins.[182]

The above modern descriptions of the human state, as 'alienated' etc., all reflect a sense of incompleteness, a felt lack of integration and a widespread judgment that human individuals in twentieth-century society have failed to live up to the hopes engendered by scientific technology. These hopes have foundered on the rock of the obduracy of self-will operating in a humanity inadequate through its own inner paralysis of will to the challenge of its newly won knowledge and power over the world. Contributing crucially to this paralysis is the failure of humanity to discern what it should be becoming – that is, what it *ought* to be. Thus it is that the greater intelligibility of a universe evolving from persons which is afforded by the postulate of the existence of God as Creator[183] is in danger of collapsing in view of the enigmatic and paradoxical nature of humanity, the persons who have been so evolved.[184] To put it more directly, what does God think he is doing in evolving the human being, this 'glory, jest and riddle of the world'[185] with such an enormous potentiality both for creative good and for degradation and evil, both self-destructive and dangerous to the rest of the created world?

The earlier accounts in this chapter of biology, genetics and psychology incline one to ground at least some of this widely intuited individual and social malaise in the levels on which these sciences focus. This serves to warn that no superficial palliatives will be able to achieve the consummation of human potentialities – transformation is needed of the total human being at the many levels of human existence in the individual and in society. What this transformation could or might be cannot be read off from even the extensive new knowledge of humanity that the sciences are yielding:

In his hope to achieve the accomplishment of his humanness the general direction of organic creation may indeed provide man . . . with a signpost and a criterion; but ultimately man has to depend on what he [and she] is not yet, but wants to be, i.e., on what is yet to come, the truly human, the uncorruptedly creatural! The divine?[186]

Furthermore, in exercising their freedom, human beings are always 'beings-on-the-way'.[187] Thus it is that philosophical and theological anthropologies are concerned with 'the realization of human nature as an emerging reality'[188] and actually shape the character of that emerging reality.[189] In this 'search' for humanity, the sciences do not provide data or even theories which can tell us what humanity should be becoming, individually and corporately. They certainly provide new information about the context in which imperatives and norms have to operate, and thereby must have a significant influence on human decisions, but they do not themselves provide those imperatives and norms.[190] So we may well ask, in what range of human inquiries might such guidance and wisdom be found?

We saw[191] that it is being increasingly urged by at least some social anthropologists that the religions of humanity have played a determinative role in the socio-cultural evolution of values, the formulation of what *ought* to be rather than what *is* so. For the power of social and personal values generated by the religions of humanity in socio-cultural evolution stems from their being grounded, so they believe, on experience of a pressing 'reality' which both transcends and inter-penetrates human self-awareness.[192]

It is at this point that the evidence accumulated by the Alister Hardy Research Centre at Oxford, from people in highly secularized Britain within and without the membership of institutional religions, is particularly relevant. It is that: '. . . a large number of people even today possess a deep awareness of a benevolent non-physical power which appears to be partly or wholly beyond, and far greater than, the individual self.'[193] Such awareness is, of course, the springboard of the great religions of the world which, in various proportions and to varying degrees, perpetuate in human society experiences of both the numinous – the awareness of the holy[194] – and the mystical – the sense of the merging of the self with a divine-ultimate reality. I cannot think that these documented experiences of a 'transcendental reality', to use Hardy's term, can simply be experiences of 'nothing-at-all'. Can these cognitive experiences of myriads of people in many ages alone out of all human experiences – those that by encountering physical, biological, social and personal realities are conducive to human survival and flourishing – have *no* contact with any reality essential for human survival and flourishing? This is not what the role of religion that is beginning to be discerned in socio-cultural evolution suggests. Nor would any of those having such experiences believe that. Nor can anyone who, not blessed with such experiences, has immersed him or herself in a religious tradition that nurtures the numinous and the mystical believe it either. These experiences and the cumulative wisdom of the religious traditions point together to a level of human cognition whereby human beings become aware of the existence of an all-encompassing Reality that transcends all, yet is immanent in all existence, their relation with which is essential for human survival and flourishing. This Reality, 'men call God', as St Thomas Aquinas would have said in English!

In this light, the religious experience of humanity is to be seen as constituted of a trial-and-error and conjecture-and-refutation process of interaction with that Reality, of encounter with God. For if that Reality exists, if there is a God, there could be nothing more important for humankind than to come into the most comprehending and comprehensive relation with him/her/it. For the establishing of such a relation would surely then be the basic condition for humanity to flourish both individually and as a species. Only thus would human beings, it would then appear, be able to satisfy those needs which go beyond the physical and biological, which it shares with its mammalian progenitors, and those social and personal needs that society might satisfy, to those distinctively human needs which arise from our possessing a free, self-consciousness.[195]

We know only too well that these needs are not satisfied within our grapplings with our biological and even our social environments and we experience a kind of 'gap' between our yearnings and the actualities of our situations. There seems to be an endemic failure of human beings to be adapted to what they sense as the totality of their environment – an incongruity eloquently expressed by that great nineteenth-century Presbyterian preacher, Thomas Chalmers, in his 1822 Bridgewater treatise:

There is in man, a restlessnss of ambition; . . . a dissatisfaction with the present, which never is appeased by all the world has to offer . . . an unsated appetency for something larger and better, which he fancies in the perspective before him – to all which there is nothing like among the inferior animals.[196]

Does not the human condition raise the profound question of what humanity's *true* environment really is? Thus it was that St Augustine, after years of travail and even despair, addressed his Maker: 'You have made us for yourself and our heart is restless till it rests in you.'[197]

If the foregoing was all there was to be said – much as this 'all' has proved to be! – then would we not be left with the feeling that it all amounts only to a kind of prelude to the rich experience that constitutes human awareness of the dealings of God with humanity? Does this not all lead to the recognition of the potential presence to us all of that all-encompassing, circumambient Reality we name as 'God' – to a recognition that the stuff of human nature is but dry, inflammable tinder, ready to ignite at the first flickering touch of the 'divine flame'.

For we have to reckon with the nature of that Reality whose name is 'God'. This 'God' is no stone idol or merely impersonal force. Such a 'God', we have to acknowledge, is in principle greater than all else of which we can conceive, and cannot therefore, as the source and meaning of all-that-is, be less than personal. God seeks to communicate both God's own meaning to us and God's own very self. We have already investigated in the previous chapter how God might be conceived of as communicating God's purposes and intentions to human beings who are part of and immersed in a world increasingly understood from the perspectives of the sciences. We therefore have every reason to take with the utmost seriousness that 'long search'[198] by humanity for wisdom about their nature and true destiny which is represented in the religious traditions. Moreover, if God is a self-communicating God (as we have earlier argued[199]) who penetrates all-that-is to convey meaning and intelligibility to human beings, then we have to reckon with the outreach of God *to* humanity and the meanings to and for humanity that God is conveying. After all, if God created us, God must be presumed to know what he wants to make of us. Indeed, since the signals concerning human fruition and consummation that come from scientific study of the natural, including the human, world are both ambiguous and indicative of danger-

ous possibilities, especially in an age of environmental degradation and nuclear hazard, we would be wise to examine what *God*
may have been communicating to humanity concerning its
fruition, consummation and even perfectibility. It might even be
that human personhood, nurtured by the natural order for this
very purpose, can only come to be what the divine purpose has
intended all along for it, if and when *God*, God's own self, comes to
human beings to bring them to the fruition of a humanity taken
up into the divine. To explore the possibility of and any evidence
for such an outreach of God to humanity must therefore be our
next concern.

CHAPTER 13

The Long Search[1] and Jesus of Nazareth

1 INTRODUCTION

We saw, at the end of chapter 11, that our understanding of the way God interacts with the world, as it is described by the sciences, was coherent with the notion that God could communicate to humanity in the world in and through events or patterns of events, including mental events occurring in the human brain. On this basis one could ground the hope that God might communicate God's own meanings and indeed his very presence to that part of the created order capable of discerning his meanings and responding personally to his presence, namely human beings.

In the following chapter (12), we explored the many-levelled nature of human being which the sciences now disclose. This implied that any development of human nature, of human 'being' – any realizable process of human 'becoming' – to be truly fulfilling, nurturing and conducive to the full flourishing of humanity would need to occur so as to penetrate to all levels in that complex which is the individual human being in society. This scientific perspective also hinted that a transformation of human being, that a new realization of human potentiality, was needed to counter the dis-ease of humanity, its inner disturbances and widely felt lack of 'fit' and harmony with its environment. This 'environment', it transpired from the signals concerning the human condition coming *inter alia* from the literature of our times,[2] extended beyond the biological, personal and social to that circumambient, creative and creating, transcendent yet immanent, Reality we have named as 'God'. That is – to speak more generally – we have to recognize, with John Macquarrie,[3] that 'the most profound anthropologies of modern times, both religious and secular have made the idea of transcendence central to their understanding of the human condition, and . . . there would be great difficulty in saying where the limits of human trans-cendence[4] lie'. This all points to the need for a profound trans-formation of human being that would involve an opening up of human existence to the transcendent in its 'environment', in the above sense, in a way that was unifying and integrative for mutual human relations and those to nature and to God.[5] Any discernment of how this need might be satisfied involves answer-ing two interlocking questions.

The first is about the direction that the 'becoming' of humanity should take – what *should* humanity become? The well-trod path of the discussion on 'natural law' leads to the recognition that 'certain basic characteristics [are] written into the context of human life which mean we cannot simply make of it whatever we choose'.[6] Yet 'Even if man's being provides the *basis* for the norms of his becoming, it should not be understood to prescribe the precise form that the becoming should take'.[7] 'Evolutionary ethics' – the attempt to read off ethical norms for humanity from the direction of change in biological, including human, evolution – is but a particular example of this kind of attempt to decide what *ought* to be the case from what *is*. It has been widely regarded by moral philosophers as generally unsuccessful, although it has to be recognized that there is certainly need for a more adequate recognition of the biological, and so evolutionary, basis for more of human behaviour than it has been customary to assume, both in moral philosophy and in moral theology.[8] For example, any postulate concerning the direction of the road along which humanity ought to travel, any putative hypothesis about human becoming, will now have to take into account the many-levelled nature of the human person which the sciences indicate. However, the question remains, 'What *should* humanity become?' and it is clearly not going to be answered from within the purview of the sciences as such. (It will be our concern in a later chapter (15)).

The second question is: what is that 'environment' of humanity with which it needs to be in harmony, to which it needs to be adapted? We have suggested above that *this* 'environment' extends 'beyond the biological, personal and social to that circumambient, creative and creating, transcendent but imma-nent, Reality we have named as "God"'.[9] If that is so, then our con-ceptions of the nature of God, of God's being and becoming, and

God's relation to and interaction with the world in general – as we have developed them in Part II – will be relevant to and shape any putative response to the question of human becoming.[10]

If God is indeed that ultimate 'environment' in which humanity is set and to which it needs to relate, there would appear to be two means whereby the answers to both these questions might be forthcoming: human search for intelligibility and meaning; and/or self-communication ('revelation') from God. The religious quest of humanity, its 'long search', may be regarded as constituting the first, though this does not rule out the possibility that the world religions might also include revelations from God. (This is the concern of the following section, 2).

With respect to the second, God's self-communication, it has already been urged[11] that any a re-formation of the human condition which could really be a profound transformation of human being would involve an opening up of human existence to the transcendent in its environment (in the broad sense in which we are using this term) in a way that was unifying and integrative for human relations: to each other, to nature and to God. *A priori* this seems unlikely of achievement by human beings themselves and to require some new creative initiative of God. That is, any self-communication, any 'revelation', or outreach of God to humanity needs to be, in the widest sense of the word, also salvific. If there were to be such a revelatory and salvific initiative from God, it would have to be of a kind that would operate within all the multiple levels that constitute the human person – for they all interact with each other and with the 'environment' in the life of that unique creature, *homo sapiens*.

So we find ourselves asking again[12] if there is any evidence that there has been any self-communication, any outreach of God to humanity to actualize that flourishing and consummation of human potentiality which humanity seems incapable of accomplishing alone and unaided. The evidence for the Christian claim in this regard will be the concern of the last section (3) of this chapter. (The following chapter (14) will consider its content and the one after (15) its implications for human becoming).

Before we embark on considering the two routes, – roughly speaking, from humanity to God and from God to humanity – it is worth noting that they constitute a reciprocal dynamic which may be overlooked in so distinguishing them. For they are two modalities of one unitary process in which human beings and God

can come into relation, can encounter each other. This feature of
the interaction is implicit in two well-known models, or images,[13]
within the Christian tradition for this mutual communication
between God and humanity, namely the concepts of God as 'Spirit'
and of God as 'Word', or *Logos*. Both refer to an all-pervasive
outreach into and presence of God in the world that is matched
and responded to by an inner movement within the hearts and
minds of human beings which is itself stimulated by that very
same movement of God into humanity.[14] God as 'Spirit' is
regarded as present in and to all-that-is but as especially
vitalizing and informing humanity at the deepest levels of the
human psyche and consciousness so that human beings are
enabled to respond to God as thus present. The *Logos*, the 'word' of
the prologue to the Gospel of John, is regarded as the very self-
expression of God which exists eternally as a mode of God's own
being as Creator and is the Source and Sustainer of all that is
created. It seems to be[15] a conflation of the, largely Hebraic,
concept of 'the word of the Lord', as the will of God in creative
activity, with the divine *logos* of Stoic thought which is the
principle of rationality as both manifest in the cosmos and in the
human reason (also *logos*). Both of these concepts of the 'Spirit'
and the 'Word' of God involve a reciprocity of interaction between
God and humanity – a matching human response being elicited,
but not compelled, by an activity of God in which God has taken
the initiative.

2 THE RELIGIOUS QUEST

We saw, towards the end of the previous chapter, that the
religious consciousness of humanity – that individual and corporate 'deep awareness of a benevolent non-physical power which
appears to be partly or wholly beyond, and far greater than, the
individual self'[16] – has played, and still plays, a crucial role in
providing individuals and societies with values and hopes that
transcend their times and their commitment to their genetic kin.
The existence of this widespread religious consciousness of
humanity and the reasons we adduced to encourage us to look for
an outreach of God in and to humanity together combine to
focus our attention on the religions of humanity as sources from
which might flow the knowledge and experience requisite for the
flourishing of human beings and the actualization of their

potentialities in their mutual relations and those to nature and God.[17]

The 'long search' of humanity in the major religions has been exercised with extraordinary vitality, ingenuity and richness of expression. This quest for meaning and intelligibility has led the vast majority of mankind to locate this in some transcendent/ immanent non-human mode of Being, variously named in the religions of the world. Adherents of these religions would regard their long search as not having been in vain. Many have followed Karl Jaspers[18] in distinguishing an 'axial period' *c.*800–200 BCE when, in the three culturally disconnected areas of the Chinese, Indian and Mediterranean peoples, there was a genuine expansion of human consciousness beyond the confines of the ancient civilizations which had gone before and been based on the river valleys of the Yellow River, the Indus and the Nile and Mesopotamia:

> What is new about this age, in all three areas of the world, is that man becomes conscious of Being as a whole, of himself and his limitations. He experiences the terror of the world and his own powerlessness. He asks radical questions. Face to face with the void he strives for liberation and redemption. By consciously recognizing his limits he sets himself the highest goals. He experiences absoluteness in the depths of selfhood and in the lucidity of transcendence . . . In this age were born the fundamental categories within which we still think today, and the beginnings of the world religions, by which human beings still live, were created. The step into universality was taken in every sense.[19]

In Western civilization (European, North American and related cultures) we stand on a road that leads from the merger of two of the trails started in this axial period in its Mediterranean manifestation – those of Greece, partly transmitted via Rome, and those of ancient Israel, as transmitted and transmuted by two thousand years of Christian interpretation and expansion. This double heritage, although now compounded with that scientific culture with whose impact on theology we are concerned, has shaped our language, art, literature, ethics, institutions and indeed science itself. It has made us Westerners the people we are and provides the principal cultural resources which we have to hand to express, articulate and formulate those intimations which have motivated that 'long search' which we share with humanity in general. But it would take a lifetime of immersion into the culture and languages of the Far East to get under the skin of, say, Buddhism or the religions of India in order for them really to come alive for us and to speak to us at all levels of our psyches and intellects, moulded as we are by this Western heritage, sympathetic and open to the insights of other cultures though we must strive to be.

Hence, when we 'Westerners' ask the crucial question of the long search, 'What can we know of God's meaning for humanity in this our culture?' we are compelled by our own history to recognize that, unique among the formative influences in *our* culture, and uniquely challenging in his person and teaching, there stands the figure of Jesus of Nazareth, however much his image may have been distorted by his professed followers. For us in 'Western' society, the figure of Jesus Christ poses a basic challenge concerning the nature and purposes of God. Being members of *this* society, and not of some other, we cannot avoid asking whether this challenge is weighty and cogent enough to be credible and coherent. The challenge, as I have expressed it elsewhere, is: 'the effect of the brief life and death of this obscure Jew, Jesus, of no distinguished parentage, in a backwater of the Roman Empire, produced an effect, first on his disciples and then on his culture, which resulted from focussing primarily on his person, and only secondarily on his teaching, and which was of a magnitude and quality that requires explanation.'[20]

However weary we may be of all that claims the adjective of 'Christian' in our society, the person of Jesus still constitutes a pivotal reference point for any Westerner seeking the meaning that God has written into the world. More particularly, we have recognized that humanity is a creature whose essence is paradoxically to be always in the mode of becoming. But we have, so far, not been able to discern the direction this 'becoming' ought to take. It is to such discernment that the nature and content of the Christian claim is supremely relevant. It is based on the belief that human beings have the potentiality of being in the image and likeness of God, but that this potentiality is not yet realized, for the image and likeness of God in humanity is incomplete, unfinished, still being formed ('defaced' is the traditional word).[21] Thus, as John Macquarrie puts it:

If then there ever came into existence a human being in whom that image was not defaced but manifested its fullness, would not that human being, precisely by being fully human, be God's existence into the world, so far as the divine can become manifest on the finite level? . . . we are talking only of possibility – the possibility of a being both human and divine. It seems to me that given the plasticity of the human being, the affinity of that being to God, and the capacity of that being for transcendence, then one can affirm that the possibility of a God-man is a real possibility within what we know of the conditions of existence in this world.[22]

The question is, then, whether or not this possibility has been actualized in Jesus of Nazareth that is, whether or not there has been a definitive revelation of God to humanity in the historical person of Jesus and in experiences centred on him. This must now be examined and interpreted in the light of that theology which we have been attempting to develop as consonant with scientific perspectives on the world.

3 WHO IS JESUS OF NAZARETH?

Anyone facing up to this question and its implications (e.g., how is he relevant to the relation of God and humanity?), if he or she is to have any intellectual integrity and so any grounds for addressing both the 'cultured despisers' of the Christian faith and the many wistful agnostics of our times, has to take into account the intensive research and scholarship which, for the last century and a half, has been invested in the study of the origins of Christianity and the person of Jesus. This result of the Enlightenment is irreversible and should be welcomed by Christian believers, for the critical pursuit of truth has priority over all other considerations with respect to the content of all our most cherished beliefs, religious or otherwise.

It is increasingly difficult for the non-expert to be well-enough informed to make judgments on many questions concerning biblical history and its associated belief-systems, particularly with regard to the New Testament – the most intensively and critically examined of the whole corpus of sacred literature. Similar remarks apply, of course, to the non-scientist confronted with the burgeoning fruits of the scientific enterprise. In both situations, the 'lay' person has to rely on the experts and try to judge where there is accord and where not. Unlike science, however, which has a much more agreed methodology for arriving at inter-subjective consent (and, it must be said, a subject matter more amenable to agreement between the immense variety of human beings), historical judgments, in general, and especially those concerned with the origins of Christianity, are fraught with ideological traps which can ensnare even the most impartial in their own pre-suppositions. The non-experts have to make their judgments on the basis both of what they can discern, on the one hand, of the arguments and evidence presented by contending historians and biblical scholars and, on the other, by their assessment of the experts' impartiality and frankness about the pre-suppositions which shape their individual inquiries and conclusions.

The literature on the New Testament and the person of Jesus is, of course, vast and even the expert can have read only a fraction. Fortunately there are reliable and careful guides[23] to help us in the task of coming to a judgment about the person of Jesus of Nazareth who is so central to our cultural and religious experience in the West – and increasingly in other cultures. We have to try to find ways of steering between the Scylla of a 'biblicism' that underestimates the nature of the ancient literature from a strange culture (not to mention the fundamentalism that woodenly takes the whole library of the biblical corpus to be literally true in every respect); and the Charybdis of a scepticism that is excessive in relation to the prevailing canons of historical judgment and literary criticism of ancient sources. When the experts disagree, which is very often on detailed exegesis, one can but take note and rely on the kind of common sense we employ when we make those judgments which determine our personal actions. Often these judgments do not have cast-iron evidence to warrant them, yet they nevertheless can be to all intents and purposes certain enough for practical action. Indeed, 'to us, probability is the very guide of life',[24] as the redoubtable Bishop Joseph Butler long since stressed. Probability can likewise be the best guide in the judgment that this inquiry necessitates.

It is from such considerations that I find myself inclined to what John Bowden,[25] following John Knox,[26] has called an *a priori* more 'trusting' attitude to the scriptures than his own *a priori* more 'sceptical' stance. This distinction of Bowden and Knox does not refer to the use of different evidence or even to interpreting it differently but to a difference 'in basic conception as to where the burden of proof lies and therefore of what is required as evidence'.[27] This may be a matter of temperament, but I myself incline to the more 'trusting' position advocated by A. E. Harvey:

It may be true that, in the light of modern critical study, there is virtually no single report of any of the words and deeds of Jesus of which we can be certain, and there is indeed quite a large number of them which are likely to be either fictitious or fashioned by the tradition into something very different from the original. But it does not follow from this that we can know nothing for certain about Jesus.[28]

He goes on to draw a parallel, rather along the lines of Bishop Butler, with the way we make judgments about people, especially those we already have good grounds for respecting. He continues,

And so it is in modern New Testament study. Attention has moved away from establishing the truth or falsity of any particular report about Jesus, and is now directed more towards the impression made by the narrative as a whole . . . The Jesus who emerges from their [the writers of the Gospels] accounts has both originality and consistency . . . Unless these authors were the most consummate and imaginative artists, able to create a striking and consistent character out of scanty and unreliable sources, we have every reason to think that, in broad outline (whatever may be the case with some of the details) the Jesus whom they portray is the Jesus who actually existed. To this extent, no New Testament scholar today would be prepared to say that we can know nothing for certain about Jesus.[29]

As is inevitable with all such purely historical matters of so long ago, *absolute* certainty eludes us and we have to recognize, with Bowden,[30] that we may often have to say 'In the end, we do not *know*', with regard to some particular assertion about the person, sayings and actions of Jesus of Nazareth. Nevertheless, following the principle of Bishop Butler, it seems much more probable that the light refracted through the no doubt distorting lenses of the Gospels (and of Paul) can help us to delineate the significant features of the apparently striking character of Jesus than it would be to assume that, suddenly in the latter half of the first century, four 'consummate and imaginative artists' appeared as it were *de novo* and simply thought up this character – so that their stories cannot be sifted and analysed now to give us any significant data about him.

The crux of the problem is, of course, in that word 'significant'. D. E. Nineham[31] has argued that the evidence of the Gospels is insufficient on many matters that would be deemed as significant[32] in any assessment of Jesus. One thinks of Jesus' supposed sinlessness, or moral 'perfection', his messianic consciousness, the closeness of his relation to God as his 'Father', and so on. Any assessments of these features of the historical Jesus will inevitably be in dispute, and we shall have much need of Butler's advice! In the following I can but set out some basic conclusions of New Testament scholarship which, listening to the experts, appear to me (and I would hope to others striving to be objective) to be sufficiently reliable to be relevant to the question at the head of this section. They will constitute for us the pieces of a jigsaw in which putatively we seek to detect any pattern of meaning through which God may be seen to have been communicating God's own self to humanity.

a Historical Foundations

'What can we really know about Jesus?' is the title of a chapter in John Bowden's *Jesus: the Unanswered Questions*[33] and he points us to what is widely agreed as one of the best modern books about Jesus, namely the historical treatment of E. P. Sanders.[34] In his Introduction to that book, Sanders lists several features, excluding sayings, about Jesus' career and its aftermath which 'can be known beyond doubt', for which 'the evidence is most secure'. They are, roughly in chronological order:

> 1. Jesus was baptized by John the Baptist. 2. Jesus was a Galilean who preached and healed. 3. Jesus called disciples and spoke of there being twelve. 4. Jesus confined his activity to Israel. 5. Jesus engaged in a controversy about the temple. 6. Jesus was crucified outside Jerusalem by the Roman authorities. 7. After his death Jesus' followers continued as an identifiable movement. 8. At least some Jews persecuted at least parts of the new movement (Gal. 1.13, 22; Phil. 3.6.), and it appears that this persecution endured at least to a time near the end of Paul's career (II Cor. 11.24; Gal. 5.11; 6.12; cf. Matt. 23.34; 10.17).[35]

Such a list is intended to present only the barest outlines of what can reliably be known about Jesus. Additionally, some authors stress what they regard as the special character of his death,[36] but that can be disputed in view of the many crucifixions that characterized the times.

There is considerable concord between the various summaries[37] of the basic 'facts' about Jesus, but they scarcely amount yet to the 'Christ of faith'. A. E. Harvey can affirm that '. . . New Testament scholars themselves (who tend to be the severest critics of their own methods) no longer regard all information offered by the Gospels as in principle untrustworthy'.[38] He goes on to describe the general assent among these scholars to one of the criteria enabling them to distinguish between material which is likely to be derived from Jesus and that which may have originated in the early church, namely:

> the sheer consistency and originality of the broad outlines of the portrait of Jesus as they emerge from the entire gospel tradition. Material which has this recurring and characteristic quality[39] . . . can be confidently regarded as having considerable historical reliability.[40]

As G. N. Stanton has put it, towards the end of his carefully objective examination of the four Gospels,

> We have seen that while certainty often eludes us, we do know a good deal about Jesus of Nazareth . . . Historians, whether Christian or not, are able to confirm that Jesus did exist and that the evangelists' portraits, for all their differences, are not wholly misleading.[41]

b Jesus' Mission, Teaching and Relation to God

At the end[42] of his impressive and astringent study, E. P. Sanders sums up his conclusions concerning the mission and teaching of Jesus, particularly in relation to the context of first-century Judaism, by placing them on a scale of degree of certainty. He concludes that *'certain or virtually certain'* are:

1. Jesus shared the world-view of 'Jewish restoration eschatology' – the expectation that Israel would be restored.[43] The key facts are his start under John the Baptist, his expectation of a new (or at least a renewed) temple, and the eschatological setting of the work of the apostles. 2. He preached the kingdom of God.[44] 3. He promised the kingdom to the wicked. 4. He did not explicitly oppose the law, particularly laws relating to Sabbath and food. 5. Neither he nor his disciples thought that the kingdom would be established by force of arms. They looked for an eschatological miracle.

Sanders concludes as *'highly probable'*: 1. The kingdom which Jesus expected would have some analogies with this world: leaders, the twelve tribes, a functioning temple. 2. Jesus' disciples thought of him as 'king', and he accepted the role, either implicitly or explicitly.

Sanders' *'probable'* list is: 1. Jesus thought that the wicked who accepted his message would share in the kingdom even though they did not do the things customary in Judaism for the atonement of sin. 2. He did not emphasize the national character of the kingdom, including judgment by groups and a call for mass repentance, because that had been the task of John the Baptist, whose work he accepted. 3. Jesus spoke about the kingdom in different contexts, and he did not always use the word with precisely the same meaning.[45]

Similarly Rowland, in concord with innumerable other New Testament scholars, locates 'the main thrust of Jesus' message and work in the proclamation of the imminent reign of God [that is, of the kingdom of God]'.[46] He also, with others, stresses that there is an implicit claim in Jesus' proclamation of the imminence of the kingdom, about the importance of Jesus' own person in the divine economy. So that

> even if we consider that the titles [e.g., as the Prophet, the Son of God, Messiah, the Son of Man] which are used of Jesus in the Gospels reflect the beliefs of the early Church rather than the mind of Jesus himself, it should not cause us any surprise that the character of his preaching caused his followers to make such claims about him . . . Jesus' activities in claiming to forgive sins (Mark 2.6f.), his teaching with authority (Mark 1.22), his conviction that God had sent him (Luke 10.16; cf. John 7.16 . . .) all point to a claim of ultimate significance.[47]

This, at least implicit, identification of Jesus' own presence as a sign of the initiation by God of his imminent kingdom, the authority of his teachings, as well as many smaller features of his life, point to Jesus having a special relationship with God which was intense and intimate. This relation is sometimes described (e.g., in *Matt.* 11.25 and parallels and *John* 5.19ff.) in terms of that between a father and son[48] and is 'a way of speaking about the intimacy of relationship, which enables such a unity of will between Jesus and God in the fulfilment of the divine purposes'.[49] We could say, in our terms, that he was exceptionally 'open' to God – 'the way in which Jesus speaks of God as Father certainly indicates that he claimed a special relationship to God'.[50]

Since 'sin' is theologically the state of alienation and separation from God, then the absence of sin must mean harmony with, openness to, God. It is this which characterizes the earthly Jesus according to the above judgments.[51] With respect to Jesus' moral character, there does, in fact, seem to be good evidence, in the tradition, of his moral sensitivity and perception; and his teaching concerning human relationships still has in its total impact a pungency and incisive power which can cut deeply into the conscience of even modern readers of the Gospels. Thus Bernard Levin, an avowedly non-Christian, could write, in relation to a projected 'biography' of Jesus, 'Is not the nature of Christ, in the words of the New Testament, enough to pierce to the soul anyone with a soul to be pierced? . . . he still looms over the world, his message still clear, his pity still infinite, his consolation still effective, his words still full of glory, wisdom and love'.[52] Of course, no historical evidence could ever establish the negative proposition that he never performed a morally dubious act.[53] Any assertion of Jesus, moral perfection, if it is made at all, could only be regarded as a deduction from beliefs about his person and not as their 'historical' ground.

c Jesus: A Complete Human Being

Since AD 451, the Definition of Chalcedon has been taken as the criterion of orthodoxy and catholicity in the Christian churches with regard to belief about the person of Jesus Christ – even though subsequent reactions to it, especially in the Eastern churches,[54] showed that it had not settled many issues, many of which are still alive today.[55] That Definition, which most churches, certainly in the West, have inherited, affirmed that Jesus was 'complete in regard to his humanity', that is, 'completely human'. This, John Robinson argued,[56] is the sense in which Jesus was a 'perfect man', 'perfect' in the sense of 'complete' – that is, fully human, but not necessarily displaying perfection in all conceivable human characteristics.[57]

For example, he could not be 'completely' human unless he had been an individual of his own times and most New Testament scholars agree that his knowledge was limited in many respects to that of his day.[58] Indeed 'limited' is too cautious a word, for he was probably mistaken about something as important as the timing of his own imminent return and establishing of the kingdom of God, if the Synoptic Gospel accounts are to be believed.[59] These limitations do not derogate at all from Jesus' penetrating, at times devastating, insights into the relations between God and humanity and those between human beings;

and to his manifesting in his life and death what obedience to the call of God involves.

If he was a complete human being, it is proper to ask what his human self-understanding was – the problem of his 'messianic consciousness', as it is usually called. Was he aware of being the 'Christ', the Anointed One, the 'Messiah?' The considered judgment of the majority of New Testament scholars is that the question of Jesus' own *self*-understanding cannot be answered historically in any unambiguous way from the evidence we have. But as R. E. Brown[60] points out 'this [absence of evidence that Jesus claimed the title of "Messiah"] would not necessarily imply that he had no consciousness of a salvific mission to men (the type of mission that the Church called Messiahship when it had reinterpreted that term in a spiritual way)'.[61] As regards the title 'Son of God', he notes that:

> it would have taken Jesus time to formulate concepts, and he might have found some of the concepts of his day inadequate to express what he wanted to say. One would then say that his knowledge was limited, but such limitation would not at all exclude an intuitive *consciousness* of a unique relationship to God and of a unique mission to men.[62]

He regards 'the way in which Jesus speaks of God as Father indicates he claimed a special relationship to God'.[63]

Thus, particular and individual as he is, and unique as he continues to be in his impact, these considerations, taken in conjunction with those in section *a*, strongly support our starting any assessment of Jesus on the basis of his being completely a human being, that is, a 'complete human being', albeit with a very special vocation and relation to God. However, this starting point is called into question by the assertion in the traditions about Jesus that there were acts of his and events associated with him that have a 'supernatural' connotation: I refer to the supposed 'miracles', both those which Jesus is said to have performed and those connected with his person. Any theology for a scientific age must come to terms with these accounts in the tradition, for they stand as a barrier to belief for many.

d Jesus' 'Miracles'

Earlier we pointed out[64] that judgments concerning the occurrence of a 'miracle', regarded as an event interpreted as 'not fully explicable by naturalistic means', would depend on 'one's *a priori* attitudes towards the very possibility of such events occurring in principle; and additionally, for the theist, on whether or not the claimed miracle is generally consistent with one's understanding of the nature of God and of his purposes for the world and for humanity'. The very width of the range of natural phenomena – physical, biological, psychological and social – over which the sciences have been able to observe regular patterns of events in intelligible relationships has inevitably enhanced scepticism about the occurrence of 'miracles',[65] in the sense defined at the beginning of this paragraph. At the same time the extent and quality of the historical evidence needed to attest their occurrence has come under the scrutiny of New Testament scholarship which has shown how the Gospel narratives have been shaped, biassed even, by the particular purposes of their authors.

Furthermore, our understanding of the nature of God, of the mode of God's interaction with the world, and indeed of God's purposes for the world and for humanity, are all deeply influenced by our new knowledge of that world which the sciences have afforded, along the lines we have been developing.[66] This means that there are now strong *theological* objections to the idea of a God who intervenes in and manipulates the world in ways that would disrupt the very fabric of relationships through which God is sustaining the world in being and continuing to create in and through it in its processes of becoming. The concepts of God and of God's interaction with the world must be coherent and God must be conceived to act consistently with God's own inferred nature and character. The really difficult question concerning 'miracles' is, of course, as C. F. D. Moule has put it, 'Within what bounds, and on what level, do we look for consistency, and how far is that consistency determinative in our judgment?'[67] On the one hand, consistency with already known regularities ('laws', even) could be too restrictive a straitjacket by assuming *all* such regularities were fully understood with respect to their boundary conditions and that no new regimes could exist, or no other determining factors could ever be operative in any particular historical situation. On the other hand, it must be taken into account that, even if God could in theory set aside any regularity or law of the created natural order at any time,[68] the whole edifice of theism in the Judeo-Christian tradition is constructed, at least for twentieth-century Christians in a scientific world, on the foundation of the experienced intelligibility and rationality of the world as indicative of the existence and nature of its Creator and that God the Creator has limited God's own self by giving the creation its autonomous, orderly existence.

This is basic to any coherent notion of a creator God and so, now for theological reasons, increases the onus on any historical evidence to convince one that any supposed intervention by God to perform a 'miracle' has actually occurred – including those associated with Jesus. 'Miracle' is still here being taken as an event 'not fully explicable by naturalistic means' because not only is this the most commonly assumed sense of the term but also because it is the sense which, in a scientific age, creates problems for belief. When the word is used in the sense of *miraculum*, a wonder, or of a 'sign' (in the general sense of St John's Gospel[69]) to refer to events or clusters of events in which God reveals himself, then no disruption of the natural order need be involved or implied and no problems arise for theology in a scientific age.[70] It will be a matter for judgment on the New Testament narratives where on a scale running between these two categories of interpretation – 'miracle' as not fully explicable by natural means to miracle as natural, yet revelatory, event – any particular 'miracle' story lies. These considerations will have to be borne in mind in any appraisal of narratives of 'miracles' said to be performed by Jesus to see if these justify any assertion about him which suggests that he was in some sense 'more than' human, while still being undoubtedly and completely human.

For our present purposes, it is useful to distinguish within the Gospel narratives two groups of miracles described as *performed by* Jesus: (1) 'miracles' of healing and exorcism; (2) 'nature miracles'. (Other 'miracle' stories which concern the person of Jesus will be discussed in the following sub-section (*e*)). It is impossible to examine (1) and (2) in any proper detail here. But it will be necessary at least to indicate what is a reasonable general judgment, in the light of our current scientific and historical knowledge, on these different kinds of 'miracle' story to see if they are relevant to any appraisal of the significance of Jesus for the relation of God and humanity.[71] We shall have to make clear the presuppositions which we today consider reasonable to bring to bear on these two groups of 'miracle' stories in order to gauge the degree of historical validation needed to warrant belief in their actual occurrence. In the light of this, the broad, but not (here) detailed, character of the available historical evidence will then have to be assessed to judge their significance for the relevance of Jesus in the 'long search'. Clearly in the present context all that is possible is only an outline of an informed response, bearing in mind our aim of constructing a theology believable in a scientific age. Such judgments have to depend on assessing what appears to be the drift of New Testament scholarship on the role of the narratives of 'miracles' in the Gospels, in particular. As before, one can but attend to the New Testament scholars[72] while making one's own judgments based on presuppositions defensible in a scientific age.

'Miracles' of healing and/or 'exorcism' recorded in the New Testament have the feature that they are not unlike events which still occur today. For there appears to be a non-eliminable residue of reliable reports of irreversible cures of organic diseases which are unexpected on the basis of the probable prognoses of medical science. Such prognoses can never be better than probable – given the complexity of many ailments – so that the chance of spontaneous recovery is never entirely ruled out by medicine. In many such cases there is a strong psychological component in the recovery and our ignorance of psychosomatic relationships is widely admitted. Hence there is no impediment to our concluding that a strong, authoritative, charismatic personality, such as Jesus undoubtedly was, could be the proximate agent initiating healing processes. Similarly, the not infrequent success of 'exorcisms' today does not so much validate the existence of a demonic world as stress the necessity for any 'exorcist' to accommodate themselves to the thought-world and convictions of the sick person that they are possessed by an external agent (a 'demon', 'devil', or whatever). Again the success of the 'exorcisms' performed by Jesus can be attributed to the strength of his personality and his sharing with the 'possessed' the general first-century belief in the existence of a demon world.

Hence the threshold of scepticism, even in a scientific age, to the possibility of sudden healings (including 'exorcisms') under these special kind of circumstances is relatively low. The relevant historical evidence that Jesus performed such healings and 'exorcisms' is correspondingly strong – at least as good as for the content of his teaching.[73] Other miracle-workers in the first century have been reported who were also believed to have performed wonder-generating acts (including the cure of diseases and rain-making!). Thus Harvey:

> It is true that Jesus by no means stands alone in his time and his culture as a doer of miraculous works; one of his own sayings acknowledges that there were other exorcists at work (Mt. 12.27) and stories are told of rabbis and charismatic teachers in Palestine, as well as of pagan wonder-workers in other lands, which are no less sensational than those told of Jesus.[74]

But

> the tradition of Jesus' miracles has too many unusual features to be conveniently ascribed to conventional legend-mongering ... many of them contain details of precise reporting which is quite unlike the usual run of legends and is difficult to explain unless it derives from some historical recollection.[75]

None of this means, of course, that we must accept all the 'miracle' stories in the Gospels, lock, stock and barrel. Each will have to be weighed by accepted criteria of exegesis which allow for the growth of legend, mis-recollection, re-telling for different purposes, subsumption into a symbolic theme or action, and so on. 'But even when a number has been excluded for these reasons we shall be left with a substantial body of material which belongs peculiarly to Jesus, which has no parallel in the ancient world, and which at the very least testifies to the surprise and wonder which he evoked on many occasions.'[76]

Thus, as a general category,[77] group (1) of the 'miracle' stories about Jesus gives rise to no special difficulty – even for a scientific age. This is certainly not the case with the second kind of 'miracle' supposed to have been performed by Jesus –

'Nature miracles' refers to those narratives in the New Testament,[78] other than healings/exorcisms, according to which events occurred that were, and still are, 'not fully explicable by naturalistic means'. These events are reported as infringing quite commonly observed regularities and stabilities – infringements of laws and regularities that are rendered even more improbable when the underlying scientific principles are explicated (namely those concerned with, for example, the laws of gravity, the conservation of matter, the stability of certain kinds of matter (water, bread, the constituents of wine), the irreversibility of biological death). So we properly approach these narratives with a

high degree of scepticism on account of both first- and twentieth-century experience of the natural world. This is compounded by theological doubts as to their validity for the reasons already adduced, namely their apparent assumption of an 'intervening' God. Furthermore, in several cases the Gospel narratives, especially those in the fourth one, carry a heavy loading of symbolic reference[79] which cannot but suggest that the evangelists were less interested in the historicity of their tales (a very post-Enlightenment pre-occupation) than in conveying insights into the significance of Jesus, of his actions and of the reactions to him. Even the apparently realistic story in the fourth Gospel of the raising of Lazarus is closely interwoven with dialogue about the relation of Jesus to the believer 'in such a way that death cannot separate them'.[80] This leaves us uncertain as to whether or not the story was ever *meant* as history in our sense. Most of these Gospel narratives, no doubt selected from many others, have a setting in which a particular point is being made about the role and ministry of Jesus and the character of his interactions with various kinds of people.

Some 'nature miracle' stories seem frankly legendary, for example, the coin conveniently found in the fish's mouth enabling Jesus to pay his temple tax! Others (like the raisings from the dead in the Synoptic Gospels) stand starkly there in the text as one-off narratives, with no other means of corroboration of an event which is so improbable on the reasonable presuppositions we have already made. One can only honestly return a *historical* verdict of 'unproven', even 'incredible'.

The 'nature miracles', therefore, are not convincing as accounts of 'what actually happened', which indeed we can never know for certain, and are included as narratives in the Gospels to convey a significance which the author wishes to attribute to some particular aspect of Jesus' ministry. In the case of the 'nature miracles' the probabilities are stacked against their historicity. All we *can* say is that, whatever did happen and, more pertinently, how it was recalled much later, constituted part of what the first-century readers of the Gospels would regard as confirmatory of the significance of Jesus for them, however problematic these stories may be for us now. We read these narratives to inform us of the reaction of these writers and readers to Jesus, but we cannot now call upon them as evidence for *us* of any special significance of Jesus, especially in the light of the tendency to attribute such wonder-working to charismatic figures of the first century. Such attribution of itself does, of course, confirm that he *was* such a figure for them and this perception of Jesus' contemporaries is at least one element in the jigsaw, whose existence and pattern we are examining. However there is another group of 'miracle' narratives relevant to any assessment of the significance of Jesus for today of which we must take serious account. They are:

e 'Miracles' Connected with the Person of Jesus

The two which occur *within* Jesus' life are stories of unusual events which appear to involve an inner (psychological/spiritual) experience, in the one case, of Jesus himself with respect to his vocation (his baptism[81]); and, in the other, of three of the disciples, with respect to their apprehension of the nature of Jesus' person (the transfiguration[82]). As reported, these stories include features and hints of much symbolic significance for a first-century Jewish reader. I can but refer the present reader to the commentaries, but for our present purposes it is, again, important to note that we have only these accounts and cannot know 'what happened' in any objective sense. However, it is clear that the story of Jesus' baptism, in its various forms, conveys convincingly the sense of a turning point in Jesus' own apprehension of his relation to God and of his mission, and the description of the event, with its various symbolisms, are an understandable reinforcing of this central theme and present no special problems, even in this scientific age. In the case of the transfiguration,[83] it is the disciples' apprehension of the ultimate significance of Jesus that is the main theme of the narratives, which are again stamped in their form with symbols meaningful to the disciples and to first-century Jewish readers. These accounts of their experience need cause us today no more difficulty that those of many other 'visionary' experiences, which always display the marks of the cultural and religious background of those having them. It seems to me that these two groups of narratives inform us of moments of spiritual insight for Jesus and for the disciples, respectively, couched in terms intelligible and meaningful in their own time. As such they must be taken as genuine evidence for the state of mind of Jesus and of the disciples' reaction to him. The issues which are raised by the narratives which describe 'miracles' connected with his birth and death, the 'virginal conception' and the 'resurrection', are of greater significance for our inquiry and merit separate treatment.

Jesus' Birth. The birth narratives in the early chapters of the Gospels of Matthew and Luke[84] have provided the principal basis for the belief that Jesus was born of his mother Mary, betrothed and later married to Joseph, without the agency of a human father, that is by the direct action of God (as 'the Holy Spirit').[85] The two Gospel narratives have been intensively studied in relation to both their historicity and symbolism[86] and to this we shall have to revert. Before doing so, it is pertinent to stress the particular issues raised by our scientific knowledge in relation to the very notion of a 'virginal conception' of Jesus – commonly called the 'virgin birth', although it is really the nature of Jesus' beginning as a living being that is involved. It is with respect to this that modern biological science poses some hard questions.

The relevant facts, determined by the biology of the last one hundred and fifty years, are as follows. Any complete human being begins life by the union of an ovum from a female human being and a spermatozoon from a male one. The sex of the fertilized ovum, and so of the baby that is born, is determined by a particular pair of chromosomes present in all the ordinary (somatic) cells of human beings – those in females being both of the same type denoted as X (so XX), and those in males being different, one X and the other of type Y (so XY). These pairs of chromosomes carry in their DNA genes for various character-istics, as do the other twenty-two pairs of chromosomes in somatic cells that do not differ in kind from male to female. In the formation of ova and spermatozoa ordinary, somatic cells split so that the members of the various pairs of chromosomes separate out into new 'half-cells' (an ovum or a sperm cell) containing one chromosome only of each pair. Human conception begins with the union of two such 'half-cells' one from each parent. The mother *always* contributes an X-type chromosome to this new line of cells while the father contributes *either* an X *or* a Y: if the former, a female combined cell (XX) results; if the latter, a male one (XY). This is how all human beings begin and this is how the sex of the resulting child is determined from its beginning.[87]

For Mary to have been pregnant with the foetus that became Jesus without the involvement of a human father – that is, without a Y chromosome coming from (say) Joseph – there are, biologically only two possibilities. Either (1) Mary provided the ovum which was then transformed by an act of God (impregnation by the Holy Spirit?) into a viable, reproducing cell, as if a sperm had entered the ovum; or (2) there was created such an impregnated ovum within her uterus with no contribution from Mary's own genetic heritage at all.[88]

According to the first possibility for a virginal conception (1), Mary would have contributed an X chromosome to the cells of Jesus but, for Jesus to be male, the Y chromosome (not coming from a human father) would have to have been created *de novo* by God. The X (and other) chromosomes in Jesus' cells would have had, through Mary's genetic predecessors, a particular inheritance as a member of the evolved species *homo sapiens*. But, we cannot avoid asking, what genetic characteristics would be created in Jesus' Y (and other) chromosomes, normally derived from the sperm of a human father? As we saw in the previous chapter, the genetic constitution of a human being is foundational to their humanity and so of their personhood. So, in case (1), really to have been human, Jesus would have to have been provided with an intact created set of human genes, on the Y and other chromosomes. What genetic information was encoded in these miraculously created genes? Did God give him a set to make his characteristics (shape of nose, colour of hair, blood group, etc.) mimic what Joseph *would* have provided had he been involved – or what? Implausible though this all sounds, this possibility at least has the merit of retaining a link of Jesus with humanity through the genetic contribution of Mary.

But even this is precluded by the possibility (2), mooted above, in which Mary is simply a vessel in which is implanted an already fertilized ovum – indeed a kind of surrogate mother.[89] In this case (2), Jesus' entire genetic constitution (carried on the X and Y and all the other chromosomes) would have had to have been created *de novo*. So the question arises *a fortiori*, what genes did God choose to put in the cells from which the embryo of Jesus developed during what is implied, in the two Gospel accounts, to be the normal gestation period? *Could* Jesus then be said to be genuinely human at all if this was his miraculous origin? Or was he just a *copy* of a human being but with all his genetic endowment, and so bodily features, not actually continuous with our evolved nature at all?

To pile Ossa on Pelion, one improbability on another, one has further to recognize what is actually being proposed in either form of the virginal conception in the light of the scientific knowledge we now have of the processes of life. This belief means that God must suddenly have brought into existence either (1) a complete spermatazoon, which then entered an ovum of Mary, or (2) a completely fertilized ovum.[90] Each of these biological entities, especially the second, is an enormously complex system of actual molecules, some very large such as DNA, engaged in dynamic biological activity in an organization as, or rather more, complex than that of any modern factory! This really would be a wonder-working magical kind of act – a 'special creation' *de novo* of exactly the type the so-called 'creationists' argue for – an act producing an entity resembling a human being but not actually sharing in our evolved humanity. Such a being would indeed be a *theios aner*, a 'divine man', which 'was a recognized type in the Hellenistic world, a man whom the gods endowed with superhuman powers'.[91]

Thus the present understanding of the biology of reproduction and of heredity reveals the doctrine of the virginal conception to be postulating an extraordinary, almost magical, divine act of suddenly bringing into existence a complex biological entity. All the evidence is that is *not* how God has created and is creating, as explained in Part I – certainly not the God whose mode of being and becoming we have here been discerning as one in whom it is possible today to believe.

In the light of our biological knowledge it is then impossible to see how Jesus could be said to share our human nature if he came into existence by a virginal conception of the kind traditionally proposed. This means that the doctrine of the virginal conception is also *theologically* inadequate if Jesus is to be relevant to our human destiny.[92] As Macquarrie has expressed it:

> . . . if we suppose Christ to have been conceived and born in an altogether unique way, then it seems we have separated him from the rest of the human race and thereby made him irrelevant to the human quest for salvation or for the true life. We would be saying not that he is the revelation of God shedding light on our darkness, but that he is an altogether unintelligible anomaly, thrust into the middle of history.[93]

Indeed it is now, in the light of the science I have been indicating, actually inconsistent with the doctrine of the incarnation which insists that it is a *complete* human nature that is united with God (as *Logos*, or as 'God the Son'). Jesus must be bone of our bone, flesh of our flesh[94] and DNA of our DNA, DNA from a human father, in order to have any salvific role for humanity. For 'what he has not assumed he has not healed'.[95]

Furthermore, these scientifically-based considerations also now show, in a way which was less obvious before they could be brought to bear on the question, that theologically speaking the doctrine of the virginal conception is actually 'docetic' in its implications.[96] For if Jesus' humanity *was* only apparent, in the biological sense described above, and so not real (indeed artificial, not natural) and if Jesus was, in some way we have yet to consider, also divine, then he would indeed have been 'a divine being . . . dressed up as a man in order to communicate revelations', which is the core of the definition of the heresy of docetism.'[97]

With these considerations in mind, the historical evidence for the virginal conception of Jesus would have to be very strong indeed and it is almost notorious now that it is not so. Indeed even the Roman Catholic scholar Raymond Brown, whose biblical investigations are critical and objective, has concluded that 'the *scientifically controllable* biblical evidence leaves the question of the historicity of the virginal conception unresolved'.[98] By 'scientifically controllable biblical evidence' he quite properly means 'evidence constituted by tradition from identifiable witnesses of the events involved, when that tradition is traceably preserved and not in conflict with other traditions'.[99] Brown's verdict of 'unresolved' would be regarded as over-cautious by other scholars less restrained by traditional dogma. Thus Macquarrie, an Anglican, affirms that '. . . our historical information is negligible . . . apart from . . . scraps of doubtful information, the birth narratives [of Matthew and Luke] are manifestly legendary in character'.[100] And C. J. Cadoux, a Congregationalist, concluded his discussion of the matter thus:

> Nor indeed is it enough for scholars to leave the issue [of the Virginal Conception] open, on the sole ground that the evidence for the miraculous birth is insufficient. If a miracle is asserted to have occurred, and cogent evidence for its occurrence cannot be adduced, and belief in it can be readily accounted for along other lines, the duty of scholars is not to leave the reality of it an open question, but to reject it, not as inconceivable, but as in all probability not true.[101]

With this last statement I concur and, indeed, the improbability of such an event is, I have been arguing, greatly increased in the light of modern biological knowledge. The historical investigations (some points of which are summarized in an endnote[102]) lead implacably to the conclusion that the two birth narratives, which transpire to be the sole evidence for a virginal conception, are best regarded as legendary stories symbolizing *inter alia*[103] that there was a divine initiative conjoined to a human response in the advent of Jesus the Christ.

Briefly, for Jesus to be fully human he had, for both biological and theological reasons, to have a human father as well as a human mother and the weight of the historical evidence strongly indicates that this was so – and that it was Joseph. Any theology for a scientific age which is concerned with the significance of Jesus of Nazareth in the 'long search' now has to start at this point.[104]

The Resurrection/Exaltation of Jesus. The situation with the other significant, postulated 'miracle' concerning the person of Jesus – that complex of events we call his Resurrection (and Ascension or Exaltation)[105] – is quite otherwise. But first we have to ask what is meant by 'resurrection' in the New Testament. According to Pheme Perkins in a carefully balanced study:

> One finds two types of resurrection affirmation [in the New Testament], that of kerygmatic formula (e.g., 1 Cor. 15:3–7; Rm 4:25) and that of the narratives that conclude the gospel accounts. Although the formulae are the oldest witnesses to resurrection belief, one cannot simply derive the later narratives from the earlier formulae. The narratives themselves contain as many points of divergence as they do of similarity. They cannot be treated as fragments of a single account . . . At the level of the gospel narrative, each account may be viewed as an integral conclusion to the story of Jesus as presented by the evangelist. Differences at this level indicate apologetic concerns and show the development of early Christian reflection on resurrection.[106]

Furthermore, the narrative traditions can be divided into those centring on the finding of the empty tomb and others on the appearances of Jesus to his disciples.

> The kerygmatic traditions of I Cor. 15:3–7 refer to appearances but not to the tomb. Each of the three streams of tradition – kerygma, appearance, tomb – has come down to us in a context of further interpretation. In Mark and Luke the finding of the empty tomb provides the occasion for the kerygmatic announcement of the resurrection by an angel. Matthew and

John, on the other hand, know traditions that combine the empty tomb and an appearance of Jesus.[107]

In this case it is not at all clear that the narratives of the 'resurrection' are sensitive to scientific considerations in the way that beliefs concerning Jesus' birth are. The only science which might have any direct bearing by its very nature on the evidence of the disciples' experience of the risen Jesus is that of psychology. But the probability that these diverse experiences of different kinds of people were due to a kind of communal hallucination or psychosis is minimal in the light of the willingness of these same witnesses, and those to whom they communicated their experiences, to suffer and die for their belief – a belief which itself involves the strongest possible ethical commitment to truth and so an onus on the truthfulness of those who hold it.[108]

The evidence is, therefore, that this was a genuine psychological experience, that is, within the consciousness of these witnesses. Note that this would not necessarily imply that they were 'merely' psychological, with no reference to reality, if they can be shown to form part of a meaningful pattern that requires a higher-level autonomous theory to render it intelligible.[109] Just as theories of, say, biology and the neurosciences, cannot be reduced in principle to purely chemical ones (even though chemical processes are the only ones occurring at one level of description in the systems in question), so that realities not present in the separated chemical components have to be depicted as having emerged in these systems[110] – so also a complex of psychological experiences, especially when they are communal, may together manifest a new reality only discernible in that particular complex combination. In the case of the resurrection experiences centred on Jesus, these include: the special character of the life, teaching and death of Jesus; current beliefs concerning resurrection; the transformation of the witnesses; the witnesses' incipient discernment of the presence of God *to* them and so *in* him. The whole complex of experiences to which the New Testament refers generated this new conceptual framework – that of 'resurrection' – to render these experiences intelligible. This concept[111] of 'resurrection' need not be reducible to any purely psychological account and the affirmations of the New Testament that propose this concept can properly be claimed to be referring to a new kind of reality hitherto unknown because not hitherto experienced. Such a proposal is parallel to those whereby emergent realities are apprehended in any hierarchy of complex systems studied by the sciences and so given at least tentative ontological status.[112] In this case the 'complex system' in question was the pattern of events which was a conjunction of all the special, historical circumstances concerning Jesus, including those of the 'resurrection' experiences: in its totality it was historical and particular. Given our understanding of how God interacts with the world and how he can communicate to human beings through meaningful patterns of events, there is every justification for regarding this 'resurrection' of Jesus as resulting from the initiative of God and so as a 'revelation' from God manifesting his purposes and intentions at least with respect to Jesus himself.

Death, the dissolution of the organization of an individual human being, is, of course, a biological event but no one doubts now that Jesus actually died 'under Pontius Pilate'.[113] Biological science unites with common experience to emphasize the irreversibility of death, a process seen in scientific terms as the breakdown of the biological organization of a living human body and the eventually wide dispersal of its atoms and molecules through disintegration and chemical processes of decay. The reversal of these processes of the human body is highly improbable, in any finite time (such as three days) to the point of appearing to be as impossible as breaking the Second Law of Thermodynamics which formalizes such irreversibility in general in natural processes. Moreover, the relevant sciences, we have noted earlier,[114] strongly indicate the psychosomatic unity of the human person. So any general bearing of science on the 'what happened' when Jesus died would, with certain amplifications, be much the same as that of common experience. It is 'what happened' afterwards that is the issue – if that can be discussed as an 'event' at all.

For we have the situation, as Pheme Perkins has put it, that 'resurrection':

> does not have a well-defined conceptual structure . . . On the one hand, transmission of such insights to the present demands more than the mere repetition of the words and images of the New Testament. It requires some explication and perhaps even systematization. On the other hand, resurrection as 'event' can only be understood in metaphorical and mythic categories.[115]

She continues by summarizing some of the central convictions underlying 'resurrection' in the New Testament as:

1. Resurrection implies some unity in the person that does not divide somatic and spiritual . . .
2. This bodily continuity ensures the identity of the exalted Lord with Jesus, who died on the cross. It also can be seen to have significance for the way in which Christians are to understand their bodies (1 Cor. 6:13).
3. Resurrection depends on the perception that the world is not as it appears. God's purposes are being accomplished even in the midst of those evils that appear to thwart them.
4. Resurrection requires some expression of the presence of the power of God in the experience or lives of the believers. The ways in which that presence is expressed is quite varied . . .
5. The experience of presence may take the form of ecstatic spiritual experiences. It may be given shape in the ritual of the community [e.g., baptism] . . . it also receives powerful expression in the paraenesis [exhortation] that calls the Christian to walk in the new life of the Spirit.
6. Resurrection is still a communal symbol, which speaks of the new life of the righteous with the Lord . . . [The faithful] expect to be 'with the Lord,' but it is often not clear whether that expectation is fulfilled after the individual's death or at the consummation of all things.[116]

The 'teaching of the universal church' which based itself on the New Testament has recently been summarized[117] as the affirmation:

that our Lord truly experienced human death; that that state of death was ended and wholly overcome; that there was genuine continuity between his dying self and his risen self; that the mode of existence of the Risen Lord was one in which his full human nature and identity, bodily, mental and spiritual, were present and glorified for eternal blessedness; and that this mode of existence was observed and experienced, and its essential secret grasped, by numbers of his disciples in personal encounter.[118]

The church's resurrection belief, it should be noted, involves the conviction that Jesus retained his identity and his human nature after the resurrection. For he communicated with his disciples after his death in a way that confirmed to them the continuation of his personal identity (many of the resurrection narratives attribute this recognizability of the risen Jesus to his possession of some kind of bodily form, though they differ in to the degree of physicality attributed to it). It is this risen Jesus, whom the disciples quickly came to call the 'Lord' and whose humanity continued to be regarded as real, who was also said,[119] after the resurrection, to have been taken 'up' into the life of God, to be 'in God'.

The church has never affirmed precisely 'what happened' in the resurrection itself – how could it? For there were no observers and the church witnesses to the reality only of the experience of the disciples of the continued livingness of Jesus in a form that escapes capture by our language. For, it is believed, Jesus' mode of existence as the risen Lord partakes of that of God's own self, and hence must be ineffable. That this postulated mode of existence of the risen Lord, the nature of the corporeality that the disciples witnessed, the degree of his physicality, was (and still is), in the proper sense of that word, mysterious is well illustrated by the struggles of Paul to find appropriate language for it.[120] The belief that Jesus is truly now fully in the presence of God entails that *for us* there is an 'ontological gap'[121] between the earthly Jesus and the risen Jesus the Christ, even as his continued identity and humanity is affirmed. Holy Saturday cannot but constitute a kind of impenetrable 'black hole' between the undoubted historical reality of Good Friday and the experienced realities of Easter Day and afterwards which no historical investigation can ever bridge.

It cannot be too strongly emphasized that belief in the resurrection of Jesus was then, and still is now, founded on the first disciples' experience of the risen Jesus. It was not for them then, and *a fortiori* cannot be for us now, based on the Gospel stories[122] that Jesus' tomb was found to be empty shortly after his undoubted burial – some two days afterwards according to these stories. For an empty tomb simply raises a question mark[123] with several possible answers themselves subject to the historical evidence.[124]

The evidence that the tomb was empty is not as strong as that for the resurrection appearances to the disciples, so there are two possible positions that might be adopted:

(1) to affirm an intimate connection between the emptiness of the tomb and the resurrection appearances – that is, to affirm that Jesus' resurrection involved some kind of fundamental transformation of Jesus' body, as buried, into his new mode of existence in his risen state;

(2) to remain agnostic, recognizing that the historical question remains open, because 'On the question whether, as a result of this divine act of resurrection, Christ's tomb that first Easter Day

was empty . . . scholarship can offer no conclusive demonstration.'[125]

Both views affirm that the whole person of Jesus was taken through death into a form in which his identity was unimpaired, in which he could express himself in a glorified state recognizably akin to his previous bodily state before death, that he now exists united with God his Father within the very being of the Godhead and that this was made known through experiences of the disciples (later described as 'appearances') to which history convincingly attests. In this instance, do we have to postulate a particular act of God in the world, of the kind to which we previously referred as an 'intervention' of God in the natural order? Earlier,[126] we pointed out that the historical evidence that such an intervention by God *has* happened would have to be especially strong.

The historical evidence for the disciples experiencing a manifestation of the person of Jesus after his death, in the terms in which we have described it, is indeed strong. Yet the complex of experiences were of such a kind that one hesitates to describe the resurrection as a 'miracle' in the sense of an 'intervention' by God *in* the natural order of events since its end-result was not a clearly defined natural state. For 'what happened' in these experiences could only be interpreted by the disciples, and so by us, as involving a mysterious, and ultimately ineffable, transition of Jesus from the natural, created order of being into a state of unity with God. Hence any language restricted to the natural order of events observed both by common sense and by the sciences is inevitably incapable of expressing the nature of such a transition. The resurrection of Jesus is perhaps better described as an experience of the disciples which they could interpret only as a disclosure by God that the human being of Jesus existed after his physical death in an entirely new mode, or level. Such a disclosure would have to have involved a transformation/ re-creation of the dead Jesus to which the regularities and 'laws' of the natural sciences and ordinary experience do not in principle apply. What *God* might be said to be disclosing will concern us later[127] but, whatever it transpires to be, the clue to it will be that it was *this* Jesus who was 'raised' – the Jesus with all the characteristics, teaching and particular features of his life which we have seen that historical scholarship can reliably adduce, the Jesus who set his face to go to Jerusalem,[128] there to meet a tragic death, abandoned by his followers and (he thought) by God his Father.[129]

It must be stressed again that *both* of the two possible forms of belief in the resurrection of Jesus, (1) and (2) above retain the essential core of Christian belief.[130] Where they differ is in their implications concerning the actual nature of the resurrection, the inner contents of that 'black hole' between the burial and the appearances, the *way* the 'ontological gap' was bridged. We are here moving in a realm of speculation for which language[131] is patently inadequate; nevertheless it is worth pursuing a little further because of our long-term interest in the fate of the natural order.

On the first interpretation (1), there must have been a transformation, amounting to some kind of de-materialization, of Jesus' dead body into a new 'risen' mode of existence, usually called that of his 'glorified body'.[132] On this interpretation (1) the resurrection of Jesus is regarded as a change of his physical body into an entirely new mode of existence, with continuity and without loss of identity. In it there would have to have been a *transformation* of matter-energy in space-time into an entirely new mode of being. It could then appropriately be seen as a sign of the ultimate destiny not only of human beings, but of the whole created order in the eternal purposes of God.[133] However, splendid though such a hope would be which this kind of interpretation reinforces, a very close linkage, such as implicit in (1), between the disappearance of Jesus' body and his risen life renders *more* problematic than does the more reticent interpretation (2) what, in the purposes of God, might eventually happen at death to other human beings. For it is only too clear that the constituents of human bodies are at death irreversibly dispersed about the globe, eventually contributing to the bodies of other, later persons (as well as other living organisms). Hence the actual transformation of individual human bodies could not itself secure the continuity of personal identity through death because the bodies of any individual human person has constituents which are not uniquely confined, in the course of time, to the body of that person. Interpretation (2), not being dependent on the disappearance of Jesus' body in the resurrection,[134] would entail what could be described as his *re-creation* into a new mode of existence. Such a *re*-creation would then relate more intelligibly to what God might be thought to be doing for other human beings in *their* individual 'resurrection', should it occur.

However, we are here moving in a realm of conjecture where the concepts of 'transformation' and 're-creation' are not so easily distinguished. For example, interpretation (1) has actually also been described as 're-creation': 'Even on the most literal understanding of the "resurrection of the body" in terms of the actual physical organism which was the vehicle of [the] historical life [of Jesus] there has to be a divine act of re-creation.'[135] Similarly, although Raymond Brown concludes from his study of the biblical evidence that 'Christians can and indeed should continue to speak of a *bodily* resurrection of Jesus'[136] (which sounds very much like (1)) he nevertheless continues in the same paragraph to stress that Jesus' body

> was no longer a body as we know bodies, bound by the dimensions of space and time . . . we should never become so defensively governed by apologetics that we do not do justice to this element of transformation and mystery. Christian truth is best served when equal justice is done to the element of continuity implied in bodily resurrection and to the element of eschatological transformation.[137]

So for Brown the notion of 'transformation' is very radical, as well as mysterious, and one cannot help thinking it merges into that of 're-creation'. However, Brown is very concerned to keep to the term 'transformation', regarding it as based on (1), in order to indicate God's ultimate plan for the world to be 'transformed and changed into the city of God'.[138] But the linkage is not so direct and one can only continue to speak of the *bodily* resurrection of Jesus if the adjective is taken as affirming that the risen Lord retained his personal identity and continuity with his earthly existence and possessed the ability for those personal interactions that we, with our limited perceptions, cannot but associate with the possession of a body. His risen 'body' can perhaps be regarded, to use a computer analogy, as some kind of divinely *newly-created* 'hardware' (hence the irrelevance of whether or not the tomb was empty) in another dimension which embodies the 'software' that was taken by God through death to continue his personal identity.[139] (We note, in this analogy, that any software program stored in hardware disappears when the hardware is switched off or is otherwise destroyed – some divine initiative is certainly therefore involved.) Hence the need to go on affirming belief in 'the resurrection of the *body*', in this extended sense, with respect to Jesus – and, because of this, belief in its possibility for all humanity whose condition he shared.

The foregoing paragraphs show how it is impossible to discuss one of the most central historical facts about Jesus – namely, that after his death, the disciples had, variously, experiences in which they became convinced that he continued to live and somehow to be *with them* – without moving into theological interpretation. This is not surprising because what is affirmed is an indivisible complex of the human reactions, and so interpretations, of the disciples to whatever it was that 'happened' in the resurrection of Jesus: and, if there is any communication by God to humanity in this focal feature concerning Jesus of Nazareth, it has to be in the whole pattern of events, *including* the reactions to the risen Jesus of the disciples. We can never expect to penetrate historically very far beyond that or ever to have history without interpretation.

The central theological claims that emerge in connection with all the diverse (New Testament) traditions have been summarized by Pheme Perkins in the following terms, paraphrasing H. Küng:

1. Resurrection cannot be described as a historical event in the ordinary sense of the word. There were no human witnesses to the resurrection itself. The New Testament consistently presents resurrection as an eschatological act of God, as part of the final transformation of the world . . . God's salvation is involved in Jesus in such a way that after Easter Jesus becomes the norm for the relationship between humanity and God.
2. Speaking of resurrection as an 'eschatological event' distinguishes it from miraculous intervention in the natural order, such as the revival of a corpse or a near-death experience. It also implies that resurrection is an event for Jesus, not merely a change of awareness on the part of the disciples. As 'eschatological', resurrection implies that Jesus is not the same as the other righteous people who have died.
3. The variety of traditions and types of witnesses makes it impossible to reduce resurrection to the projection of the disciples' need to recover the 'heady intimacy' of their fellowship with Jesus.
4. Finally, 'eschatological event' implies that the 'bodily' reality involved is discontinuous with the material reality we experience. One might even say discontinuous with our experience of bodily death such as we might discover through medical studies.[140]

Let us conclude this discussion of the resurrection with the penetrating statement of C. F. Evans of its essential significance, which we shall have to think about again later:

> The core of resurrection faith is that already within the temporal order of existence a new beginning of life from God, and a living of life under God, are possible, and are anticipatory of what human life has it in it to be as divine creation; and that this has been made apprehensible and available in the life and death of Christ regarded both as divine illumination of human life and as effective power for overcoming whatever obstructs it. This is cosmic in its scope and also reaches to the depths of the human person.[141]

f 'Who do you say I am?'

This was the question that the Synoptic Gospels report[142] as being addressed by Jesus to his disciples at Caesarea Philippi at a crucial point in his ministry. Across the centuries we still feel the sharp edge of its challenge, a challenge implicit in the less personal form of the question we have been addressing in this section, 'Who is Jesus of Nazareth?'.

We have been setting out, as it were, the pieces of the jigsaw of what we know about Jesus historically. On any reckoning it is indeed a remarkable person whom we encounter in a nexus of powerful personal interactions the consequences of which have spread through history. Even when we have had, in all intellectual honesty, to abandon the more 'super-naturalist' features in the Gospel accounts of Jesus and in the general past traditions of the Christian church – for the most part pre-scientific and pre-critical – we can nevertheless understand how these stories became attached to someone whose spiritual quality and power made such a very great impact, and still does. This apprehension of the compellingly attractive nature of Jesus' life, teaching and death (and even resurrection) is not confined to Christians. He has always been regarded as one of the great prophets of Islam, the Hindu religion readily recognizes divine incarnation in him, Buddhism resonates with his spiritual teaching and even some Jews – in spite of what the centuries of Christendom have done to them – are coming to hear in him an authentic rabbinic voice of one of their own people. He certainly bestrides the world religions 'like a Colossus'. His presence in history constitutes a turning point in that long search of humanity for God. His story will not leave us alone. Its distinctive challenge to us, as for his first disciples, is that he evokes in us a sense, less that in him we find a path *to* God, but rather that in him we encounter a self-communication *from* God to us – and above all in the resurrection experienced by his disciples.

We now have to examine if the pieces of the jigsaw can in fact be assembled to form for us today in a scientific age a coherent, discernible pattern which, by being a self-communication of God to humanity, is also a clue to the answer to our earlier question concerning what human beings should be becoming.[143] What should be the method whereby we can piece together the jigsaw of the 'things about Jesus' into such a meaningful pattern? We clearly need some kind of framework (as might be provided by lines, to be joined up, on the reverse sides of the pieces of a jigsaw) to interpret today what critical historical scholarship has made available about Jesus for our generation. To change the metaphor – it is as if we have been collecting scattered pieces of coloured glass through which we view different facets of the many-hued person of Jesus of Nazareth and of his impact on his contemporaries. We need a framework, such as is provided by the thin strips of lead in a stained-glass window, to assemble these pieces into an image through which we can receive any intelligible light that will illuminate our perception of God, of humanity and of their inter-relation.

Such a framework could well be afforded us by those apprehensions for a scientific age of natural and divine being and becoming which we have earlier been developing. Any insight into what the remarkable pattern of events involving Jesus of Nazareth can mean for us will have to be coherent with and illuminate those earlier inferences – about God, about God's interaction with and self-communication to the world, and about the many-levelled nature of apparently incomplete humanity – for it to be intelligible and believable in our own milieu of thought today. This inquiry will be the concern of the next chapter.

CHAPTER 14

Divine Being Becoming Human

'The Word of God, our Lord Jesus Christ who, of his boundless love, became what we are . . .'[1]

1 'THE JESUS OF HISTORY AND THE CHRIST OF FAITH'

There has been a continuous, and in recent years an increasingly intensive, study of the historical process whereby the 'Jesus' that is uncovered by historical scholarship, as summarized in the previous chapter, developed during the first few centuries of the Christian church into the 'Christ of faith', expressed in terms of that doctrine of the union of God with humanity which is known as that of the 'Incarnation'. This doctrine found its classical expression in the Definition of Chalcedon of AD 451.[2] These studies have generated keen debate both about the extent to which this classical christological formulation and its later developments and extensions can be properly inferred and extracted from the New Testament (by virtue both of its historical status and its own theological interpretations of Jesus); and about their validity today for expressing the significance of Jesus and his relation to God in a framework of thought totally different from the cultural milieu within which the Definition was propounded.[3]

As regards the former, the role of the New Testament in the emergence of the 'Christ of faith', there has been an increasing recognition that the understanding of Jesus in the New Testament is pluriform and diverse and that the use of the concept of 'incarnation' to interpret the significance of the life, teaching, death and resurrection of Jesus emerges only towards the end of its period (roughly that of the first century AD) in the Johannine writings, i.e., the Fourth Gospel and the three epistles of John.

Thus, in a widely respected study, J. G. Dunn, asking 'How did the doctrine of the incarnation originate?' concludes:

> It did *not* emerge through the identification of Jesus with a divine individual or intermediary being whose presence in heaven was already assumed . . . It did *not* emerge from an identification of Jesus as Elijah or Enoch returned from heaven – exaltation to heaven was not taken necessarily to presuppose or imply a previous existence in heaven . . . It did *not* emerge as an inevitable corollary to the conviction that Jesus had been raised from the dead or as part of the logic of calling Jesus the Son of God . . . It did *not* emerge as a corollary to the conviction that Jesus had been divinely inspired by the eschatological Spirit, a concept of inspiration giving way imperceptibly to one of incarnation . . . *The doctrine of the incarnation began to emerge when the exalted Christ was spoken of in terms drawn from the Wisdom[4] imagery of pre-Christian Judaism* . . . only in the post-Pauline period did a clear understanding of Christ as having pre-existed with God before his ministry on earth emerge, and *only in the Fourth Gospel can we speak of a doctrine of the incarnation.*[5]

Dunn points out that

> Initially at least Christ was not thought of as a divine being who had pre-existed with God but as *the climactic embodiment of God's power and purpose* – his life, death and resurrection understood in terms of *God himself reaching out to men*. Christ was identified . . . with *God's* creative wisdom, *God's* redemptive purpose, *God's* revelatory word . . . – *God's clearest self-expression, God's last word.*[6]

He argues that the use of 'wisdom' and 'word' imagery meant that in these early formulations of the significance of Jesus what was being affirmed was that:

> *Christ showed them what God is like, the Christ-event[7] defined God more clearly than anything else had ever done . . . Jesus had revealed God* not the Son of God, not the 'divine intermediary' Wisdom, but God. *As the Son of God he revealed God as Father . . . As the Wisdom of God he revealed God as Creator-Redeemer . . .* 'Incarnation' means initially that *God's* love and power had been experienced in fullest measure in, through and as this man Jesus, that Christ had been experienced as God's self-expression, the Christ-event as the effective, re-creative power of God.[8]

A. E. Harvey stresses the constraint of their monotheism on the New Testament writers (and, I would add, also on *us*): 'The New Testament writers appear to have submitted to this constraint, and to have avoided using the word 'god' or 'divine' of Jesus . . .

[they] are similarly insistent about the absolute oneness of God, and show no tendency to describe Jesus in terms of divinity.'[9]

He agrees with Dunn that the early application of Wisdom-language to Jesus precedes the doctrine of the incarnation and makes the further point that, even if the language of 'pre-existence' is in fact applied to Jesus in the Fourth Gospel,[10] this does not in any case imply divinity. For 'Wisdom's presence at the creation was a way of saying that no part of creation is an afterthought: it was all there from the beginning. So with Jesus.'[11]

Neither of these authors is especially radical in his handling of the New Testament data and the rather more conservative R. E. Brown, who thinks that there are three instances[12] in which the New Testament calls Jesus God and five probable ones, agrees that 'there is no reason to think that Jesus was called God in the earliest layers of New Testament tradition . . . the use of "God" for Jesus belongs to the second half of the period [of 30–100 AD., i.e., 65 AD onwards]'.[13] So Brown clearly recognizes a development[14] *into* the usage of calling Jesus God, even if he charts it differently from Dunn and Harvey.

The widely acknowledged diversity of ideas, words and images in first-century Christian writings concerning the nature of Jesus and his relation to God has been broadly interpreted in two ways, with many gradations in between.[15] It has been seen[16] either as a 'development', meaning 'growth, from immaturity to maturity, of a single specimen from within itself'; or as an 'evolution', meaning 'the genesis of successive new species by mutations and natural selection along the way'. C. F. D. Moule makes a strong case that whatever came later was already there in the early experience of Jesus by others and was not an unwarranted accumulation of supernatural qualities from other cults. He argues that there was for the early believers a finality, ultimacy, uniqueness (as well as originality) about Jesus' revelation of God.[17] But we may well question if a sharp contrast between 'development' and 'evolution' can be maintained in the light of contemporary understandings of doctrinal history which take account of general philosophies of historical existence and interpretation ('hermeneutics').[18] What is clear is that the great diversity of christological formulations in the New Testament impel us to acknowledge that

christology should not be narrowly confined to one particular assessment of Christ, nor should it play off one against another, nor should it insist in squeezing all the different NT [New Testament] conceptualizations into one particular 'shape', but it should recognize that from the first the significance of Christ could only be apprehended by a diversity of formulations which though not always strictly compatible with each other were not regarded as rendering each other invalid.[19]

New Testament scholars have therefore uncovered a rich treasury of ways in which the impact of Jesus on his first disciples and their followers was interpreted and have clarified enormously both their relative independence as well as their inter-relations. What the New Testament vouchsafes is not an intellectual synthesis but a kaleidoscopic variety of poetic insights.

The synthesizing and systematizing activity of the Christian intellect was fully exercised in the following centuries leading to the Chalcedonian Definition and subsequent elaborations. These ramifications cannot be entered into here, except to recognize that what emerged in these centuries of the 'Fathers' has come to have classical, even normative, status concerning God and Jesus when it was enshrined in the formulations of church councils of the first five centuries AD. What they did is a task still incumbent upon us now in our own historical and cultural milieu.[20] It is this which generates the second aspect of the contemporary debate, mentioned at the start.

The real problem for us today is how much of this subsequent development/evolution of doctrine, especially that of the first five centuries AD concerned with the relation of God and Jesus, can be of help to our interpreting and understanding today.[21] Inevitably those classical doctrinal formulations were closely integrated with the philosophy and theology of the prevailing Hellenistic culture (mainly neoplatonic) and were expressed in terms such as 'nature', 'substance' and 'person' in an ontological framework quite other than our own – and certainly not that of a culture dominated by modern science. All of which is widely recognized and has led to an intensive debate, at least in Britain, in the last decade or so, beginning with the publication in 1977 of *The Myth of God Incarnate*, about how to formulate today Jesus' relation to God and to the rest of humanity.[22]

However, much of this intensive debate about how to formulate Jesus' relation to God and to the rest of humanity has been confused, in my view, by not being based on an intelligible and believable account of the issues we have been dealing with in previous chapters. These issues were: how we are to conceive of God's being and becoming, of God's interaction with the world, of God's communication with humanity and of what human being is constituted. They were there all considered in the light of what the sciences now tell us of the being and becoming of the natural, created world, including humanity.

It is in *this* contemporary theological framework that we have to re-consider the 'things about Jesus' which we examined in the last chapter in order to formulate what significance Jesus could have for us today. J. G. Dunn could sum up John's contribution in the New Testament to the beginnings of christology thus: 'John is wrestling with the problem of how to think of God and how to think of Christ in relation to God in the light of the clarification of the nature and character of God which the Christ-event afforded.'[23] This leads him to urge the taking up today of this same task as did John in his day, in the following terms: 'We honour him most highly when we follow his example and mould the language and conceptualizations in transition today into a gospel which conveys the divine, revelatory and saving significance of Christ to our day as effectively as he did to his.'[24]

To do this we shall have to employ that theological framework which we have been developing as viable, intelligible and defensible in the light of the sciences. Is the concept of the 'incarnation', initiated apparently by this same 'John', intelligible enough in *this* framework still to be credible today as a justifiable interpretation of those 'things about Jesus' which have a historical basis? It may be the case that, in the end, we shall find ourselves asking the question which D. Nineham poses in the penultimate paragraph of *The Myth of God Incarnate*:

> Is it necessary to 'believe in Jesus' in any sense beyond that which sees him as the main figure through whom God launched men into a relationship with himself so full and rich that, under the various understandings and formulations of it, it has been, and continues to be the salvation of a large proportion of the human race?[25]

We shall have to see. But, even if it transpires that more can be said than Nineham suggests, we shall have to accept that there is a certain indivisibility about the 'Christ-event', as the New Testament scholars tend to denote the 'things about Jesus'. We have no option, in view of the once-for-all givenness of our historical sources, but to take as *our* starting point the whole complex of the life, teaching, death and resurrection/exaltation[26] of Jesus *together with* its impact on his first-century followers that led to the formation of the first Christian community. This is indeed what is meant by the 'Christ-event'.[27]

Generations of Christians have shared in the experiences of the early witnesses through the continuous life of the ensuing Christian community, as expressed in its liturgy, literature, visual arts, music and architecture; in a nexus of transformed personal relationships; and through their direct apprehension of God through Christ, revered as the universalized human Jesus 'raised' to the presence of God.[28] Thus that arrow which was shot into history in the Christ-event lands fairly and squarely here today and we are ourselves challenged to interpret it. 'Revelation' is, of course, relative to circumstances – that is, the meanings which God can express in his creation and in human history are relative to the receptiveness and outlook, the hermeneutical horizons, of those to whom God is communicating. So however strong a case may be made out for a 'high', ontological christology having its roots in the Christ-event, we cannot avoid asking whether what they saw in him, we can see too. Even if we were to accept that the New Testament represents a 'development' of seeds of judgment and reflection on Jesus, rather than an 'evolution' with mutations, we would still be bound to ask about Jesus 'What must the truth have been and be if that is how it looked to people who thought and wrote like that?'[29]

2 *How* COULD GOD COMMUNICATE THROUGH JESUS?

God's interaction with the world has been characterized earlier[30] as a holistic, top-down continuing process of input of 'information', conceived of broadly, whereby God's intentions and purposes are implemented in the shaping of particular events, or patterns of events, without any abrogation of the regularities discerned by the sciences in the natural order. Amongst the constituents of that world are human beings who are persons. These too can be 'informed' by God through the nexus of events, which includes events in human-brains-in-human-bodies. When the recipient of such an 'input' from God is conscious of it, it is properly called 'religious experience'. I argued that such an understanding of God's interaction with human beings can be regarded as revelatory and as fully personal as that between human beings, in spite of the apparently abstract limitations of the terminology of 'information input' and of computer science.[31]

How, in the light of this, might we then interpret the experience of God that was mediated to his disciples and to the New Testament church through Jesus? That is, how can we understand the Christ-event if God's self-communication is to be conceived of in these terms developed in order to make intelligible God's interaction with a world now perceived through the natural and human sciences? We need to explicate in these terms the conclusions of scholars about the understanding in New Testament times of Jesus the Christ – as represented, for example, in that earlier quotation[32] from J. G. Dunn that 'Initially Christ was thought of . . . as *the climactic embodiment of God's power and purpose . . . God himself reaching out to men . . . God's* creative wisdom . . . *God's* revelatory word . . . *God's clearest self-expression, God's last word.'*

These descriptions of what Jesus the Christ was to those who encountered him and to the early church are all, in their various ways, about God *communicating* to humanity, and so, in the broad sense we have been using the terms,[33] about an 'input of information'. This process of 'input of information' from God we earlier also denoted, more conformably with the actual content of human experience, as the conveying of 'meaning' from God to humanity.[34] We argued then that God can convey his meanings through events and patterns of events in the created world – those in question here are the life, teaching, death and resurrection of the human person, Jesus of Nazareth as reported by these early witnesses. As the investigations of the New Testament show, they experienced in Jesus, in his very person and personal history, a communication *from God*, a revelation of God's meanings for humanity. So it is no wonder that, in the later stages of reflection in the New Testament period, there was a conflation, by John, of the concept of divine Wisdom[35] with that of the *Logos*, the 'Word' of God, in order to say what he intended about the meaning Jesus the Christ had for the early witnesses and their immediate successors. The *locus classicus* of this exposition is, of course, the prologue to his Gospel.[36] The 'beauty and aptness' in this expression, 'Word' or *Logos*, when applied to Jesus has recently been emphasized by John Macquarrie.[37] For, in addition to carrying undertones of the image of 'Wisdom', it conflates two other concepts: the Hebrew idea of the 'word of the Lord' for the will of God expressed in utterance, especially to the prophets, and in creative activity;[38] and that of '*logos*' in Hellenistic Judaism, especially in Philo – the Divine *Logos*, the creative principle of rationality operative in the universe, and especially manifest in human reason, and which is formed within the mind of God and projected into objectivity.[39]

I have already spoken of what we have called God's 'input of information' into the world as more appropriately denoted by the notion of God communicating his 'meaning'. As mentioned previously,[40] Macquarrie has in fact attempted to interpret for our times the import of Word/*Logos* in the prologue to John's Gospel by substituting 'Meaning' for it. His paraphrase, now published in full, is worth quoting for it does succeed in conveying in our own terms to us today something of what it meant for its first readers (numbers refer to the paraphrased verses of *John* 1):

(1) Fundamental to everything is Meaning. It is closely connected with what we call 'God', and indeed Meaning and God are virtually identical. (2) To say that God was in the beginning is to say that Meaning was in the beginning. (3) All things were made meaningful, and there was nothing made that was meaningless. (4) Life is the drive toward Meaning, and life has emerged into self-conscious humanity, as the (finite) bearer and recipient of Meaning. (5) And meaning shines out through the threat of absurdity, for absurdity has not overwhelmed it. (9) Every human being has a share in Meaning, whose true light was coming into the world. (10) Meaning was there in the world and embodying itself in the world, yet the world has not recognized the Meaning, (11) and even humanity, the bearer of Meaning, has rejected it. (12) But those who have received it and believed in it have been enabled to become the children of God. (13) And this has happened not in the natural course of evolution or through human striving, but through a gracious act of God. (14) For the Meaning has been incarnated in a human existent, in whom was grace and truth; and we have seen in him the glory toward which everything moves – the glory of God. (16) From him, whom we can acknowledge in personal terms as the Son of the Father, we have received abundance of grace. (17) Through Moses came the command of the law, through Jesus Christ grace and truth. (18) God is a mystery, but the Son who has shared the Father's life has revealed him.[41]

The substitution of 'Meaning' for Word/*Logos* helps to convey better the effect of what was then being affirmed as having happened in creation and in Jesus the Christ.

For, as we have seen,[42] conveying of meaning, in the ordinary

sense, is implemented initially by an input of 'information' –
the constrained and selected elements among all possibilities
that sufficiently delimit signals (i.e., language and other means
of human communication) so that they can convey meaning. As
John Bowker has put it:

> How do we arrive at the sense of anything? How do we construct
> meaning on the basis of information which arrives at our receptor
> centres in the form of sensation, or which occurs in the internal process?
> The biological and neurological answer lies in the (initially latent)
> structured ability of the brain to code, store, and decode signals and
> represent (re-present) them *as* information. This implies that 'meaning'
> is constituted not by the quantitative amount of information, but
> by a qualitative selection (control into restriction), which enables
> meaning . . . to transcend the mathematical base of its constituent
> elements . . . The way [in which 'meaning' does this] . . . does not mean
> that there is an automatic, radical disjunction between quantitative (in
> a semiotic sense) and qualitative information.[43]

The use of the concept of 'information input' to refer to the way
God induces effects in the world was, to the best of my knowledge, pioneered by Bowker. It has furthermore been used by
him to render intelligible the idea of God expressing himself in
and through the human being of Jesus:

> . . . it is credibly and conceptually possible to regard Jesus as a wholly
> God-informed person, who retrieved the theistic inputs coded in the
> chemistry and electricity of brain-processes for the scan of every situa-
> tion, and for every utterance, verbal and non-verbal . . . the result
> would have been the incarnating (the embodying) of God in the only
> way in which it could possibly have occurred. No matter what God may
> be in himself, the realization of that potential resource of effect would
> have to be mediated into the process and continuity of life-construction
> through the brain-process interpreted through the codes available at
> any particular moment of acculturation . . . There is no other way of
> being human, or indeed of being alive, because otherwise consciousness
> ceases . . . That is as true of Jesus *de humanitate* as of any one else.
> But what seems to have shifted Jesus into a different degree of
> significance . . . was the stability and the consistency with which his
> own life-construction was God-informed . . .
>   It is possible on this basis to talk about a wholly human figure,
> without loss or compromise, and to talk also, at exactly the same
> moment, of a wholly real presence of God so far as that nature (what-
> ever it is in itself) can be mediated to and through the process of the
> life-construction in the human case, through the process of brain

behaviour by which any human being becomes an informed subject –
but in this case, perhaps even uniquely, a wholly God-informed
subject.[44]

This illustrates how the notion of God communicating himself,
expressing himself, through a human being, through the complete person of Jesus the Christ, is consistent with all that we have
been saying concerning the nature of God's interaction with and
self-communication to the world and is thereby rendered intelligible in a way that seemed to be impossible for its critics in *The
Myth of God Incarnate*.[45]

At this juncture in our enterprise, recognition that God has, in
fact, communicated God's own self to humanity in this way – that
is, acceptance of the belief, given its intelligibility, that God was
in this sense 'incarnate' in Jesus – must be left to the judgment of
the reader. That judgment has to rest on the reader's assessment
not only of its intrinsic intelligibility but also:[46] of its moral and
religious significance; of the Christ-event in the light of the New
Testament evidence which we have assembled (albeit in a starkly
summarized fashion); of whether or not the church's teaching
down the ages is to be regarded as providentially guided; and of
the experience of Christ as a living and active presence of God in
the church and in the world.

The present writer judges that these considerations are com-
pelling, so – hoping the reader is prepared to continue with him, at
least provisionally, in this belief – we shall proceed by exploring
its implications and its relation to that more general theology for
a scientific age we have been developing. This belief in the
incarnation was founded on the whole complex of what we have,
following others, clumsily and for want of a better designation,
called the Christ-event.[47] Those who were actually involved
historically in the interpretation of Jesus the Christ came to
believe that in the completely human person of Jesus, it was *God*
whose self-expression they experienced.[48] In the following section, we pursue the question of what it is that, according to this
Christian belief, God may actually be said to have communicated
to humanity about God's own self in and through Jesus the Christ,
the 'Word made flesh'. In doing so, we shall be responding to our
earlier concern[49] about ascertaining if what the disciples and
early church saw in Jesus we can see too in our very different
milieu of thought and presuppositions.

3 GOD'S SELF-EXPRESSION IN JESUS THE CHRIST

Any communication of the nature of God's own self believed to
have been transmitted in and through Jesus the Christ will have
to be related to those insights into what we have been able to
discern of divine Being and Becoming from our more general
reflections based on the character of natural being and becoming.
We look, of course, not for proof but for a consonance which might,
at least, consolidate the insights of such a 'natural' theology.
However, if Jesus the Christ really is a self-communication *from*
God and the self-expression *of* God in a human person, as the
church in concord with the early witnesses has affirmed, then we
can hope for much more. What were glimmers of light on a distant
horizon might in him become shafts of the uncreated light of the
Creator's own self. Hints and faint echoes of the divine in nature
might, then, in Jesus the Christ become a resonating word to
humanity from God's own self, a manifest revelation of God. Jesus
the Christ would then indeed be the very Word of God made
human flesh as the early church came to assert. What is only
implicit and partially and imperfectly discerned of God in the
created world would then be explicit and manifest in his person.
We shall therefore need to reflect on what the Christian community affirmed as their experience of God in Jesus the Christ
(through the Holy Spirit, as they would put it), in its paradigmatic
and archetypal early form, in the light of what we have here been
able to discern[50] of divine Being and Becoming from natural being
and becoming.

a God as Continuous and Immanent Creator

From the continuity of the natural processes, we inferred[51] that
God is continuously creating, as the immanent Creator, in and
through the natural order. For the processes of the world exhibit
an intelligible continuity in which the potentialities of its
constituents are unfolded in forms of an ever-increasing complexity and organization. These forms are properly described as
'emergent' in that they manifest new features which are irreducible to the sciences which describe that out of which they have
developed. That qualitatively new kinds of existence come into
being is one of the most striking aspects of natural becoming. We
witness the seeming paradox of discontinuity generated by

continuity. For nature adopts new forms of being that appear to be discontinuous, at least in some respects, with those from which they originate. Hence belief in God as Creator involves the recognition that this is the character of the processes whereby God actually creates new forms, new entities, structures and processes that emerge with new capabilities, requiring distinctive language on our part to distinguish them. God is present in and to this whole process whose discontinuities are grounded in its very continuities.

This has important consequences for the way in which we might understand and express the way in which God might be said to manifest himself in the human person of Jesus, of 'informing' the human personhood of Jesus so that God could be said to be expressing God's own self in and through his humanity. For when we reflect on the significance of what the early witnesses reported as their experience of Jesus the Christ, we have found ourselves implicitly emphasizing both the *continuity* of Jesus with the rest of humanity,[52] and so with the rest of nature within which *homo sapiens* evolved; and, at the same time, the *discontinuity* constituted by what is distinctive in his relation to God and what through him (his teaching, life, death and resurrection) the early witnesses experienced of God.[53] This paradox is already present in that peak of christological reflection of the New Testament period that comes to expression in the Prologue to the Gospel of John. For in that seminal text,[54] the Word/*Logos*, which both is God and was with God in creating (vv. 1–3) and which becomes human 'flesh' (v. 14), is the same 'Word' that is all the time 'in the world' (v. 10) and giving 'light' (v. 4–6) to humanity, even though unrecognized (v. 10). God had been and was already in the world expressing God's meaning[55] in and through his creating, but says the author, this meaning was hidden and suppressed and only in Jesus the Christ has it become manifest and explicit, so that its true 'glory' (v. 14) has become apparent.

This encourages us now to understand the 'incarnation' which occurred in Jesus as exemplifying that emergence-from-continuity which characterizes the whole process whereby God is creating continuously through discontinuity. There is both continuity with all that preceded him, yet in him there has appeared a new mode of human existence which, by virtue of its openness to God, is a new revelation of both God and of humanity. Taking the clue from the Johannine Prologue, we could say that the manifestations of

God which Jesus' contemporaries encountered in him must have been a manifestation emanating from within creation, from deep within those events and processes which led to his life, teaching, death and resurrection. That is to say, in the light of our understanding of God's creation and presence in the world, we must understand 'incarnation' not to involve any 'descent' into the world of God conceived of as 'above' (and so outside) it – as so many Christmas hymns would have us believe – but as the manifestation of what, or rather the One who, is already in the world but not recognized or known. The human person Jesus is then to be seen, by virtue of his human response and openness to God, as the locus, the *ikon*, in and through whom there is made open and explicit the nature and character of the God who has never ceased to be present continuously creating and bringing his purposes to fruition in the order of energy-matter-space-time. Because of this continuity of the creative activity of God throughout time and acting through the inherent, created, creativity of the universe, it seems to me that we have to come to see Jesus the Christ, not as a unique invasion of the personhood of an individual human being by God conceived of as wholly transcendent, but rather as the distinctive manifestation of a possibility always inherently there for human beings in their potential nature, that is, by virtue of what God had created them to be and to become. Such a joint emphasis on continuity (corresponding to 'immanence') as well as on emergence (corresponding to 'incarnation') we shall later[56] see also to be vital to any understanding of Jesus the Christ which is going to make what he *was* relevant to what we *might* be. For this interpretation of the 'incarnation' entails that what we have affirmed about Jesus is not, in principle, impossible for all humanity – even if, as a matter of contingent historical fact, we think that manifest 'incarnation' is only fully to be seen in him, it is not excluded as a possibility for all humanity.[57]

In proposing a recovery of an active sense, too much suppressed for the last three hundred years in the West, of the significance of God's immanence in the world as the context for thinking about the 'incarnation', we must nevertheless continue to recognize the transcendence of God. Admittedly this has often so dominated thought on the 'incarnation' that the very concept has seemed to many inconsistent with our talk about God and even nonsensical. However, the fact is that in Jesus the Christ his Jewish followers encountered, especially in the light of his resurrection, a dimension of that divine transcendence which, as devout monotheists, they attributed to God alone.[58] But they also encountered him as a complete human being and so experienced an intensity of God's immanence in the world different from anything else in their experience or tradition. Thus it was that the fusion of these two aspects of their awareness that it was *God* acting in and through Jesus the Christ gave rise to the conviction that in him something new had appeared in the world of immense significance for humanity – as *we* might say, a new emergent had appeared within created humanity. And thus it was, too, that they ransacked their cultural stock of available images[59] and models, at first Hebraic and later Hellenistic, to give expression to this new non-reducible distinctive mode of being and becoming that the teaching, life, death and resurrection of Jesus the Christ instantiated.

b God as (at least) Personal, or 'Supra-Personal', and Purposive

We have noted earlier[60] that the operation of natural selection in biological organisms has an inbuilt tendency (following Popper, we called it a 'propensity') to favour, because of their survival-value, increasing complexity, information-processing and -storage ability – those foundations for sensitivity to pain, consciousness, and even self-consciousness which must also be reckoned to have survival value. This process – albeit by the zigzag, random path carved out by the interplay of chance and law – reaches its maximum development, to date, in the emergence of the human-brain-in-the-human-body, which has that distinctive and emergent feature we call being a 'person'. We drew attention to the 'anthropic' features of the universe which allowed the emergence through evolution of human persons and so the appearance of *personal* agency.[61] This would seem to justify tentatively the description of the universe as a 'personalizing universe',[62] in the sense that 'the whole is to be understood as a process making for personality and beyond'.[63] Reflecting on what could constitute the 'best explanation' of such a universe, we concluded[64] that God is (at least) personal, or 'supra-personal'. The awkward term '*supra*-personal' was introduced to indicate that, while wanting to emphasize that the nature of human personhood, with its transcendence-in-immanence, was the 'least misleading' pointer to the nature of God the Creator as the source of all-that-is, yet we also recognized that any extension of the language of human personhood inevitably, like all analogies based on created realities, must remain inadequate as a *description* of the nature of that ineffable, ultimate Reality which is God.

However, tentative as any use of personal language when applied to God must be, even when properly qualified ('at least . . .', 'supra-'), yet it remains the most consistent and the least misleading of any that might be inferred from our reflections on natural being and becoming. Furthermore, consideration of the emergence of the experience of transcendence-in-immanence that characterizes evolved human personhood, led us to conjecture (hope, even) that

> in humanity immanence might be able to display a transcendent dimension to a degree which would unveil, without distortion, the transcendent-Creator-who-is-immanent in a uniquely new emergent manner – that is, that in humanity (in a human being, or in human beings), the presence of God the Creator might be unveiled with a clarity, in a glory, not hitherto perceived.[65]

and we went on to ask the question

> Might it not be possible for a human being so to reflect God, to be so wholly open to God, that God's presence was clearly unveiled to the rest of humanity in a new, emergent and unexpected manner?[66]

It was the affirmation of the early church, and continues to be its affirmation that, on the grounds of the New Testament experience, in Jesus the Christ this has actually happened.[67] That is, in the human person, Jesus the Christ, God has been able to self-express God's own self in a way that validates the attribution to God of personal language, even as we recognize its inherent limitations. For in Jesus the Christ, God has apparently taken the initiative to reveal his presence to humanity in and through a completely human *person*. The early disciples, and subsequent members of the Christian church, have no doubt that in Jesus the Christ, it is God they encounter and God who is made known to them in that human *person* – that in his personhood,[68] God has, and still does, convey his meanings to and for humanity.

Meanings which persons wish to communicate are conveyed through words and the concept of the Word/*Logos* of God, which we have seen has been especially appropriated to understand the significance of Jesus the Christ, is therefore an essentially personal one. We have already had our understanding of the prologue to St John's Gospel[69] enriched by Macquarrie's substitution of 'Meaning' for Word/*Logos*. The 'Meaning' so communicated transpires, within the pages of the New Testament, to be principally about the significance of the personal, of a personal relation to God as 'Love' and of loving interpersonal relationships. Hence John Robinson's paraphrase of the prologue, in which he substitutes the concept of the 'personal' for Word/*Logos*, is particularly illuminating:

(1) The clue to the universe as personal was present from the beginning. It was found at the level of reality which we call God. Indeed, it was no other than God nor God than it. (2) At that depth of reality the element of the personal was there from the start. (3) Everything was drawn into existence through it, and there is nothing in the process that has come into being without it. (4) Life owes its emergence to it, and life lights the path to man. (5) It is that light which illumines the darkness of the sub-personal creation, and the darkness never succeeded in quenching it . . . (9) That light was the clue to reality – the light which comes to clarity in man. Even before that it was making its way in the universe. (10) It was already in the universe, and the whole process depended upon it, although it was not conscious of it. (11) It came to its own in the evolution of the personal; yet persons failed to grasp it. (12) But to those who did, who believed what it represented, it gave the potential of a fully personal relationship to God. (13) For these the meaning of life was seen to rest, not simply on its biological basis, nor on the impulses of nature or the drives of history, but on the reality of God. (14) And this divine personal principle found embodiment in a man and took habitation in our midst. We saw its full glory, in all its utterly gracious reality – the wonderful sight of a person living in uniquely normal relationship to God, as son to father.
(16) From this fullness of life we have all received, in gifts without measure. (17) It was law that governed the less than fully personal relationships even of man; the true gracious reality came to expression in Jesus Christ. (18) The ultimate reality of God no one has ever seen. But the one who has lived closest to it, in the unique relationship of son to father, he has laid it bare.[70]

In this perspective, the experience of Jesus the Christ was, and still is, in essence a personal encounter with God in and through the human person of Jesus the Christ. The meaning that God communicated to humanity about God's own self in Jesus the Christ was therefore an explicit revelation of the significance of personhood in the divine purposes – an insight only partially and incompletely discernible from our reflections on natural being and becoming. The Creator God in whom the world exists has all

along been instantiating, 'incarnating' God's own personalness
in that world and this has been made supremely and explicitly
manifest in particular in Jesus the Christ. Again we must note
that this is being affirmed as the contingent historical reality
that is Jesus the Christ: but this affirmation does not confine the
incarnating of God the Word to him alone and does not preclude
the possibility of such language being the appropriate description of at least some other human beings – and perhaps,
potentially at least, of all.

To speak of the 'personal' as if it were an end in itself is not
enough. For we saw earlier[71] that what is distinctive of human
beings *qua* persons is that they are potential carriers of values
which they seek by purposive behaviour to embody in their
individual and social life. It was one of the well-attested features
of the experience of Jesus the Christ that he was seen not only to
seek to inculcate values in his disciples through his teaching, but
that he also exemplified them in his life and, as they came to
realize afterwards, more especially in his suffering and death, in
view of the circumstances under which and the reasons for which
these were inflicted on him. What these values were, and are, we
shall eventually have to consider (especially in the next chapter);
here we simply note that it is not just *any* kind of personhood,
any kind of personal life, that we can now see as the purpose of
God to bring into existence. For acceptance of Jesus the Christ as
the self-expression of God in a human person compels the
recognition that it is the eliciting of persons embodying values
which is the underlying purpose of the divine creative process.
Persons can only be carriers of values if they are self-conscious
and free, so that the 'propensities' of the biological, evolutionary
process, to which we have again referred above,[72] have their
ultimate limiting form in *this* person, Jesus the Christ. So the
'incarnation' which occurred in Jesus the Christ may then
properly be said to be the consummation of the creative and
creating evolutionary process. That is, the implication of belief
in Jesus the Christ as the Word of God 'made flesh', the self-
expression of God's meaning, is that the evoking in the created
world of the kind of personhood manifest in him, with his
particular embodiment of values, is unveiled as the purpose of
God in creation.

c God as Exploring in Creation through Its Open-Endedness

Our earlier recognition that God as Creator acts through chance operating under the constraints of law and that many of the processes of the world are open-ended (they are irreducibly unpredictable), together with a renewed emphasis on the immanence of God in the creative and creating processes of the world, led us to suggest[73] that it was legitimate to speak of God the Creator as *exploring* in creation. It transpired that by the assertion that 'God the Creator explores in creation' was meant that God improvisingly responds to and creates on the basis of eventualities which are irreducibly unpredictable in advance. The operation of human free will is, of course, a particularly notable, and 'unpredictable' feature of the world which demonstrates God's willingness to let it have this open-ended character, while concomitantly being a world in which God exercises providential guidance and influence in the ways we came to see as intelligible.[74]

Jesus, a completely human being, exercised his free will to be entirely open to God to such a distinctive degree that his disciples came to designate him as the 'Christ' and their successors to develop an understanding of what was happening in him as the 'incarnation' of God, God's very self-expression in a human person. That same Jesus risked his all on the faithfulness of God in the hazardous events of his times and thereby united himself with God in that painful process, and hope, of bringing into existence God's reign, the 'kingdom of God'. This means that, in Jesus the Christ, the open-endedness of what is going on in the world, self-consciously and overtly by the willing act of a created human being united itself with the purposes of God for the still open future. In Jesus' oneness with God his Father, we see the open-endedness of the creative process operative in him as a human person becoming united fully and self-consciously with the immanent activity of God – God who is the source of the open future which is the medium of expression of God's intentions for humanity and the world. But is not this just that very close linkage between the advent of Jesus and the initiation of the kingdom of God ('God's reign') which is so well testified[75] as distinctive of Jesus' own teaching?

The historical evidence is indeed that Jesus *was* so open to God, that he entrusted his whole future to God unequivocally to the point of abandoning at his death even his sense of God's presence to himself.[76] The historical Jesus, the evidence attests, staked all on God's future for God's kingdom and thereby made possible the resurrection wherein God was able to reveal further the way ahead for Jesus, as 'Jesus the Christ', to draw all humanity after him into a full relation with God. Thus it is we can now see Jesus the Christ as a new departure point in the creative process, the beginning of a new possibility for human existence in which new potentialities of human life are actualized in those willing to share in Jesus' *human* and *open* response to God.

d God as 'Self-Limited' and as Vulnerable, Self-Emptying, Self-Giving, and Suffering Love

Earlier[77] we attributed 'self-limitation' to God with respect to God's own power over all events and knowledge of the future. We arrived at this conclusion because of certain inherent, yet created, unpredictabilities in many systems of the natural world. These included *inter alia* the operations of the human-brain-in-the-human-body, and so of the deliberations of human free will. This led to the notion that God had allowed himself not to have power over and knowledge of such systems because God wanted them to possess a degree of autonomy that could develop into self-conscious, free human beings.

Now, if Jesus the Christ is the self-expression of God in a human person, this inevitably involves a self-limitation of God. For only some aspects of God's own nature are expressible in a human life. In particular, God's omnipotence and omniscience would have to be further restricted and confined if expressed in the limits of the human person of Jesus, whose complete humanity certainly restricted his power and knowledge.

This 'self-emptying' (*kenosis*) of God when 'incarnate' in Jesus the Christ has been much discussed since its revival as 'kenotic christology' in the nineteenth century to reinterpret the classical doctrine of the incarnation.[78] It was predicated on a somewhat over-cautious acceptance of the full humanity of Jesus[79] and was heavily dependent on the interpretation of certain key passages[80] in St Paul's writings as indicating the pre-existence of 'Jesus Christ' himself, regarded as the God-man. There are many difficulties[81] with this view, including exegetical ones,[82] and there is considerable confusion about what and to whom the notion of 'pre-existence' refers. Suffice it to say for our present purposes, that God, or the Word/*Logos* of God as a mode of God's being, and hence God's intentions and purposes, can all be coherently conceived as pre-existent in relation to the human Jesus. Furthermore, on the interpretation of created natural being and becoming that we have been advancing, God is all-the-time self-limiting in his immanent, creating presence in the world. Indeed, we found ourselves having to speak of the self-emptying (*kenosis*) and self-giving of God in creation.[83] So the eventual self-expression of God, in 'the fullness of time', in the restricted human personhood of Jesus can be seen as an explicit manifestation and revelation of that perennial (self-limiting, -emptying, -giving) relation of God to the created world which was up till then only implicit and hidden. The only temporal pre-existence, relative to the Jesus who was in history, implicit in this insight is that of *God*, whose transcendent Being is of such a kind that God creatively expresses God's self in immanent Becoming in the world all of created time. In any case, God always has ontological priority.

Because of the interplay of chance and law in the processes of creation we also inferred[84] that God may be regarded, as it were, as 'taking a risk' in creating and therein making himself and his purposes vulnerable to the inherent open-endedness of those processes. This vulnerability of God extended, more particularly, to the effects of the possession of free will by human beings, an outcome of that inbuilt open-endedness. Such a suggestion could be only a conjecture, an attempt to make sense of certain features of natural processes that were also seen as created by God. But this suggestion is reinforced, indeed overtly revealed – that is, communicated by God – if God truly self-expressed God's own self in Jesus the Christ. For his path through life was pre-eminently one of vulnerability to the forces that swirled around him, to which he eventually innocently succumbed in acute suffering and, from his human perception, in a tragic, abandoned death.

Because sacrificial, self-limiting, self-giving action on behalf of the good of others is, in human life, the hallmark of love, those who believe in Jesus the Christ as the self-expression of God's own self have come to see his life as their ultimate warrant for asserting that God is essentially 'Love', in so far as any one word can accurately refer to God's nature. Jesus' own teaching concerning God as 'Abba', Father, and of the conditions for entering the 'kingdom of God' pointed to this too, but it was the person of Jesus and what happened to him that finally, and early, established this perception of God in the Christian community.

We see therefore that belief in Jesus the Christ as the self-expression of God in the confines of a human person is entirely consonant with those conceptions of God, previously derived only tentatively from reflection on natural being and becoming, which affirm that God, in exercising divine creativity, is self-limiting, vulnerable, self-emptying and self-giving – that is, is supremely Love in creative action. On this understanding Jesus the Christ is the definitive communication from God to humanity of the deep meaning of what God has been effecting in creation – and that is precisely what the Prologue to the Fourth Gospel says in terms of God the Word/*Logos* active in creation and as now manifest in the person of Jesus the Christ.

Furthermore, we inferred,[85] even more tentatively, from the character of the natural processes of creation that God has to be seen as suffering in, with and under these selfsame processes with their costly, open-ended unfolding in time. But if God was present in and one with Jesus the Christ, then we have to conclude that *God* also suffered in and with him in his passion and death. The God whom Jesus therefore obeyed and expressed in his life and death is indeed a 'crucified God'[86] and the cry of dereliction can be seen as an expression of the anguish also of God in creation. If Jesus is indeed the self-expression of God in a human person, then the tragedy of his actual human life can be seen as a drawing back of the curtain to unveil a God suffering in and with the sufferings of created humanity and so, by a natural extension, with those of all creation, since humanity is an evolved part of it.[87] The suffering of God, which we could glimpse only tentatively in the processes of creation, is in Jesus the Christ concentrated into a point of intensity and transparency which reveals it to all who focus on him.

What the disciples and their followers experienced[88] in Jesus the Christ and the more general notions of God's continuing relation to the world which we provisionally inferred from natural being and becoming (in the terms such as those which head this last section) clearly render each other more intelligible and mutually enrich and enhance each other. In him, we might say, general and special revelation of God converge, coincide and reinforce each other. This experience, as interpreted by them, and down the centuries by the church, has immense significance for our perceptions of human potentialities[89] and to these we must now turn.

CHAPTER 15

Divine Meaning and Human Becoming

'. . . to make us what even he himself is'[1]

We have seen that it is intelligible and coherent to affirm that in Jesus the Christ God has expressed Godself in a human person and we have reported the historical grounds on which this is affirmed. This enabled us, in the previous chapter, to develop various insights into the nature of God which we had only provisionally inferred from reflection on natural being and becoming. It now behoves us to examine the meaning of and meanings for *human* being and its potential becoming which God may be regarded as communicating in the light of the capacity of humanity, in the person of Jesus the Christ, actually to be the vehicle of God's self-expression. For this self-communication of God in and through a completely human person, this 'incarnation' of God in a human person, has crucial implications for human being and becoming.

1 THE DIVINE MEANING OF CREATED HUMAN BEING

We saw earlier[2] that human beings consist of and operate at various levels which are the foci of the different clusters of sciences (physical, biological, behavioural, social); and that these levels merge into that of human culture and its products. We recognized[3] that no other part of the observed universe appears to range over so many levels as do human beings and that this is the sense in which a human being might now be said to be a 'microcosm' of the 'macrocosm', of all-that-is. Human beings, at one level, are 'nothing but' atoms and molecules (or, quarks, etc.), yet they operate at numerous other, even more complex, levels up to the finest flowering of human genius in the expression of the values (*inter alia*) of truth, beauty and goodness and of their converse – falsity, ugliness and moral degradation.

The uniqueness[4] for us of this comprehensive unity-in-diversity and diversity-in-unity that is a human being is encapsulated in our use of the term 'person' applied to human beings, as denoting both the integrated sum, as it were, over all these discriminable levels and that elusive, mysterious almost, nature of the whole person to which we earlier drew attention.[5] The Christian affirmation is that, contingently and historically, in at least one such human 'person' – Jesus the Christ – God explicitly expressed God's own nature and purposes within the created world. This involved, we suggested,[6] God totally operating in, 'informing', the human person of Jesus and this must have been at all levels of his created humanity – that is, at every level from his atoms and molecules, via his DNA and genetic constitution and physiology to his behaviour, psychology and social enculturation. This 'informing' of Jesus' humanity by God must have been coincidental and co-ordinate *pari passu* with the human response to God of the whole person of Jesus in his openness and obedience to God his 'Father'. So much so that we can properly say that Jesus, by becoming a channel of God's presence and power into the world, unveils through this openness to God the character of God's intentions and purposes in creation. These are manifested in his life, death and resurrection and in the formation of the kind of community these inspired. In this way, Jesus (now seen entitled 'Christ') throws light on the divine meaning of the multiple levels of the created world which were present in him and most of which came into existence in evolution before the species, *homo sapiens*, to which he himself belonged. For he unveiled a definitive aspect[7] of the 'meaning' of these multiple levels, namely, their place in God's unfolding purpose which is effected through the divine exploration of their creative possibilities by their integration into higher complexes through evolution. Through these unitive and unifying processes of the world there have emerged self-conscious persons whose ultimate potentialities, as we shall see, are revealed through Jesus the Christ. Hence the significance and potentiality of all levels of creation, as they are incorporated into created personhood, may be said to have been unfolded in Jesus the Christ who in his relation as a created human person to God the Creator thereby 'mediates' to us the *meaning* of creation.[8]

Through him we learn that for which all things were made and this understanding of his mediatorial role is coherent with the way that God has been shaping creation for the emergence of persons.[9] For the meaning which God communicates through Jesus the Christ, through the Christ-event, is the meaning of God both *about* humanity as well as *for* humanity. For the meaning he (Jesus) discerns, proclaims, expresses and reveals is the meaning that he himself *is*.

But in much traditional Christian thought, this meaning of God revealed in Jesus the Christ also takes on a more cosmic significance as 'disclosing the ultimate meaning of the whole indivisible process of creation, nature and history'.[10] When the meaning of God that is communicated through Jesus the Christ is related to the meaning God has and is conveying through the creation itself, in the way we have been attempting to depict, we can then recognize that the Christ-event is itself the focus of many shafts of meaningful light dispersed throughout the multiple levels of creation. Jesus the Christ may then be seen as a specific, indeed for Christians a unique, focal point in which the diverse meanings written into the many levels of creation coalesce like rays of light with an intensity that so illuminates for us the purposes of God that we are better able to interpret God's meanings communicated in his creative activity over a wider range of human experience of nature and history. This is the import of the whole notion of 'incarnation' as we have been developing it here and has also been well expressed by John Macquarrie.

> ... incarnation was not a sudden once-for-all-event ... but is a process which began with the creation. If I were to offer a definition of 'incarnation', I would say that it is the progressive presencing and self-manifestation of the Logos in the physical and historical world. For the Christian, this process reaches its climax in Jesus Christ, but the Christ-event is not isolated from the whole series of events. That is why we can say that the difference between Christ and other agents of the Logos is one of degree, not of kind.[11]

The apparent tension in this interpretation of 'incarnation' between the meanings hidden in the events and processes of nature and history and *the* meaning disclosed in Jesus the Christ is also present in the prologue to St John's Gospel. There, on the one hand, the Word/*Logos* through whom 'all things came to be'

(v. 3) which (who) is omnipresent (v. 4) is also that localized, temporally constricted Word/*Logos* which 'became flesh' whose 'glory' was seen in history (v. 14). The latter is local, historical, and particular and is the focus, the paradigm, the definitive illuminating exemplar of, and clue to, the former which is dispersed, perennial and general. What Jesus the Christ was and what happened to him can, in this perspective, be seen as a new source and resource for reading God's meaning for humanity in all the levels of creation leading to and incorporated into humanity – the clue that points us to a meaning beyond itself, a key that unlocks the door on to a more ample vista, a focus of rays coming from many directions, a characteristic gesture from the hand of God revealing his meaning and purpose.[12]

2 THE DIVINE MEANING FOR HUMAN BECOMING

We have been considering 'human being' but, as Macquarrie has pointed out,

> we are all *becoming* human, in the sense that we are discovering and, it may be hoped, realizing what the potentials of a human existence are . . . our humanity is simply not a natural endowment (as felinity is to a cat) but has to be discovered and realized.[13]

That is, we should, he suggests, 'speak not of a "human being" but of a "human becoming", awkward though this usage would be';[14] for 'the nature of the human being is the as yet unfinished humanity which is emerging and taking shape in the history of the race and in the existence of the individual'.[15]

Again we cannot help recognizing the paradoxical character[16] of this 'as yet unfinished humanity' and its need to discern what it *ought* to be and become. We concluded that there was little hope of ascertaining this from our new knowledge of what humanity *is* that the sciences now provide. From then on[17] we have been joining in the 'long search' of humanity and this has led us to the Christ-event, to Jesus the Christ, as the concentrated point of God's self-communication to humanity both about God's own nature and that of humanity. As regards this latter, our present concern, it transpired that the notion of God totally 'informing' a human person, being 'incarnate' in that person, was not only intelligible but also that there were grounds for recognizing that it had actually happened in the multiple levels of the complete humanity of Jesus the Christ. So we have now to ask, if 'God was in Christ', what does the Christ event tell us about God's ultimate purposes for human nature,[18] for human becoming – that is, for the realization of human potential, for human fulfilment, flourishing and even consummation?

The claim that Jesus was 'sinless' is often proffered by Christians as the answer to this question, with the concomitant assumption that by 'sinless' is meant moral perfection.[19] But historical evidence could never prove such a negative proposition, even if that available was much more ample than it actually is in the four gospels. Even from them it is not clear that Jesus was not sometimes, for example, angry or just irritated. In any case the quest for 'perfection' in humanity is liable to be the pursuit of a chimera because of the many ambiguities of the concept[20] and the impossibility of knowing what we really mean by it.

Perhaps we could simply attribute 'greatness' to the human Jesus of Nazareth? But he was not a great philosopher, scientist, artist, musician, statesman, writer – or any of the other spheres of human life to which the word 'great' is usually applied. The gospel evidence indicates that he was certainly very intelligent, quick in debate, skilled in pungent narrative and in pithy, often ironic, parables and exceptional in his effects on his contemporaries and in his personal relations – not least in his positive and open treatment of women, children and other second-class citizens of his times. And, as we have seen, he was certainly a devoted follower, if a radical one, of the commandments of the Law of the people of Israel, true faithfulness to which he called his fellow Jews. However, his distinctiveness does not lie even in this, for there were prophets before and noble rabbis after him who said as much. What is distinctive about Jesus was his openness to and intimacy with God his Father and his complete self-offering obedience to the will of God to the point of his ultimate surrender to and acceptance of death by crucifixion – *and* that his disciples had grounds for believing that after his very real death his life, *his* particular life of *that* kind, had been taken in its full identity and personhood through death 'up' into the very Being of God.[21] It was this resurrection,[22] and so transformation/re-creation,[23] of the Jesus-whom-they-knew that led to him being designated as the Christ, as 'Lord' and later as 'Son of God'. It was this which generated the conviction that his whole life, death and resurrection had an ultimate significance both as a window into, an *ikon* of, God's own nature and as revealing what humanity was meant by God to become – namely, united to God in self-offering love for God and others. His early disciples, their immediate followers including the New Testament authors, and subsequently the church through the ages have seen in the human Jesus who so responded to God and in the distinctiveness of that response not only a paradigm[24] but also the unique paragon[25] and archetype[26] of what it is for a human being to become united in self-offering will and purpose with God his Creator, his 'Father'. They saw that it was *God* who had acted in his resurrection and this endorsed what they had apparently only previously intuited – namely, that it was the presence of God in him which had made his teaching, life and death as remarkable as it was. Jesus' resurrection demonstrated to them, and so to us, that it is the union of *his* kind of life with God which is not broken by death and capable of being taken up into God. For he manifested the kind of human life which can become fully life with God, not only here and now, but eternally beyond the threshold of death.

But this has consequences for all humanity – and very early we find Paul expressing his conviction that what happened to Jesus is of significance for the possible ultimate destiny of all humanity. Jesus' resurrection emerges as the warrant and basis for the possibility of *our* ultimate life with God.[27] Indeed the Letter to the Hebrews speaks of the risen Jesus as the 'pioneer' of the salvation of the 'many children' brought to 'glory' through his being made 'perfect through sufferings'.[28] This is entirely consonant with Jesus' characteristic call to discipleship – 'Follow me'[29] – and with the earliest members of the church being described as 'of the Way'.[30] Clearly what happened to him, Jesus saw *could* happen to all. From what we subsequently know about him, his imperative 'Follow me' now constitutes for us a call for the transformation of humanity into a new kind of human being – and becoming.

In this perspective, Jesus the Christ, in the whole Christ event, has shown us what is possible for humanity. The actualization of this potentiality can properly be regarded as the consummation of the purposes of God in the evolution of humanity. To become one with God, to be fully open to God in self-offering love, is now to be perceived as the ultimate realization of human potential. Hence Jesus the Christ occupies in 'spiritual' history (that is, the history of the relationship of humanity with God) the place that a

mutation does in biological evolution – an irreversible transformation into a new kind of existence allowing the actualization
of new possibilities. In this sense, all humanity can aspire to
becoming 'Christlike' and can hope, as Paul puts it, to 'take the
shape/form of Christ'.[31] Those who become 'Christlike' in this
sense may be deemed to constitute a new kind of humanity,
almost a new 'spiritual species'. The consequence of welding
together these, then relatively recent, insights into human
evolution with a strongly incarnational theology was noted as
long ago as 1889 by J. R. Illingworth in *Lux Mundi*:

> . . . in scientific language, the Incarnation may be said to have introduced
> a new species into the world – a Divine man transcending past humanity,
> as humanity transcended the rest of creation, and communicating His
> vital energy by a spiritual process to subsequent generations of men.[32]

Such an idea is consistent with those passages in the 'New'
Testament that refer to the 'new creation' that has occurred in
Jesus the Christ.[33] It is an act of new *creation* because the
initiative is from God within human history within the responsive
human will of Jesus inspired by that outreach of God into
humanity traditionally designated as 'God the Holy Spirit'.[34]
Jesus the Christ can indeed be regarded as the progenitor of a new
possibility for humanity, a veritable 'second Adam' in a sense that
now enriches and gives a new dimension to this significant phrase
of St Paul for whom it was so pivotal in his understanding of
Christ and his role. As Wolfhart Pannenberg has recently
expressed it:

> . . . it takes a renewal of the human creature, a new Adam, to achieve what
> the human vocation has been from the beginning: to exist in the image of
> God. It is the Son incarnate who embodies that goal for which human
> beings have been created.[35]

Jesus the Christ is then seen, in the context of the whole Christ
event, as the supreme paragon and original archetype of what God
intends for all human beings, of the potential which God wishes to
see become actual in all humanity – the potentiality of responding
to, being open to, the God who is, in Jesus' own language, our
Father-Creator (and, in our contemporary perceptions, also our
Mother-Creator) and who calls us into unity with God's own
future.[36]

When we were surveying the perspectives of the sciences on human being we had to acknowledge that the sciences can give only limited help in providing any signposts for the direction of human becoming. We quoted Gunter Altner's assertion[37] to the effect that to be truly human, humanity must reach out beyond itself, that is, to be transcendent[38] – stretching towards 'the divine', he mooted – and we then turned to examine the 'long search' of humanity for God. Thereby we came to Jesus the Christ and in him, in the Christ event, we can now discern God's self-communication to humanity within the patterns and fabric of human history, in full accordance with the way in which we also found we had to conceive of any such divine self-communication in general.[39] In Jesus the Christ, God unveiled God's own 'meanings', his intentions and purposes for humanity in the form of a human being who *became* united with the ultimate Being and Becoming of God. That is the destiny and hope for humanity made known to us in Jesus the Christ.

But how can what happened in and to him, there and then, actually happen in us, here and now?

3 THE DIVINE INITIATIVE FOR HUMAN BECOMING

We have seen that in Jesus the Christ God has, as it were, unmistakably shown his hand, has unveiled further the purposes he has written into the cosmos for humanity. God in and through Jesus the Christ has afforded a new definition of what it is, or rather might be, to be and become fully human. In Jesus the Christ we see what kind of life it is (and the kind of death he suffered was specific to and a direct consequence of the character of his life) that can be taken up by God into the very being of God, so that death becomes the gateway into a new kind of existence, emergent from yet transcendent with respect to the matrix of matter-energy-space-time and the finitude of the individual person. It is a life of openness to God, of oneness with God's purposes to bring his kingdom into the life of humanity, of unstinting self-offering love of humanity through love of God.

So in Jesus the Christ we now have revealed the consummation of God's creative purposes for humanity. But how can what happened in and to him, happen in us? Is what happened in and to him in any way effective in and effectual for bringing the rest of humanity along the same 'Way'? Can it have any effects here and now, some two thousand years later, in a way that might actually enable us to live in harmony with God, ourselves and our fellow human beings – that is, experience the fulfilment for which human nature yearns?

Any possibility of answering such questions in the affirmative will have to be grounded on our sharing a common humanity with this Jesus. For only on this basis can we see Jesus the Christ, as we earlier suggested, as a 'distinctive manifestation of a possibility always inherently there for human beings in their potential nature, that is, by virtue of what God had created them to be and become'.[40] Such a joint emphasis on continuity (corresponding to 'immanence') as well as on emergence (corresponding to 'incarnation') we then also suggested would prove to be vital to any understanding of Jesus the Christ which is going to make what he *was* relevant to what we *might* be. For the interpretation of the 'incarnation' we have been propounding entails that what we have affirmed happened in and to Jesus is possible for all humanity – that is the basis of our hope. What is pivotal here is our joint affirmation both of the *continuity* of the human Jesus with the rest of creation, including humanity, with its concomitant stress on the meaning of that continuous action and self-communication of God in creation which is focussed, realized, unveiled and illuminated in him; and of the *emergence* in him through the divine initiative of what is new and irreducibly distinctive ('incarnation') in the relation of his created human nature to God. Because of the continuity we can conjecture that what happened in and to him could happen in and to us. But because, also, it was through the fusion of his human response and the divine initiative that Jesus of Nazareth became the 'Christ', with all that the title has come to imply, we have to inquire further about how the Christ event, the 'things about Jesus', could be operative in relation to *our* wills and to the divine initiative so that our transformation into harmony with God, ourselves and our fellow human beings becomes possible.

'God was in Christ reconciling the world to himself',[41] St Paul attested and the working out of how this might be so has been historically the intention of theories of the 'atonement', the 'at-one-ment'. This is the term used to refer to the reconciliation and the reconciling of God and humanity – both the condition of being 'at one' and the means whereby it is attained. It is often referred to as the 'work of Christ' and we must now inquire how it could be such in the light of the theology we have been developing here. Before we attend to the possible models that have been, or might today be, deployed to explicate such an at-one-ment we must remind ourselves of features in our scientific perspectives that might bear upon the way in which any such 'work of Christ' could be conceivable and credible. These appear to be:

(1) Biological death of the individual, as the means of the evolutionary creation of new species by natural selection, cannot *pace* St Paul be attributed to human 'sin', whether understood in a purely moral sense (i.e., as 'sins') or, more fundamentally, as alienation from God and humanity;[42]

(2) The evidence is all against human beings ever in the past having been in some golden age of innocence and perfection from which they have 'fallen'. Furthermore the frequent traditional emphasis in seeing in the Adam and Eve myth a connection between the human 'fallen' condition and the acquisition of sexual awareness has also been demolished by the evolutionary history of other sexual living organisms.[43] Hence that myth can now only be accepted as an existential insight into the human condition. That it is a significant and shrewd one we have indeed recognized[44] but now it has to be considered on its merits and 'inference to the best explanation'[45] requires that we also take into account other considerations, including those from the sciences. These latter constrain us to postulate that, whatever models or metaphors we eventually deploy to understand the 'work of Christ' in atonement, they must enable us to see how what happened in and to Jesus the Christ, with regard to (1) above, liberates us from the finitude which is constituted by the boundary of biological death; and, with regard to (2), can actually effect our release here and now from the bonds of that paradoxical state of frustrated incompleteness and alienation from God and humanity which we have already noted as our contemporary experience of 'original sin', and can thereby actually enable us to come into greater harmony with God and humanity.[46]

With these considerations in mind, let us now investigate briefly how the atonement, the 'work of Christ', has been broadly perceived hitherto. What first strikes any investigator is the multiplicity of models and metaphors which have been used to attempt to make this intelligible to the followers of Jesus the Christ from the beginning. For example, just to report the labours of one leading New Testament scholar, in expounding 'the concept of grace and the reality of salvation to which it refers', E. Schillebeeckx has distinguished as many as 'sixteen key concepts which occur repeatedly in all parts of the New Testament' and which give us an idea of its 'understanding of what redemption through Jesus Christ is from and what it is for'.[47]

In spite of this pluriformity within the New Testament, there has been continual pressure, not least in Anglican theology, to interpret the atoning efficacy of the *death* of Jesus as a 'sacrifice' with meanings developed out of those inherent in Old Testament rituals, as fully investigated in the recent Durham Essays in Theology.[48] However, as I. U. Dalferth reminds us in that volume, although 'there is abundant evidence that the New Testament uses sacrificial language with reference to the atoning death of Christ',[49] it is also necessary to pay attention to at least three features of its usage; 'its devaluation of the sacrificial cult, its spiritualizing use of the theme of sacrifice, and the limited function of the sacrificial symbolism in the Christian language of salvation'.[50] Thus, with respect to the last-mentioned, 'the astonishing multiplicity of ways, not always and in every respect compatible with each other, in which the New Testament writers express and communicate their understanding of salvation' is 'significant, for it resists all attempts at reduction'. In any case, Dalferth insists, 'the historically prior is not necessarily for this reason also the more true'.[51]

The Nicene Creed subsequently simply affirmed baldly that Christ 'was crucified *for us* under Pontius Pilate. He suffered and was buried'. This reticent 'for us' encompasses a very wide range of interpretations, of which the understanding of Jesus' death as a sacrifice is only one and not a necessary consequence of believing that the at-one-ment of God with humanity was accomplished in the Christ event. It is important to be clear about this because sacrificial interpretations of the 'work of Christ' are almost totally unintelligible, even if not actually repulsive, to people today who, by and large, are not enculturated into, or sympathetic with, the sacrificial system of the ancient Hebrew people in Old Testament times. Too much cultural water has flowed under the bridges for there to be much hope of the sacrificial images and metaphors ever again having a vital and evocative impact on those nurtured in a predominantly scientific culture. This is not to say that profound insights into the meaning of Christ's passion and death cannot be salvaged from such language,[52] but such images and metaphors are not going to be readily accessible to the average denizen of our contemporary culture dominated by scientific perspectives. It is really available only to the biblical scholars and professional theologians. However, this is *not* to say that any sense of Christ dying 'for us' has to be irretrievably lost with this demise of the communicability of sacrificial language.

Indeed, there is another distinctive strand of New Testament interpretation of the 'work of Christ' which appears *prima facie* to be capable both of giving an intelligible meaning to Jesus the Christ dying 'for us' and of being coherent with a credible theology along the lines we have been trying to develop. I refer to the notion of Jesus the Christ as the *representative* of humanity in his suffering and death. This is strongly argued by Morna Hooker as being the essence of St Paul's understanding of the atonement:

> It is as man's *representative*, rather than as his substitute, that Christ suffers, and it is only as one who is fully human that he is able to do anything effective for mankind, by lifting man, as it were, into an obedient relationship with God. The work of reconciliation between God and man is not achieved by the work of an outside Saviour (though, of course, it originates in the purpose of God), but is the working-out of utter love and obedience in human nature. The result is that *in Christ* men become what they were intended to be from the creation. In Christ there is a new creation, so that men now bear his image, as they have borne the image of Adam. They share this relationship with God by themselves becoming sons of God, and so finding blessing, righteousness, and glory. In other words they become truly human.[53]

For Morna Hooker, this notion of Christ as 'representative' of humanity is an aspect of a wider concept of Paul, namely, that of participation in Christ (cf. his use of the phrases 'in Christ' and 'with Christ'), which she designates by the, admittedly not wholly satisfactory, term 'interchange in Christ', meaning a mutual participation.[54] 'It is *not* that Christ and the believer change places, but rather that Christ, by his involvement in the human situation, is able to transfer believers from one mode of existence to another.'[55] She believes Paul's statements concerning 'interchange' in this sense 'offer the real clue to Paul's understanding of the atonement'[56] and, indeed, also of what was later called the 'incarnation'.[57]

J. D. G. Dunn also prefers the term 'representation', rather than 'substitution', to describe Paul's view of Jesus' death because he considers the latter too one-sided. For the latter 'tends to conjure up pagan ideas of Jesus' standing in man's place and pleading with an angry God'[58] and does not 'emphasize *with equal or greater weight* that in Paul's thought Jesus in his death also substituted *for God* in the face of man's sin'.[59] Any emphasis on Christ substituting for humanity in receiving on the cross a 'penalty' from God has not only the moral defect of representing God as inflicting punishment on the innocent, but also has a graver one, namely 'the blasphemy of supposing that God inflicts retributive justice like a hanging judge'.[60] In the parables of Jesus God accepts sinners by sheer grace and in Jesus' own dealings with sinners, he declares the divine forgiveness and receives them into fellowship with himself – 'God accepts men as they are, without conditions'[61] and this, G. W. H. Lampe argued, runs counter to much of the traditional teaching on the atonement for in that teaching the 'Cross is no longer the point at which the paradoxical love of God embraces men at the moment when they are supremely unlovable'.[62]

Thus 'penal substitution' interpretations of the atonement have fatal flaws, but is Paul's notion of Jesus as 'representative' really viable for us today? Minimally it includes the idea that Jesus shares our humanity (otherwise he could not even begin to represent us in any sense whatever), but how can what happened in and to him actually be effective for, have any effect on, *us*? In response to such questions, the concept of human 'solidarity' is often evoked and associated ideas of Christ being a 'corporate' or 'inclusive' personality.[63] Although such an essentially Hebraic concept undoubtedly underlies New Testament ideas of the believer being 'in Christ' and 'with Christ',[64] it is hard to see what ontological basis it actually has – over and beyond merely *asserting* that what happened in and to Jesus Christ can be regarded as happening in and to us. But this begs the very question at issue. So such talk does not solve the problem and appears to me to be the Achilles heel of the undoubtedly Pauline notion of Jesus being our 'representative' in any sense that goes beyond the simple affirmation that he shares our humanity. However, this limited assertion may prove to be enough, as I hope we shall see.

The ideas of Jesus' solidarity with us and of his being our representative in his sufferings and death have often been invoked as the basis for ascribing a *universal* significance for the 'work of Christ'. By universal there is meant 'the particularity of

the Christ event is *constitutive* of universal reconciliation', as
V. White has recently argued.[65] That is, on his view, what Jesus
accomplished through his suffering and death is effective in
principle for all humanity, past, present and future, whether or
not they consciously hear and receive the Christian message. But
if the notions of the 'solidarity' of humanity, and so of Christ
having in some sense an 'inclusive' personality, cannot be given
an intelligible content, then Jesus' representation of humanity
cannot have an 'objective', 'constitutive', ontological, universal
effect – even though we accept that his humanity was actual, real
and complete, so what happened in and to him could and might
happen in and to us. Hence the question of *how* this could or might
be so remains. An alternative possible basis for the sought-after
'universality', in the sense above, might reside in there being a
change in *God* so that God's relation to humanity is thereby
irreversibly changed for all eternity. This is the presumption of
many of the 'theories of the atonement' which have been propounded, unsatisfactory though it is fundamentally, as we shall
see.

Although the church, in its many branches, has never officially
endorsed any one particular theory of the atonement, one way of
interpreting the work of Christ 'for us', yet a number of such
theories have become classical in the sense of being widely
disseminated doctrinally, liturgically and devotionally. They
continue to attract the attention of contemporary theologians of
many different persuasions.[66] All that is possible to do here is to
draw some conclusions from these critical and wider surveys. The
central models and metaphors of these classical theories of the
atonement which are regarded as representing what was effected
in the Christ event, God's 'saving' action in Jesus the Christ,
include:

– a vicarious sacrifice (already alluded to);
– a demonstration of justice in which 'satisfaction' is made of the
demands of justice (Anselm);
– a decisive victory over hostile evil powers (revived in 1931 by
G. Aulen in his *Christus Victor*);
– an act of love (Abelard).

Of these theories[67] of the atonement (the sources quoted must be
consulted for a fuller exposition) all, apparently except the last,
are susceptible to a 'constitutive' interpretation. For they all
postulate something as having happened irreversibly on the cross

which is of universal significance in the relation of God and humanity. Equally, all, except the last, involve some kind of change within God as a result of the 'work of Christ'.

F. W. Dillistone rightly reminds us that the writings of leading Christian theologians at successive periods of Christian history should be 'necessarily viewed within the context of the cultural assumptions and interests of their own time'[68] and that we should draw upon the

> nature of alienation and estrangement which seems to have been uppermost at the time. At-one-ment only becomes meaningful when there is some sense of brokenness, of disruption, of things being 'out of joint', of falling short, of estrangement from the ideal self, from social well-being, from God.[69]

These last are certainly features of the human condition as experienced in this scientific age, as we have already observed.[70]

We today have the duty to re-assess ideas concerning the atonement in the light of our own judgment on the paradoxes of humanity as we perceive them in our times. The historical perspective should make us sympathetic to past theories of the atonement which nevertheless now seem so inaccessible to us – admittedly sometimes even absurd and morally repelling.

When the revisable nature of the metaphors, and models, of theological language is properly taken into account,[71] it is, in fact, possible to accept more readily and to discern more clearly the realities to which the 'constitutive' theories were attempting to refer. Recent authors, such as C. Gunton and P. Fiddes,[72] have been properly sensitive to the way in which metaphors operate in these theories and have enabled past generations to depict, however falteringly, the reality of God's action in Christ to which they seek to refer.[73] However, because these theories were so culturally conditioned, they are not readily available to most of us in an age dominated by other perceptions, such as those of science, which generate new constraints on and provide new insights for our thinking (e.g., (1) and (2) above).

To begin with, we note that the 'constitutive' theories (i.e., all except the last, Abelardian one) in their different ways, depict the 'work of Christ' in his suffering and death on the cross as involving a transformation at that time of the status of humanity in its alienation from God[74] to a new status in which the relation has once-for-all been restored and death has been universally overcome. The dominating concept in these theories is of an irreversible, ontological change of the status of humanity before God at a point of time (the Cross) which reverses the effects of an historical 'Fall', including its supposed consequence of biological death. This change of status is regarded as somehow universally applicable to all humanity. These 'constitutive' (or 'objective') theories of the atonement therefore rely heavily on the very two pre-suppositions which are no longer tenable in the light of well-founded science (namely, (1) and (2) above). Not surprisingly, they also fail to incorporate our sense – which we derive from the vista of cosmological, biological and human evolution which the sciences unfold before us – of humanity as emerging, with concomitant positive and negative consequences, into individual and corporate consciousness and self-consciousness; into an awareness of values; into social cooperation and transmission of human culture; and into a sense of and awareness of God. This is not to deny the possibility of new modalities of human becoming beyond the purview of the sciences, as such. Indeed this limitation of the sciences is precisely the point at which the Christian perspective can come into play with its full force.

But it is also at this very point that the classical, 'constitutive' theories of the atonement fail to express any dynamic sense of the process of human *becoming* as still going on. They fail to meet the requirement that any effective transformation of humanity, whether in its relation to God or in its mutual relationships, needs to be a continuous shaping and moulding of a *humanum* still in the process of becoming what God intends. We are incomplete, paradoxical creatures needing the continuous creative action of God to bring us into harmony with God's own self, our fellow human beings – and, increasingly, it seems, with nature too. We need a 'theory of the atonement' which really shows how God's action in Jesus the Christ actually can contribute to that process here and now.[75]

Another serious defect, in my view, of all these classical 'constitutive' theories of the atonement, except the Abelardian, is that they fail to make clear how the human response which is an essential part of the reconciliation between God and humanity is evoked. For, as Fiddes puts it, 'that human response must actually be part of the act of salvation, not merely a reaction to it afterwards'.[76] So the question which was posed at the end of the previous section and with which this one began needs to be reframed as: how can what happened in and to Jesus the Christ actually evoke in us the response that is needed for our reconciliation to God and actually enable us to live in harmony with God and humanity here and now?

This question may be answered most effectively, it seems to me,[77] by seeing the life, suffering and death of Jesus the Christ as an *act of love*, as Fiddes[78] expounds it – an act of love *of God*. Recognition of the continuity of Jesus the Christ with ourselves has already enabled us to see him as the forerunner, the first realization and instantiation of, a new possibility for human existence. We perceive in him that this is not a mere possibility but can actually be the case in a human response of costly obedience and of openness to God which was itself an initiative of God in his outreach to humanity – that is, God as Holy Spirit, immanent within the created world.

But in the suffering and death of Jesus the Christ, we now also concomitantly perceive and experience the suffering, self-offering love of God in action, no more as abstract knowledge, as might well have been the case in our previous reflections on God as Creator suffering in, with and under creation. For we have recognized too that the openness and obedience of the human Jesus to God enabled him to be a manifest self-expression in history, in the confines of human personhood, of God as creative Word/*Logos*/'Son'.[79] In and with the suffering and cross of Jesus the Christ we witness *God* explicitly in history undergoing that suffering which God's vulnerable, self-offering Love eternally invests in his work of ongoing creation, with all the self-limitation that involves.[80]

From this perspective, we now see in the life, suffering and death of Jesus the Christ, in his humanly experienced anguish, *God* going to the ultimate in suffering love on behalf of humanity, an act of Love 'for us'. Thereby is uniquely and definitively revealed the depths of the divine Love for humanity and the cost of God's gracious outreach to us as we are, 'sinners', alienated from God, humanity and ourselves. As such this love of God *engages*[81] us. That is to say, the cross, as the culmination of that particular human life, with its teaching, character and suffering, is not only a statement about God's love and about perfect human love, but is rather a proposal *of* love and *as such* engages our response. Once we have really come to know that it was God's love in action 'for us' in the Christ event, then we can never be the same again. For in ordinary human life, an act or expression of love, once perceived as such, has an irreversible effect on the one loved, so that the relation is fundamentally changed – a new bond and harmony is proffered which, if responded to, itself transforms the relationship by establishing the basis of a new flourishing and deepening of it. So it is *a fortiori* with our experiencing the love of God as revealed in the self-offering of the one human person, Jesus the Christ, who alone could be and was the transparent lens through which was focussed the self-offering, suffering Love of God towards humanity and all creation. For, if the response to human love can have such a transformative power on human relationships, how much more must response to the outreach of ultimate Love make an irreversibly profound, difference existentially, here and now, to our communion and harmony with God?

The same God in that outreach to humanity, as Holy Spirit, which united the human Jesus with the Father, his Creator, now kindles and generates in us a love for God our Creator and for the humanity for whom Jesus died, as we contemplate God in Christ on the cross. What is being proposed here is that this action of God as Holy Spirit in us is itself effecting our at-one-ment, is itself salvific, actually making us whole, making us 'holier' – that is, it saves and sanctifies us, restoring us in our right relationships to God, humanity and ourselves. 'Through the Holy Spirit he has given us, God's love has flooded our hearts.'[82]

Through the 'work of Christ' and God as Holy Spirit, human beings now: know that they can live their lives in and with God through the self-offering of themselves in love and obedience to the God and Father of our Lord Jesus Christ; and are also enabled to do so by the action within them of that selfsame God as 'Holy Spirit' as they immerse themselves in the contemplation of the life, death and resurrection of God incarnate in *that* human life of Jesus the Christ. Thereby we are enabled to share in Jesus Christ's own life of obedience towards his and our Father, of becoming open to God in the way he himself was. That is our potential transformation here and now which can constitute our at-one-ment with God, our fellow human beings and ourselves.

In this understanding, atonement is no longer conceived of in static terms, as some abstruse transaction effected by God whereby his attitude towards us is changed, as in the 'constitutive' theories – the correcting of some debit in the divine balance sheet, or the removing of a penalty in a divine law court, etc.

Rather, it is seen as a manifestation of God's perennial, loving gracious intention to actualize the potential he has given us of a full and enriched personhood by bringing humanity into his own life through that self-offering and suffering love for God which God's own self kindles in us through his immanent presence as Holy Spirit – as we respond to that Love revealed in Jesus the Christ. It is a path costly to God and costly to us.[83]

This has been, in fact, a recurrent theme in the Christian reaction to Jesus' suffering and death, for example, in its still popular expression in Isaac Watts' hymn:

> When I survey the wondrous Cross
> on which the Prince of glory died
> My richest gain I count but loss
> And pour contempt on all my pride.
> . . .
> Were the whole realm of nature mine,
> That were an offering far too small;
> Love so amazing, so divine,
> Demands my soul, my life, my all.

The case for such an understanding of how atonement is the effect of the Christ event has recently been cogently argued, indeed re-vivified, by Paul Fiddes[84] who shows that this basically Abelardian[85] approach is not a purely 'subjective' interpretation of the 'work of Christ' nor merely an 'exemplarist' view of the significance of Jesus' humanity for us today. Fiddes sets out to demonstrate, to me it seems successfully, that Abelard is pointing us towards something much more objective than the power of the love of God revealed in the cross to *move* us to similar love – namely, 'the power of the divine love to *create* or generate love within human beings'.[86] In his expansion of Abelard's theme, Fiddes calls upon psychology (R. Niebuhr and R. S. Lee) to:

> supply insights into psychological processes through which the story and image of Christ – teacher and crucified one – can transform the mind. Whether 'shattering' the self-centredness of the ego or healing the conflict between conscious and unconscious levels of the mind, the [psychological] theories [of the atonement] show that the effect of revelation is much deeper than a mere moving of the emotions.[87]

> . . . the revelation of love's truth is at the same time a generation of love.[88]

Why the love of God can be demonstrated finally in the *death* of Christ is rendered intelligible if one accepts, as Abelard did not, but as we have done in this volume,[89] that the *divine* nature can suffer as well as the *human* nature of Jesus – so that *God* suffers in the human suffering and death of Jesus the Christ. As Fiddes puts it, 'God himself undergoes the bitter depths of human experience in the cross. God, we may say, shows his love by enduring to the uttermost the estrangement of his own creation. This is the depths of God's identification with us.'[90]

Fiddes finds one weakness of Abelard's approach to be its apparently excessive individualism, for the transforming power of God's love is postulated as happening as the individual self comes into confrontation with a story of unique revelatory force. However a sense of the corporate character of the salvation, which the whole complex of the human world alienated from God requires, can be included[91] in it if adequate account is taken of the following: the new kind of 'corporate life' which can come into existence between those so transformed by God's love and between them and God; the corporate character of the 'means of grace'[92] through which the Christ event impinges on the individual; and the relational reality that is the new kind of human being which is Jesus the Christ, who is the 'beyond in the midst of life', in the centre and not at the boundaries (Bonhoeffer) – where there is suffering and oppression in which God participates. 'So the presence of Christ, conforming us to himself, is intimately bound up with the cross whether he is met in the community of the church or the community of the wider world.'[93]

This conceiving of the 'work of Christ', this achieving of at-one-ment by the Christ-event, as an act of and engagement with us of God's suffering, self-offered Love at no point depends on assuming a past historical 'Fall'. Since it conceives of our salvation and sanctification as the initiation and continuation of a process whereby God as Holy Spirit kindles love for God and humanity in us here and now as we face what God did there and then in Jesus the Christ, it coheres with our present evolutionary perceptions that the specifically human emerged and still emerges only gradually and fitfully in human history.

Furthermore, since God took Jesus through death into his own life, there is implied in the initiation and continuation of this process in us, that we too can thereby be taken up into the life of

God, can be 'resurrected' in some way akin to that of Jesus the Christ.[94]

> Now if this is what we proclaim, that Christ was raised from the dead, how can some of you say that there is no resurrection from the dead? If there is no resurrection, then Christ was not raised; and if Christ was not raised, then our gospel is null and void, and so too is your faith.[95]

At this point we recall[96] that all we can with assurance affirm about the resurrection of Jesus is that he was apprehended as having been taken through death with his personhood and identity intact and as having been 'taken up' into the presence of God. Since that happened to him, Paul is saying, it *could* happen to us and that is the ground of our hope for our individual future and that of humanity corporately. The virtue of being agnostic about the relation between the empty tomb and the risen Christ here becomes apparent. For, within a relatively short time after our own biological death, our bodies will lose their identity as their atomic and molecular constituents begin to disperse through the earth and its atmosphere, often becoming part of other human beings. So within a few years, there are no physical remains that could, logically, possibly be the vehicle of any continuity for our particular identity. This would constitute an insuperable, logical gulf – even for God – between what could happen to us and what happened to Jesus if *his* resurrection consisted of a transformation of his physical body, for the nature of his resurrection would then be unique and irrelevant to what might happen to us.[97]

If, on the other hand, we confine our assertions about the resurrection to the experience of the disciples that the whole person of Jesus has become the risen/exalted Christ after his death, with continuity of his personal identity – coupled with no particular assertion about what happened to his body – then, if God so wills it, what happened to him *could* in principle happen to us. It would then be for us, as it was for Jesus, an act of God supervening beyond the natural order, in which our physical bodies are the vehicles of our personal identity, by providing us, after our biological death, with a new mode of expression of our individual personhood and identity. This would have to be a new kind of what we can only call 'embodiment' of that individual personhood of ours which, in this life, is expressed in and through, and in some sense *is*, our bodies.[98]

Furthermore the interpretation[99] of the death and resurrection of Jesus as manifesting uniquely the quality of life which can be taken up by God into the fullness of God's own life implicitly involves an affirmation about what the basic potentiality of all humanity is. It shows us that, regardless of our particular human skills and creativities – indeed regardless of almost all that the social mores of our times applauds – it is through a radical openness to God, a thoroughgoing self-offering love for others and obedience to God that we grow into such communion with the eternal God that *God* does not allow biological death to rupture that essentially timeless relation.

Moreover, while our sufferings, and even more the sufferings of those close to us and of the millions we only hear about, remain an opaque mystery, what happened in and to Jesus the Christ begins at least to make them more bearable as we come to realize that God is suffering in and with us and them. God has experienced human suffering in the passion of the human Jesus whom he indwelt and so can know and share our sufferings here and now. There is a sense in which the sufferings of Jesus the Christ now exist within God's own self and it is to God as so apprehended that we can turn in our distress.

This way of understanding the 'work of Christ', of at-one-ment, therefore appears as not only consistent with evolutionary perspectives (which include features (1) and (2) above) but also shows how, in and through Jesus the Christ, God acted to meet those needs of humanity which stem specifically from our unique self-awareness,[100] namely, our needs *inter alia*: to come to terms with death and with finitude; to bear suffering in ourselves and in others; to realize our potentialities; and to steer our paths through life.[101]

Now the possibility of these needs being met rests entirely on the nature and character of God as revealed through his activity and presence in Jesus the Christ. But *to* whom has this been revealed? Those human beings who have had access to the revelation of this explicit activity of God can consciously appropriate its benefits and consequences by responding to it, if they so will. Yet the vast majority of those who have ever lived, and indeed of those living today, have not had such access. Even in societies in which Christian churches have long existed, the pressures of secularization and of a science-dominated (or, rather, a 'scientistic'-dominated) culture[102] restrict such access especially when the churches themselves fail to present the revelation in credible terms. It is such reflections that, quite rightly, generate the pressure to attribute some kind of 'constitutive', universal effect of the atonement which will be operative for all humanity regardless of whether or not they have known of the revelation that is in Jesus the Christ. We have rejected those theories of the atonement which imply an event that changed God's attitude and relation to humanity; yet it is on this basis that 'universal' effects for the atonement in Christ have usually been predicated.[103] How can seeing the atonement as an 'act of love' respond to that proper pressure for any theory to have a universal scope?

We recall that, in this interpretation, the establishing of a relationship with God depended on our response in love, through the action of God as Holy Spirit in us, to God revealing himself and experienced as self-offering, suffering Love in the Christ event. Note that it was *God* as Word/*Logos*/'Son', God in the modality of God's own self-expression in the created world, God as universally operative and perennially within the created order, who is the One who is incarnate in Jesus of Nazareth. Furthermore, it was God as thus understood who, in the words of the Prologue to St John's Gospel, 'was life, and that life was the light of mankind. The light shows in darkness and the darkness never mastered it.'[104] This 'light' never ceases to illuminate humanity at all times in all places, so all human beings have the opportunity of seeing at least some of its gleams and to respond to God as Word/*Logos*/'Son' through the images and symbolic resources of their various cultures (including entirely 'secular' ones). Whatever positive response is made by a human being to such self-expressions of the God who is Love cannot but be salvific for them, that is, effective in the process of at-one-ment with God – by whatever name God is named, whether in a 'religious' context or not. Such at-one-ment, on the understanding we have espoused here of its being effected through an 'act of love' and revelation of God in the Christ event, is of universal significance for it is the explicit manifestation of what the *eternal* love of God is doing at all times and places to reach out to all humanity, past, present and future. It is *that* Love which can elicit a healing, salvific response at all times and all places and in all cultures, however difficult it is for Christian believers to identify it across cultural barriers.[105] This encourages such believers to pass on to others the revelation that they have received in Jesus the Christ but it should also prevent them from placing restrictions on the scope of God's loving, communicating activity in the world. There is therefore no need to evoke 'theories' of the atonement which will render it 'constitutive' and so 'universal' in ways that presume to change God's attitude to humanity. For even if the suffering and death of Jesus the Christ change God's *experience*, God's *nature* as Love remains eternal and unchanging in character – and 'for all'.

It seems to me that this understanding of the at-one-ment – of what has traditionally included 'redemption', 'salvation', and 'sanctification' – is wholly consistent with both the revelation in Jesus the Christ and with that evolutionary perspective warranted by the sciences. It affords, I would suggest, the Christian faith a way of communicating to a generation to whom the older language, based on other models and theories of the atonement, is often totally incomprehensible and unbelievable – even when they are not actually morally repellent, as is the 'penal substittion' theory. Those who have been nurtured in the bosom of the church and steeped in biblical language and models (e.g., that of 'sacrifice') may still be able to appropriate the language of such traditional 'theories of the atonement' and make them their own so that they have a significance for their devotional lives. But for most of our contemporaries, and especially those who take seriously the scientific accounts of human origins, such language is not available and is often totally mystifying and incomprehensible, even for believers in God.

It is imperative that the church starts talking about at-one-ment (salvation, redemption, sanctification) in a credible manner – yet still in a way true to Christian insights down the centuries. Salvation is about making whole – about health, wholeness, wholesomeness.[106] It is about living in and with God in such a way that our alienation from God, from other human beings and from ourselves is overcome by the life God can now live in us as we respond to what God in Christ revealed to us – the gracious, costly, suffering love of God for us and for our fulfilment as God's creation. So the 'good news' is all about living our lives in and with God; about being taken into the presence of God and being re-shaped after the image of Christ so that God begins to 'take over' our inner lives and our humanity begins to become what God intended. Thus we can become a God-transformed human being, which is, after all what Christ was and still is. Thus it is Paul yearns for the Galatians that 'Christ be formed' in them, that they 'come to have the form of Christ'.[107] As, through God's action in us, this process continues, we can hope to become more and more one with the resurrected Jesus the Christ who is now present within the life of the Godhead. This seems, in short, the way to make what happened to Jesus there and then have significance for us here and now.

In this volume, I have been attempting to work out a theology which is both rooted in the Judeo-Christian tradition and also consonant and coherent with those scientific perspectives on the world which are well-established enough in our culture to form the pre-suppositions of most of our thinking, at least in the 'West'. The result is, I would hope, a reasonable locating and exposition of the basic essentials of the Christian revelation within that context of a world profoundly influenced by and indebted to the perspectives of the sciences. It has been my hope that this approach might encourage genuine inquirers to take with utter seriousness at least the putative reasonableness of the claim that in Jesus the Christ there has been a revelation in incarnation of the God who is eternally the transcendent-immanent Creator whose fundamental nature is best described as that of Love. And that such unprejudiced inquirers might, furthermore, come to see that Jesus the Christ is the consummation both of the creative work of God in evolution and of the revelation of God made to the people of Israel; that in and through him human beings can receive insight into the potentialities of their own being and becoming; that through their response to the revelation of God as Love, made explicit in the Christ event, God can also effect in them a re-orientation of their self-understanding and a transformation of their relation to God; and that thereby they can begin to become what God intended them to be and become, namely, one with God, in harmony with God's own self and purposes in the world.

This has been the major objective of this work and whether or not it has been achieved at this stage must be left to the readers. However, we have arrived at no resting stage in any inquiry that is adequate to our themes. For having established, as I hope, why human becoming might legitimately be represented as a process of growing into God in Christ through the Holy Spirit, one still needs to determine the means for effecting this process and to formulate how its end is best conceived. Such tasks are beyond the scope of a volume of this compass. But, since the pervasive influence of scientific perspectives cannot be absent from any reasonable and believable expositions even of what constitute the divine means and end of human becoming, some consideration of these matters is needed in this context to send inquirers on their way. The next chapter will be concerned to indicate briefly some of the issues involved and the resources for pursuing such a quest.

CHAPTER 16

L'ENVOI: The Divine Means for and the End of Human Becoming

In the previous chapter, we considered human becoming in terms of at-one-ment, of humanity being reconciled to God through Jesus the Christ, of human beings becoming 'one with God, in harmony with God's own self and purposes in the world'.[1] To speak thus is to refer to the divine 'end' of human becoming in two relevant senses of that word: the 'end of human becoming' as God's *purpose* expressed in the process of human becoming; and union with God as the *terminus* of this process which human beings ultimately hope to attain and to which human becoming converges.

The 'end of human becoming' in the first sense provokes inquiry into the means whereby this process of human becoming is facilitated and consolidated; and how these means might also be conceived of as *divine* activities in the light of our understanding of how God interacts with the world and communicates with humanity. The 'end of human becoming' in the second sense relates both to a significant element in traditional Christian thought (that of 'deification', *theosis* in the Eastern Church)) and, if only by contrast, to scientific projections concerning the future of *homo sapiens*, of the Earth and of the universe. In this concluding, dispatching, chapter we consider the divine means for and end of human becoming in order to sketch out briefly how the theology for a scientific age propounded here might be applied and extended both existentially in the life of the church and as the basis of eschatological hope.

The divine means for human becoming for those who have responded to the love of God manifest in Jesus the Christ and who have set out on the transforming process of human becoming intended by God the Creator are traditionally known as the 'means of grace'.[2] They include the Bible, prayer, worship and the sacraments. It is worth considering briefly how their role and operation might be understood in the light of our earlier proposals concerning God's interaction with the world and God's communication with humanity.[3] It was suggested that God, and only God, can affect patterns of events within the world by exerting 'top-down'/'whole-part' constraints or influences, including those that affect the brain events, consciousness and thinking, feeling, etc., of human beings – for these human experiences are themselves mediated through the world of objects (Popper's[4] world 1) and of cultural artefacts (his world 3), as in human inter-personal communication.

From this perspective, the *Bible*, as the communally selected, and preserved, library of the Judeo-Christian tradition and as a record of classic human experiences of God, often in events that have proved to be seminal, is a unique and irreplaceable resource. For in it we meet human beings attempting to discern patterns of events *as* of divine origin and responding, or in many cases not responding, to them. As the reader judges the extent to which he or she may discern the activity of God in the events and experiences it records, the Bible has an uncanny ability also to judge the reader. It is moreover unique in providing awareness of the milieu and experiences of God into which Jesus the Christ entered in history so that its role as a 'means of grace' can never be underestimated. As itself a human 'world 3' artefact, it exists within the world of human culture with all its limitations, but this does not diminish by one whit its value as a means whereby God communicates to humanity, for all such communication is mediated through the 'broken vessels' of human individuals and societies. The traditional role of the Bible as a 'means of grace' is therefore entirely intelligible within the understandings we have developed in this work. As such, the value of the biblical literature will depend crucially on critical analysis of its contents united with sensitive discernment – as with all great classical literature – for none of the activities of God in the world or God's communications to human beings comes ready-labelled as 'made in heaven'!

In *prayer* individuals, either alone or corporately, believe themselves to be in communication with God – they feel themselves to be 'in the presence of' God. Prayer involves states of consciousness (Popper's 'world 2') which are conditioned and evoked to some extent by objects in the natural world ('world 1') and the heritage of cultural artefacts ('world 3'), but are primarily successions of mental states ('world 2': thoughts, feelings, intentions, etc.) that have the character of being experiences of God, sometimes in a distinctive personal modality (but not always so[5]). As successions of mental states, they are also successions of brain states and so susceptible to the influence both of earlier brain states of the individual praying and also of the 'top-down'/whole-part' action of God in the past and during prayer itself. Hence prayer falls within the scope of the way in which we have proposed that God interacts with the world and can shape the patterns of its physical events (including patterns of brain activity or memory, and so mental states); and also within the range of modes of God's communication with human beings in such a world. That experience of God in prayer should often have the character of being like a *personal* interaction is also intelligible in this framework of thought for we have already seen that personal interactions between human beings are entirely mediated by the natural entities, structure and processes of the world which, of course, include the human, cultural artefacts of 'world 3'. The 'varieties of religious experience', discussed earlier in these terms,[6] therefore subsume this major feature of prayer as personal communion with God.

However, recent discussion[7] has focussed more on the nature of *intercessory/impetratory* prayer, in which human beings ask God that particular events may occur, and therefore involve how one considers God to 'act in' the world. In such prayer the individual, or group, praying are *ipso facto* altering the situation, the pattern of events (including the brain events of those praying) with which God is being asked to interact. Hence the very act of praying provides God with a different situation from that which would prevail if the prayer(s) had not been offered – and so provides an opportunity that God would not otherwise have had to interact with the total situation by his 'top-down'/whole-part' interaction to bring about a different outcome, if God so wills it. Any such response of God of this holistically interactive kind may not only not be readily obvious in its complexity to our limited discernment, but is also likely to operate over a much longer time span than our impatience would naturally demand. For the validity of this kind of prayer does not have to imply any crudely 'interventionist' understanding even of God's positive responses to it.

In communal *worship*, groups of people focus their attention on God's revelation and intentions for them and the world (including other people) and together seek to relate to God as a group in various modes – praise, thanksgiving, adoration, confession, celebration, etc. Such worship may also be regarded as itself a particular pattern of events occurring in a community of individual human beings, each with their own brain/mental states, but now, in this situation, with specific inter-personal relationships occurring communally which would not otherwise be present. Again, such particular kinds of situation could make it possible for God to interact distinctively (in a 'top-down/'whole-part' manner, as we have proposed) both with the worshipping community and with the world in which they exist so that new situations and relationships, not otherwise possible, can occur. And this would be anticipated with some confidence if the worshipping community had reason to believe that God had indicated to them, most likely through their tradition pointing back to seminal events and experiences, that such communal action would evoke a response from him.

This is especially true of the *sacraments* which originate, directly or indirectly, within the complex of experiences of the early Christian communities that the Christ event generated. For one in particular, the eucharist, there is good historical evidence that it is an act authorized by Jesus himself.[8] In the sacraments, the Christian church takes 'entities, structures and processes'[9] of the natural world, often transformed by human activities – such as bread, wine, oil – and attributes to them a divine instrumental function, whereby God effects changes within the participant(s) characteristic of and particular to the designated situation; and also a symbolic function, wherein God signifies particular features of his continuing relation to human beings transformed by the Christ event. These are the two aspects of how we earlier, following O. C. Quick,[10] thought God can be regarded as being broadly related to the world. The 'entities, structures and processes' of the world have, we suggested, an instrumental function of being the means whereby God effects his purposes; and also a symbolic function wherein God signifies and expresses God's own nature. These are aspects both of God's presence in the world in general and of sacramental acts, in particular. As such, sacramental acts are particular, focussed representations and manifestations of a universal character of God's relation to the created world.

Within the life of the Christian church, a sacramental act is a particular pattern of events which has been given this kind of significance in a tradition believed to be divinely authorized, directly or indirectly. Any sacramental action in its totality is then regarded as having an irreducible, holistic significance as the medium and means of God's gracious activity in and upon those specifically involved in the act, which always has a communal dimension. As such, sacramental actions are intelligible in terms of the way we have regarded God as interacting generally with the world (in a 'top-down'/whole-part' manner) so as to affect the patterns of events, and as communicating with humanity in the world – but, in these instances, with the added feature that such patterns of sacramental activity are regarded as having been divinely designated as the medium of God's self-communication to humanity. It is entirely appropriate that sacraments involve created 'entities, structures and process' of the world for, through the divinely sustained evolutionary process, they have in humanity emerged to become the vehicle of the personal, and so of the mental and of the spiritual – the capacities to be thinking and be self-consciousness, and consciously to relate to God.[11] Indeed the whole approach of this book can, at this stage, be regarded as a working out of the William Temple's notion of the universe itself as sacramental[12] – and encouragement for its pertinence to our situation today is to be found in the related notion that human 'life is sacramental' expounded in the concluding pages of Bernard Cooke's significant recent contribution to sacramental theology.[13]

The Christian sacraments are an activity which the church as a *community* is specifically authorized to implement. This reminds us that the nature of the community of those who have responded to the love of God manifest in Jesus the Christ, and in whom God as Holy Spirit engenders love for God and humanity, is an essential element in the way the Christ event is appropriated by the individual. That community, the 'church', is more than the sum of its individual members; it is a collective 'system' and has itself a quality and character that is *sui generis* to which the New Testament terminology of the church as, in some sense, the 'Body' of Christ draws pointed attention. More research is merited than has yet been carried out on the relation of the concepts operative in modern evolutionary biology, social psychology and sociology to this and other images, models and metaphors attempting to depict the nature of the 'church'. This does not have to be carried out with reductionist intentions, any more than does the study of the psychology of religion void religious experience and the reality of its referent. For example, when we were discussing the 'divine meaning for human becoming' in the previous chapter,[14] we tentatively mooted the idea of humanity become 'Christlike' as a new kind of humanity, a new 'spiritual species', an idea found as long ago as 1889 when Illingworth adopted the language of Darwinian evolution for human spiritual development.[15] Hence it is intriguing to find John Zizioulas, in a study of personhood and the church from an essentially patristic viewpoint,[16] posing the question 'How do we see this new biological hypostasis of man[17] realized in history?' and answering 'In the Church'. It would be interesting to investigate further the relation between these parallel but apparently converging approaches to the holistic nature of that new entity, the church, which emerged out of, and beyond, the biological evolution of *homo sapiens*.

Furthermore, the relation of that community to human creativity and culture and to the natural world has too often been overlooked. We need the recovery of the motivations and sense of *Christian humanism* and of human beings as *co-creators* with God, as I have urged elsewhere.[18] The latter has received extensive expression and development in Philip Hefner's study of human beings as 'created co-creators'[19] with God.[20] The enterprise of co-creating with God as creatures, could also provide the basis for a new mode of interaction of science and Christian theology. For those who aspire to co-create *with* God in nature – working harmoniously with the grain, as it were, of the natural order – will need more and better-informed science and technology in order simultaneously to provide for human needs and to respect the rest of the world, living and non-living. This, it seems to me, is the direction which we should be looking for a sound basis for that 'creation-centred' spirituality and a theo-centric ecological ethic[21] which many in our contemporary society are now seeking.

The divine end of human becoming has been encapsulated for the exposition in this book in the phrase of Irenaeus: '. . . to make us what even he [Jesus the Christ] is'. For the definition of human beings to be seen in Jesus the Christ is not merely a *self*-definition: it constitutes not what they begin as, but that to which God intends to bring them. However we may define and describe humanity from the viewpoint of the sciences, this is no match for a definition coming, as it were, from the direction of the Other who is God the Creator. In this sense Jesus the Christ is the definition of the divine end of humanity – he defines humanity not by its origins in the physical, biological and social worlds but in terms of what God intends humanity to become. In and through Jesus the Christ we have come to see what human personalness can amount to. In his life and death and, supremely, in his resurrection, we see a concentration of the activity of the immanent Creator to bring created personalness out of materiality into the divine life.

We here come very close to patristic teaching on the 'deification' (Gk. *theosis*) of humanity as the goal, the 'end' in this sense, of the Christian life – to become 'like' God, to share in the divine nature in the sense of 'sharing in God's energies which, however, are truly God in his action and self-disclosure.'[22] It is important to note that the 'deification' of humanity

does not mean absorption into God, since the deified creature remains itself and distinct. It is the whole human being, body and soul, who is transfigured in the Spirit into the likeness of the divine nature, and deification is the goal of every Christian, to be reached by the faithful following of Christ in the common life of his body the church.[23]

From the perspective of the Christian revelation, the ultimate destiny of humanity is to be 'in God', to be vouchsafed that beatific vision so nobly expressed in the last stanzas of Dante's *Paradiso*. This is the basis of the Christian hope in the human future. In my earlier *Creation and the World of Science*, I examined the understanding of the basis of hope in some contemporary Christian theologians. I concluded,[24] and still judge, that for the 'theologians of hope' (e.g., C. Braaten, W. Pannenberg, J. Moltmann), hope becomes for them the attitude appropriate to the experience engendered when we look towards God in the present; that for Teilhardian theologians, hope is located on the axis which runs between humanity and God, rather than along the 'ordinary' time-scale; and that process theologians locate 'the ultimate horizon of hope' as 'situated not in the end of history but in the present experience of God'.[25]

This agreed understanding of hope, as consisting in our movement towards and into God beginning *in the present*, quite cuts across, indeed 'transcends' in the strict sense of that term, the now-familiar predictions of the future on the physical (clock) time-scale which scientists can provide.[26] These are: the virtual certainty of the disappearance of the planet Earth (and so of all life, including human life, on the Earth) in about 4000 million years' time when the Sun runs out of the fuel provided by its hydrogen atoms; and the possible destinies of the universe as a whole – namely, continuous expansion to a heat-death or a slowing down of expansion of the universe, followed by a contraction to a very small volume (the 'big crunch'), and then, possibly, by further cycles of expansion and contraction.

The common factor in all of these predictions is the disappearance of the conditions for human life as we now know it, or could even imagine it to be. Some, such as Freeman Dyson[27] and Frank Tipler,[28] have tried to speculate, purely on the basis of physics, how intelligence, in the sense of information-processing capacity might conceivably be able to survive the demise of the Earth and even of this galaxy and universe as we know it. But they have no reasons from within the sphere of the sciences for believing that intelligent life *must* survive. Any such hope would have to be based elsewhere and this grounding they do not provide. Moreover the ultimate destiny of the universe, in Tipler's 'Omega Point', for example, which preserves in its infinite computer-like 'memory' all that has ever been thought and done by human beings (and any other intelligences), has no inbuilt system of values. So that the ultimate destiny of humanity, and of all forms of intelligent life that may succeed it, will be a state in which all the past evils and inhumanities that have been perpetrated in our known history (Auschwitz, Stalin's pogroms, the lot) will be for ever present in this final state. There can be no hope there.[29]

The Christian hope is quite otherwise – it is in the nature of God as the self-offering faithful creating Love revealed in the life, death and resurrection-exaltation of Jesus the Christ, God the Word/*Logos*/'Son' incarnate. Through him we discover and experience that we can begin to participate in the life with God, even here and now, and can share in God's work of creation by God's presence as Holy Spirit within and between us in the community of those who have responded to that Love. And our End will be our Beginning – God's own self.

> We shall not cease from exploration
> And the end of all our exploring
> Will be to arrive where we started
> And know the place for the first time.[30]

POSTSCRIPT

In concluding the last chapter, our experience of God was very readily expressible implicitly in the language of the so-called 'economic' Trinity,[1] the manifestation for humanity 'in order' of God's Being and Becoming in the world; *from* God the Father, *through* God the Word/*Logos*/Son, *in* God the Holy Spirit. How – indeed, whether or not – this threefold experience of God in God's creative and salvific outreach to the world is related to any differentiation within God's inner being and becoming (the so-called 'essential'[2] Trinity) is still a matter for much hard thinking and clarification.[3] Certainly earlier, in Part II,[4] we found that, since God is regarded as creating a world of immense diversity yet with an underlying unitary rationality, *God is One* and also a *Being of unfathomable richness* – that is, God must be a unity-in-diversity and a diversity-in-unity to be the source of the being and becoming of such a world.

The revelation of God in incarnation in Jesus the Christ evoked the consequent experience of those who responded and respond to it that God is present within the individual and operates in community *between* individuals to create unity. So the one God whom Jesus and his followers worship as a Unity is also experienced in a triple activity: as (1) Transcendent, (2) Incarnate, and (3) Immanent; as (1') Creator, (2') Redeemer-Liberator, and (3') Sanctifier-Unifier; and hence as Father, Word/*Logos* /'Son' and Holy Spirit. The triple character of this Christian experience of God has frequently and reasonably been taken as pointing to a differentiating threefoldness in the very nature of God's Being and Becoming, that is, God is believed to be 'essentially' Triune. It is as if the three kinds of activity represent various dimensions (like the cross-sections of a solid form) which reveal the inner threefold diversity within the unity of the Godhead.

It is tempting to relate the triply-formulated concepts which denote ways in which God is understood to relate to the world specifically to the three traditional *personae* of the Trinity, that is, to Father, Word/*Logos*/'Son' and Holy Spirit. But if God is to be one in all of God's interactions with the world, and if the *personae* are recognized (with Barth) as 'modes of being' (*Seinsweise*) of the one *personal* God,[5] then we are impelled towards affirming that *'God'* in God's own unity must still be the subject of those verbs which represent God's relation to the world ((1) to transcend over, (2) to be incarnate in, (3) to be immanent in); and also of those verbs which represent the relation of God to humanity in the Christian revelation ((1') to create, (2') to redeem/liberate/atone/reconcile, (3') to sanctify/come into union with).[6] God, in God's own triune unity, is active in all these triple modalities, even if we, because of our experience and the way we have come to make these distinctions within the Godhead, associate each kind of activity more particularly with one mode (Father or Word/*Logos*/'Son' or Holy Spirit) of God's being and becoming rather than with another.

There is, it seems, an ineffable richness, analogous to that of personal communion, within the divine life, a diversity within a fundamental unity, that escapes precise articulation. At this point in any discussion of the Trinity, a kind of intellectual vertigo begins to set in[7] and J. P. Mackey's judgment seems pertinent: 'No doubt the intellectual "unpacking" of this central Christian credal conviction [of the doctrine of Trinity] will always require some tentative account of what much contemporary trinitarian theology calls God's self-differentiation, and as long as the demonstrative nature of doctrine is acknowledged in whatever is retained or emerges – its ability, that is to say, to point out and to point to the life, death and Lordship of Jesus as the *locus* of encounter with God and of such dark knowledge of God as we may here possess – all will be well.'[8]

It is related that one of the greatest theologians of the Christian era, St Thomas Aquinas, suspended work on the third part of his great *Summa Theologiae*, telling his secretary that, after an experience while saying Mass in December 1273, he would write no more for, he said, 'All that I have written seems to me like so much straw compared with what I have seen and with what has been revealed to me.'[9] Theology that is not fed by and consummated in prayer and worship is indeed sterile and can deteriorate into a merely intellectual exercise. Who, writing on the profundity that is God, cannot but feel with St Thomas that the bricks of his or her constructions are made only of straw? Nevertheless, we are commanded to love God with our minds and so such an enterprise as this is worthwhile if its limitations are recognized – that talk about God, theo-logy, is but ancillary to prayer, worship and action. But to pray and to worship and to act we need supportable and believable models and images of the One to whom prayer, worship and action are to be directed. This volume is offered as a necessarily inadequate contribution to that pressing and perennial task of refurbishing our images of God – and of humanity.

NOTES

Other works by the author cited in the notes are abbreviated as follows:

SCE   Science and the Christian Experiment (Oxford University Press, London, 1971)
CWS   Creation and the world of Science (Clarendon Press, Oxford, 1979)
IR   Intimations of Reality: Critical Realism in Science and Religion (University of Notre Dame Press, Indiana, 1984)
PCBO   An Introduction to the Physical Chemistry of Biological Organization (Clarendon Press, Oxford, 1983; repr. as pbk, with supplementary references, 1989)
GNB   God and the New Biology (Dent, London, 1986)

NDCT refers to *A New Dictionary of Christian Theology* ed. A. Richardson and J. Bowden (SCM Press, London, 1983)

Introduction: The Theological and Scientific Enterprises

1   B. Martin and R. Pluck, *Young People's Beliefs* (General Synod of the Board of Education of the Church of England, 1977), pp. 22, 24, 59.
2   Lesslie Newbigin, *Foolishness to the Greeks* (World Council of Churches, Geneva, and Wm B. Eerdmans, Grand Rapids, Michigan, 1986), *passim.*
3   Thomas Sprat, *The History of the Royal Society of London for the Improving of Natural Knowledge* (London, 1702, 2nd edn), pp. 370–2.
4   See, for example, John Durant, 'Darwinism and divinity: a century of debate', in Darwinism and Divinity, ed. John Durant (Basil Blackwell, Oxford, 1985), pp. 18–23, and references therein.
5   For it has been claimed that the Judeo-Christian milieu of Western Christendom, through its belief that the natural world had a contingent order, afforded a congenial matrix, to say the least, for the rise of modern science – though a direct causality is less easily

established and is probably, in any case, unprovable. For a critique of the widely held belief in this supposed historical causal relation, see Rolf Gruner, 'Science, Nature and Christianity', *Journal of Theological Studies*, 26 (1975), pp. 55–81.

6 For a careful account of the meaning of this term (which in English can be misleadingly translated as 'human sciences') and its history, see W. Pannenberg, *Theology and the Philosophy of Science*, trans. F. McDonagh (Darton, Longman and Todd, London, and Westminster Press, Philadelphia, 1976), pp. 72ff.

7 What we are to mean by 'God' can only transpire later. But I refer here to those experiences, to use the phraseology of Alister Hardy and the Centre named after him, of an 'awareness of a benevolent non-physical power which appears to be partly or wholly beyond, and far greater than, the individual self' (see Alister Hardy, *The Spiritual Nature of Man*, Clarendon Press, Oxford, 1979, p. 1). 'Religious experience', of course covers a far wider range than this, as reference to the literature of that same Centre reveals.

8 John Passmore, *Science and its Critics* (Duckworth, London, 1978), p. 57.

9 ibid., p. 96.

10 H. Harris, 'Rationality in science', in *Scientific Explanations*, ed. A. F. Heath (Clarendon Press, Oxford, 1981), p. 40.

11 Taking this in the broad sense, see n. 7.

12 See *IR* and references therein; A. R. Peacocke, 'Science and theology today: a critical realist perspective', *Religion and Intellectual Life*, 5 (1988), pp. 45–58. A helpful account of critical realism as a philosophy of science and an analysis of, and apologia for, its significance for systematic theology has been given by W. van Huysteen in *Theology and the Justification of Faith* (Wm B. Eerdmans, Grand Rapids, Michigan, 1989), ch. 9. See also Michael Banner, *The Justification of Science and the Rationality of Religious Belief* (Clarendon Press, Oxford, 1990).

13 J. Leplin, 'Introduction', in *Scientific Realism*, ed. J. Leplin (University of California Press, 1984), p. 1.

14 ibid., p. 2.

15 Ernan McMullin, 'The case for scientific realism', in Leplin, *Scientific Realism*, p. 26.

16 ibid., p. 30.

17 Janet Martin Soskice, *Metaphor and Religious Language* (Clarendon Press, Oxford, 1984), ch. 7.

18 W. H. Newton-Smith, *The Rationality of Science* (Routledge and Kegan Paul, London, 1981), pp. 164–74.

19 Soskice, *Metaphor*, p. 159.

20 Ian Barbour, *Issues in Science and Religion* (Harper and Row, New York, 1971, pbk edn), p. 158.

21 See *IR*, p. 30, for further discussion and references.

22 See n. 12 above.

23 See, for example, B. G. Mitchell, *The Justification of Religious Belief* (Macmillan, London, 1973); D. Pailin, 'Can the theologian legitimately try to answer the question: is the Christian faith true?', *Expository Times*, 84 (1973), pp. 321–9; J. R. Carnes, *Axiomatics and Dogmatics* (Christian Journals, Belfast, 1982), ch. 5 (his criteria are: coherence, economy, adequacy and existential relevance – these overlap those cited in the text); and Banner, *Justification of Science*.

24 ibid.

25 I cannot trace the reference.

26 Hans Küng in 'Paradigm change in theology', a lecture given at the University of Chicago in 1981; published in a different form in *Paradigm Change in Theology* ed. Hans Küng and David Trace (T. & T. Clark, Edinburgh, 1989), pp. 3–33. See H. Küng, *Theology for the Third Millennium – an ecumenical view*, transl. P. Heinegy (Doubleday, New York, 1988 and Harper Collins, London, 1991), ch. 3 II on 'Paradigm Change in theology and science' especially pp. 161–2 in relation to pp. 17–18 of the main text here.

27 cf. D. C. MacIntosh, 'Experimental realism in religion', in *Religious Realism*, ed. D. C. MacIntosh (Macmillan, New York, 1931).

28 I cannot avoid here betraying my conviction that the traditional reliance of the Anglican communion *inter alia* on a judicious use of the resources of scripture and tradition, viewed in the light of reason based on experience (the 'three-legged stool'), affords the most viable way of developing a defensible and believable expression of Christian faith. Such an expression of faith might unite Christians and convince the post-Enlightenment, 'post-modern' world of its truth – that is, that it genuinely depicts realities (or, rather, *the* Reality that is God in Christ through the Holy Spirit). It is such a weaving of this threefold cord (Scripture, tradition and reason based on experience) in a united church yet-to-be in which authority is dispersed, collegial and non-coercive, essentially dialogical, that, I would submit, can provide any long-term future for Christian faith in a not unjustifiably sceptical world.

29 See chs. 2–4.

30 John Bowker, *Licensed Insanities* (Darton, Longman and Todd, London, 1987), p. 13.

31 See *IR*, pp. 18–22, for references.

32 See *IR*; van Huysteen, *Theology*; Banner, *Justification of Science*; McMullin, 'The case for scientific realism'.

33 A. R. Peacocke, 'Introduction', in *The Sciences and Theology in the Twentieth Century*, ed. A. R. Peacocke (Oriel Press, Stocksfield and London, and University of Notre Dame Press, Notre Dame, Indiana, 1981), pp. ix–xviii.

34 R. J. Russell, 'A critical appraisal of Peacocke's thought on religion and science', *Religion and Intellectual Life*, 2 (1985), pp. 48–58.
35 ibid., p. 50.
36 Ernan McMullin, 'Realism in theology and science: a response to Peacocke', *Religion and Intellectual Life*, 2 (1985), pp. 39–47.
37 See *CWS*, ch. 1 and references therein.
38 See also *GNB*, chs. 1, 2.
39 See chs. 8 and 10.
40 See the useful discussion of these ideas by Eric T. Juengst, 'Response: carving nature at the joints', *Religion and Intellectual Life*, 5 (1988), pp. 70–8.
41 And in relation to the person of Jesus the Christ; see Part III, chs. 13–15.
42 If the referent of theology is, then, to that which is 'The Transcendent-in-the-Immanent', could not its relation to other disciplines be regarded as that of a highly democratized constitutional monarchy, something like the 'Queen-in-Parliament' of the constitution of the United Kingdom?

CHAPTER 1: INTRODUCTION

1 Herbert Butterfield, *The Origins of Modern Science* (Bell, London, 1968), p. vii.
2 ibid., pp. vii, viii.
3 Introduction, n. 10.

CHAPTER 2 WHAT'S THERE?

1 Stephen Hawking, 'The direction of time', *New Scientist*, 115 (9 July 1987), pp. 46–9; *A Brief History of Time* (Bantam and Transworld, London, 1988), p. 14.
2 See, for example, Hawking, *Brief History of Time*, n. 1; Steven Weinberg, *The First Three Minutes* (André Deutsch, London, 1977); Paul Davies, *The Runaway Universe* (Dent, London, 1978); and the account in *SCE*, ch. 2.
3 H. K. Schilling, *The New Consciousness in Science and Religion* (SCM Press, London, 1973), p. 126.
4 I refer to such books as: Peter Atkins, *The Creation* (Freeman, Oxford and San Francisco, 1881); Adam Ford, *Universe: God, Man and Science* (Hodder and Stoughton, London, 1986); and *SCE*, chs. 2 and 3.

5   F. H. C. Crick, *Of Molecules and Man* (University of Washington Press, Seattle and London, 1966), p. 10.
6   See *GNB*, for a fuller discussion of this whole matter.
7   James P. Crutchfield, J. Doyne Farmer, Norman H. Packard and Robert S. Shaw, 'Chaos', *Scientific American*, Dec. 1986, pp. 48–49.
8   J. S. Bell, 'On the Einstein-Podolsky-Rosen Paradox', *Physics* 1 (1964), pp. 95–200; J. F. Clauser and A. Shimony, 'Bell's theorem; experimental tests and implications', *Reports on Progress in Physics*, 41 (1978), pp. 1981–1927; Bernard d'Espagnat, 'The Quantum Theory and reality', *Scientific American*, 241 (Nov. 1979), pp. 128–40; Abner Shimony, 'The reality of the Quantum World', *Scientific American*, 258 (Jan. 1988), pp. 46–53.

CHAPTER 3   WHAT'S GOING ON?

1   R. Harré, *The Principles of Scientific Thinking* (Macmillan, London, 1970), ch. 4.
2   e.g., see Henri Poincaré, *Science and Method*, tr. F. Maitland (Thomas Nelson, London, 1914), p. 68.
3   Michael Berry, 'Breaking the paradigms of classical physics from within', 1983 Cercy Symposium, *Logique et theorie des catastrophes*.
4   ibid.; James P. Crutchfield, J. Doyne Farmer, Norman H. Packard and Robert S. Shaw, 'Chaos', *Scientific American*, Dec. 1986, p. 49.
5   See Crutchfield et al., 'Chaos'; *PCBO*, chs. 2, 4, 5; and Paul Davies, *The Cosmic Blueprint* (Heinemann, London, 1987), chs. 3–6; see also, John Polkinghorne, *Science and Creation* (SPCK, London, 1988), ch. 3.
6   So the plots that mathematicians customarily use to depict changes in the state of a system (diagrams in phase-space) keep on revealing complexities and sequences of states at every level of magnification. In other words, they look like the pictures illustrating 'fractals' with which Mandelbrot has familiarized us. Indeed, mathematically the regions in the phase-space to which the systems gravitate (the states they tend to take up in ordinary language) can be proved to be fractals, having non-integer dimensions and revealing more detail as they are progressively magnified. The line depicting the state of the system continuously folds back on itself, going through states close to, but never identical with, previous ones – like dough, containing a drop of dye, that is neaded by a baker. Such systems possess what is provokingly called a 'strange attractor' to distinguish it from the more ordinary 'attractors', the points, lines or regions in phase-space towards which non-linear systems may move in time. This 'fractal' charac-

ter of the mathematical representation of these particular non-linear systems is another way of expressing that special feature of their exquisite sensitivity to the values of their distinctive parameters which makes very close states in time lead to widely different results. In other words, small fluctuations in the system can lead to very large effects (the 'butterfly effect' again), with loss of all predictive power.

7   See *inter alia*, Ilya Prigogine, *From Being to Becoming* (W. H. Freeman, San Francisco, 1980); Ilya Prigogine and Isabelle Stengers, *Order Out of Chaos* (Heinemann, London, 1984); and *PCBO*, ch. 2.

8   Crutchfield et al., 'Chaos', p. 48.

9   Donald T. Campbell, '"Downward causation" in hierarchically organised systems', in *Studies in the Philosophy of Biology: Reduction and Related Problems*, ed. F. J. Ayala and T. Dobzhansky (Macmillan, London, 1974), p. 179–86.

10   Roger W. Sperry, *Science and Moral Priority* (Blackwell, Oxford, 1983), ch. 6.

11   Another example from another area of science, a computer programmed to rearrange its own circuitry through a robot that it itself controls, has been proposed by Paul Davies (*The Cosmic Blueprint*, Heinemann, London, 1987, pp. 172–4 and fig. 32) as an instance of what he called 'downward causation'. In this hypothetical (but not at all impossible) system, changes in the information encoded in the computer's software (usually taken as the 'higher' level) downwardly cause modifications in the computer's hardware (the 'lower' level) – an example of software-hardware feedback.

12   Michael A. Arbib and Mary B. Hesse, *The Construction of Reality* (Cambridge University Press, Cambridge, 1986), p. 64.

13   F. J. Ayala, 'Introduction' in Ayala and Dobzhansky, *Studies in the Philosophy of Biology*, p. ix.

14   Arbib and Hesse, *Construction of Reality*, p. 65.

15   ibid., p. 66.

16   Sperry, *Science and Moral Priority*, pp. 88, 90–6.

17   Arbib and Hesse, *Construction of Reality*, p. 64.

18   See *PCBO*, ch. 5.

19   M. Eigen, 'The self-organization of matter and the evolution of biological macromolecules', *Naturwissenschaften*, 58 (1971), p. 519.

20   F. Jacob, *The Logic of Living Systems* (Allen Lane, London, 1974), p. 13.

21   Campbell, 'Downward causation', pp. 181–2.

22   Elisabeth Vrba, 'Patterns in the fossil record and evolutionary processes', in *Beyond Darwinism*, ed. M. W. Ho and P. T. Saunders (Academic Press, London, 1984), p. 121.

23 ibid., pp. 121–2, see for further references and discussion.

24 R. C. Lewontin, 'Gene, organism and environment', in *Evolution from Molecules to Men*, ed. D. S. Bendall (Cambridge University Press, Cambridge, 1983), pp. 273–85.

25 Sir Alister Hardy, *The Living Stream* (Collins, London, 1985), pp. 161ff., 189ff.

26 Section 2(b), above.

27 D. M. Mackay, 'The interdependence of mind and brain', *Neuroscience*, 5 (1980), pp. 1389–91.

28 J. Searle, *Minds, Brains and Science* (Harvard University Press, Cambridge, Mass., 1984), p. 26.

29 Sperry, *Science and Moral Priority*, pp. 93–6; and by Donald Mackay, see 'Interdependence of mind and brain' for brief statement, with full references.

30 *SCE*, chs. 2, 3; *CWS*, ch. II; Holmes Rolston III, *Science and Religion: A Critical Survey* (Random House, New York, 1987), chs. 2, 3.

31 The depiction of this process as 'nature, red in tooth and claw' (a phrase of Tennyson's that actually pre-dates Darwin's proposal of evolution through natural selection) is a caricature for, as many biologists have pointed out (e.g., G. G. Simpson in *The Meaning of Evolution*, Bantam Books and Yale University Press, New Haven, 1971 edn, p. 201), natural selection is not even in a figurative sense the outcome of struggle, as such. Natural selection involves many factors that include better integration with the ecological environment, more efficient utilization of available food, better care of the young, more cooperative social organization – and better capacity of surviving such 'struggles' as do occur (remembering that it is in the interest of any predator that their prey survive as a species).

32 For a fuller discussion of this, see *GNB*, Appendix.

33 Section 2(b), above.

34 R. Winkler and M. Eigen, *Laws of the Game* (Knopf, New York, 1981, and Allen Lane, London, 1982).

35 See *CWS*, ch. III; D. J. Bartholomew, *God of Chance* (SCM Press, London, 1984); John Polkinghorne, *Science and Creation* (SPCK, London, 1988) chs. 3, 4; *Science and Providence* (SPCK, London, 1989), ch. 3.

36 J. Wicken, *Journal of Theoretical Biology*, 72 (1978), pp. 191–204; *GNB*, Appendix, pp. 141–2.

37 Karl Popper, at the World Philosophy Congress, Brighton, August 1988, reported in *The Guardian*, 29 August 1988.

38 W. McCoy, *Journal of Theoretical Biology*, 68 (1977), p. 457.

39 J. Maynard Smith, in *Towards a Theoretical Biology, 2 Sketches*, ed. C. H. Waddington (Edinburgh University Press, Edinburgh, 1969), pp. 88–9.

40   P. T. Saunders and M. W. Ho, *Journal of Theoretical Biology*, 63 (1976), pp. 375–84); 90 (1981), pp. 515–30; W. McCoy, ibid.; C. Castrodeza, *Journal of Theoretical Biology*, 71 (1978), pp. 469–71.

41   For fuller discussion, see *GNB*, Appendix; and *PCBO*, ch. 6.

42   H. A. Simon, 'The architecture of complexity', *Proceedings of the American Philosophical Society*, 106 (1962), pp. 467–82.

43   E.g., G. G. Simpson, *The Meaning of Evolution* (Bantam Books, Yale University Press, New Haven, 1971 edn), p. 256.

44   Holmes Rolston (ibid.) has developed this characteristic of biological evolution in what he calls 'cruciform naturalism' (p. 289ff.). Sentience, he argues, evolves with a capacity to separate the 'helps' from the 'hurts' of the world: with sentience there appears caring (p. 287). With the appearance of life, organisms can now view events as 'pro-' or 'anti-life' and values and 'disvalues' appear – the world becomes a 'theatre of meanings' and nature may be variously judged as 'hostile', 'indifferent' and 'hospitable' (p. 244). 'The step up that brings more drama brings more suffering' (p. 288). But 'pain is an energizing force' so that 'where pain fits into evolutionary theory, it must have, on statistical average, high survival value, with this selected for, and with a selecting against counterproductive pain' (p. 288). 'Suffering . . moves us to action' and 'all advances come in contexts of problem solving, with a central problem in sentient life the prospect of hurt. In the evolution of caring, the organism is quickened to its needs' (p. 288). 'Suffering is a key to the whole, not intrinsically, not as an end in itself, but as a transformative principle, transvalued into its opposite' (p. 288).

45   C. Isham, 'Creation of the universe as a quantum tunnelling process', in *Physics, Philosophy and Theology: A Common Quest for Understanding*, ed. R. J. Russell, W. R. Stoeger and G. V. Coyne (Vatican Observatory Publication, Vatican State, 1988), p. 397.

46   J. B. Hartle and S. W. Hawking, *Physical Reviews*, D28 (1983), p. 2960; see Isham's account, 'Creation of the universe', and Stephen Hawking, *A Brief History of Time* (Bantam and Transworld, London, 1988) ch. 8.

47   Isham, 'Creation of the universe', p. 400.

48   For a fuller discussion, see *CWS*, ch. VIII; and J. Polkinghorne, *Science and Creation* (SPCK, London, 1988), pp. 64ff.

49   Freeman Dyson, *Disturbing the Universe* (Pan Books, London, 1981); see also ch. 16 and its reference to the 'Omega Point' of F. J. Tipler (n. 27).

CHAPTER 4   WHO'S THERE?

1   For further accounts, see *SCE*, pp. 99–106; *CWS*, pp. 72–4; and
    Holmes Rolston III, *Science and Religion: A Critical Survey*
    (Random House, New York, 1987), chs. 4, 5.
2   For a recent survey, from scientific, philosophical and theological
    viewpoints, of a wide range of conceptions of the human person and
    of what constitutes personality – in various combinations of
    naturalism, reductionism, existentialism, dualism and theism –
    see *Persons and Personality*, ed. Arthur Peacocke and Grant Gillett
    (Blackwell, Oxford, 1987); see also the magisterial survey of John
    Macquarrie, *In Search of Humanity: A Theological and Philosoph-
    ical Approach* (SCM Press, London, 1982).
3   For an account of these ideas on evolutionary epistemology and
    their philosophical import, see Peter Munz, *Our Knowledge of the
    Growth of Knowledge* (Routledge and Kegan Paul, London, 1985).
4   Such a mutually defined account of (a) the relation of conscious-
    ness to brain activity and (b) the evolution of consciousness, so
    defined, has recently been given by Michael A. Arbib and Mary
    B. Hesse, (*The Construction of Reality*, Cambridge University
    Press, Cambridge, 1986, pp. 76–7) in terms of schema theory. In
    that theory a 'schema' is a unit of representation of reality and it
    views 'language as metaphorical, having its meaning within the
    open schema networks of the participants in a discourse' (p. 67).
5   Richard Tur, 'The "person" in law', in Peacocke and Gillett, *Persons
    and Personality*, pp. 116–29.
6   Konrad Lorenz, *Behind the Mirror: A Search for a Natural History
    of Human Knowledge* (Methuen, London, 1977, English trans.)
    p. 113.
7   I. T. Ramsey, 'Human personality', in *Personality and Science*, ed.
    I. T. Ramsey and Ruth Porter (Churchill Livingstone, Edinburgh
    and London, 1971), p. 128.
8   John Barrow and Frank Tipler, *The Anthropic Cosmological
    Principle* (Clarendon Press, Oxford, 1986), p. 16.
9   J. H. Crook, *The Evolution of Human Consciousness* (Clarendon
    Press, Oxford, 1980), p. 35.
10 ibid., p. 36.
11 Lorenz, *Behind the Mirror*, p. 6.

CHAPTER 5   WHAT DOES IT ALL MEAN?

1   F. Hoyle, *The Nature of the Universe* (Blackwell, Oxford, 1960),
    p. 103.

2 See *PCBO*, ch. 6.
3 A. Einstein, *Out of My Later Years* (repr. Greenwood Press, Westport, Conn., 1970), p. 61.
4 H. K. Schilling, *The New Consciousness in Science and Religion* (SCM Press, London, 1973).
5 Victor Weisskopf, *Knowledge and Wonder* (Doubleday, Garden City, NY, 1962), p. 100.

CHAPTER 6   ASKING 'WHY?': THE SEARCH FOR INTELLIGIBILITY AND MEANING

1 Introduction, section 3.
2 J. J. Shepherd, *Experience, Inference and God* (Macmillan, London, 1975), p. 76.
3 M. K. Munitz, *The Mystery of Existence* (Appleton-Century-Crofts, New York, 1965).
4 Keith Ward, *The Turn of the Tide* (BBC Publications, London, 1986), ch. 3.
5 Keith Ward, *The Concept of God* (Blackwell, Oxford, 1974), p. 148.
6 Introduction, section 1.
7 To be more precise: 'necessary for the existence of sentient entities'.

CHAPTER 7   'GOD' AS RESPONSE TO THE SEARCH FOR INTELLIGIBILITY AND MEANING

1 Keith Ward, *The Turn of the Tide* (BBC Publications, London, 1986), p. 67.
2 Introduction, section 3.
3 See Introduction, n. 23.
4 John R. Carnes, *Axiomatics and Dogmatics* (Christian Journals, Belfast, 1982), ch. 5.
5 ibid.
6 ibid.
7 Richard Swinburne, *The Coherence of Theism* (Clarendon Press, Oxford, 1977); *The Existence of God* (Clarendon Press, Oxford, 1979); *Faith and Reason* (Clarendon Press, 1981); Ward, *Turn of the Tide*; Alvin Plantinga, 'Reason and belief in God', in *Faith and Rationality*, ed. A. Plantinga and N. Wolsterstorff (University of Notre Dame Press, Notre Dame, Indiana, 1983), pp. 16–93.
8 Anthony Kenny, *The God of the Philosophers* (Clarendon Press, Oxford, 1979); J. L. Mackie, *The Miracle of Theism* (Clarendon Press, Oxford, 1982).

9 Mackie, *Miracle of Theism*; Richard Swinburne, 'Mackie, induction, and God', *Religious Studies*, 19 (1983), pp. 385–91.
10 Swinburne, ibid., p. 385.
11 Swinburne, *Existence of God*, p. 8.
12 Here, and in the phrases that follow, the wording of Swinburne (ibid., p. 8) is followed, denoted by quotation marks.
13 Swinburne, *Existence of God*, p. 8, n. 1. Here I would prefer to regard God as 'personal', or as 'at least personal', rather than as 'a person', since to call God 'a person' seems to me to indicate a greater insight into the mystery of the ultimate Reality that is God than is warrantable. One is trying to express the experience believers have that God relates to them personally and that God is 'something like' (see the quotation from E. McMullin, Introduction p. 12 and n. 15) a personal agent in their lives and, it will be argued, in the world. Theological language, as was stressed in the Introduction, is inevitably metaphorical so that qualifying adjectives ('at least personal') and adverbs ('personally') are preferable, in my view, to unqualified nouns ('a person') in referring to God.
14 Swinburne, p. 92.
15 ibid., p. 93.
16 Swinburne, 'Mackie, induction and God', p. 385.
17 Swinburne, *Existence of God*, p. 32.
18 Swinburne, 'Mackie, induction and God', p. 391.
19 *The Concept of God*, ed. Thomas V. Morris (Oxford University Press, Oxford, 1987).
20 ibid., pp. 6, 7.
21 *Believing in the Church – The Corporate Nature of Faith*, a report by the Doctrine Commission of the Church of England (SPCK, London, 1981).
22 *We Believe in God*, a report by the Doctrine Commission of the Church of England (Church House Publishing, London, 1987).
23 For a fuller consideration of the nature and significance of Jesus Christ see chs. 13–15; and the Postscript for a briefer one on trinitarian doctrine.

CHAPTER 8 THE CONCEPT OF GOD: IMPLICATIONS OF SCIENTIFIC PERSPECTIVES

1 See Ch. 10 for a further discussion of this distinction; cf. also the 'dipolar' concept of God in process theology.
2 Ch. 7, section 1.
3 See Part I, above, and references therein; see also John Polkinghorne, *One World* (SPCK, London, 1986), pp. 22ff., 44ff.
4 Ch. 2, sections 1 and 2.
5 Ch. 2, section 4.

6   Ch. 2, section 3.
7   Ch. 5, nn. 1, 3.
8   Ch. 3, sections 1(d), 3(a).
9   Ch. 2, section 1.
10 *Summa Theologiae* I.2.3.
11 Ch. 2, section 1.
12 ibid.
13 Using (*faute de mieux*), here and elsewhere, the traditional male pronoun in English, but not thereby intending to exclude 'feminine' aspects of God.
14 Ch. 3, section 3.
15 This chapter, section 2.
16 Ch. 7, section 1.
17 e.g., Richard Swinburne, *The Existence of God* (Clarendon Press, Oxford, 1979), p. 8 and *passim*.
18 Ch. 7, section 2.
19 Ch. 4, section 2.
20 P. W. Atkins, *The Creation*, (W. H. Freeman, Oxford and San Francisco, 1981).
21 D. J. Bartholomew, *God of Chance* (SCM Press, London, 1984), pp. 64–5.
22 H. Montefiore, *The Probability of God* (SCM Press, London, 1985); John Polkinghorne, *Science and Creation* (SPCK, London, 1988).
23 See for example, the discussion of J. Leslie, 'How to draw conclusions from a fine-tuned universe', in *Physics, Philosophy and Theology: A Common Quest for Understanding* (Vatican Observatory publication, Vatican City State, 1988, distributed by University of Notre Dame Press), pp. 297–311; see also his *Universe* (Routledge and Kegan Paul, London and New York, 1989).
24 Montefiore, *Probability of God*; Polkinghorne, *Science and Creation*.
25 *CWS*, pp. 67–72.
26 ibid., pp. 70–1.
27 Ch. 4, section 1.
28 A. N. Whitehead, *Science and the Modern World* (Mentor Books edn, New York, 1949), p. 56.
29 John Durant, on 'Is there a role for theology in an age of secular science?' in *One World: Changing Perspectives on Reality*, ed. J. Fennema and I. Paul (University of Twente and Kluwer Academic Press, 1990), pp. 161–72.
30 Ch. 4, section 1 and *CWS*, pp. 70–1.
31 See ch. 2, section 3.
32 Here following *CWS*, pp. 72–3.
33 G. E. Pugh, *The Biological Origins of Human Values* (Basic Books, New York, 1977); see *CWS*, p. 154, n. 13, for more details.

34   See R. Trigg, *The Shaping of Man* (Blackwell, Oxford, 1982); and ch. 12, section 4, p. 226 and especially n. 82.

35   Ch. 3.

36   Ch. 2, section 2, and ch. 3, section 3(a).

37   Ch. 8, section 1.

38   C. Darwin, *The Origin of Species* (Thinkers Library, Watts London, 6th edn), p. 408.

39   *Genesis* 1:31.

40   *CWS*, pp. 108–11.

41   Manfred Eigen and Ruthild Winkler, *The Laws of the Game* (Knopf, New York, 1981 and Allen Lane, London, 1982).

42   Ch. 3, section 1.

43   See for example, Ilya Prigogine and Isabelle Stengers, *Order Out of Chaos* (Heinemann, London, 1984); and *PCBO* for other references.

44   Ch. 3, section 2(a).

45   See ch. 3, section 1(b).

46   Ch. 3, section 2(b).

47   Jacques Monod, *Chance and Necessity* (Collins, London, 1972).

48   Bartholomew, *God of Chance*.

49   A. R. Peacocke, 'Chance, potentiality and God', *The Modern Churchman*, 17 (n.s. 1973), pp. 13–23; and in *Beyond Chance and Necessity*, ed. J. Lewis (Garnstone Press, 1974), pp. 13–25; 'Chaos or cosmos', *New Scientist*, 63 (1974), pp. 386–9; *CWS*, ch. 3.

50   *CWS*, p. 94.

51   Ilya Prigogine, *From Being to Becoming* (W. H. Freeman, San Francisco, 1980); Prigogine and Stengers, *Order Out of Chaos*. For some recent accounts of the scientific work of the Brussels school and its significance, see *GNB*, appendix on 'Thermodynamics and Life', pp. 133–60, and *PCBO*, esp. ch. 2.

52   Eigen and Winkler, *Laws of the Game*; M. Eigen and P. Schuster, *The Hypercycle* (Springer-Verlag, Berlin, 1979); see also *PCBO*, ch. 5.

53   Richard Dawkins, *The Blind Watchmaker* (Longmans, Harlow, 1986).

54   *CWS*, pp. 105–6.

55   ibid., pp. 108–11.

56   ibid., p. 95.

57   Bartholomew, *God of Chance*, p. 97.

58   ibid.

59   ibid., p. 98.

60   ibid.

61   ibid., p. 102.

62   Ch. 8, section 1.

63   Ch. 3, sections 1 and 2.

64   Ch. 7, section 1.

65 J. Moltmann, *The Crucified God* (SCM Press, London, 1974); C. Hartshorne, *The Divine Relativity* (Yale University Press, New Haven, 1948) and *Creative Synthesis in Philosophical Method* (SCM Press, London, 1970); W. H. Vanstone, *Love's Endeavour, Love's Expense* (Darton, Longman and Todd, London, 1977).

66 Bartholomew, *God of Chance*, p. 138. Some of the things, he argues (pp. 139ff.), which one might expect a creative God to wish to do are: to act in 'the springs of creative thought in the human mind'; to be involved in, a party to, human decision making; to be at work at those junctures where man makes mistakes, or threatens to do so; to be active on the side of reconciliation between warring factions; to communicate his presence in critical circumstances: and, perhaps, to engineer coincidences in 'very special circumstances'. All of these concern the problem of the nature of God's interaction with the world and will have to be discussed, and not necessarily accepted, later.

67 This chapter, section 1(g).

68 Cf. ch. 15, section 3, p. 331.

69 Ch. 3, section 3, *CWS*, pp. 198–202, 213–14, 229–30.

70 Paul S. Fiddes, *The Creative Suffering of God* (Clarendon Press, Oxford, 1988) p. 3 (italics in original).

71 ibid., p. 45 (see also ch. 2 *passim*).

72 I hint here at my broad acceptance of John Hick's 'Irenaean' theodicy in relation to 'natural' evil (see 'An Irenaean theodicy', in *Encountering Evil*, ed. Stephen T. Davis (T. & T. Clark, Edinburgh, 1981), pp. 39–52; and his earlier *Evil and the God of Love* (Macmillan, London, 1966), especially chs 15 and 16) and the position outlined by Brian Hebblethwaite in ch. 5, 'Physical suffering and the nature of the physical world', of his *Evil, Suffering and Religion* (Sheldon Press, London, 1976).

73 cf. this chapter, section 1, *passim*.

74 For both his personhood and his ability to act in the world, see J. R. Lucas, *A Treatise on Time and Space* (Methuen, London, 1973), chs 55, 56; Nelson Pike, *God and Timelessness* (Routledge and Kegan Paul, London, 1970); Keith Ward, *Rational Theology and the Creativity of God* (Blackwell, Oxford, 1982).

75 See Lucas, *Treatise on Time and Space*, chs 55, 56; Pike, *God and Timelessness*; Ward, *Rational Theology*; P. T. Geach, 'The future', *New Blackfriars*, 54 (1973), p. 208.

76 This chapter, section 1(e), p. 105.

77 Lucas, *Treatise on Time and Space*, ch. 17, *passim*.

78 Ward, *Rational Theology*, p. 151–2.

79 John Polkinghorne, *Science and Providence* (SPCK, London, 1989) p. 82.

80 ibid. See now the discussion of C. J. Isham and J. C. Polkinghorne on 'The Block Universe' in the Proceedings of the Second Vatican

Observatory Conference (1991), entitled *Quantum Cosmology and the Laws of Nature*, eds. R. J. Russell, N. Murphy, C. J. Isham (Vatican Observatory and University of Notre Dame Press 1993). Since no light signals can emanate from a particular event until it has happened in its own frame of reference, there is a sense in which that event has a universally denotable future with respect to all other frames of reference, including God's.

81   'It is therefore true to say that when you [God] had not made anything there was no time, because time itself was of your making', *Confessions* xi.14, trans. R. S. Pine-Coffin (Penguin Classics edn, Harmondsworth, London, 1961), p. 263.

82   Ward, *Rational Theology*, p. 160.

83   See discussion in this chapter, pp. 121–3 and above, and ch. 7, section 1.

84   H. K. Schilling, *The New Consciousness in Science and Religion* (SCM Press, London, 1973), p. 126.

85   cf. R. Swinburne, *The Coherence of Theism* (Clarendon Press, Oxford, 1977), p. 175, where he develops an account of omniscience not as knowledge of everything true but as knowledge of everything true it is logically possible to know. He suggests the following understanding of omniscience: 'A person P is omniscient at a time t if and only if he knows of every true proposition about t or an earlier time that it is true *and* also he knows of every true proposition about a time later than t, such that what it reports is physically necessitated by some cause at t or earlier, that it is true. On this understanding of omniscience, P is omniscient if he knows about everything except those future states and their consequences which are not physically necessitated by anything in the past; and if he knows that he does not know about those future states.'

86   See above, ch. 7, section 1, where the phraseology of R. Swinburne, in *The Coherence of Theism* and *The Existence of God* (p. 8), is reproduced.

87   For a philosophically more thorough exposition of an understanding of God's relation to time very close to that in the text, see Ward, *Rational Theology*, ch. 7. This section in the text is much indebted to the expositions of both Keith Ward and John Lucas.

88   As R. Swinburne *inter alia* has argued (in *The Coherence of Theism*, pp. 211–15).

89   *We Believe in God*, a report by the Doctrine Commission of the Church of England (Church House Publishing, London, 1987), p. 160.

90   ibid., pp. 159–60.

91   Ch. 3, section 3(b); Stephen Hawking, *A Brief History of Time* (Bantam and Transworld, London, 1988), ch. 8; J. B. Hartle and S. W. Hawking, *Physical Reviews*, D28 (1983), p. 2960.

92   Hawking, *Brief History of Time*, pp. 134–6.

93 ibid., p. 135.
94 ibid., p. 136.
95 ibid., p. 174.

CHAPTER 9 GOD'S INTERACTION WITH THE WORLD

1 Michael J. Langford, *Providence* (SCM Press, London, 1981), p. 6.
2 John Macquarrie, *Principles of Christian Theology* (SCM Press, London, 1966), p. 219.
3 Christoph Schwöbel, 'Divine agency and Providence', *Modern Theology*, 3 (1987), pp. 225–44, esp. p. 241.
4 ibid., p. 241.
5 Vernon White, *The Fall of a Sparrow*, (Paternoster Press, Exeter, 1985), pp. 54–5.
6 Langford, *Providence*, p. 41.
7 ibid., p. 42.
8 Thomas F. Tracy, *God, Action and Embodiment* (Eerdmans, Publishing Co., Grand Rapids, 1984), p. xii.
9 ibid.
10 Langdon Gilkey, 'Cosmology, ontology, and the travail of Biblical language', *Journal of Religion*, 41 (1961), pp. 194–205; rep. in *God's Activity in the World*, ed. Owen C. Thomas (Scholars Press, Chico, Cal., 1983; page numbers refer to this edn), p. 37. Italics added.
11 ibid., pp. 42–3.
12 David Brown, *The Divine Trinity* (Duckworth, London, 1985), pp. 5, 33. In this context, theology might well take a hint from philosophical discussions of the mind–body problem, in which some authors (e.g. Donald Davidson, 'Mental events', in *Experience and Theory*, ed. L. Foster and J. W. Swanson, University of Massachusetts Press, 1970) speak of mental events as 'supervenient' upon the neuronal activities of the brain, rather than 'intervening' in them – meaning by this that mental events can at least be affirmed to have a controlling, directing, supervisory influence on brain events without entailing reducibility to, or in any way being disruptive or interruptive of, them. To be fair to Brown's position, it should be noted that in the Introduction (p. xv) to *The Divine Trinity* he says that intervention as 'part of the normal pattern of divine activity' is what he is aiming to establish. He has subsequently further clarified his position in an article, 'God and Symbolic Action' (in *Divine Action: Studies Inspired by the Philosophical Theology of Austin Farrer*, ed. B. Hebblethwaite and E. Henderson, T. & T. Clark, Edinburgh, 1990), where he concedes that his position might be better described as 'inter-

actionist', for he is chiefly concerned to allow God at least the same power and dignity of action as we are prepared to ascribe to ourselves in relation to others.

13 William P. Alston, 'God's action in the world', in *Evolution and Creation*, ed. Ernan McMullin, University of Notre Dame Press, Notre Dame, Indiana, 1985, pp. 197–220.

14 ibid., pp. 213–14.

15 ibid., p. 217.

16 Far from all; see also Alston, ibid., pp. 210–14.

17 David E. Jenkins, *God, Miracle and the Church of England* (SCM Press, London, 1987), p. 64.

18 ibid., pp. 63–4.

19 Schubert M. Ogden, 'What sense does it make to say, "God Acts in History"?', ch. VI of *The Reality of God and Other Essays* (Harper and Row, New York, 1963; repr. in O. C. Thomas, *God's Activity*, pp. 77–100).

20 Gordon D. Kaufman, *God the Problem* (Harvard University Press, Cambridge, Mass., 1972).

21 Such criticisms of Ogden's position were made by James Wm. McClendon, in 'Can there be talk about God-and-the-world?', (*Harvard Theological Review*, 62 (1969), pp. 33–49), and by David H. Kelsey, in 'Can God be an agent without a body?' (*Interpretation*, 27 (1973), pp. 358–62). The former remarks (n. 12) that 'in making the distinction, which modern philosophy owes to Descartes, between "inner" and "outer", Ogden opens the door to a host of troubles'; and the latter (p. 359) 'that Ogden seems to have a dualistic view of "person"... It sometimes seems to come to expression in a mind/brain dualism.' There have been criticisms on a similar score of Kaufman's position, calling it 'residual Cartesianism' (E. Michael McLain, 'On theological models', *Harvard Theological Review*, 62 (1969), pp. 155–87), to which Kaufman has replied in the preface to *God the Problem* (n. 20).

22 Tracy, *God, Action and Embodiment*, pp. xv, xvi.

23 See, for example, the illuminating and thorough article by R. Ellis, 'God and 'Action'', *Religious Studies*, 24 (1989), pp. 463–82. (I am grateful to Dr Ellis and Cambridge University Press for permission to reproduce the quotation below.) Ellis usefully identifies and enumerates (pp. 475–6) fifteen theses concerning human action that emerge from current philosophical analysis. He goes on – pertinently to our present purposes – to relate these analogically to the notion of God's 'action'. Since this analysis is presupposed in the discussion here I cannot do better than to summarize it in his own words (pp. 478–81; the bracketed small Roman numerals refer to the fifteen theses, as he enumerated them):

'... for God to be said to *act* in the fullest sense ... he should have (i) an intention for a particular state of affairs. God's act (ii) is his intention for an event . . . God is able (iii) to think about his acts far more rationally and with much greater vision than we. God's intention has (iv) future reference ie. (xv) it is directed to a specifically desired state of affairs: he intends this, not that. God (v) is conscious of his intention, and (vi) statements of his intentions are the way of giving answers to questions 'why?' asked of certain events. (vii) All God's intended acts are voluntary . . . The only ways in which God's acts can be considered involuntary are perhaps (a) because of states of affairs in the world which God wishes were not so, and which he must 'take into account' in acting . . . (b) if the best for a given situation which God is able to intend for it will still bring inevitably discord and suffering . . .

God is responsible (x) for all events which occur according to his intention for them and as a result of his intention for them. Such an act is *his* act . . . He is also responsible for effects which he could reasonably have been expected to have prevented from occurring, i.e. if they were not beyond his control . . . For an act to be God's act he must have intention for it and have made it what it was.

. . . (xi) the distinction between basic and complex actions. God's basic actions are the simple offerings of himself to his creatures in love, in which he may offer (though it will not often be acknowledged consciously) his intention and influence. God acts in this basic way on every existing thing at every instant . . . Such would be the content of much of our talk about providence . . . But God also acts in a complex way, involving the realising of his intention through other free agents . . . we are here talking of 'Double Agency'. God can act (xiv) through the free agency of another, and yet we may still say that it is properly and mostly *his* act . . .

We must recall what was said concerning the nature of complex actions: they bring with them the increasing possibility of failure (viii, xiii) . . .

. . . when we propound a theory of God's complex action in history, using a variety of free agents, then the task seems to demand our recognition that as acts get more complex, they also get more 'risky' . . . it may be useless to attempt a conception of God's agency unless we envisage this agency as operative among other autonomous agents . . .

God's basic actions cannot fail, but his complex actions are inevitably more precarious. We suggest then, that 'action' may well include within it the notion of possible failure . . .

God's aim and intentions are constant, and he is always acting (basic) and seeking to act (complex) according to his constant love.'

24 Richard Swinburne appears to be unusual among contemporary philosophical theologians in arguing for a dualistic interpretation of the mind/body problem (in *The Evolution of the Soul* (Clarendon

Press, Oxford, 1986), in which the 'soul' is regarded as a distinct entity, but not naturally immortal) and this shapes very directly his understanding of God's action in the world.

25   D. J. Bartholomew, *God of Chance* (SCM Press, London, 1984), p. 123; and see above, ch. 3(b).

26   Thomas, *God's Activity*, pp. 234–5.

27   ibid., pp. 235–6.

28   The approach which regards accounts in scientific and theistic languages as simply two alternative perspectives, equally valid in their respective 'language games'. The weakness of this approach is that, if one takes the critical-realist view of both scientific and theological affirmations, one cannot ignore the relation of what the two languages are asserting about the one actual, real world.

29   Thomas, *God's Activity*, ch. 14.

30   Thus no general attempt will be made here to classify authors according to their different approaches.

31   See nn. 19 and 20, above.

32   G. D. Kaufman, *God the Problem* (Harvard University Press, Cambridge Mass., 1972).

33   The response of process theologians to 'how?' questions C and D ('To what effect?' and 'to what extent?') is more a part of their account of God's purposes than of how they envisage God as involved in actual processes.

34   Maurice Wiles, 'Religious authority and divine action', *Religious Studies*, 7 (1971), pp. 1–12: reproduced in Thomas, *God's Activity*, pp. 181–94.

35   It is true that Wiles (n. 37, below), does distance himself from those who view the world as 'a closed deterministically ordered system' (*God's Action in the World*, p. 65) and from 'extreme dualists' in their 'understanding of the human person' (p. 30). He attributes, by analogy, mentalistic properties, such as 'intentions' and 'purposes', to God as manifest in God's one, continuous, act of creation. Even so, he does not elaborate the kind of causality that operates when human ('mentalistic') intentions manifest themselves as actions in a physical world. This is crucial for making the analogy of God's agency to that of persons plausible with respect to the nexus of physical events in the world. Moreover the unpredictability of many macroscopic systems (see ch. 3, section 1) is not taken into account by Wiles or any of the other authors, even while some (it appears) do recognize the indeterminacy of the physical world at the quantum level.

36   Kaufman, *God the Problem*, p. 137.

37   Maurice Wiles, *God's Action in the World* (SCM Press, London, 1986), pp. 20, 28–9, 93.

38   Austin Farrer, *Faith and Speculation* (A. & C. Black, London, 1967).

39 Kaufman, *Problem of God*, preface; Brian L. Hebblethwaite Providence and divine action', *Religious Studies*, 14 (1978), pp. 223–36; David Galilee, 'The Remaking defended', *Theology*, 78 (1975), pp. 554–5.

40 Farrer, *Faith and Speculation*, p. 159.

41 Brian Hebblethwaite has called Farrer's analogy 'the paradox of double agency, the hidden hand of God making the creature make itself, in and through the interaction of each created energy, at each level of complexity, thus realising specific divine purposes in the evolution of man, in the history of our salvation, and in men's lives as they open themselves up to the will of God, and become the vehicles of God's action to each other' 'Providence and divine action' n. 39, p. 229).

42 Farrer, *Faith and Speculation*, p. 66.

43 Maurice Wiles, 'Farrer's concept of divine agency', *Theology*, 84 (1981), p. 248.

44 Langford, *Providence*, p. 76.

45 ibid.

46 ibid., p. 87.

47 ibid.

48 ibid., p. 89.

49 See also this chapter, section 3b.

50 Langford, *Providence*, p. 90.

51 ibid.

52 White, *Fall of a Sparrow*, p. 108.

53 The resort of Vernon White (ibid., pp. 104–5), and indeed of D. J. Bartholomew (*God of Chance*, p. 142), to the ill-established claims that 'psychokinetic' phenomena occur, can only be regarded as a counsel of despair, if not as an outright aberration.

54 Vincent Brummer, *What Are We Doing When We Pray?* (SCM Press, London, 1984).

55 ibid., p. 64.

56 See ch. 3, section 1.

57 For a discussion of the irreducible unpredictability of non-linear dynamical systems at the macroscopic level, see pp. 50–3.

58 John Polkinghorne, *Science and Providence* (SPCK, London, 1989), p. 31.

59 John V. Taylor, *The Go-between God* (SCM Press), 1972, p. 28.

60 Polkinghorne, *Science and Providence*, p. 31.

61 ibid., p. 32. Polkinghorne is not here referring to the randomness of individual *quantum* events as the basis for divine action within the 'flexible process' of macroscopic events – a proposal he rightly, in my view, rejects (ibid., p. 27). The 'small triggers' (ibid., p. 32) which 'could generate large effects' (ibid., p. 32) and which he suggests (in the phrases quoted on p. 154 of the main text) could be the location of divine immanent action, cannot but be changes (i.e.

fluctuations) in small regions in those initial conditions to which the macroscopic events are so sensitive (e.g. concentrations of certain molecules). Such an alteration by God of these localized conditions would be an action within the casual nexus at this micro-level. However, Dr Polkinghorne informs me that such an 'interventionist' understanding of what he has written would be a misinterpretation.

62   I, too, with both Taylor and Polkinghorne, wish to stress emphatically that God interacts continuously with the world to implement his purposes, but I suggest that his influence on events is by means of a continuous top-down causative input on the world as a whole in the way elaborated later in this section. I agree with John Polkinghorne that this 'input', in my approach regarded as into the system as a whole, may best be conceived of as that of information, but I furthermore accept that energy exchange usually accompanies such an input (as we saw, Hawking has also argued that there can be no storage of information without expenditure of energy (ch. 2, section 1 and n. 1)). Even 'the bead at the top of a vertical smooth U-shaped wire' (Polkinghorne, *Science and Providence*, p. 32) cannot require less than one quantum of energy to make it go to one side rather than the other. One can never escape entirely the conundrum of the 'causal joint'! Although the *concept* of information is clearly distinguishable from that of energy, in the real world we seem to know of no transfers of information that do not involve exchanges of matter/energy, however small relatively to the scale of the systems in question.

63   Ch. 8, section 2.

64   For the reasons why the majority of physicists reject the existence of 'hidden variables' underlying the probabilistic predictions of quantum theory which would make the theory deterministic, see J. C. Polkinghorne, *The Quantum World* (Penguin Books, Harmondsworth, 1986), chs. 5 and 7. See also our earlier discussion on divine knowledge (ch. 8, section 2(c)) for what such 'self-limitation' of God's knowledge might mean.

65   Ch. 3, section 1.

66   Ch. 8, section 2(c).

67   Ch. 3, section 3(a).

68   Karl Popper, lecture to the World Philosophy Congress, Brighton, August 1988; reported in *The Guardian*, 29 August 1988.

69   Bartholomew, *God of Chance*, p. 138.

70   Ch. 8, section 2(b).

71   Ch. 3, sections 1 and 2.

72   Ch. 3, section 1(d).

73   Ch. 3, section 2(b).

74   Ch. 3, section 2(c).

75   e.g., the present author in *CWS*, pp. 45, 141, 201, 207, 352, where

this way of speaking is denoted as 'pan-*en*-theism'. This term is defined (*Oxford Dictionary of the Christian Church*, 2nd edn, revised, ed. F. L. Cross and E. A. Livingstone, Oxford University Press, Oxford, 1983, p. 1027) as 'The belief that the Being of God includes and penetrates the whole universe, so that every part of it exists in Him but (as against pantheism) that His Being is more than, and is not exhausted by, the universe.' Since it was first defined by K. C. F. Krause (1781–1832) it seems to have incurred some disfavour for reasons not readily apparent. In our century it has been particularly espoused by process theologians. However, the basic concept, as defined in this text and by the definition in the *Oxford Dictionary of the Christian Church*, seems to me to be not at all dependent on that particular metaphysical system and to be entirely consistent with Christian theism as a useful spatial model.

It does not, in my usage at least, have any implication (cf. John Polkinghorne, *Science and Creation*, SPCK, London, 1988, p. 53) that the world is in some sense a *part* of God, that is, of the same kind of being as God. This would indeed deny the ultimate otherness of God from that which he has created and imply that the world was of the same stuff or 'substance' as God himself. But this does not follow from the definition of the term which allows there to be an ontological gap in mode of being between God and the world while at the same time stressing two essential features of that relation – the accessibility of all-that-is to God and God's ultimate ontological 'beyondness', expressed by a spatial metaphor in the model. Because of misconceptions surrounding the word 'pan-en-theism', I shall, as far as possible, avoid its use, but not the idea itself, as defined above.

David Pailin in his *God and the Processes of Reality* (Routledge, London and New York, 1989, ch. 5) has given a useful exposition of the idea of 'panentheism' following mainly the expositions of Charles Hartshorne. They both contrast it with 'classical pantheism' and with 'classical (immured) theism'. For classical pantheism, 'the divine being is constituted by the sum total of all that truly is' (ibid., p. 77), the divine is totally receptive of all events in the world, and it also 'involves a denial of God's genuine independence of the world' (p. 77). For classical theism, 'God and the constituents of the world have each an appropriate degree of autonomy and the nature of the divine is such that no significant reciprocity is possible between them' (p. 78); it denies any dependence of God on the world. This God of 'classical theism', as both Hartshorne and Pailin denote it, is necessary, absolute and perfect – like the God of some philosophers. Neither of these theisms corresponds to the God of Christian belief, as we inferred earlier (ch. 7, section 2, and ch. 8), and I share their desire to affirm both that God is causally independent of the world, that the world has a derivative existence, and is thereby dependent on God, *and* that God interacts continuously with the world. So 'panentheism is not a new position but a new appreciation of the proper conceptual structure of a dominant tradition of religious faith in God' (p. 81). The technical term 'panentheism' for Christian theism, awkward thought it is, at least expresses an overt desire to hold together both the transcendence and the immanence of God in relation to the world. Moreover Pailin, in concord with Hartshorne, regards their 'dipolar panentheism' as a 'concept of God as Eternal-Temporal Consciousness, Knowing and including the World (ETCKW)' (p. 84).

Some or all of these attributes of God have been variously deduced by others (e.g., by R. Swinburne; see ch. 7, section 1) on grounds, it should be noted, that do not invoke the metaphysics of 'process thought', with which the term 'panentheism' has, in my view, been unfortunately too closely tied. I think process theology has tended to over-emphasize God's *total* receptivity to all events in the world in a way that seems to allow God little discrimination. In my own past usage of the term 'panentheism', I have not wanted to imply an equally direct involvement of God in all events nor that all events equally and in the same sense affect God – as often appears to be an implication of process theology.

76   *Acts*, 17:28 (AV).
77   *Confessions*, VII.7, tras. E. B. Pusey (from *Great Books of the Western World*, vol. 18, ed. R. M. Hutchins, Encyclopaedia Brittanica, Inc., Chicago, 1952, p. 45).
78   See, *inter alia*, C. Blakemore, *The Mechanics of the Mind* (Cambridge University Press, Cambridge, 1976); the articles assembled in the *Scientific American* publication *The Brain*, (W. H. Freeman, San Francisco and Oxford, 1979); and the comprehensive information in *The Oxford Companion to the Mind*, ed. Richard L. Gregory (Oxford University Press, Oxford, 1987).
79   cf. the earlier quotation from I. T. Ramsey, a Christian philosopher of religion, ch. 4, section 1, and n. 7.
80   A. R. Peacocke, *CWS*, pp. 119–22, 128–31; idem, 'A Christian materialism?', in *How We Know*, ed. M. Shafto (Harper and Row, San Francisco, 1985), pp. 146–68.
81   ibid. pp. 147–9, 163–4.
82   Ch. 3, section 2(c).
83   p. 61.
84   This chapter, section 4, ch. 11 and also *The Science and Theology of Information*, eds. C. Wassermann, R. Kirby and B. Rordorff (Editions Labor et Fides, Geneva, 1992), the Proceedings of the Third European Conference of Science and Theology at Geneva in 1990.
85   Kaufman, *God the Problem*; Wiles, *God's Action in the World*.

86 Hugh Montefiore, *The Probability of God* (SCM Press, London, 1985), p. 98.
87 e.g. in *CWS*, pp. 104ff., 210, *passim*.
88 In *GNB*, pp. 97ff.
89 However, this response did not satisfy David Pailin (in *God and the Processes of Reality*, Routledge, London and New York, 1989), who considered that an emphasis on the inherent creativity of natural processes still cannot avoid implying 'that while God initially established the potentialities of the constituents of that [evolutionary] process, *it develops automatically . . .* this way of understanding divine creativity suggests that God does not affect what particular forms of being emerge in the natural order . . . God on this view seems to have neither direct nor even indirect influence on what happens – until, perhaps, human beings . . . appear' (p. 136, emphasis added).

But if, as I am here suggesting, God is interacting with the whole world system in a top-down causative influence on the whole, then this: (a) would be discernible by us only through the actualizations of the potentialities of the fundamental entities of the universe and of the natural processes they undergo, as manifest in their inbuilt propensities towards complexity, sensitivity and open-endedness (and so towards consciousness and freedom); and (b), at the same time, could be the means whereby God effected his purposes by steering events towards particular instantiations of these selfsame potentialities, and as particular manifestations of their inbuilt propensities – yet without any 'intervention by God' occurring at any level lower than that of the whole, that is, at any of the lower levels analysed by the particular sciences appropriate to them.

I would suggest that this 'top-down' causal interpretation of God's continuous interaction with the world as a whole provides a coherent way of combining a strong emphasis on the immanence of God in and the transcendence of God over the world and its processes, both of which I have previously argued (in *CWS* and *GNB*) must be held together for a satisfactory conception of God's relation to the world. This combination of the ideas of immanence and top-down causation (and of the other considerations in the main text) seems to me to be more coherent with the ability of the natural sciences to interpret the processes of the natural world at many observable levels than is the postulate of process theology that there is some kind of direct divine influence on *all* particular natural events (often called a 'lure', as if all events had a mental component).

On the view proposed here, God's general interaction with the world as a whole can, but not must, have particular consequences, if God wills them in accord with his general purposes for the universe and its creatures, without any intervening (or 'giving an aim', or 'luring', in process terminology) at the level in the whole system of natural processes at which the particular event to be influenced occurs.

90 See p. 145, above.

91 See n. 62 above.

92 David Galilee and Brian Hebblethwaite, 'Farrer's concept of double agency: a reply', *Theology*, 35 (1982), pp. 7–10.

93 ibid., p. 9.

94 ibid.

95 Ch. 8, sections 1 and 2.

96 John Macquarrie, 'God and the World', *Theology*, 75 (1972), pp. 394–403.

97 ibid., p. 394.

98 ibid., pp. 394–5.

99 See Sallie McFague, *Models of God* (SCM Press, London, 1987), pp. 63ff. For McFague the patriarchal associations of the monarchical models rule them out of consideration, but I think this dismissal is unwarranted. for these models incorporate a sense of the personal transcendence of God over the world that is essential to the concept of God, even when any false notion of 'maleness' in the Godhead is, quite rightly, expunged.

100 *We Believe in God*, report of the Doctrine Commission of the Church of England (Church House Publishing, London, 1987), pp. 148ff.

101 ibid., p. 149.

102 ibid.

103 McFague, *Models of God, passim.*

104 e.g., the present author in *CWS* (pp. 141ff.), in which I point out that if in some sense the world is 'within' God (a spatial metaphor), God is 'more than' the world and God is creator *of* the world, then a natural analogy is that of a mother bearing a child within her, with the obvious limiting ('is not') feature of this metaphor, namely that God is the source of being of that which God creates within 'herself', whereas a human mother is not the *creator* of the growing embryo she carries within her.

105 *We Believe in God*, p. 154.

106 For fuller expositions see *IR* (ch. 1) and A. R. Peacocke, 'Science and theology today: a critical realist perspective', *Religion and Intellectual Life*, 5 (1988), pp. 45–58 and references therein; also Janet Martin Soskice, *Metaphor and Religious Language* (Clarendon Press, Oxford, 1985) and McFague, *Models of God*.

107 McFague, *Models of God*, pp. 69–78; Grace Jantzen, *God's World, God's Body* (Darton, Longman and Todd, London, 1984).

108 According to Julius Lipner, it could also, if taken seriously by Christians, be of great value in dialogue with Hinduism, in the light of the theology of Ramanuja, an eleventh- to twelfth-century

(CE) Tamil Brahmin (J. J. Lipner, 'The world as God's 'body': in pursuit of dialogue with Ramanuja', *Religious Studies*, 20 (1984), pp. 145–61.

109   Our stress is on models of the *creative* activity of God in the world. But, of course, these do not exhaust the range of metaphors that have been employed to represent God's general activity in the world. I. T. Ramsey, for example, in *Models for Divine Activity* (SCM Press, London, 1973), demonstrates how 'Spirit' (= 'wind' or 'breath') has been developed and grown in the Judeo-Christian tradition as a model of God's activity. *'Spirit is a noun* whose logical tradition is more reliably a verb: *being active, God active.* It tells of a becoming, not a *being*' (p. 14). He also shows how the model of 'economy' (with its senses of administration, provision for need and discipline) was once used widely by Christian theologians as a model for God's activity, but has fallen into desuetude. Finally, he develops the model of God's ubiquity or omnipresence that is provided by talk of God's locatable presence, which may be impersonal or personal – and the latter connotation, of God's personal presence, has been employed by M. Wiles (*Faith and the Mystery of God*, SCM Press, London, 1982, pp. 122ff.) to express God's action in the world in relation to both prayer and to the concept of 'spirit' and, following G. W. H. Lampe (*God as Spirit*, Oxford University Press, 1977), in relation to the Incarnation.

110   Macquarrie, *Principles*, pp. 200–9.

111   ibid.

112   Stephen Hobhouse, *The Selected Mystical Writings of William Law* (C. W. Daniel & Co., London, 1938), p. 250.

113   From William Law, *An Appeal* (1740), reproduced in Hobhouse, *Selected Mystical Writings*, p. 36.

114   Macquarrie, *Principles*, pp. 200–9.

115   e.g. Macquarrie, *Principles*, p. 202; and, more recently, this model has been endorsed as helpful and suggestive in *We Believe in God*, n. 77, pp. 151ff.

116   Dorothy Sayers, *The Mind of the Maker* (Methuen, London, 1941), p. 23.

117   ibid., p. 97.

118   ibid., p. 28. She stresses that 'Idea' in this quotation is not used in the traditional philosopher's sense but in the sense in which it is used by a writer when he says 'I have an idea for a book'; and 'energy' and 'power' are similarly used in their everyday, non-physicist's, sense.

119   ibid., p. 42.

120   Austin Farrer, *A Science of God?* (Geoffrey Bles, London, 1966), p. 76.

121   Wiles, *God's Action*, p. 37; see also the discussion of Wiles'

      suggestion by John Polkinghorne, *Science and Providence* (SPCK, London, 1989), p. 84.

122 *We Believe in God*, p. 151.

123 Sayers, *Mind of the Maker*, pp. 45–7.

124 Quoted by Karl Popper in his 'intellectual autobiography', *Unended Quest* (Fontana/Collins, London, 1976), p. 59; see p. 206, n. 59 for details.

125 ibid.

126 See *CWS*, pp. 82–4.

127 Ch. 3, section 3(a).

128 cf. *CWS*, pp. 105–6.

129 This and the preceding follow closely paragraphs in *IR*, pp. 72–3.

130 The fascinating nature of music has also provided Colin Gunton with concepts useful in interpreting the Christian doctrine of the Incarnation (in *Yesterday and Today: A Study of Continuities in Christology*, Darton, Longman and Todd, London, 1983, pp. 115ff.); and it has proved to be a rich quarry for M. Eigen and R. Winkler in explicating aspects of modern biology and other sciences (*Laws of the Game*, Knopf, New York, 1981, and Allen Lane, London, 1982), as well as many otherwise baffling features of modern physical concepts of the world (see also A. R. Peacocke, 'The theory of relativity and our world view', in *Einstein: The First Hundred Years*, ed. M. Goldsmith, A. Mackay and J. Woudhuysen, Pergamon Press, Oxford and London, 1980, esp. pp. 87–9, where reference is made to the use of musical imagery by M. Capek, *The Philosophical Impact of Contemporary Physics*, Van Nostrand, Princeton, 1961, pp. 371ff.).

131 T. S. Eliot, 'The Dry Salvages', *The Four Quartets*, 11. 210–12.

132 For an earlier exposition of this suggestion, see *SCE*, pp. 194–6; and *CWS*, ch. 7, esp. pp. 304–11.

133 I am indebted to Sir David Lumsden, for his helpful contributions to my thinking in this paragraph and, indeed, this whole section on musical creativity.

134 Some of the ideas in this section were originally presented in *CWS*.

135 *Psalm* 33:6.

136 See ch. 3, section 2; ch. 9, section 2(b), (c).

137 John Macquarrie, 'God and the world: one reality or two?', *Theology*, 75 (1972), pp. 394–403.

138 ibid., p. 400–1.

139 ibid., p. 401.

140 Ch. 3, section 1.

141 C. E. Raven, *Natural Religion and Christian Theology*, Gifford lectures, 2nd series, 1952, *Experience and Interpretation*, (Cambridge University Press, Cambridge, 1953), II, p. 157.

142 cf. *CWS*, pp. 208–9.

143 Grace M. Jantzen, *God's World, God's Body* (Darton, Longman and Todd, 1984), p. 98.
144 Ch. 8, section 2(c).
145 See above, p. 135.
146 Langford, *Providence*, pp. 13–24; Macquarrie, *Principles*, ch. XI.
147 Langford, *Providence*, p. 17.
148 ibid., p. 18.
149 ibid., p. 19.
150 This chapter, section 1.

CHAPTER 10   CONCLUSION TO PART II

1   John Macquarrie, *Principles of Christian Theology* (SCM Press, London, 1966), p. 101.
2   'Lets-be' in the terminology of Macquarrie, ibid.
3   For an interesting exposition and analysis of these terms in the context of the theologies of Charles Hartshorne and Karl Barth, see Colin E. Gunton, *Being and Becoming* (Oxford University Press, Oxford, 1978).
4   See David A. Pailin, *God and the Processes of Reality* (Routledge, London and New York, 1989), esp. ch. 7. Pailin takes a stronger line than is adopted here, namely, that God is *necessarily* creative: '. . . "If God, then creator" seems a necessary entailment (for a being which is not the creative ground of all reality would not satisfy the definition of what it is to be 'God'); and "If creator, then continually and universally involved in events" seems a plausible implication (for a God who initiated the creative process and then carelessly abandoned it to its own devices . . . is hardly a proper object of worship) . . . To cast doubt . . . on the possibility of talking significantly about God as creator is to cast doubt on the significance of theistic understanding' (p. 123). 'As personal . . . the divine must be held to be related to what is other than Godself, since it is only possible to be personal in relation to others. Similarly, it may be argued that as ultimate in value God must be considered to be loving . . . and that to be loving requires objects for its expression . . . God cannot be coherently considered to be without a world and so must be regarded as necessarily creative' (p. 126).
5   A. Louth in *The Origin of the Christian Mystical Tradition* (Clarendon Press, Oxford, 1981, p. 91) quotes Gregory of Nyssa: 'for he is invisible by nature, but becomes visible in His energies, for He may be contemplated in the things that are referred to Him' (*Hom.* VI, 12690, in H. Graef's translation). Louth goes on to make the point that, for Gregory of Nyssa, to know God is to possess him not to be informed about him. The soul is a mirror reflecting the

divine image and therefore contemplates God by contemplating the divine image present within itself. 'In the darkness of unknowability the soul contemplates God in the mirror that it is' (Louth, *loc. cit*).

6 According to Rowan Williams, *The Wound of Knowledge*, (Darton, Longman and Todd, London, 1979), pp. 54–5.

7 ibid., p. 54.

8 cf. *CWS*, pp. 131ff.

9 cf. *CWS*, pp. 212–13.

CHAPTER 11   GOD'S COMMUNICATION WITH HUMANITY

1 Ch. 9, section 2, pp. 161–3; and section 4, p. 179. The concept of flow of 'information' in relation to God's interaction with the world has recently been perceptively explored by J. C. Puddefoot in 'Information and Creation', a contribution to the Proceedings of the 3rd European Conference on Science and Theology, Geneva, 1990. *The Science and Theology of Information*, eds. C. Wassermann, R. Kirby and B. Rordoff (published by the Faculty of Theology of the Univ. of Geneva, Editions Labor et Fides, 1992), pp. 7–25. For a brief account of his analysis of the meaning of the term 'information', see n. 31, ch. 14.

2 Ch. 9(2).

3 Oliver C. Quick, *The Christian Sacraments* (Nisbet, London, 1927, repr. 1955), ch. 1.

4 ibid., p. 3.

5 ibid., p. 6. 'Instrumentality is primarily the relation of act to purpose, and is extended to include the relation to purpose of any thing with which action is performed' (pp. 8–9). However 'a symbol is essentially a means of expression' although 'every constructed symbol has been an instrument from the first' (p. 9). On closer examination (p. 12) he concluded that 'Instrumentality is the relation of a thing to that which is effected by it; significance [capability of signifying to the human mind a reality other than itself] is the relation of a thing to that which is suggested by it'.

6 ibid., p. 16.

7 Ch. 9, sections 2 and 3.

8 See p. 180.

9 Cf. pp. 158–9.

10 See p. 159.

11 Karl Popper, 'Epistemology without a knowing subject', in *Logic, methodology and philosophy of sciences, III* ed. van Rostelaar and Staal (North-Holland Publ. Co., Amsterdam, 1968) – quoted and represented diagramatically in Fig. 34 in *Facing Reality* by

J. C. Eccles (Longman, London, 1970) and more recently as Fig. 4.2 of his *Evolution of the Brain: Creation of the Self* (Routledge, London and New York, 1989).

12 Popper calls them 'World 1', 'World 2' and 'World 3', but I consider this to be a misleading division of what is essentially only *one* world, so have preferred to refer to them, in this chapter, as 'constituents' 1, 2 and 3 of the world.

13 In more detail, Eccles, *Evolution of the Brain* (1989) lists the following in each category.
(1) *Physical objects and states.*
1. Inorganic – matter and energy of the cosmos
2. Biology – structure and actions of all living beings – human brains
3. Artefacts – material substrates of human creativity, of tools, of machine, of books, of works of art, of music.
(2) *States of consciousness*
Subjective knowledge
Experience of: perception, thinking, dispositional intentions, memories, dreams, creative imagination.
(3) *Knowledge in objective sense*
Cultural heritage coded on material substrates: philosophical, theological, scientific, historical, literary, artistic, technological
Theoretical systems: scientific problems, critical arguments.
It seems to me that 'theoretical systems' should not be included under (3) but (2) and I have assumed this transposition in my discussion in the text.

14 See n. 13 above.

15 See pp. 160ff.

16 See p. 41.

17 See pp. 53–5.

18 See below, section 3(b), for an elaboration of what is involved in such communciation.

19 See p. 181.

20 Rowan Williams, 'Trinity and Revelation', *Modern Theology* 2 (1986) p. 200.

21 ibid.

22 A suitable definition of 'revelation' for the present purposes is that given by David Pailin (*NDCT*, p. 504–6): 'By 'revelation' is generally meant the disclosure of what was previously unknown or only uncertainly apprehended. In theology such disclosure is normally regarded as caused by the agency of God ... and as making known hidden aspects of the character and purposes of God, of humanity in its relationship with God and of what is to occur in the future through the providence of God. This unveiling of what was concealed may be either through some means of communicating information on these topics or in the form of what is

taken to be a self-manifesting encounter with God. In either case God is the agent who reveals and human persons are the subjects who receive revelation' (p. 503). The former of these two aspects of revelation corresponds to the briefer definition of Basil Mitchell when he writes of God 'finding ways of communicating to his creatures fundamental truths about his nature and purposes which they otherwise could not discover' (in 'Does Christianity need a Revelation? A Discussion' by B. Mitchell and M. Wiles, *Theology* 83 (1980), p. 103).

23   Ch. 9; denoted by the double-shafted arrows in Figure 1.

24   Because there is a sense in which all genuine knowledge of God is fundamentally revelatory (Pailin, *Revelation*, p. 506), the distinction between 'general' revelation to all humanity and 'special' revelation to particular individuals or communities is preferred to that between 'natural' and 'revealed' theology. For the latter – although it could be regarded as consistent with St Paul in *Romans* – depends on an oversharp and insupportable distinction between truths determinable by 'unaided human reasoning and other truths which cannot be apprehended . . . unless they are disclosed by God' (ibid., p. 504). See also n. 38 below and the quotation from Pailin cited at that point in the text to which it refers.

25   *Romans* 1:19, 20 (NEB). See also James Barr, *Biblical Faith and Natural Theology* (Gifford Lectures 1991, Clarendon Press, Oxford, 1993), esp chs. 3, 6 and 10.

26   See n. 1 above.

27   'Conspicuous Sanctity and Religious Belief', in *The Rationality of Religious Belief*, eds. W. J. Abraham and S. W. Holtzer (Clarendon Press, Oxford, 1987), p. 122.

28   See p. 16.

29   See p. 181.

30   R. Williams n. 21 above and the quotation in the main text to which it refers.

31   See pp. 15ff.

32   David Brown, *The Divine Trinity* (Duckworth, London, 1985), pp. 52–98.

33   ibid., p. 70.

34   Ch. 9; and, in this connection, see particularly the latter part of n. 12 to ch. 9.

35   David Brown, 'God and Symbolic Action' in *Divine Action: Studies inspired by the philosophical theology of Austin Farrer*, eds. B. Hebblethwaite and E. Henderson (T. & T. Clark, Edinburgh, 1990).

36   Cf., p. 3.

37   See: David Hay, *Religious Experience Today: studying the facts* (Mowbray, London, 1990) especially pp. 56–7, 79–85, for details and references. The two questions given in the text were devised for

different surveys but they have been shown to evoke the same response (Hay, ibid., p. 69).

38 ibid., p. 57.

39 ibid., Table 5, p. 83.

40 See, D. Pailin, 'Revelation', (n. 22), p. 506.

41 ibid.; cf. earlier, p. 15 of the Introduction.

42 Nicholas Lash, *Easter in Ordinary: Reflections on Human Experience and the Knowledge of God* (SCM Press, London, 1988) p. 7.

43 Where 'experience of God' must include the 'deep awareness of a benevolent non-physical power which appears to be partly or wholly beyond, and far greater than, the individual self' (Alister Hardy, *The Spiritual Nature of Man*, Clarendon Press, Oxford, 1979, p. 1) which the Alister Hardy Research Centre has shown to be so widespread, even in contemporary Britain. See p. 3 and Hay, *Religious Experience*, n. 37 above.

44 The cautionary inverted commas will be omitted henceforth on the understanding that the text here indicates the necessary reservations about and limitations of this term.

45 Basil Mitchell, *The Justification of Religious Belief* (Macmillan, London, 1973); Richard Swinburne, *The Existence of God* (Clarendon Press, Oxford, 1979) ch. 13; David Brown, *The Divine Trinity*, pp. 33–51; Caroline Franks Davies, *The Evidential Force of Religious Experience* (Clarendon Press, Oxford, 1989) ch. 4, esp. pp. 108–114; William J. Abraham, 'Cumulative Case Arguments for Christian Theism' in *Rationality of Religious Belief*, Abraham and Holtzer, pp. 17–37.

46 As discussed in ch. 9, section 2 and depicted in Fig. 1.

47 ibid.

48 I have included his category (4) under the 'Unmediated' heading, since I cannot see how it could be 'mediated' in his sense, since it involves sensations 'not of a kind describable by normal vocabulary' (Swinburne, ibid., p. 251).

49 R. Swinburne, *The Existence of God*, ch. 13.

50 ibid., p. 252.

51 D. Brown, *The Divine Trinity*, pp. 33–51 (see his *n.* 75, p. 36, for a comparison of his classification with that of Swinburne). Caroline Franks Davies (*Evidential Force*, ch. 2) gives another classification which overlaps with those of Figure 2. Since it covers much the same range of experience it is not necessary for our present purposes also to reproduce her classification, useful though it is.

52 R. Swinburne, *Existence of God*, p. 246.

53 Cf. the definition of Alister Hardy, n. 43, above. I myself would demur from Swinburne's phrase 'some other *supernatural thing*'.

54 See n. 50 above.

55 Earlier (Introduction, pp. 15–16), allusion was made to the distinction between 'positive' and 'negative' theology (between the

via positiva and the *via negativa*). The former dares to articulate our understanding of God in words, symbols, images and models (as we are trying to do here); the latter retreats into silence before the inscrutable nature of God, the Ineffable. In Figure 2, 'positive' theology covers roughly (1), (2) and (3), and I and II; and negative theology (4) and (5), and III and IV.

56   See n. 13 above.
57   See n. 1 above.
58   See n. 13 above.
59   See ch. 2, section 3.
60   A similar point has been made by Russell Standard (*Grounds for Reasonable Belief*), Scottish Acad. Press, Edinburgh, 1989, pp. 277ff, para. 18.9). Cf. also the quotation from W. P. Alston, on p. 141 (n. 14, ch. 9).

   In Fig. 1 the pairs of single-headed arrows which represent interactions between human beings may therefore be regarded as subsets of the effects represented by the single-shafted, double-headed arrows (the solid ones being human effects on the non-human world, and the dashed ones *vice versa*), provided it is recognized that they are also distinctive in that they are the means of communicating information concerning states of consciousness (intentions, desires, purposes, memories, etc.) between human beings – and so are irreducibly personal and social.

61   Cf. ch. 12, section 5, p. 238 and n. 121.
62   See ch. 2, section 3.
63   These means include all the constituents 3 of Popper (n. 13).
64   See n. 13 above.
65   Such mutual and social relationships are, at every level of intensity, essential to the emergence and flourishing of the individual person (see p. 74).
66   See ch. 9, section 2 and Fig. 1.
67   See n. 1 above.
68   D. Brown, *The Divine Trinity*, p. 37, expounded on pp. 42–51.
69   Swinburne, *Existence of God*, p. 251. These constitute Swinburne's category (4) and are located where they are in Figure 2 for the reasons given in n. 48.
70   ibid.
71   What has graphically been called the 'divine laser-beam' by David Jenkins, (*God, Miracle and the Church of England*, SCM Press, London, 1987, p. 4).
72   See p. 183.
73   Ch. 4, section 1 and ch. 9, section 2(c).
74   See n. 13 above.
75   pp. 195–6.
76   The righthand side of Figure 2.
77   *Psalm* 46:10.

78 Swinburne, *Existence of God*, p. 252.
79 Ch. 9, section 2.
80 See p. 183.
81 Some readers may be surprised that at no point have I invoked the supposed evidence for non-physical communication between human beings (e.g., extra-sensory perception) and even between human beings and matter (e.g., psychokinesis, etc.). The evidence for these is still highly disputed, not least amongst the scientific community, so that they cannot form the basis of any generally accepted reliable model for understanding inter-human communication, let alone that of God with humanity (for a recent survey see *Parapsychology: the controversial science*, by R. Broughton (Rider, London, 1992). If they ever were proven to general assent, they would then fall into the category of natural features of the world and the arguments in the text would then also apply to them – they could then be one of the modes whereby God communicates with humanity. But while their status is still widely held to be *sub judice*, and indeed inconsistent with what we know about the world through the sciences, they cannot form the basis of any of our theological models. The validity of religious experience, that is, the authenticity of God's communicating with humanity does not depend on, and certainly has no vested interest in, the reality of such phenomena and even less in that of the so-called occult in general.

CHAPTER 12   NATURAL HUMAN BEING

1 Ch. 4, section 1.
2 Ch. 2, section 3.
3 Ch. 3, section 2(c).
4 Ch. 3, sections 1(e), 2(b).
5 For an earlier attempt at this, see 'What is man in the light of the sciences?' *CWS*, pp. 149–154.
6 Based on Figure 8.1 of W. Bechtel and A. Abrahamsen in *Connectionism and the Mind* (Blackwell, Oxford and Cambridge, Mass., 1991).
7 *CWS*, p. 68.
8 Sir Bernard Lovell, 'In the centre of immensities', *Advancement of Science*, NS, 1 (1975) p. 6.
9 D. Levy, *Encyclopedia of Philosophy*, Vol. 5 (Collier-Macmillan, London, 1972 [1967], p. 121.
10 John Macquarrie, *In Search of Humanity* (SCM Press, London, 1982), pp. 255–6.
11 For example, in *GNB*, Figure 2, I depicted a series in which each 'whole' was constituted by 'parts' successively, namely:

(1) Ensembles of eco-systems; (2) eco-systems; (3) populations (of living organisms); (4) individual organisms; (5) cells and organelles; (6) biological macromolecules and small molecules; (7) molecules and atoms; (8) atomic structures and sub-nuclear 'particles'. The corresponding scientific disciplines (those directly focussed on humanity in italics) were: (1) terrestrial ecology, *social anthropology*; (2) community ecology, zoo- and plant-geography, *sociology*; (3) population ecology, population genetics, ethology, *sociology*; (4) cell biology, physiology, ethology, *psychology*; (5) cytology, cell physiology; (6) biochemistry and biophysics; (7) chemistry; (8) physics.

12   J. G. Miller, *Living Systems* (McGraw Hill, New York, 1978); expounded briefly, with some of his diagrams, in *PCBO*, pp. 7–11.

13   Bechtel and Abrahamsen, *Connectionism* pp. 283–4.

14   Such as that described in n. 11.

15   ibid., p. 256.

16   See Bechtel and Abrahmsen, pp. 256–9; and A. A. Abrahamsen, 'Bridging boundaries versus breaking boundaries: psycholinguistics in perspective', *Synthese* 72 (1987), pp. 355–88.

17   See n. 6 above.

18   See n. 38 below.

19   Ch. 11, section 1, nn. 11, 13.

20   Bechtel and Abrahamsen, *Connectionism*, p. 258.

21   The vertical arrows indicate 'that a lower level subdiscipline may obtain specialized descriptions of the domain from a higher-level discipline' and that 'the higher-level discipline may use the lower level discipline as a source of explanation, constraint, and ancillary evidence' (ibid., pp. 259).

22   Macquarrie (*Humanity*, p. 254) discusses the extent to which 'a fairly good case can be made out for thinking of the human being as a miniature cosmos'. He draws attention to the chemical basis and evolutionary origins of human life, and this parallels the involvement of humanity in levels (1) and (2) of Figure 3 which we have already noted. But how far participation in those 'spiritual' qualities that are associated with being a person (possessing freedom, reason, conscience, etc.) 'allows us to think of the human being as somehow reflecting God as well as the natural universe is a matter of debate' (ibid.). However Macquarrie goes on to suggest that this 'affinity between the life of humanity and the wider reality within which life is set' can help construct what he calls an 'anthropological argument for the existence of God' (p. 256).

23   *Genesis* 3:19 (AV).

24   This does not mean that there are not major discoveries of a conceptual as well as of an experimental kind to be made in order to understand the pattern-forming and developmental capacities of the matter in complex systems such as are living organisms. Some

of these are beginning to appear but there is a long way to go in understanding the often baffling ability of living organisms to develop and change (see *PCBO*, chs. 4 and 6).

25 Ch. 2, section 3; more fully argued in *GNB*, chs. 1 and 2.

26 Ch. 3, section 3(a).

27 Q.v., Stephen J. Gould, *Wonderful Life: the Burgess shale and the nature of history* (Penguin Books, London, 1989), p. 49.

28 ibid., p. 51, and *passim*.

29 Cf. Ch. 8, section 2(b).

30 A useful account of the general story of human evolution, especially concentrating on the development of the brain, and the concomitant use of tools and cultural activities, has been given by John C. Eccles in *The Evolution of the Brain: creation of the self* (Routledge, London and New York, 1989), ch. 2.

31 For more details, see *SCE*, pp. 71–2.

32 See ch. 3, section 2(b), 3(a).

33 Ch. 8, section 2(a).

34 Cf. ch. 3, p. 63 and the author's 'The Challenge of Science to Theology and the Church' in *The Weight of Glory*, eds. D. W. Hardy and P. H. Sedgwick (T. & T. Clark, Edinburgh, 1991), p. 45.

35 *Romans* 6:23 (REV).

36 See Karl J. Narr, 'Cultural achievements of early man' in *The Human Creature*, ed. G. Altner (Anchor Books, Doubleday, Garden City, New York, 1974), pp. 115–7: '. . . a marked evolutionary expansion manifests itself after around 30,000 BC, at the beginning of the upper Palaeolithic. The new picture that emerges can be characterized by such terms as accumulation, differentiation and specialization. There is an increase and concentration of cultural goods, a more refined technology with greater variety in the forms of weapons and tools produced and corresponding specialization of their respective functions, more pronounced economic and general cultural differentiation of individual groups'. (pp. 115–6).

37 K. Jaspers, *The Origin and Goal of History* (Routledge and Kegan Paul, London, 1953); see below ch. 13, section 2.

38 P. S. Churchland and T. J. Sejnowski, 'Perspectives on Cognitive Neuroscience', *Science*, 242 (1988), pp. 741–5.

39 The levels of organization of the nervous system depicted in Figure 3 are those distinguished by Churchland and Sejnowski, 'Cognitive Neuroscience', Fig. 1), as (with physical scale): molecules (10^{-10}m.); synapses (10^{-6}m.); neurones (10^{-4}m.); networks (10^{-3}m.); maps (10^{-2}m.); systems (10^{-1}m.); CNS (1m., in human beings). They instance the following as selected examples of the kind of scientific accounts appropriate to particular levels: of *systems*, the processing hierarchy of the visual areas in the

monkey visual cortex; of *networks*, a small network model for the synthesis of oriented receptive fields of simple cells in the visual cortex; of *synapses*, the structure of a chemical synapse.

40   Churchland and Sejnowski, 'Cognitive Neuroscience', p. 742.

41   D. Marr and T. Poggio, 'From understanding computation to understanding neural circuitry', as reported in *Neurosci. Res. Program Bull.* 15 (1977), 470–488.

42   Bechtel and Abrahamsen, *Connectionism*, n. 2, p. 259, regard levels 2, 3 and 4 of Figure 3 in the text here (based on their Fig. 8.1) as corresponding, respectively, to the implementation, algorithm, and computational levels of analysis of D. Marr (*Vision*, Freeman, San Francisco, 1982; and n. 39 above). See also Churchland and Sejnowski, 'Cognitive Neuroscience', *n.* 2, p. 745, for an account of the development of these ideas of levels of analysis. These latter also identify another notion of 'level' in this field, in addition to those of 'analysis' and 'organization', namely, the level of *processing* – for the greater the distance from those cells that respond to sensory input, the higher the degree of information processing.

43   The terms 'cognition' and 'cognitive' here refer to a range of mental processing, including, not only reasoning and memory but also language, perception and motor control (Bechtel and Abrahamsen, *Connectionism*, p. 1).

44   Churchland and Sejnowski, 'Cognitive Neuroscience', p. 741.

45   Bechtel and Abrahamsen, *Connectionism*, p. 259.

46   Even in 1976, studies of the visual control of orientation behaviour in the fly led W. Reichardt and T. Poggio to affirm 'The behaviour of a complex system, composed of many elements, cannot be easily understood in terms of a simple extrapolation of the properties of its components. New properties appear and their understanding requires an independent approach which is as fundamental to its nature as any other' (in 'Visual control of orientation behaviour in the fly', *Quart. Rev. Biophys.* 9 (1976), p. 313).

47   'Properties not found in components of a lower level can emerge from the organization and interaction of these components at a higher level. For example, rhythmic pattern generation in some neural circuits is a property of the circuit, not of isolated pacemaker neurons. Higher brain functions (e.g., perception, attention) may depend on temporally coherent functional units distributed through different maps and nuclei.' (T. J. Sejnowski, C. Koch and P. Churchland, *Science* 241 (1988), p. 1300).

48   Churchland and Sejnowski, 'Cognitive Neuroscience', p. 744.

49   Cf. ch. 2, section 3.

50   AI is 'the science of making machines do the sorts of things that are done by human minds . . . AI helps one to realize how enormous is the background knowledge and thinking (computational) power needed to do even . . . everyday things. The 'machines' in question

are typically digital computers, but AI is not the study of computers. Computers are its tools because its theories are expressed as computer programs . . .' (Margaret Boden, article on 'Artificial Intelligence', in *The Oxford Companion to the Mind*, ed. R. L. Gregory. Oxford University Press, Oxford and New York, p. 48). The cognitive science that emerged along with the 'cognitive turn' that occurred (see below, pp. 232ff.) in the behavioural sciences (level 3, Fig. 3) increasingly adopted the idea that cognition involves the manipulation of symbols referable to external phenomena. The symbols were conceived of as storable in and retrievable from memory and as transformable by rules (i.e., algorithms) which thereby governed cognitive performance. Such a concept suggested that it should be possible for cognitive processes to be modelled by those of digital computers which also manipulate symbols according to prescribed algorithms. From this notion sprang the expanding exercise of AI. Its achievements cannot be doubted and there are kinds of human mental operation that are certainly illuminated by its successes. Whether or not the human brain functions *only* as a digital computer, indeed if at all, is widely questioned (for example by the mathematical physicist R. Penrose in *The Emperors New Mind* (Oxford University Press, Oxford, 1989)). The argument continues (e.g., in *Behavioral and Brain Sciences* 13, no. 4 (1990), 643–705) and it is still too early to assess other developments, such as connectionism (see n. 51). Meanwhile recognition of the character of their successes, especially with respect to their rapidity and capacity, is matched by the acknowledgment of the width of the gap between what computers can do and quite ordinary human mental operations.

The AI research programme has significance for the philosophical mind-body problem because, as Margaret Boden puts it, 'modelling a psychological phenomenon on a computer is a way of showing that – and how – it is *possible* for that phenomenon to arise in a physical system . . . [AI] could (and should be) interpreted . . . as showing how it is possible for material systems (which, according to the biologist, we are) to possess such characteristic features as subjectivity, purpose, freedom, and choice.' (Boden, 'Artificial Intelligence', pp. 49, 50).

51 In the 1980s, there has developed an alternative way of understanding cognition, not as a manipulation of symbols, as in AI, but as the differential and dynamical activation (the 'problem') of a network of connected units that can mutually cross-excite and cross-inhibit each other, until a stable state is reached (the 'solution' of the 'problem'). This approach is based on models that have been called 'connectionist', 'parallel distributed processing' (PDP) or 'neural network' models. (See Bechtel and Abrahamsen,

Connectionism, ch. 1, for an account of its development, and their ch. 8, for an appraisal of its significance).

52   Ch. 3, section 1(d).

53   J. P. Crutchfield, J. D. Farmer, N. H. Packard and R. S. Shaw, 'Chaos', *Scientific American*, (December) 1986, 49.

54   Ch. 9, section 2(c).

55   This ch., section 2.

56   M. Boden, 'Artificial Intelligence', p. 50.

57   ibid.: 'The central theoretical concept in AI is *representation*, and AI workers ask how a (programmed) system constructs, adapts, and uses its inner representations in interpreting – and changing – its world. On this view, a programmed computer may be thought of as a subjective system (subject to illusion and error much as we are) functioning by way of its idiosyncratic view of the world. By analogy, then, it is no longer scientifically disreputable, as it has been thought for so long, to describe people in these radically subjective terms also. AI can therefore counteract the dehumanizing influence of the natural sciences that has been part of the mechanization of our world-picture since the scientific revolution of the sixteenth and seventeenth centuries.'

58   J. Maynard Smith, in 'The birth of sociobiology' (*New Scientist* 28 (1985), pp. 48–50) has described its basic ideas, which are used in the analysis of animal, bird and insect societies as: (i) societies consist of relatives between whom cooperation and 'altruistic' (self-sacrificing) interactions are more likely to occur; (ii) both partners in a cooperative interaction may benefit, so neither would gain by defection; and (iii) the most evolutionarily stable strategy for the behaviour of the individual organism can be derived by the application of the theory of games. These ideas, with the experimental studies they suggest, have been applied to a wide range of behaviour – 'altruistic', aggressive, sexual, parental, feeding, etc. – with considerable success.

59   *GNB*, ch. 4.

60   J. H. Crook, *The Evolution of Human Consciousness* (Clarendon Press, Oxford, 1980), pp. 189–90.

61   For a fuller discussion, see *GNB*, ch. 8, 'God and the selfish genes'; and also the author's 'Sociobiology and its theological implications', *Zygon* 19 (1984), pp. 171–184.

62   E.g., ch. 8, section 1 (e), (f); for some implications in relation to contemporary 'evolutionary naturalism', see *GNB*, pp. 109–110.

63   E.g., *inter alia*: E. O. Wilson, *Sociobiology: the new synthesis* (Belknap press, Cambridge, Mass., 1975), and *On Human Nature* (Harvard University Press, Cambridge, Mass. 1978); R. Dawkins, *The Selfish Gene* (Oxford University Press, Oxford, 1976) and *The Blind Watchmaker* (Longmans, Harlow, 1986).

64 As, for example, by R. Trigg in *The Shaping of Man* (Blackwell, Oxford, 1982) and in *CWS*, ch. 4 and appendix C.

65 L. J. Eaves, H. J. Eysenck and N. G. Martin, *Genes, Culture and Personality: an empirical approach* (Academic Press, London, New York, 1989), p. 3.

66 The first text in this area was apparently that of J. L. Fuller and W. R. Thompson, *Behavior Genetics* (Wiley, New York, 1960); for a history see D. A. Hay, *Essentials of Behaviour Genetics* (Blackwell, Melbourne, Oxford, London, 1985), pp. 18–21.

67 Hay, *Behaviour genetics*, p. 1.

68 ibid., p. 22; see also pp. 24–5.

69 ibid., p. 4, quoting J. R. Vale, *American Psychologist*, 28 (1973), p. 872.

70 L. J. Eaves and L. M. Gross, in 'Theological reflection on the cultural impact of human genetics' (*Insights* (Chicago Center for Religion and Science), 2 (1990) p. 15–6) speak of the 'growing investment of researchers and research funding in genetic paradigms for the understanding of human behaviour ... studies designed to uncover the *genetic* basis of human differences. These research programs do not just focus on physical diseases ... but also on psychiatric and social disorders ... even normal differences in habits, lifestyles and behaviour ... "Behavior genetics" and its clinical counterpart "psychiatric genetics" have emerged as a coherent discipline on the frontier between genetics and psychology which is not to be confused with "sociobiology" but has its own body of strong empirical findings.'

71 Here, as in other areas of science, the dictum 'garbage in, barbage out' applies; see Hay, *Behaviour Genetics*, pp. 8–17.

72 Eaves, Eyseneck and Martin, *Genes*, pp. 8–11. They name three 'major dimensions of personality' or 'super-factors' as 'psychoticism', 'extraversion' and 'neuroticism' and list the clusters of traits that go to make up these factors. They claim that the condition that 'these three dimensions, in one form or another, should emerge from the great majority, if not all, statistical studies carried out in this field' (ibid., p. 10) is met – even though there is no agreement about their labelling.

73 J. Kagan, 'The meanings of personality predicates', in *American Psychologist*, 43 (1988), pp. 614–20, has pointed out that the theoretical meaning of a descriptive word for any quality is derived from its source of evidence, which in most cases in the study of human personality is that of self-reporting. Relying on Frege's distinction between sense and referential meaning, he suggests that 'theoretical meanings can change when the referent changes and [he] criticizes the practice of treating personality concepts as unchanging essences that transcend all assessment contexts' (p. 614). Taking account of this would undoubtedly complicate the

task of investigators, who have already had to reckon with the problems in behaviour genetics generated by the process of change in their human subjects of study (Eaves, *et. al.*, *Genes*, pp. 413–4).

74   Eaves, Eyseneck and Martin, *Genes* p. 415.

75   Ch. 3, section 2(b).

76   The names of G. v. Wahlert and W. Wickler should also be added to those already given, according to G. Altner, 'The Human Creature?', in Altner, *The Human Creature*, p. 422.

77   ibid., p. 423–4.

78   J. Huxley, 'The evolutionary process', in *Evolution as a Process*, ed. J. Huxley, A. C. Hardy, and E. B. Ford (Allen and Unwin, London, 1954).

79   Ch. 4, section 1.

80   Altner, *Human Creature* p. 424.

81   For an account, see A. G. N. Flew, *Evolutionary Ethics* (Macmillan, London, 1967).

82   M. Ruse and E. O. Wilson, 'Moral philosophy as applied science', *Philosophy*, 6 (1986) 173–92; M. Ruse, 'Evolutionary ethics: a phoenix arisen', *Zygon*, 21 (1986) pp. 95–112; idem, *Taking Darwin Seriously: a naturalistic approach* (Blackwell, Oxford, 1986).

One such complex of ideas surrounds their metaphorical use of the word 'altruism', which in ordinary usage means 'regard for others, as a principle of action: opposed to egoism and selfishness' (*Shorter Oxford English Dictionary*, (Clarendon Press, Oxford, 1973 edit.). In sociobiology, *biological* 'altruism' includes (according to Ruse, 'Evolutionary ethics', p. 97), behaviour in which an individual sacrifices some immediate interest for the sake of another individual, or group, possessing some of its own genes; and also behaviour in which mutual benefits are exchanged reciprocally, again for the perpetuation of the genes of the organisms involved. The suggestion is that 'moral (literal) altruism might be one way in which biological (metaphorical) "altruism" could be achieved . . . To make us cooperate for our biological ends, evolution has filled us full of thoughts about right and wrong, the need to help our fellows and so forth . . . Our moral sense, our altruistic nature, is an adaptation – a feature helping us in the struggle for existence . . .' (Ruse, ibid., p. 98, 99). On this view, no objective reference is possible for ethics, whether theological or philosophical: 'Ultimately there is no reasoned justification for ethics in the sense of foundations to which one can appeal in reasoned argument . . . What is really important to the evolutionist's case [i.e., this case] is the claim that ethics is illusory inasmuch as it persuades us that it has objective reference . . . We think morality has objective reference even though it has not . . . It is precisely because we think that morality is more than mere subjective desires, that we are led to obey it' (Ruse, ibid., pp. 102–3).

I have elsewhere (*GNB*, pp. 113–4) argued against this view and have raised the question of whether it does really provide a new basis for understanding ethics as such, our actual ethical beliefs. For the content of moral reasoning has its own standards and cannot itself be genetically determined, even if the motives, impulses and attitudes (e.g., our propensity to favour our genetic kin) between which moral reasoning attempts to arbitrate are themselves the result of our evolutionary history and so of our genetic endowment.

83 *GNB*, p. 114.

84 Ch. 8, section 1(f).

85 Ch. 4, section 1.

86 Eaves and Gross, 'Theological reflection on the cultural impact of human genetics', p. 17.

87 *CWS*, pp. 179–184.

88 E.g., Peter Morea: 'It is certainly odd that we do not feel at home in the only home we have – Earth. We are part of nature, subject to its laws, to growth, decay and death; but at the same time we feel ourselves strangers on Earth, like ships in dry dock.' (*Personality; an introduction to the theories of psychology*, Penguin Books, London, 1990, p. 166).

89 D. R. Davis, article on 'Psychology', in *The Oxford Companion to the Mind*, ed. R. L. Gregory (Oxford University Press, Oxford, 1987), p. 650.

90 Jung and Adler, of course, opposed many of Freud's ideas, but they share this feature of stressing the unconscious and down-playing conscious experience.

91 R. W. Sperry, 'Psychology's Mentalist Paradigm and the Religion/Science Tension', *Amer. Psychologist* 43 (1988), p. 607.

92 E.g., B. J. Baars, *The Cognitive Theory of Consciousness* (Cambridge University Press, Cambridge, 1988):
'. . . we view conscious experience . . . as a theoretical construct that can often be inferred from reliable evidence; and as a basic problem needing solution.' (p. 9);
'. . . scientific psychologists have once again begun to speak of meaning, thought, imagery, attention, memory, and, recently, conscious and unconscious processes – all inferred concepts that have been tested in careful experiments and stated in increasingly adequate theories. Our view here is that *both* conscious and unconscious processes involve inferences from publicly observable data.' (p. 10);
'We may have a better chance to understand human conscious experience now than ever before.' (p. 10).

93 Cf. Ch. 8, section 1 (g), especially the remarks of J. Durant (p. 110). As the psychologist Peter Morea has put it (in *Personality*, pp. 154–5): 'Personal, subjective experience has not yet been

accounted for, and it is difficult to know how it could be by any advance in brain research. An objective description in terms of brain-cells and chemistry cannot explain (or explain away) what can be known only in the first person – my experience, as I feel pain and hope and believe and love and remember. As yet, the experience of being human cannot even be captured other than by poets, novelists and dramatists; it certainly cannot be described scientifically.'

94 R. W. Sperry, 'Psychology's Mentalist Paradigm', p. 608.

95 Even cognitive scientists such as Bechtel and Abrahamsen (*Connectionism*, pp. 287–9) have to recognize the increasing inability of human observers to track the human reality without resorting to the mentalist language of what they call 'folk psychology', the attributions made by people of propositional attitudes to other people as whole persons and the use of these attributions to predict and explain behaviour (p. 288).

96 Ch. 4, section 1.

97 See the concluding paragraph of this section.

98 For some discussion of a possible intelligible physical matrix for 'freedom' to be attributable to human brain states, see Arthur Peacocke, 'Natural Being and Becoming – the chrysalis of the human', in *Individuality and Cooperative Action*, ed. J. E. Earley (Georgetown University Press, Washington, DC, 1991), pp. 91–108. See also earlier, ch. 3, section 2(c), p. 61.

99 M. A. Jeeves, 'Minds and Brains: then and now', *Interdisc. Sci. Revs.* 16 (1991), p. 70.

100 ibid., p. 79. Cf. the view, which he quotes, of the US National Institute of Mental Health report ('The neuroscience of mental health', Dept of Health and Human Services, Washington, DC, 1985): 'Restraint must be exerted against extremes in taking a reductionist approach to synaptic events and brain function . . . To understand normal and abnormal behaviour research needs to be pursued *at all levels of analysis.*'

101 See Ch. 9, section 2(c).

102 Sperry, 'Psychology's mentalist paradigm', p. 609.

103 Ch. 13, section 3(e), and ch. 15, section 3.

104 Consistently with what we have argued earlier concerning 'top-down' or 'downward' causation (Ch. 3, sections 1(e) and 2(c)), Sperry (ibid., p. 609) also asserts that 'The consciousness revolution of the 1970s . . . represents . . . a further undermining of opposed dualistic thinking in philosophy and theology by explaining and accepting mind and the subjective entirely within a monistic framework . . . Instead of excluding mind and spirit, the new outlook puts subjective mental forces near the top of the brain's causal control hierarchy and gives them primacy in determining what a person is and does.'

105 Holmes Rolston III, *Science and Religion: a critical survey* (Random House, New York, 1987) points out – and this is relevant particularly to psychology – that when scientists are using their brains to understand their brains 'we run afoul of a new kind of indeterminacy, a new limit to our resolving power, namely, that a system of great complexity can perhaps not be wholly understood, predicted, and controlled either by itself or by some observer of the same type and complexity' (p. 152).

106 ibid., p. 158.

107 Introduction, section 3.

108 Don S. Browning, *Religious Thought and the Modern Psychologies; a critical conversation in the theology of culture* (Fortress Press, Philadelphia, 1987) *passim.*

109 Up to this point in his text, those of Freud, humanistic psychologies (C. Rogers, A. Maslow, F. Perls) and B. F. Skinner.

110 ibid., p. 122 emphasis as in the original.

111 ibid., p. 125.

112 ibid., p. 7.

113 ibid.

114 B. F. Skinner, whose ideas have also been applied, may be classified as 'experimental', prescinding from his deterministic metaphysics.

115 ibid., p. 31.

116 Thus Browning (*Religious thought and modern psychologies*) has perceived in each of the psychological theories the existence of an 'horizon' – the 'larger, often vague and incomplete, view of the world that surrounds the more central key psychological concepts' as 'revealed in its deep metaphors and implicit principles of obligation' (ibid., p. 29). He summarizes these cultural horizons thus: Freud, civilized detachment; humanistic psychologies, expressive joy; Skinner, total justice; Jung, sacred egoism in a culture of joy; Erikson and Kohut, care (ibid., pp. 30–1, for an expansion of these cryptic terms).

117 Morea, *Personality*. He summarizes the results of his survey thus: 'Theories of personality present us with a variety of perspectives. Freud's angry, sexual baby, adult on the outside . . . Skinner's mindless organism . . . Roger's flower people, seeking to be human . . . Fromm's caring liberals, free but lonely . . . social behaviourism's actors, playing life's roles . . . Kelly's applied scientists . . . Confronted by these views, none obviously nonsense, our reaction may well be one of wonder . . . But at times the theories scarcely appear to be describing the same human animal, and at other times plainly contradict one another' (ibid., p. 155).

In support of the contention of this last quoted sentence, he cites the disagreement between the psychologies on such fundamental issues as: whether or not the human mind is illusion; the existence and nature of human freedom; what human morality is and even whether it is desirable (pure self-interest, or simply good frustrated, or good but distorted, or human beings as blank slates waiting to be written upon, or as agents and centres of a conflict of needs, or as integrators of the needs of self and society, or . . .?). They often conflict with common sense, even though 'Theories of personality would falter and fail without . . . unrecognized recourse to common sense' (ibid., p. 161).

118   Rolston, *Science and Religion*, ch. 4.

119   Browning, *Religious Thought and Modern Psychologies.*, *passim*.

120   Browning *Religious Thought and the Modern Psychologies*, ch. 7, reports on the new interest in Jung in the light of sociobiology, neurobiology (this especially under the influence of A. Stevens' *Archetypes: the natural history of the self* (William Morrow, New York, 1982)), ethology, and the social sciences.

121   See pp. 230–32, section 4, above; and p. 77.

122   ibid., pp. 193–4.

123   Morea, *Personality*, pp. 161–2: 'Personality is a puzzle, not because of the shortcomings of present theories, soon to be remedied by bigger and better ones, but because of the nature of what we are studying. We end up with a kaleidoscope of one-dimensional perspectives because of the nature of personality . . . The real difficulty lies in not being able to step back and consider personality objectively . . . Personality is something each of us is . . . The French philosopher Gabriel Marcel distinguished between a problem and a mystery. Personality is not a problem to be solved, like building a bridge, because it is not a problem at all. It is, in Marcel's terms, a mystery.'

124   ibid., p. 170.

125   ibid., p. 171.

126   ibid. 'Evolution seems to have played a nasty trick, bringing into existence human beings vast in their desire and potential, but minute in their fulfilment and satisfaction'.

127   Even as a purely biological species the situation of *homo sapiens* is manifestly paradoxical, as David Jenkins pointed out: 'It begins to look as if man has somehow and by his own boot-straps, so to speak, pulled himself out of the ecological niche in which he evolved but that he is not collectively capable of doing what is necessary to keep things sufficiently under control to construct the new ecology and environment which would permit him any sort of stable existence' (*What is Man?*, SCM Press, London, 1970, p. 45). But the problem is not purely biological and has a moral basis: 'Man can be seen as constantly failing to measure up to, and again and again making harmful uses of, the possibilities and powers that come his way. He seems to prefer his degradation, to choose for instance to consider

himself rather as a naked ape than as a responsible human being.'
(ibid., p. 54).

128 Cf. *CWS* pp. 181–2 and 185.

129 Those of S. Freud, B. F. Skinner, C. Rogers, E. Fromm, G. H. Mead
and G. Kelly.

130 *Genesis* 1:27. Humanity also has a claim to be the 'microcosm of the
macrocosm'. See above, section 1 and n. 22.

131 Though in what respect(s) humanity is regarded as made 'in the
image of God' in the biblical literature has been a subject of much
study and little agreement (see *CWS*, pp. 189–90, 283–5).

132 Morea, *Personality*, p. 174.

133 Introduction, section 3.

134 Ch. 4, section 1, p. 73.

135 This chapter, section 3, n. 82.

136 Donald T. Campbell, 'On the conflicts between biological and social
evolution and between psychology and moral tradition', *Zygon* 11
(1976), pp. 167–208.

137 ibid., p. 192.

138 Rolston, *Science and Religion*, Ch. 5 on 'Culture: religion and the
social sciences'. His comments on the psychological human sciences
in general, including psychology, are worth noting: 'The human
sciences have been all too anxious to borrow from the natural
sciences both their paradigms and their associated methods.
Meanwhile, the two main branches of the human sciences have in
fact unique paradigms of their own. Psychology has the category of
mind, the psychic unity. Social science has the paradigm of the
cultural community. They both sell themselves short by groping for
mechanistic, organic, causal, equilibrating, functional, or even
cybernetic models, since mind and community are richer processes
than can be fully illuminated by lesser models.' (ibid., pp. 233–4).

139 ibid., p. 234.

140 Bechtel and Abrahamsen, *Connectionism*, p. 256.

141 ibid., p. 258. They instanced how a sentence uttered, say, by a child
could come into the focus of the linguist in level 4, of the
psycholinguist in level 3, the neurologist in level 2 and of the
acoustic physicist and physiologist in level 1.

142 Ch. 11, section 3(b).

143 Ch. 11, section 3(c).

144 G. Steiner, *Real Presences* (Faber and Faber, London and Boston,
1989), p. 4.

145 ibid., p. 4. I cannot forbear quoting from some of his concluding
pages (226–7): 'To summarize: it is, I believe, poetry, art and music
which relate us most directly to that in being which is not ours . . .
It is counter-creation and counter-love, as these are embodied in
the aesthetic and in our reception of formed meaning, which puts us
in touch with that which transcends, with matters "undreamt of" in

our materiality ... All good art and literature begin in immanence. But they do not stop there. Which is to say, very plainly, that it is the enterprise and privilege of the aesthetic to quicken into lit presence the continuum between temporality and eternity, between matter and spirit, between man and the "other" ... The questions: "What is poetry, music, art?", "How can they not be?", "How do they act upon us and how do we interpret their action?", are, ultimately, theological questions'.

146   As Bechtel and Abrahamsen deflatingly call them (n. 140 above)!
147   See n. 141 above.
148   This chapter, sections 3 and 4.
149   See n. 91 above.
150   In the old reduced sense of 'materialism'.
151   Quoted by G. Altner, *The Human Creature*, p. 427–8.
152   Cf., *inter alia*, *SCE*, pp. 174–6; *CWS* pp. 308ff.
153   Though we can be grateful for the comprehensive attempts of, for example, John Macquarrie in *In Search of Humanity: a theological and philosophical approach* (SCM Press, London, 1982) to which I am much indebted.
154   A. Pope (*Ep.* ii (1733), 1.1): 'The proper study of mankind is man'.
155   This chapter, section 2.
156   Ch. 3, section 3(a), pp. 65–9.
157   Ch. 3, section 3(a) and ch. 8, section 2(b).
158   Gould, *Wonderful Life*, p. 35.
159   ibid., p. 44.
160   This chapter, section 1.
161   Cf. n. 80, ch. 9.
162   Ch. 9, section 2(c).
163   This chapter, section 3, especially in relation to the cognitive sciences; and section 4, with respect to psychology.
164   Ch. 11, section 3(b).
165   Ch. 11, section 3(c).
166   Note that this 'is not meant to be at all dismissive of the significance of the non-human creation. For at every level in the operation of the creative process, something is reflected in its own measure of the divine purpose' (*CWS*, pp. 197–8). In this connection, I went on to quote Charles Raven: 'from atom to molecule to mammal and man each by its appropriate order and function expresses the design inherent in it and contributes, so far as it can by failure or success, to the fulfilment of the divine purpose' (*Natural Religion and Christian Theology*, 2nd series of Gifford lectures on *Experience and Interpretation* (Cambridge University Press, Cambridge, 1953), vol. ii, p. 157).
167   See *SCE*, pp. 151–3 for a discussion of this with references.
168   This chapter, section 3.
169   This chapter, section 4, p. 231 and n. 86.

170 This chapter, section 2.

171 Ch. 8, sections 1(c) and 2(a).

172 See *SCE*, pp. 174–6 and *CWS*, pp. 306–311 for discussion of a 'Christian humanism'; and for the need for a theo-centric ecological ethic, see *CWS*, ch. VII and also ch. 16 in this volume where the concept of humanity as 'co-creators' is discussed (p. 342).

173 This chapter, section 3, pp. 221–3.

174 The same is true of human sexuality. For sexuality appeared in evolution in remote earlier ancestors of *homo sapiens* and developed primarily as a result of the pressures of natural selection since it enhanced *inter alia* the variability of individuals. Hence any notion of linking sexuality, as such, with 'sin' is untenable, in spite an ancient Christian prejudice to this effect. Our sexuality is as God-given and as capable of God's blessing as our eating and drinking, indeed our lives in general – for it is part of the way God brought humanity into existence and continues to give it life.

175 This chapter, section 3, pp. 222–3; and Arthur Peacocke, 'The challenge of science to theology and the church', in *The Weight of Glory*, eds. D. W. Hardy and P. H. Sedgwick (T. & T. Clark, Edinburgh, 1991), pp. 45–46.

176 See ch. 15, section 3(a).

177 This chapter, section 4, pp. 231–2.

178 Morea, *Personality*, p. 171.

179 For a contemporary theological interpretation, see *SCE*, pp. 148ff., 169–70; and in *CWS*, pp. 190–1, 284–5.

180 Alan Richardson, article on 'Adam, Man' in *A Theological Word Book of the Bible*, ed. A. Richardson (SCM Press, London, 1957), p. 14.

181 Cf. *CWS*, pp. 174–184.

182 Cf. *CWS*, pp. 191–2.

183 Ch. 8, *passim*.

184 Cf. *CWS*, p. 197; cf., also pp. 185–6, 196–203.

185 A. Pope, *An Essay on Man*, Epistle ii, 1.28.

186 Altner, *The Human Creature*, p. 426.

187 J. Macquarrie, 'A theology of personal being', in *Persons and Personality*, eds. A. Peacocke and G. Gillett (Blackwells, Oxford, 1987), pp. 172–5. For further elaboration of this theme, see J. Macquarrie, *In Search of Humanity*, e.g., 'If we are to speak of human "nature" at all, then we should have to understand the word in a much more fluid way, going back to something like its root meaning . . . *Natura* is that which is arising or coming to birth and the nature of the human being is the as yet unfinished humanity which is emerging and taking shape in the history of the race and in the existence of each individual' (p. 3).

188 J. Macquarrie, *In Search of Humanity*, p. 3.

189 ibid., p. 4.
190 Cf., the discussion in section 4 of this chapter on sociobiology and ethics.
191 This chapter, section 6.
192 ibid., the quotation from D. Campbell, p. 241, n. 137.
193 Sir Alister Hardy, *The Spiritual Nature of Man* (Clarendon Press, Oxford, 1979), p. 1.
194 In the sense of R. Otto, *The Idea of the Holy* (Oxford University Press, 1923).
195 See pp. 230–32 above; ch. 4, section 1, p. 77; and *CWS*, pp. 179–184.
196 T. Chalmers, 'The Power, Wisdom and Goodness of God, as manifested in the adaptation of external nature to the moral and intellectual constitution of man', First Bridgewater Treatise, 1822, p. 308.
197 Augustine, *Confessions*, Book 1 [1] 1.
198 This was the title of a notable series of BBC television and radio programmes in 1977.
199 Ch. 9, section 4, and ch. 11.

Chapter 13   The Long Search and Jesus of Nazareth

1 The 'long search' is the search for God, the religious quest of humanity (see n. 198, ch. 12).
2 Ch. 12, section 9.
3 J. Macquarrie, *Jesus Christ in Modern Thought* (SCM Press, London, 1990), p. 370. The philosophical anthropologies to which Macquarrie refers in this quotation, and which he has analysed in the preceding pages, are: existentialism (Jean-Paul Sartre, Friedrich Nietzsche); Marxism and the neo-Marxist (Herbert Marcuse, Ernst Bloch); process philosophy (A. N. Whitehead); and transcendental Thomism (Bernard Lonergan, Karl Rahner).
4 Earlier (ibid., pp. 362–3) Macquarrie has pointed out that, 'etymologically, to "transcend" means to climb over, to cross a boundary. So "transcendence" is a "metaphor" of advancing into new areas, perhaps overcoming obstacles on the way. We could say it is moving from one horizon to another. Wherever one stands, there is a horizon at the limit of vision, but as one advances toward that horizon, the horizon itself recedes. It is not a barrier, but discloses new horizons beyond. So the notion of transcendence seems to contain not just the idea that one can move out from where one happens to be, but that there is no limit.' (p. 363).
5 This is what traditional Christian theology would characterize as 'redemption from sin' and 'sanctification'. Such language now has little currency in Western societies and, insofar as it is still in use,

too often has a strongly ethical connotation, instead of denoting the rectification of that vast and tragic range of human dis-ease and unease which the literature of our times so accurately reflects (Ch. 12, section 9, pp. 248–50).

6 M. Wiles, *Faith and the Mystery of God* (SCM Press, London, 1982), p. 109.

7 ibid., p. 110. Wiles is here referring to a statement to the effect that 'man's being is the basis of the norms of his becoming' by Richard A. McCormick, in 'Human significance and Christian significance', in *Norm and Context in Christian Ethics*, ed. G. H. Outka and Paul Ramsey (SCM Press, London, 1968), p. 247 – quoted by Wiles, ibid., p. 109.

8 For discussion of these issues, see *inter alia* A. M. Quinton, 'Ethics and the Theory of Evolution', in *Biology and Personality*, ed. I. T. Ramsey (Blackwell, Oxford, 1965), pp. 107–30; A. C. N. Flew, *Evolutionary Ethics* (Macmillan, London, 1967); P. Hefner, 'Is/ Ought: a risky relationship between theology and science', in *The Sciences and Theology in the Twentieth Century*, ed. A. R. Peacocke (Oriel Press, Routledge and Kegan Paul, Stocksfield and London, and University of Notre Dame Press, Notre Dame, Indiana, 1981) pp. 58–78; and *GNB*, pp. 112–4.

9 Above, p. 254.

10 This will emerge more particularly in the attempt we shall be making to interpret the relation of Jesus the Christ to humanity and to God (chs. 14 and 15).

11 Ch. 12, section 9.

12 ibid.

13 And indeed the parable of the prodigal son, in which the son's decision to return meets a father who *runs* to meet and embrace him (*Luke* 15:20).

14 For further comments on these models relevant to this point, see *CWS*, pp. 205–7, where the emphasis is adopted of G. W. H. Lampe in *God as Spirit* (Oxford University Press, Oxford, 1977) – on the 'Holy Spirit' as Godself considered in respect of God's personal outreach and immanence in the cosmos, especially as active towards and in God's human creation. See also earlier in this work, p. 165, and n. 109 to ch. 9.

15 This is but an inadequately terse summary of concepts that are both subtle and profound: see *CWS*, pp. 205–7 for further references. The Word/*Logos* became identified in the course of a complex development (strongly influenced by the Fourth Gospel) with 'God the Son' – that second *persona* of the Triune but One God who was manifest as incarnate.

16 Sir Alister Hardy, *The Spiritual Nature of Man*, Clarendon Press, Oxford, 1979, p. 1.

17 Cf. the quotation from John Bowker on p. 18.

18 K. Jaspers, *The Origin and Goal of History*, Routledge and Kegan Paul, London, 1953.

19 ibid., p. 2.

20 *CWS*, p. 219.

21 Traditionally, of course, this notion was cast in a narrative form in which a 'Fall' followed the creation by God of human beings perfectly in his 'image and likeness', an image subsequently defaced by disobedience, 'sin'. For reasons already given (ch. 12, section 8), this way of expressing the truth of human alienation has to yield to terminology more in accord with an evolutionary account of human origins.

22 Macquarrie, *Jesus Christ*, p. 371.

23 Useful bibliographies, as well as informed and balanced comment, are to be found in the articles on 'Jesus' (by J. Bowden), 'Christology' (by G. Newlands), and on 'Incarnation' (by B. Hebblethwaite) in NDCT. The best, recent survey of both the historical, philosophical and theological issues in assessing for today the significance of Jesus is John Macquarrie's *Jesus Christ in Modern Thought* (SCM Press, London, 1990) in which he has covered a vast range of the literature, and not only that of the twentieth century. The two great treatises of E. Schillebeeckx on *Jesus* and *Christ* (Seabury Press, New York, 1979 and 1980) contain comprehensive bibliographies, especially valuable with respect to the non-English language literature. Other works the author has relied upon will be cited subsequently. Useful lists of references are to be found in the endnotes referring to the beginnings of the various sub-sections in *Christian Origins* (SPCK, London, 1985) by Christopher Rowland. References to the discussion of whether the genesis of the early church's understanding of Christ is to be regarded, to use the terminology of C. F. D. Moule (in *The Origin of Christology*, Cambridge University Press, Cambridge, 1977), as a 'development' (growth from immaturity to maturity from within itself) or as an 'evolution' (genesis of a new species, as it were, of belief by mutations and selection) are to be found in *CWS*, pp. 223–7.

24 Joseph Butler, in the Introduction to *The Analogy of Religion* (1736). The surrounding passage is worth recalling: 'Probable evidence, in its very nature, affords but an imperfect kind of information; and is to be considered as relative only to beings of limited capacities . . . to us, probability is the very guide of life. From these things it follows, that in questions of difficulty, or such as are thought so, where more satisfactory evidence cannot be had, or is not seen; if the result of examination be, that there appears on the whole, any the lowest presumption on one side, and none on the other, or greater presumption on one side, though in the lowest degree greater; this determines the question, even in matters of speculation; and in matters of practice, will lay us under an

absolute and formal obligation, in point of prudence and of interest, to act upon that presumption or low probability, though it be so low as to leave the mind in very great doubt which is the truth. For surely a man is as really bound in prudence to do what upon the whole appears, according to the best of his judgment to be for his happiness, as what he certainly knows to be so.'

25   John Bowden, *Jesus: the unanswered questions* (SCM Press, London, 1988), pp. 44ff.

26   John Knox, *The Death of Jesus* (Abingdon Press, 1958, and Fontana, Collins, 1958).

27   See n. 25 above.

28   A. E. Harvey, *Jesus and the Constraints of History* (Duckworth, London, 1982), p. 4.

29   ibid., p. 5. Harvey recognizes that the idea of 'certainty' needs clarifying in this context: 'The appropriate comparison today is not with statements which may be believed to be true on divine authority [as, Harvey says, it was for biblical statements for most of Christian history], but with other historical statements made on the basis of comparable evidence. What we have to ask is not whether a given statement is true with a kind of supernatural certainty but whether the fact which it reports may be regarded as at least as well established as any other fact which comes down to us from antiquity. On this test we shall find that the evidence for at least the main facts of the life and death of Jesus is as abundant, circumstantial and consistent as is the case with any other figure of ancient history.' (ibid., p. 5–6).

30   Bowden, *Jesus*, p. 45.

31   Dennis Nineham, 'Epilogue' to *The Myth of God Incarnate*, ed., J. Hick (SCM Press, London, 1977), pp. 186–204. This article pinpoints very clearly, in referring to some distinctions made by N. Perrin (in *Rediscovering the Teaching of Jesus*, SCM Press, London, 1967), the problems and dilemmas of a contemporary assessment of the figure of Jesus of Nazareth in the light of the knowledge (or rather the dearth of it, relative to traditional expectations) that is forthcoming from New Testament studies.

32   As M. Wiles has put it: ' . . . it is essential that the doctrinal theologian recognizes the real position with which he has to deal. He has to recognize that the kind of information about Jesus that theology has so often looked to New Testament scholars to provide is not available . . . The information the theologian has traditionally looked for is simply not the kind of information that can properly be expected to be drawn from the evidence at our disposal by historical means.' (*The Remaking of Christian Doctrine* SCM Press, London, 1974, p. 48).

33   Bowden, *Jesus*, pp. 32ff.

34   E. P. Sanders, *Jesus and Judaism* (SCM Press, London, 1985).

35   Sanders, *Jesus and Judaism*, p. 11. It is interesting to compare with this A. E. Harvey's statement of 'those facts about Jesus which, by any normal criterion of historical evidence, it would be unreasonable to doubt' (*Jesus and the Constraints of History*, p. 6). They are; 'that Jesus was known in both Galilee and Jerusalem; that he was a teacher; that he carried out cures of various illnesses, particularly demon-possession, and that these were widely regarded as miraculous; that he was involved in controversy with fellow-Jews over questions of the Law of Moses; and that he was crucified in the governorship of Pontius Pilate.' (loc. cit.).

   Macquarrie (*Jesus Christ*, pp. 51–2) also deduces a 'bare outline' concerning the historical Jesus from the writings of Paul, which precede the writing of the Gospels by at least two or three decades. It is (abridged): 1. Jesus existed as a human being, born of a woman (no mention of a virgin birth), born under the law, a member of the race of Israel and a descendant of David. 2. Jesus had brothers, one of whom was called James. 3. Jesus had followers – in particular the 'Twelve'. 4. Jesus' ministry had been directed to the Jews. 5. Jesus instituted the eucharist on the night when he was betrayed. 6. Jesus was crucified. 7. His death was brought about by the Jews. [8. He was raised on the third day].

   This last point (8) was bracketed by Macquarrie because 'it is arguable whether the resurrection of Jesus, even if one believes in it, can properly be regarded as an event in the historical order.' (p. 52).

36   Jurgen Moltmann, *The Crucified God* (SCM Press, London, 1974), pp. 146–7.

37   See n. 35, above.

38   Harvey, *Jesus and the Constraints of History*, p. 8.

39   He instances (p. 8): 'the mixed – and to many of his contemporaries shocking – company kept by Jesus, his unprecedented attitude towards children *as* children, the importance he attached to the sharing of a meal, both for promoting the solidarity of his followers and for conveying religious truth'.

40   Harvey, *Jesus*, p. 8.

41   Graham N. Stanton, *The Gospels and Jesus* (Oxford University Press, Oxford, 1989), p. 272.

42   E. P. Sanders, *Jesus and Judaism*, pp. 326–7. The wording in the text is almost, but not quite, *verbatim* from these pages of Sanders.

43   This overriding factor or constraint has been well expressed at the end of Stanton's study of the four gospels: 'The key to the story [of Jesus] is its ending. Jesus went up to Jerusalem for the last time not simply in order to "minister" to its inhabitants. He went to Jerusalem in order to confront the religio-political establishment with his claim that the kingdom of God was at hand. On the basis of his convictions about the presence, power, and will of God, Jesus

called for a reordering of Israel's priorities. In that sense he sought the renewal of Judaism. Renewal movements generally involve a rediscovery of basic principles and a call for loyalty to an inherited tradition. The "Jesus movement" was no exception ... Jesus believed that he had been sent by God as prophet to declare authoritatively the will of God for his people: acceptance or rejection of him and of his message was equivalent to acceptance or rejection of God (*Matt.* 10:40 = *Luke* 10:16.' (Stanton, *Gospels*, p. 274).

44 *Cf.* Raymond E. Brown, *Jesus God and Man* (Collier Macmillan, London, and Macmillan, New York, 1967), p. 97: '. . . it seems that an irreducible historical minimum in the Gospel presentation of Jesus is that he claimed to be the unique agent in the process of establishing God's kingship over men. He proclaimed that in *his* preaching and through *his* deeds God's kingship over men was making itself felt.'

45 Sanders (*Jesus and Judaism*, pp. 326–7)) concludes as '*possible*': 'He [Jesus] may have spoken about the kingdom in the visionary manner of the "little apocalypse" (*Mark* 13 and parallels), or as a present reality into which individuals enter one by one – or both.' As '*conceivable*': '1. He may have thought that the kingdom, in all its power and might, was present in his words and deeds. 2. He may have given his own death martyrological significance. 3. He may have identified himself with a cosmic Son of man and conceived his attaining kingship in that way.' As '*incredible*': '1. He was one of the rare Jews of his day who believed in love, mercy, grace, repentance, and the forgiveness of sin. 2. Jews in general, and Pharisees in particular, would kill people who believed such things. 3. As a result of his work, Jewish confidence in election was "shaken to pieces", Judaism was "shaken to its foundations", and Judaism as a religion was destroyed.'

46 C. Rowland, *Christian Origins*, p. 244. *Cf.*, again, R. E. Brown, *Jesus God and Man*, p. 59: '. . . there is an important religious area where the teaching attributed to Jesus was unique, outdistancing the ideas of his time – the area of his own mission and the proclamation of the kingdom of God.'

47 ibid., p. 174.

48 This can still be affirmed, even though Jesus' use of the term 'Abba' now proves not to have the significance which it was once widely thought to have, especially in the treatment of J. Jeremias, *New Testament Theology* (SCM Press, London, 1971), Vol. 1, pp. 63ff. Appealing though this treatment was, it now appears to be confuted by James Barr: 'There is no evidence that the "Abba" of Paul is dependent on Jesus; it cannot be proved that Jesus used "Abba" only and always in all his addresses to his Father; it is likely that he used other terms which specified "my" or "our" Father; and,

above all, the nuance of "Abba" was not at all the nuance of childish prattle, but the nuance of solemn and responsible adult speech.' (*Theology* 91 (1988) 179; his more fully argued case, 'Abba isn't Daddy', is in *J. Theolog. Studies NS* 39 (1988), 28–47).

49 C. Rowland, *Christian Origins*, p. 179.

50 R. E. Brown, *Jesus God and Man*, p. 91.

51 Cf., J. Macquarrie, in 'The sinlessness of Jesus', *Christian World*, 25 May 1978, p. 16.

52 Bernard Levin, *The Times*, 6 June 1991.

53 Cf., D. E. Nineham, 'Epilogue', p. 188.

54 For a brief account, see Kallistos Ware, 'Eastern Christendom', in *The Oxford Illustrated History of Christianity*, ed. J. McManners (Oxford University Press, Oxford, 1990), p. 140–2.

55 Witness the conroversies ensuing from the publication of *The Myth of God Incarnate*, ed. J. Hick, (SCM Press, London, 1977).

56 John A. T. Robinson, *The Human Face of God* (SCM Press, London, 1973), p. 68 and n. 3.

57 ibid., ch. 3.

58 ibid., p. 71, where Robinson enlists support from a Roman Catholic scholar, R. E. Brown (*Jesus God and Man*, pp. 39–102), and a Protestant, C. K. Barrett (*Jesus and the Gospel Tradition*, SPCK, London, 1967, pp. 105–8.

Thus, R. E. Brown (loc. cit.) concludes that his knowledge was limited with respect to: the ordinary affairs of life; religious matters, such as his knowledge of the scriptures of the Old Testament, his acceptance of the common religious concepts of first-century Judaism (e.g., the supposed nature of the afterlife, demonology, apocalyptic); and the future (in regard to his own person and the 'Parousia', taken variously as the coming of the 'son of man', his own return and the coming of the kingdom of God in power).

59 *Mark* 13:30 (and par.): 'Truly the present generation will live to see it all.' (REB), Here the 'all' refers to a complex of political, astronomical, meteorological events accompanying the coming of the 'Son of Man'. Even if these are not the actual words of Jesus, the evangelists were clearly reporting him as predicting something that had not happened. See K. Ward on this in his *A Vision to Pursue* (SCM Press, London, 1991) pp. 16–20, 43f., 52f.

60 I have deliberately emphasized R. E. Brown's appraisal as that of a distinguished scholar from within the Roman Catholic tradition who accepts that tradition's later interpretations of Jesus.

61 R. E. Brown, *Jesus God and Man*, p. 94. As John Macquarrie puts it in another, more recent, careful analysis of the state of scholarly study of this question, '. . . we have to leave the question of Jesus' self-understanding as not clearly answerable, but that is not very important from a theological point of view. However, if someone

were to say that we just have no understanding at all of how Jesus thought of himself or of his message, I do not think that would be a probable judgment either. He was conscious of a vocation from God to proclaim the kingdom, and the record shows him as single-mindedly devoted to that vocation, even to the point at which it brought him to death.' (*Jesus Christ*, p. 354).

62 Brown, *Jesus God and Man*, p. 95.

63 ibid., p. 91. He continues interestingly for our later discussion, 'But it remains difficult to find in the Synoptic account of the public ministry an incontrovertible proof that he claimed a unique sonship that other men could not share.'

64 Ch. 9, section 4, p. 182.

65 The single inverted commas will be used around the word 'miracle' to denote that it is being used putatively with the meaning of an 'event not fully explicable by naturalistic means'.

66 Chs. 8 and 9.

67 C. F. D. Moule, 'Introduction' to *Miracles*, ed. C. F. D. Moule (Mowbray, London, 1965), p. 14.

68 Cf. p. 183.

69 *John* 2:11: '. . . signs which revealed his [Jesus'] glory and led his disciples to believe in him' (REB).

70 Such revelatory clusters of events would constitute that self-communication of God through God's mode of interaction with the world which we have already elaborated (ch. 8, section 4; ch. 11).

71 Until the nineteenth century, the 'miracles' described in the Gospels as having been performed by Jesus were regarded as evidence for his presumed divinity – not an argument that is often heard today because of a cultural background so strongly imbued with a scientific awareness of the order of nature and the questions, discussed in the main text, which this evokes.

72 For fuller references concerning the 'miracle' stories of the Gospels see, for example: A. Richardson, *The Miracle Stories of the Gospels* (SCM Press, London, 1956 [1941]); Moule, *Miracles*, 1965; ch. 5 on 'The intelligibility of miracles' in Harvey, *Jesus and the Constraints of History*; Sanders, *Jesus and Judaism*, ch. 5, 235ff. Sanders' conclusion to his chapter (5) on 'Miracles and crowds' is worth noting as indicating the milieu in which and for which these 'miracle' stories were recounted. They are '1. We do not learn with certainty what Jesus thought of himself, although it is reasonable to think that he, as well as his followers, saw his miracles as testifying to his being a true messenger from or agent of God. 2. The miracles . . . doubtless contributed greatly to his ability to gather crowds, and they thus help explain why he was executed. It was not just that his words, abstractly considered, were challenging to the authorities, but he attracted attention and commotion. 3. "Outsiders" probably regarded Jesus as a charlatan, a magician.

4. Jesus cannot be considered simply a teacher. The miracles do not require us to think that he was an eschatological prophet, but they are compatible with that view.' (p. 173).

73   E.g., about one third of the earliest Gospel, that of *Mark* (omitting ch. 13, the 'Marcan Apocalpyse') is concerned with 'miracle' and/or 'exorcisms', indeed 47% of the pre-Passion narrative (Richardson, *Miracle Stories*, p. 36). *Mark* 1 implies that the healing miracles *were* the new teaching.

74   Harvey, *Jesus and the Constraints of History*, p. 99–100.

75   ibid., p. 100.

76   ibid., p. 100–1.

77   This is not to say that there will not be a sliding scale of credibility determined by the joint operation of the criteria of antecedent probability (related to generic similarity to contemporary healings and 'exorcisms'); and of detailed exegesis of, and historical judgment upon, any particular narrative. There can be no blanket acceptance of the historicity of the narratives *in toto*.

78   These include, in the Synoptic Gospels: the miraculous catch of fishes (*Luke* 5:1–11); the stilling of the storm (*Mark* 4:35–41 and parallels); the feedings of the 5000 and of the 4000 (*Mark* 6:30–44 and par.; *Mark* 8:1–10 and par.); the walking on the water (*Mark* 6:45–52 and par.); the cursing of the fig tree (*Mark* 11:12–14, 20–5 and par.); raisings of the dead (*Mark* 5:22–3, 35–43, and par.; *Luke* 7:11–17); the coin in the fishes' mouth (*Matt.* 17:24–7). In St John's Gospel: the water into wine at Cana (2:1–11); the feeding of the 5000 (6:1–13); the walking on the water (6:16–21); the raising of Lazarus from the dead (11:1–44).

79   Such symbolic reference as: the sea and/or storms to anti- (pre-) creation forces of chaos and evil; the vine (and so wine) to Israel; wine and bread to life.

80   J. C. Fenton, *The Gospel according to John* (Clarendon Press, 1970) p. 119, where the historicity of this story is also discussed.

81   *Mark* 1:9–11 and parallels.

82   *Mark* 9:2–8 and parallels.

83   Many scholars think this might be a transposed 'resurrection' appearance of Jesus, that is, occurring after his death – but this would not affect the point made here.

84   *Matt.* 1:18 to 2:12; *Luke* 1:26–56 and 2:1–20.

85   It has also been inferred as congruent with, and a deduction from, the affirmation of Jesus as *being* both 'God and man', that is the doctrine of the Incarnation in its most explicitly ontological form. However, according to the Roman Catholic scholar Raymond E. Brown 'Both Protestant and Catholic theologians have stated clearly that the bodily fatherhood of Joseph would not have excluded the fatherhood of God' (*The Virginal Conception and Bodily Resurrection of Jesus*, Paulist Press, New York, 1973, p. 42)

and (in a footnote, 56) quotes the 'relatively conservative' Catholic theologian, J. Ratzinger: 'According to the faith of the Church the Sonship of Jesus does not rest on the fact that Jesus had no human father: the doctrine of Jesus' divinity would not be affected if Jesus had been the product of a normal marriage. For the Sonship of which faith speaks is not a biological but an ontological fact, an event not in time but in God's eternity.' (*Introduction to Christianity*, Herder and Herder, New York, 1969, p. 208.)

86   The most thorough study is that Raymond E. Brown, *The Birth of the Messiah* (Geoffrey Chapman, Cassell, London and Macmillan, New York, 1977) which has comprehensive references to the extensive literature on this subject. See also his *Virginal Conception and Resurrection*, 1973, and *An Adult Christ at Christmas* (The Liturgical Press, Collegeville, Minnesota, 1978).

87   Note that, if no male is involved, as in insect parthenogenesis, the offspring are female, because no Y chromosomes are available. It is no use calling upon cases of *natural* parthenogenesis to support the virginal conception of a *male* Jesus!

88   As D. Stanesby has put it, in a trenchant analysis of what the virginal conception really implies: 'Biologically, either Mary provided the ovum for impregnation by the Holy Ghost and so contributed to her son's genetic inheritance, or she was simply a vessel containing and nourishing the divinely implanted seed, that is, a surrogate mother' ('Notes on Biology and Salvation', in the Annual Review of St George's House, Windsor, 1990, p. 28; see also his article on the 'Nature of Jesus and his genes', *Times*, 12 December, 1987 for a similar statement).

89   As Stanesby has pointed out (ibid., n. 88). Indeed this understanding of the nature of human reproduction, in which the man provided the 'seed' and the woman was a mere receptacle, by analogy with the relation of the seeds of, say, cereals to (note) 'mother' earth, was widespread until relatively recently. It is only within the last century or so that there has been an accurate understanding of the processes of human, and indeed of all, reproduction. This misunderstanidg of the processes of human reproduction and gestation must have contributed to the possibility of rendering a virginal conception even thinkable.

90   Since the gestation period is presented as being of the usual length, Jesus' embryo must have started with only one or a few cells.

91   Macquarrie, *Jesus Christ*, p. 80.

92   *Cf.* D. Stanesby: 'In summary, a divine set of genes nurtured by a surrogate mother would hardly result in the Incarnate Lord of the Christian faith. If the world, including man, has an evolutionary history, then incarnation (for salvation) must involve identification with, not dissociation from, that history.' (St George's House, 'Notes . . .', *n.* 88, above).

93   Macquarrie, *Jesus Christ*, p. 393.

94   *John* 1:14.

95   Gregory of Nazianzus, *Ep. 101*, Nicene and Post-Nicene Fathers, Parker, 1894 (quoted in H. Bettenson, *Documents of the Christian Church*, Oxford Univ. Press, London, 1943, repr. 1956), p. 64.

96   Ironically, according to Raymond Brown, the credal 'born of the virgin Mary' was intended, by shifting the emphasis to birth, the signal 'that *part* of the interest was now on the reality of Jesus' humanity against a docetic heresy: the proof of his humanity is that we know the agents of his birth (Mary) and death (Pontius Pilate)' (*NDCT*, p. 598). Today, in the light of biology – and of historical studies – it has an opposite, docetic, tendency.

97   'Docetism (from Greek *dokeo* = I seem) refers to the doctrine that the manhood of Christ was apparent not real . . . a divine being dressed up as a man in order to communicate revelations, but was not really involved in the human state and withdrew before the passion', Frances Young, on 'Docetism', in *NDCT*, p. 160. The adjective 'docetic' is widely used to denote doctrines or views that tend in this direction, those which imply that the humanity of Jesus was not real.

98   Brown, *Birth of the Messiah*, p. 527, emphasis in his text.

99   ibid. (1978), p. 527, *n*. 26a.

100   Macquarrie, *Jesus Christ*, pp. 392, 393.

101   C. J. Cadoux, *The Life of Jesus* (Penguin Books, West Drayton, Middx., 1948), p. 30.

102   The doubts about the historicity of the virginal conception of Jesus arise from many cogent considerations, *inter alia*: the only two narratives which suggest it are those in the early chapters of Matthew and Luke, which were written *ca.* 70–80 AD, are mutually irreconcilable, symbolic and legendary in style, and not always consistent with other parts of the same Gospel (e.g., with respect to Mary's knowledge of Jesus' vocation or the status of Joseph as father); it is not mentioned anywhere in the earliest Gospel (Mark); nor in the fourth Gospel (John) with its 'high' christology; nor elsewhere in the New Testament, including the letters of Paul, the earliest of its authors, who could hardly avoid mentioning it, if known to him, in his intensive expositions of the significance of Jesus as the Christ; etc. The genesis of the stories is understandable in the light of the (on the whole false) biological ideas of the time and in the context of the growth of an increasing emphasis on the divine initiative in the whole of Jesus' life, even to the pre-existence of that divine intention. So that Jesus' divine commissioning moves back progressively as the century unfolds in the minds of these early Christians from Jesus' baptism (Mark), to his birth (the narratives in Matthew and Luke) and eventually to his pre-existence as the Word of God (the Prologue to the Gospel of

John). This process of development in the 'christology' of the first-century church is widely discussed by scholars (see, for example, C. F. D. Moule, *The Origin of Christology*, Cambridge University Press, Cambridge, 1977; James D. G. Dunn, *Christology in the Making*, SCM Press, London, 1980).

103 For an accessible account of their profound, and indeed beautiful, resonances, see Raymond E. Brown, *An Adult Christ at Christmas, essays on the three biblical Christmas stories, Matthew 2 and Luke 2* (The Liturgical Press, Collegeville, Minnesota, 1978).

104 For members of the Church of England, it is worth putting on record that the 1938 Commission on Doctrine of that church, under the chairmanship of William Temple, after noting the traditional view of the 'virgin birth' (as they preferred to call it) also went on to note that some of the Commission held that 'a full belief in the historical Incarnation is more consistent with the supposition that our Lord's birth took place under the normal conditions of human generation'; and agreed to 'recognise that both of the views outlined above [as also described above here] are held by members of the Church, as of the Commission, who fully accept the reality of our Lord's Incarnation, which is the central truth of the Christian faith.' ('Doctrine in the Church of England', The Report of the Commission on Christian Doctrine, SPCK, London, 1938, pp. 82–3; reprinted, with a new introduction by G. W. H. Lampe, SPCK, London, 1982). Ever since this Report belief in the virgin birth has been optional in the Church of England, although this was not generally realized in the controversies which surrounded the views of Professor David Jenkins when he was appointed Bishop of Durham. As a consequence of that controversy, the House of Bishops of the General Synod of the Church of England eventually made a 'Statement and Exposition' of 'the Nature of Christian Belief' (Church House Publishing, London, 1986) and on this matter: 'It needs to be clearly acknowledged that those who feel compelled to regard the virginal conception as symbolic legend rather than history may do so in support of belief in the Incarnation, and regard the symbol of such conception as pointing to an unquestionably objective divine reality' (p. 32.) Divergences of views on the relation of the virginal conception of Jesus to the mystery of the Incarnation were recognized as existing in the House of Bishops (as in the earlier Commission on Doctrine) – however all accepted that ' . . . this belief [in the virginal conception] as *expressing* the faith of the Church of England and of its historic teaching, affirming the truth that in Christ God has taken the initiative for our salvation by uniting our human nature with himself, so bringing into being a new humanity.' (p. 33, emphasis added). Clearly the word 'expressing' allows the same flexibility and freedom of interpretation as did the 1938 Commission on

Doctrine, which means the position is, mercifully for the intellectual integrity of that church, as it was then in the Church of England – namely that belief in a literal, historical virginal conception is not required either for clergy or laity.

105   'Resurrection' will be used from here on, for brevity, to denote the whole series of events/experiences which led the disciples to believe that the human Jesus had 'risen' from his death to be in the immediate presence of God his Father – recognizing that there are different theological emphases in the terms – Resurrection, and Ascension/Exaltation. The traditions of an 'Exaltation', a 'taking up', an elevation, of Jesus to God (*Phil.* 2:9; *Eph.* 4:10; *I Timothy* 3:16) and those of Jesus' Resurrection are independent in the New Testament. 'One cannot be deduced from the other' (Pheme Perkins, *Resurrection: New Testament Witness and Contemporary Reflection*, Geoffrey Chapman, London, 1984, p. 20, referring at this point to R. E. Brown, *Virginal Conception and Bodily Resurrection of Jesus*, p. 74). Undoubtedly an author such as Paul believed both that Jesus had been raised from the dead and that he had been exalted into the glory of God, the latter being the completion of the former. Even so 'The independence of exaltation traditions suggests that certain Christian beliefs are not dependent on resurrection as a necessary condition, though it may be a sufficient condition for their appearance. Thus, one learns the following from this distinction: a. It is possible to speak of Jesus' return to the Father without resurrection language. b. The sending of the Spirit is more closely tied to Jesus' exaltation than to resurrection. c. Resurrection is not a necessary prelude to exaltation. In many traditions the One manifested as risen is already exalted. d. Exaltation serves just as well as resurrection to relativize death.' (Perkins, ibid.).

106   Pheme Perkins, *Resurrection*, pp. 19–20.

107   ibid.

108   As the bishops' Statement (see n. 104) puts it: 'The psychological, moral and spiritual transformation of Jesus's close followers . . . was a remarkable fact, calling for an appropriate cause. This cause must at least have been a powerful event, or series of events, which they could interpret only as meaning that Jesus was alive.' (para., 36, p. 19).

109   Cf. *GNB*, ch. 1 on 'The sciences and reductionism'.

110   See pp. 39–41.

111   Or, rather, concepts since it includes a number of distinct strands – see n. 105.

112   The train of thought developed here rests on the general view I have developed of the putative non-reducibility of theological concepts to those pertaining to less complex and less subtle levels in the hierarchies of being (as expounded in: *CWS*, Appendix C; *GNB*,

p. 30; and, this volume, pp. 22–3). Its particular application here to the question of the status of the 'resurrection' of Jesus is based on that of Dr Christopher Knight, of Jesus College, Cambridge, in his article on 'Hysteria and Myth: the psychology of the resurrection appearances' (*Modern Churchman*, 31 New Series (1989), pp. 38–42) and in an unpublished article on 'Resurrection, religion and "mere" psychology' which he was kind enough to make available to me.

113 See the earlier summaries of the basic historical foundations concerning Jesus, section 3(a).

114 Ch. 9, section 2(c), pp. 160–3.

115 P. Perkins, *Resurrection*, p. 318.

116 ibid., p. 319.

117 'Nature of Christian Belief' (see n. 104), para. 49, p. 25.

118 The evidence for this belief is clearly and admirably summarized in the bishops' statement (ibid., paras. 32ff.) The evidence consists of: (1) the otherwise inexplicable transformation of the disciples from fear and terror into a dynamic movement proclaiming 'The Lord is risen' (paras. 35, 36); (2) the general witness of Christian experience of the living Christ (para. 37); (3) the stories of the Empty Tomb (para. 38), though the Statement recognizes that this does not constitute proof of the Resurrection (paras. 39, 40); (4) the meetings of various disciples, individually and in groups, with the Risen Christ, reported not only in the Gospels but very early by Paul (paras. 41, 42). For the literature on the subject see P. Perkins, *Resurrection*, the article by C. F. Evans in *NDCT*, p. 501–3 and the interesting discussions of Macquarrie, in *Jesus Christ*, pp. 405–410, 412–4, and of Raymond Brown, in *Virginal Conception and Bodily Resurrection of Jesus*, ch. 2.

119 Luke says there was a final appearance in which this was revealed, the 'Ascension' (*Acts* 1:6–11).

120 In that important passage in his letters which begins with his crucial early account of the first of those to encounter the Risen Lord, *I Cor.* 15.

121 Cf., ch. 9, section 1(g), p. 148ff.

122 *Matt.* 28:1–10; *Mark* 16:1–8; *Luke* 24:1–11; *John* 20, v. 1–10.

123 Cf., Raymond E. Brown, 'Of itself . . . the empty tomb was probably not at first a sign of the resurrection, and the emptiness of the tomb was not formally a part of Christian faith in the risen Jesus . . . Christians believe in Jesus, not in a tomb.' (*Virginal Conception and Bodily Resurrection*, p. 126–7); and the 'Nature of Christian Belief' (n. 104): 'That the message of the angels in the Easter stories includes an explanation of the emptiness of the sepulchre as due to the divine miracle of resurrection reflects, among other things, the simple fact that the Empty Tomb was not itself a proof of such resurrection.' (para. 39, p. 20).

124   'Nature of Christian Belief' (n. 104): 'Some scholars have argued that the Empty Tomb formed no part of the very first preaching of Easter, pointing to its absence from the tradition in *I Cor.* 15 . . . Others, who see the Easter faith as having arisen from an intense awareness in the circle of disciples of Jesus' living and personal spiritual presence with them, interpret the Tomb stories as the result of a conviction that Jesus' body must have been involved in the Resurrection, in accordance with some Jewish conceptions of the future life. Others draw attention to the significance of Old Testament prophecies for the elaboration of Christian belief' (para. 40, pp. 20–1).

125   ibid., para. 50, p. 25.

126   See p. 183.

127   Ch. 15, section 2.

128   *Luke* 9:53.

129   'And at the ninth hour Jesus cried with a loud voice, "Eloi, Eloi, lama sabachthani?" which means, "My God, my God, why hast thou forsaken me?"' (*Mark* 15:34).

130   As indeed the bishops said when they all, although variously adopting (1) or (2), acknowledged the belief that Christ's tomb was empty as '*expressing*' their faith 'that in the resurrection life the material order is redeemed, and the fulness of human nature is taken into God's eternal destiny for his creation.' (para. 50, p. 26). Here the word 'expressing' clearly allows both interpretations, the more literal (1) and the more symbolic (2).

131   Cf. P. Perkins *Resurrection*, p. 320): 'The problem of recovering significant speech about resurrection for own day is acute. Many Christians . . . hold resurrection as an item in a creed, but it has no revelatory power and certainly no ordering relevance to their lives . . . This loss of resurrection as an effective symbol has its epistemological correlation. We cease to perceive the world of time and history as having a meaning beyond that which we are able to assign to it in the ordinary dimensions of human experience . . . We live out of a three-way conflict between the facticity of our everyday language, the conceptual language of the metaphysical traditions that gave shape to most Christian systematization of belief, and the language of metaphoric consciousness in which the Bible operates.' (see ibid., pp. 23–4, for an elaboration of the distinctions between these three types of language).

132   In the sense of the 'spiritual body' of *I Cor.* 15:42ff.

133   As possibly adumbrated by Paul in *Romans* 8:18–24, where he expresses the hope that 'the universe itself is to be freed from the shackles of mortality and is to enter upon the glorious liberty of the children of God'. (v. 21, REB).

134   Cf., H. Küng: 'Today . . . historical criticism has made the empty tomb a dubious factor and the conclusions of natural science have

rendered it suspect. To maintain the identity God does not need the relics of Jesus' earthly existence. We are not tied to physiological ideas of the resurrection. There can be identity of the person even without continuity between the earthly and the "heavenly", "spiritual" body. Resurrection is not tied to the substratum – *a priori* constantly changing – or the elements of this particular body. The corporality of the resurrection does not require the tomb to be empty. God raises the person in a new, different, unimaginable "spiritual" corporality." . . . the decisive thing is the new, eternal life in that ultimate, hidden reality which we call God.' (*On Being a Christian*, Collins, London and Doubleday, New York, 1976; reissued SCM Press, London, 1991, p. 366).

135 'Nature of Christian Belief' (n. 104), para. 48, p. 24–5.
136 *Virginal Conception and Bodily Resurrection*, p. 127.
137 ibid., p. 127–8. Earlier he has described the resurrection of Jesus, along with his exaltation and giving of the Spirit, as 'an eschatological event – the beginning of the end-time'. (p. 125).
138 Brown, *Virginal Conception and Bodily Resurrection*, p. 128.
139 Cf. the quotation from H. Küng, n. 134.
140 P. Perkins, *Resurrection*, pp. 29–30, referring to Hans Küng, *On Being a Christian*, pp. 344–61.
141 C. F. Evans, article on 'Resurrection' in *NDCT*, p. 503.
142 *Mark* 8:27–33 and parallels.
143 Introduction to this chapter.

CHAPTER 14   DIVINE BEING BECOMING HUMAN

1 Irenaeus, *Adversus Haereses* v. praef.
2 It read as follows, 'Therefore, following the holy Fathers, we all with one accord teach men to acknowledge one and the same Son, our Lord Jesus Christ, at once complete in Godhead and complete in manhood, truly God and truly man, consisting also of a reasonable soul and body; of one substance (homoousios) with the Father as regards his Godhead, and at the same time of one substance with us as regards his manhood; like us in all respects, apart from sin; as regards his Godhead, begotten of the Father before all ages, but yet as regards his manhood begotten, for us men and for our salvation, of Mary the Virgin, the God-bearer (Theotokos); one and the same Christ, Son, Lord, Only-begotten, recognized in two natures, without confusion, without change, without division, without separation; the distinction of natures being in no way annulled by the union, but rather the characteristics of each nature being preserved and coming together to form one person and subsistence

(hypostasis), not as parted or separated into two persons, but one and the same Son and Only-begotten God the Word, Lord Jesus Christ; even as the prophets from earliest times spoke of him, and our Lord Jesus Christ himself taught us, and the creed of the Fathers has handed down to us.' (from H. Bettenson, *Documents of the Christian Church*, Oxford University Press, London, 1956 [1944], p. 73).

What it set was boundary conditions within which christological discourse should be located by the Christian community when set alongside the evidence of the New Testament.

3   For an accessible and readable account, see John Macquarrie, *Jesus Christ in Modern Thought* (SCM Press, London, 1990).

4   Wisdom was conceived of as 'personification of divine action' in pre-Christian Judaism rather than as 'a divine being in some sense independent of God' (James D. G. Dunn, *Christology in the Making*, SCM Press, London, 1980, p. 262). Wisdom was especially conceived as being present at and in the divine action of creation.

5   ibid., pp. 258–9 (Dunn's emphasis).

6   ibid., p. 262 (Dunn's emphasis).

7   'The Christ event is both the coming of Jesus which the disciples proclaimed – that is, the content of the *kerygma* [what is recoverable as the original core of the Christian gospel], and the formation of the Christian community on the basis of Easter – that is, the occurrence of their faith. The Christ event signifies for the disciples both the new understanding of Jesus as Messiah, and of themselves as new creatures.' (H. Weiss, article on 'Christ event' in *NDCT*, p. 93–4).

8   Dunn, *Christology*, p. 262 (his emphasis).

9   A. E. Harvey, *Jesus and the Constraints of History* (Duckworth, London, 1982), p. 157.

10   Something which Dunn disputes (ibid., p. 38–45).

11   Harvey, *Jesus and the Constraints of History*, p. 178.

12   *Hebrews* 1:8–9; *John* 1:1; *John* 20:28 – though these are not undisputed.

13   Raymond E. Brown, *Jesus God and Man* (Collier Macmillan, London, 1967), pp. 30–1.

14   Brown attributes this development to liturgical usage, having its origin in the worship and prayers of the Christian community (ibid., p. 34).

15   For a brief discussion, see *CWS*, pp. 222–7.

16   C. F. D. Moule, *The Origin of Christology* (Cambridge University Press, Cambridge, 1977), p. 2.

17   More recently, Moule has drawn attention to Jesus' 'tacit assumption that he had direct knowledge of the will of God and that where he was, there God's sovereignty was in action' ('Jesus, Judaism, and Paul' in *Tradition and Interpretation in the New Testament*, ed.

Gerald F. Hawthorne with Otto Betz, Mohr, 1987, p. 50). He also argues that it was this immediateness and directness of the representation of the Divine in the human that seemed blasphemy to the Judaism of his time and was the real gravamen of the charge brought against him at his trial ('The gravamen against Jesus', in *Jesus, the Gospels and the Church*, ed. E. P. Sanders (Mercer University Press, Macon, Georgia, 1987, pp. 177–95).

18 Cf., W. O. Chadwick, *From Bossuet to Newman: the idea of doctrinal development* (Cambridge University Press, Cambridge, 1957); N. Lash, article on 'Development, Doctrinal', in *NDCT*, p. 155–6; M. F. Wiles, *The Remaking of Christian Doctrine* (SCM Press, London, 1974).

19 Dunn, *Christology*, pp. 266–7 (a passage emphasized in the original). Dunn also stresses that, within such general considerations, 'one point in particular should perhaps be singled out for special mention – that is the consistent emphasis in NT christology on the importance of the resurrection of Christ. For on the one hand all the NT writings give prominence to the resurrection/exaltation of Christ . . . On the other hand the diminution of the resurrection's role in Christ's becoming in the Fourth Gospel poses the danger that a subsequent orthodox christology . . . will give insufficient attention to the resurrection in the assessment of Christ. (ibid., p. 267) . . . where the resurrection is recognized to have christological significance, as a becoming in *Christ's* own relation with God, the gospel has to include much more of Jesus' own call for conversion . . . – where the slogan is not so much "Become what you are", but "Become what you are becoming".' (ibid., p. 267–8). Cf. the similar stress of A. M. Ramsey: 'The Resurrection is a true starting-place for the study of the New Testament . . . It is therefore necessary both theologically and historically to "begin with the Resurrection".' (*The Resurrection of Christ*, Fontana Books, Collins, London, 1961, pp. 1, 2).

20 See James P. Mackay 'The task of systematic theology', in *New Testament Theology in Dialogue*, James D. G. Dunn and James P. Mackay (SPCK, London, 1987), pp. 27–53. The whole volume is relevant to our themes here, especially the chapters on christology by the two authors, a New Testament scholar and systematic theologian, respectively.

21 Cf., Wiles, *Remaking*, especially ch. 1.

22 *The Myth of God Incarnate*, ed. J. Hick (SCM Press, London, 1977); *The Truth of God Incarnate*, ed., M. Green (Hodder and Stoughton, London, 1977); *God Incarnate: story and belief*, ed. A. E. Harvey (SPCK, London, 1981) – and many other sequels. The debate was not confined to the English-speaking world, as witness the publication of *inter alia* W. Pannenberg's *Jesus – God and Man* (SCM Press, London, 1968 – originally in German, 1964) and

E. Schillebeeckx's *Jesus – an experiment in Christology* (Seabury Press, New York, 1979) and *Christ – the experience of Jesus as Lord* (Seabury Press, 1980).

23   Dunn, *Christology*, p. 265 (emphasis omitted).

24   ibid.

25   D. Nineham, in *The Myth of God Incarnate*, ed. J. Hick, pp. 202–3.

26   Henceforth in this chapter we shall, for brevity, use the term 'resurrection', unless otherwise stated, to denote *both* the 'resurrection' *and* the 'exaltation' of Jesus the Christ, following the usage of *n.* 105 of ch. 13.

27   See above n. 7.

28   Cf. C. F. D. Moule's evidence that the individual Jesus of history turned out, after the resurrection, to be one who transcended individuality – an unconfined, unrestricted, inclusive personality, the universal 'Christ' to all humanity (see his *The Phenomenon of the New Testament*, SCM Press, London, 1967, ch. II; and *The Origin of Christology*, ch. 2).

29   The hermeneutical question posed by Leonard Hodgson in *For Faith and Freedom* (Oxford University Press, Oxford, 1956, p. x). The proviso of J. A. Baker has to be added to this question: 'when as far as possible we know what the words meant to them then as far as possible we know what the truth was to them' (in *The Foolishness of God*, Darton, Longman and Todd, London, 1970, pp. 364–5).

30   Ch. 9.

31   See ch. 9, section 4, p. 179; ch. 11, sections 2(a), 3(b) and 3(c). Some further consideration of the term 'information' (and also of 'inform' and 'input of information') is overdue. The relation between the different usages of 'information' has fortunately been usefully clarified by J. C. Puddefoot in 'Information and Creation' (see ch. 11, n. 1), p. 15. He distinguishes three senses relevant to the present context (my numbering):

   (i) 'Information' in the physicists', communication engineers' and brain scientists' sense, that of C. E. Shannon – the sense in which 'information' is related to the probability of one outcome, or case selected, out of many, equally probable, outcomes or cases. In this sense it is, in certain circumstances, the negative of entropy (see *PCBO*, pp. 259ff. for a brief exposition of this sense of 'information' in relation to the concept of 'complexity'.).

   (ii) 'Information' in the sense of the Latin *informo, -are*, meaning 'to give shape or form to'. Thus, 'information' is 'the action of informing with some active or essential quality [sense II]', as the noun corresponding to the transitive verb 'to inform', in the sense (II) of 'To give "form" or formative principle to; hence to stamp, impress, or imbue *with* some specific quality or attribute' (quotations from the *Shorter OED*).

(iii) 'Information' in the ordinary sense of 'knowledge' – 'that of which one is appraised or told' (*Shorter OED*, sense I.3).

Puddefoot points out that information (i) must shape or give form to our minds, so giving us information (ii), in order to convey information (iii). In the main text here, and at the other points elsewhere cited at the beginning of this note, the term 'information' (and its associates) is being broadly used to represent this whole *process* of (i) modulating to (ii) modulating to (iii). However the endpoint of this process may be not the mere acquisition of 'knowledge' as such for the possibility arises, though not the certainty, that when persons acquire such 'knowledge', *meaning* is also disclosed. As Puddefoot says: 'Without minds all information is meaningless. Yet even with minds information can remain meaningless; minds are necessary but not sufficient for the perception of meaning' (p. 15).

Hence the usage of information (i) by physicists, communication engineers and brain scientists in relation to, respectively, thermo-dynamics, telecommunications and brains (biological information-processing systems) can properly be regarded as explicating the underlying processes ('input of information') which 'inform' (sense (ii)) our mental experiences giving us knowledge, information (iii), describable only in non-reducible mentalistic terms. Thus the language pertinent to information (i) is one possible, but basic, description of the conscious information (iii) that we acquire and such 'knowledge' has the further potentiality of generating discernment of meaning.

Puddefoot develops his analysis of information-transfer in relation to the concepts of 'creation' and 'incarnation' along lines parallel to those expounded here in the main text – in both cases without any reductionist intentions or implications.

The concept of information (i) has often been used to attempt to define living entites (q.v., *PCBO*, pp. 259–263; J. D. Barrow and F. J. Tipler (The *Anthropic Cosmological Principle*, Clarendon Press, Oxford, 1986, p. 515); F. J. Tipler 'The Omega Point as *Eschaton*: answers to Pannenberg's questions for scientists' (*Zygon* 24 (1989), p. 222). Tipler develops this into a future cosmic projection (an 'Omega-point') for 'life' entirely defined in such terms without, he claims, reductionist intentions with respect to ordinary human experience (ibid., p. 223). See ch. 16, p. 344 and n. 28.

32 This ch., p. 290, and n. 6.
33 See n. 31 above.
34 Ch. 9, section 4 and ch. 11, *passim*, and n. 31, above.
35 See, n. 4 above and J. G. Dunn, *Christology*, ch. VI.
36 For reference, here is the translation of the Revised English Bible (Oxford and Cambridge University Presses, 1989): '(1) In the begining the Word already was. The Word was in God's presence,

and what God was, the Word was. (2) He was with God at the beginning, (3) and through him all things came to be; without him no created thing came into being. (4) In him was life, and that life was the light of mankind. (5) The light shines in the darkness, and the darkness has never mastered it . . . (9) The true light which gives light to everyone was even then coming into the world. (10) He was in the world; but the world, though it owed its being to him, did not recognize him. (11) He came to his own, and his own people would not accept him. (12) But to all who did accept him, to those who put their trust in him, he gave the right to become children of God, (13) born not of human stock, by the physical desire of a human father, but of God. (14) So the Word became flesh; he made his home among us, and we saw his glory, such glory as befits the Father's only Son, full of grace and truth . . . (16) From his full store we have all received grace upon grace; (17) for the law was given through Moses, but grace and truth came through Jesus Christ. (18) No one has ever seen God; God's only Son, he who is nearest to the Father's heart, has made him known.' (*John* 1:1–5, 9–14, 16–18).

37   Macquarrie, *Jesus Christ*, p. 108.

38   E.g., The Word of the Lord created the heavens . . . For he spoke, and it was' (*Psalm* 33:6, 9; REB).

39   Cf. C. H. Dodd, *The Interpretation of the Fourth Gospel* (Cambridge University Press, Cambridge, 1953), p. 277. Scholars differ as to the weight to be given to the contribution of these two concepts in the thought of 'John' but both would clearly be in the minds of his readers, no doubt to varying degrees, depending on their cultural milieu. See above, n. 4.

40   Ch. 9, section 4, pp. 179–80.

41   Macquarrie, *Jesus Christ*, pp. 106–7 (verse numbers added, see *n*. 36).

42   See n. 31 above.

43   J. Bowker, *The Sense of God* (Clarendon Press, Oxford, 1973), p. 95).

44   John Bowker, *The Religious Imagination and the Sense of God* (Clarendon Press, Oxford, 1978), pp. 187–8. The whole passage (section 3 of his ch. II) should be read to amplify this necessarily abbreviated quotation.

45   See n. 22 above.

46   The grounds on which a distinctively Christian doctrine of the Incarnation in Jesus Christ, that is inclusivist and not exclusivist, might commend itself (cf. Brian Hebblethwaite, the end of his article on 'Incarnation', in *NDCT*, pp. 289–91).

47   Henceforth, I shall refer to 'Jesus the Christ' to encapsulate what this phrase refers to (see n. 7). Thereby I hope to ensure also that sight is not lost of the fact that the revelation of God and humanity

in the 'Christ-event' was personal in content and through an historical person.

48 Cf. J. G. Dunn's summary above (p. 290 and n. 6) of what was being affirmed in the early formulations of the significance of Jesus.

49 This ch., section 1, pp. 292–3. An earlier stage in the development of what follows is to be found in *CWS*, ch. VI – and some of its wording is reproduced here.

50 Part II, especially ch. 8.

51 Ch. 8, section (1).

52 Cf. Ch. 13, setion 3(c).

53 As summarized in our earlier quotation from J. G. Dunn, p. 290 and nn. 6, 8.

54 See n. 36 above.

55 Cf. Macquarrie's 'translation' of *Logos* as 'meaning', p. 296 above.

56 Ch. 15.

57 The advantage of the use of 'Spirit' language for elaborating the significance of Jesus the Christ, as advocated by G. W. H. Lampe (in *God as Spirit*, Oxford University Press, Oxford, 1977), becomes apparent in this context. For, in this way of speaking, God who as 'Spirit' is manifest in Jesus the Christ is clearly the same mode of the God's being who *as* 'Spirit' reaches out to all humanity and can dwell in the inner life of human beings – that is, can be immanent in human persons.

58 See n. 53.

59 'Christ', 'Son of God', 'Lord', 'Wisdom', '*Logos*', etc.

60 Ch. 3, section 3(a), pp. 66–8.

61 Ch. 4, section 3(a) and ch. 8, section 1(g).

62 A phrase which John A. T. Robinson in *Exploration into God* (SCM Press, London, 1967, p. 83) attributes to Teilhard de Chardin.

63 ibid., p. 97.

64 Ch. 8, section 1(g), pp. 111–2.

65 ch. 10, p. 187.

66 ibid.

67 Ch. 13, section 3.

68 See *Truly a Person, Truly God* (SPCK, London, 1990) by Adrian Thatcher for a recent investigation emphasizing the centrality of the concept of the person for any adequate understanding of the incarnation. See also his 'Christian Theism and the Concept of a Person' in *Persons and Personality*, eds. Arthur Peacocke and Grant Gillett (Blackwell, Oxford, 1987), pp. 180–190.

69 See n. 36 above.

70 Robinson, *Exploration*, pp. 98–9 (numbers refer to the verses of *John* 1, see n. 36).

71 Ch. 8, section 1(h) (pp. 112–3).

72 This sub-section, p. 302.

73 Ch. 8, section 2(b), esp. p. 121.

74   Chs. 9 and 11.
75   Ch. 13, section 3(b).
76   The 'cry of dereliction' ('My God, my God, why has thou forsaken me?' of *Mark* 15:34).
77   Ch. 8, section 2(c), pp. 121–3.
78   For a recent discussion, see Macquarrie, *Jesus Christ in Modern Thought*, pp. 245–50.
79   ibid., p. 250.
80   *Phil.* 2:6–11, and *II Cor.* 8:9.
81   Macquarrie, *Jesus Christ*, pp. 388–92.
82   J. G. Dunn, for example, (in *Christology*, esp. pp. 114–121) shows that the previously widely accepted interpretation of both of these passages has presumed the classical, and later, understanding of the incarnation and has not taken into account the background which would have been presumed by Paul's readers and which becomes clear from a study of the Pauline corpus. Dunn shows that this is the contrast between Adam and Christ: between Adam who was made in the image/form of God (according to *Genesis* 1:26) and who, by disobediently grasping at equality with God in eating the forbidden fruit, lost that likeness and so represents sinful humanity; and Jesus Christ who chose instead to empty himself of Adam's glory, obediently to embrace Adam's lot to the death that Adam experienced as punishment. The whole passage, he argues, is through and through an expression of 'Adam christology' and '... no implication that Christ was pre-existent may be intended. If Christ walks in Adam's footsteps then Christ need be no more pre-existent than Adam' (p. 119).
83   Ch. 8, section 2(d), pp. 123, 124.
84   ibid.
85   Ch. 8, section 2(f), pp. 126–7.
86   The title of Jurgen Moltmann's profound book (*The Crucified God*, SCM Press, London, 1974).
87   Cf. *CWS*, pp. 229–30.
88   In this chapter, I have for the most part been thinking about Jesus the Christ in relation to how and what God was communicating through him – in particular, what God was expressing about God's own self in and through his person and personal history. In this perspective, Jesus the Christ by virtue of his openness to God as his 'Father' and Creator was able to express in a distinctive way the transcendence of the Creator who is immanent in the world process. Thus his disciples, and their followers, encountered in him a presence of God which fused God's transcendence and immanence in a way that engendered the language of 'incarnation'. However, when such 'incarnational' language becomes confined to assertions about Jesus' 'nature' and about what kind of 'substance(s)' do, or do not, constitute him, then it loses its force to convey significant

meaning to many today who are concerned not so much with what Jesus was 'in himself', but rather with the dynamic nature of the relation between God's immanent creative *activity* focussed and unveiled in him and the *processes* of nature and of human history and experience, all of which are 'in God' and so from which God is never absent.

89 The whole concept of 'incarnation', of what happened in Jesus the Christ, also has very important implications in relation to the significance of the natural world, and so for a theology *of* nature. I have discussed this elsewhere (*SCE*, pp. 157, chs. 6 and 7, *passim*; *CWS*, pp. 233–8, ch. VII, *passim*).

CHAPTER 15 DIVINE MEANING AND HUMAN BECOMING

1 Irenaeus, *Adversus Haereses* v. praef.
2 Ch. 12.
3 Ch. 12, section 3.
4 As far as we have been able to observe in this, 'our', universe.
5 Ch. 12, section 5, pp. 238–9.
6 Ch. 14, section 2.
7 But only the aspect of their meaning of relevance and significance for human perspectives. As we have already emphasized (ch. 8, section 2(a), pp. 113–5), the creator God must be presumed to have not only inscrutable purposes but also joy in the rich variety of the non-human creation.
8 These considerations now place in a fuller context our earlier discussion (Ch. 9, section 4, pp. 180–1) of the meaning(s) that God might be intending to convey through the different levels of creation.
9 Cf. H. Berkhof ('God in nature and history', in *Faith and Order Studies*, 1964–7, World Council of Churches, Geneva, 1968, Faith and Order Paper No. 50), 'To take seriously the final events in Christ must also mean that it is confessed as the ultimate secret of *creation* . . . what is revealed in history is no unrelated incident, but the realization of a condition which had been God's purpose from the beginning. The crucified and risen Jesus is the key to the understanding of the meaning of the whole created world . . . This close connection of what God meant in creation and what he accomplished in Christ was expressed by . . . [the authors of John 1, Colossians 1 and Hebrews 1], using contemporary patterns of thought, in the confession that the world was created in and through Jesus Christ . . . Most classical theologians . . . saw the Incarnation as the great emergency-measure by which God de-

cided to bring the world back to its original perfection. A minority, however, maintained that Christ is more than that, that he is also the crown of creation, the new man for which creation had been waiting from the beginning . . . When a choice has to be made, the decision has to be in favour of the second doctrine, because the first cannot give a satisfactory explanation of the three passages in the New Testament [as above] which deal with Christ as the mediator of creation' (pp. 12–3). For further discussion of what could possibly be meant by speaking of Jesus Christ as the 'mediator' and 'agent' of creation, see *CWS*, pp. 233ff.

10 ibid.

11 Macquarrie, *Jesus Christ*, p. 392. This passage occurs at the end of a section on the traditional idea of the 'pre-existence' of Christ. He argues there, as I have done elsewhere (*CWS*, pp. 233ff.), that the only coherent sense that may be attributed to this term is that of God having from eternity the intention and purpose of consummating in a human being the work of creation, that has proceeded in the evolution of the cosmos, human history and in God's self-communication, particularly through the people of Israel. Indeed that is the meaning given to 'pre-existence' in Judaism (*CWS*, p. 234, *n*. 113). It is the only sense in which the person 'Jesus' might be said to pre-exist his actual birth. It is only *God*, as Word/*Logos* (or 'Son of God', eventually in Christian thought) who can be said to pre-exist a particular historical event or process.

12 Cf. *I John* 1:1–3 (NEB): 'It was there from the beginning; we have heard it; we have seen it with our own eyes; we looked upon it, and felt it with our hands; and it is of this we tell. Our theme is the word of life. This life was made visible; we have seen it and bear our testimony; we here declare to you the eternal life which dwelt with the Father and was made visible to us. What we have seen and heard we declare to you so that you and we together may share in a common life, that life which we share with the Father and his Son Jesus Christ.' The sequence of thought in the main text here follows approximately *CWS*, pp. 236–8).

13 John Macquarrie, *In Search of Humanity* (SCM Press, London, 1982), p. 2.

14 ibid.

15 ibid., p. 3.

16 Ch. 12, section 9.

17 Ch. 13, section 1.

18 And, indeed, also for nature in general, the whole of creation (see the discussions in *SCE*, p. 157, and *CWS*, pp. 287–91).

19 Though if by 'sin' is meant alienation and separation from God, as is proper theologically speaking, the Jesus' openness to God

can be interpreted as an absence of 'sin' and so 'sinlessness', in *this* sense. See the earlier discussion, ch. 13, section 3(c).

20 As unravelled by J. Passmore in *The Perfectibility of Man* (Duckworth, London, 1970); see *CWS*, p. 247 for discussion of his analysis.

21 Cf. ch. 13, section 3(e).

22 Here, as before, 'resurrection' denotes both 'resurrection' and 'exaltation' – cf. n. 105, ch. 13 and n. 26, ch. 14.

23 See ch. 13, section 3(e), pp. 284ff.

24 'A pattern, exemplar, example' (*Shorter OED*).

25 'A pattern of excellence; a person or thing of supreme excellence' (*Shorter OED*).

26 'The original pattern from which copies are made' (*Shorter OED*).

27 *I Cor.* 15:12–19.

28 *Hebrews* 2:10 (NRSV).

29 E.g., *Matt.* 4:19; 8:22; 9:9; *Mark* 2:14; *Luke* 5:27; 9:23; *John* 1:43; 12:26; 21:19.

30 *Acts* 9:2.

31 *Gal.* 4:19 (NEB/REB).

32 J. R. Illingworth, 'The Incarnation and Development' in *Lux Mundi*, ed. C. Gore (John Murray, London, 1889 [12th edit. 1891]), pp. 151–2.

33 *II Cor.* 5:17; *Gal.* 6:15.

34 The basis for a 'Spirit Christology' such as that of G. W. H. Lampe in *God as Spirit* (Clarendon Press, Oxford, 1977).

35 Wolfhart Pannenberg, *An Introduction to Systematic Theology* T. & T. Clark, Edinburgh, 1991), p. 61.

36 For earlier discussions of the understanding of the significance of Jesus the Christ for what humanity should become, see *SCE*, pp. 160 – 176; and *CWS*, pp. 244 – 253.

37 See p. 250, n. 186.

38 Cf., the use of the concept of transcendence to characterize the human condition by Karl Rahner, *Foundations of Christian Faith* (Darton, Longman and Todd, London and Crossroad, New York 1982, Eng. transl.), *passim*.

39 Ch. 11.

40 Ch. 14, section 3(a), p. 301.

41 *II Cor.* 5:19 (REB).

42 Ch. 12, section 3, pp. 221–2.

43 Q.v., ch. 12, n. 174.

44 Ch. 12, section 9.

45 Introduction, p. 15, 17.

46 Ch. 12, section 9.

47 These are (E. Schillebeeckx, *Christ: the experience of Jesus as Lord*, SCM Press, London and Seabury Press, New York, 1980, pp. 477ff.): salvation and redemption; being freed from forms of

servitude and slavery; redemption as liberation through purchase for a ransom; reconciliation after dispute; redemption as satisfaction/peace; redemption as the expiation for sins through a sin-offering; redemption as the forgiveness of sins; justification and sanctification; salvation in Jesus as legal aid; being redeemed for community; being freed for brotherly love; being freed for freedom; renewal of man and the world; life in fullness; victory over alienating 'demonic powers'; grace leading to celebration. (From and for what humanity is freed in redemption through Jesus Christ are listed by him on p. 513, ibid.)

48 Q.v., *Sacrifice and Redemption: Durham essays in theology*, ed. S. W. Sykes (Cambridge University Press, Cambridge, 1991).

49 ibid., p. 303.

50 ibid., p. 304.

51 ibid., p. 309.

52 E.g., see below with respect to the work of C. Gunton.

53 Morna D. Hooker, *From Adam to Christ* (Cambridge Press, Cambridge, 1990), pp. 22–3. In a footnote, she reports that a similar view was maintained by G. W. H. Lampe in his *Reconciliation in Christ* (Longmans, Green & Co., London, 1956, esp. pp. 61–6) and by D. E. H. Whiteley, 'St Paul's thought on the atonement', *JTS*, NS 8 (1957), pp. 240–55.

54 To express whast she means by this, Hooker frequently cites the quotation from Irenaeus which stands at the heads of Part III and of chapters 14 and 15 of this volume.

55 ibid., p. 5. She continues: 'Underlying this understanding of redemption is the belief that Christ is 'the last Adam' (*I Cor*. 15:45), the true 'image of God', who by sharing fully in humanity's condition . . . opens up the way for men and women to share in his condition, by being 'in Christ'.

56 ibid., p. 22.

57 ibid., p. 27.

58 J. D. G. Dunn, in Sykes, op. cit., p. 51, and earlier in 'Paul's understanding of the death of Jesus', in *Reconciliation and Hope*, ed. R. J. Banks (Paternoster Press, Exeter, 1974), pp. 125–141.

59 ibid., emphasis original. '"Substitution" does not give sufficient prominence to the point of primary significance – that God was the subject . . .' (p. 51).

60 G. W. H. Lampe, 'The Atonement: law and love', in *Soundings*, ed. A. R. Vidler (Cambridge University Press, Cambridge, 1963), p. 187.

61 ibid., p. 181.

62 ibid., p. 182.

63 Q.v., the discussion of this idea in *SCE*, pp. 171–2.

64 Q.v., C. F. D. Moule, *The Origins of Christology* (Cambridge University Press, Cambridge, 1977), ch. 2.

65 V. White, *Atonement and Incarnation – an essay in universalism and particularity* (Cambridge University Press, Cambridge, 1991), p. 8. Elsewhere instead of 'reconciliation' in this assertion about universality, White substitutes 'saving significance' or 'saving efficacy' or just 'salvation', but the general sense and intention is apparently the same.

66 E.g., in addition to those already mentioned: F. W. Dillistone, *The Christian Understanding of the Atonement* (Nisbet, London, 1968), also his illuminating article 'Atonement' in *NDCT*, pp. 50–3, ending with a useful bibliography: C. E. Gunton, *The Actuality of Atonement* (T. & T. Clark, Edinburgh, 1988); R. Swinburne, *Responsibility and Atonement* (Clarendon Press, Oxford, 1989); P. Fiddes, *Past Event and Present Salvation the Christian idea of atonement* (Darton, Longman & Todd, London, 1989); and a 1980 prescient essay by Geoffrey Lampe, very much along the lines of what is argued here and by P. Fiddes (loc. cit.), on 'Salvation: Traditions and Reappraisals' (repr. in his *Explorations in Theology 8*, SCM Press, London, 1981, pp. 14–29).

67 F. W. Dillistone wisely points out in his article on 'Atonement' (see previous note) that, literally, a 'theory' is a 'viewing' – in this instance 'trying to see the particular event of the death of the Messiah within the wider context of what is believed to be true of the relations between God and man' (p. 51).

68 ibid., p. 53.

69 ibid.

70 Ch. 12, section 9.

71 Introduction, pp. 14ff.

72 See n. 66.

73 These authors, together with F. W. Dillistone, should be consulted for expositions which demonstrate a possible continuing life for the models of these theories.

74 This alienation is conceived variously as impurity, uncleanliness before God (sacrifice theories); as guilt through infringement of God's laws (judicial theories); and of bondage to evil powers (liberation/victory theories).

75 According to V. White (*Atonement and Incarnation*) these classical theories of the atonement also fail, from his viewpoint, even in the hands of Gunton and Fiddes, who effectively transform their metaphors, for they too, he argues, fail to provide a constitutive, universal, objective, ontological significance for the Christ event in the strong sense which White regards the tradition as having asserted. White himself proposes that there is a transition within God's own self which occurs in the Christ event, so that 'unless and until God himself has experienced suffering, death, and the temptation of sin, and overcome them, as a human individual, he has no moral authority to overcome them in and with the rest of

426 *Notes to pp. 327–328*

humanity.' (p. 39). We have already argued (ch. 8, section 2(f), pp. 126–7) that any understanding of God, in the light of the created order as we now perceive it through the sciences, has to acknowledge that God suffers in, with and under the creative processes of the world – and there are also other grounds on which this is being adduced today (p. 127). But if it is the eternal nature of God to be self-offering, suffering, vulnerable Love then the Christ event cannot consist in a new transition in God's relation to humanity, but rather be an explicit manifestation of what is eternally true of God's relation to humanity (cf. ch. 14, section 3(d)). God's suffering in and through the life of the human being, Jesus the Christ, who was completely open to God and thus the embodiment of God in his outreach to humanity (i.e., God as Holy Spirit) was a new experience in content (but not in kind) for God historically and contingently, but not eternally – because that is the way God was, is and always will be in relation to humanity and the world.

It seems to me that White does not distinguish clearly enough between the eternal *nature* of God as Love and the ongoing enriching of his *experience* with his human creatures embedded in time – an enriching which would have been uniquely intense in the person of Jesus the Christ. I also find the moral dimension in White's atonement model somewhat baffling for it fails to take account of the sheer grace of God's dealings with humanity – that God accepts us as we are, *as* sinners (cf., the quotation from Lampe, above, *n.* 61, and sections IV and V in Lampe's article in *Soundings, n.* 60). Thus his model is unconvincing in establishing a basis for the kind of universality which he seeks in any atonement model – namely, that the atonement effects a change in the human status before God that applies to all humanity in all times and places. But this is not the only kind of 'universality' possible, as will transpire.

76   Fiddes, *Past Event and Present Salvation*, p. 15.
77   See A. Peacocke, 'The Challenge of Science to Theology and the Church', in *The Weight of Glory*, eds. D. W. Hardy and P. H. Sedgwick (T. & T. Clark, Edinburgh, 1991), pp. 37–53, esp. pp. 49–51 (a fuller version of an article under the same title in *The New Faith-Science Debate*, ed. J. M. Magnum (Fortress Press, Minneapolis and WCC publns., Geneva, 1989); and also the critique, to which I am much indebted, of Duane H. Larson, 'Peacocke, Christ, Atonement', Bulletin of the Center for Theology and the Natural Sciences, Berkeley, vol. 6, no. 3 (1986) pp. 1–7.
78   Fiddes, *Past Event and Present Salvation*, ch. 7.
79   Including now in this cypher the later (see ch. 13, n. 15) designation of 'God the Son' as that 'mode of being', that *persona*, of God which was incarnate in Jesus the Christ. Fiddes, remarks on this: 'Early Christian thought moved from a 'sonship of function' to a

'sonship of being' with the help of Jewish ideas of wisdom. In our age we might reflect upon the meaning of persons, and the artificiality of dividing 'being' from 'doing'. Persons are not ready-made products but become what they are because of their relationships and actions; if there really were someone who was completely open to God in trust as a son, and who was totally transparent to the loving activity of God, then such a communion would be so close that we could not think of the being of God without this person' (ibid., p. 56–7).

I recall the first line of the brave attempt of David Jenkins to put into simple words what Christian believers are affirming about the pattern of the possibilities that God has revealed and promised:

'God is. He is as he is in Jesus. So there is hope.

God is. He is for us. So it is worth it.'

(*God, Jesus and Life in the Spirit*, SCM Press, London, 1988, p. 8).

80 Ch. 8, section 2(c).

81 A word used by Duane H. Larson, (n. 77) to describe my understanding of the atonement. The *Shorter OED* says 'to engage' can mean *inter alia*: 'to attract and hold fast; to involve; to lay under obligation; to urge, induce; to gain, win over'. This is the pertinent sense in this context.

82 *Romans* 5:5 (REB).

83 That there is a *cost* of forgiveness, initially in the forgiver and subsequently in the forgiven, in human relations as well as the need to expunge guilt, and so, by analogy, in the relation of God and humanity is fully recognized and incorporated into the revised Aberlardian understanding of the atonement presented here. The reader is referred to chapters 7 ('The act of love') and 8 ('The cost of forgiveness') of Paul Fiddes' *Past Event and Present Salvation* for a penetrating and, to my mind, an entirely convincing account of how the atonement generates forgiveness and removal of guilt.

84 ibid., ch. 7.

85 Fiddes (ibid., p. 140) quotes a well-known passage from the commentary on the Epistle to the Romans of Peter Abelard (1079–1142): 'Now it seems to us that we have been justified by the blood of Christ and reconciled to God in this way: through this unique act of grace manifested to us – in that his Son has taken upon himself our nature and persevered therein in teaching us by word and example even unto death – he has more fully bound us to himself by love; with the result that our hearts should be enkindled by such a gift of divine grace, and true charity should not now shrink from enduring anything for him.' (full reference in Fiddes, op. cit., *n*. 1, p. 231).

86 ibid., p. 141. See his ch. 7 for the full working out of this argument.

87 ibid., p. 150.

88 ibid., p. 148.

89 See ch. 8, section 2(f), and n. 75 above.

90   Fiddes, *Past Event and Present Salvation*, p. 157.

91   ibid., pp. 160–6.

92   The public means of grace are usually taken to be worship and the sacraments; the private ones, prayer and the Bible.

93   ibid., pp. 165–6.

94   Cf. *CWS*, pp. 244–6.

95   *I Cor.* 15:13–4 (REB).

96   Ch. 13, section 3(e).

97   Cf., G. W. H. Lampe: '. . . if his [Jesus'] body was raised physically from the grave and did not see corruption, or if his body was transformed after death into something different, in such a way that in itself it was annihilated, then he did not experience the whole of human destiny. His entry into life beyond the grave was different from what we may hope may be our own. For it is demonstrable that our bodies of flesh and blood will be dissolved . . .
  . . . if the story of the empty tomb were true, Christ's door into God's kingdom would not be ours. We should be confronted by another door through which he has never entered; into a darker room which his presence has never lightened.' (in G. W. H. Lampe and D. M. MacKinnon, *The Resurrection*, Mowbray, London, 1966, p. 59).

98   Hence the affirmation in the Apostles' Creed, 'I believe in . . . the resurrection of the body', where 'body' can only mean 'the whole person' and not the physical body, as such, for the reasons I have given.

99   See above, this chapter, section 2 pp. 315–16.

100   See ch. 12, section 9; *CWS*, pp. 179–184.

101   These two last-mentioned are the concern of ch. 16.

102   See Introduction, p. 8, *re* scientism.

103   E.g., by V. White, *Atonement and Incarnation*, see n. 75.

104   *John* 1:4–5 (REB).

105   I find myself sympathetic in this regard to the approach to other religions of Keith Ward in his *A Vision to Pursue* (SCM Press, London, 1991).

106   Cf., the use in the New Testament (q.v., 'heal' in *A Theological Word Book of the Bible*, ed. A. Richardson, SCM Press, London, 1957, p. 103) of the Greek word *sozo* as meaning 'to save', both in the religious sense of salvation (from evil, sin, damnation, etc.), and in the sense of healing a disease – 'to make whole'; and the older English use of 'health' to signify *inter alia* 'spiritual, moral or mental soundness; salvation' (*Shorter OED*).

107   *Gal.* 4:19 (RSV and REB).

CHAPTER 16 L'ENVOI: THE DIVINE MEANS FOR AND THE END OF HUMAN BECOMING

1 Ch. 15, p. 335.
2 'Grace' is the term for a gift of God, distinct from God's gift of human life, whereby God gives God's own self to human beings 'so that they can know him and love him, so entering into a relationship with him which totally exceeds the relationship of creature to Creator, and is therefore totally undeserved . . . unless God had implanted an affinity to or aptitude for grace, grace would be irrelevant to human nature and not a transformation of it.' (E. J. Yarnold, on 'Grace', in *NDCT*, p. 245).
3 Chs. 9, section 3 and 4, and ch. 11.
4 See, ch. 11, section 1, p. 193. We revert here to Popper's terminology (see ch. 11, nn. 11, 12).
5 E.g., the experience of the holy in Isaiah, ch. 6 (q.v., R. Otto's classic work on *The Idea of the Holy*).
6 Ch. 11, section 3(a).
7 For example: I. T. Ramsey, *Our understanding of prayer* (SPCK, London, 1971; Peter Baelz, *Does God answer prayer?* (Darton, Longman and Todd, London, 1982); V. Brummer, *What are we doing when we pray?* (SCM Press, London, 1984); J. Polkinghorne, *Science and Providence* (SPCK, London, 1989), ch. 6; K. Ward, *Divine action* (Collins, London, 1990), ch. 9.
8 N.B. The very early evidence, *ca.* 55–6 AD, in Paul's letter to the Corinthians (*I Cor.* 11:23ff.), in which he refers back to his earlier visit to Corinth *ca.* 51 AD, when he informed them of what he had himself been told some ten years before, *ca.* 40 AD – which brings it within approximately seven years of Jesus' death in 33 AD. (See, for example, G. Ogg, 'The chronology of the New Testament' in *Peake's Commentary on the Bible*, eds. M. Black and H. H. Rowley, Nelson, London, 1962 edition).

   There is less agreement about whether the command of Jesus to his disciples to baptize people 'of all nations' (*Matt.* 28:19) are *ipsissima verba* of Jesus, though there is no doubt that baptism was the rite of Christian initiation from the outset.
9 As we have earlier collectively denoted the contents of the natural world (Part I, *passim*).
10 Ch. 11, section 1, pp. 191–2. See also *GNB*, pp. 116–8.
11 For a fuller working out of this, see *GNB*, ch. 9. There is a provocative discussion by Paulos Gregorios of sacramental attitudes to the natural world, holding those of 'mastery' and 'mystery' in a proper tension, in 'Technology and sacrament', part of ch. 7, 'Mastery and Mystery' in *The Human Presence: an Orthodox view of nature* (World Council of Churches, Geneva, 1978), pp. 85–9.

12   William Temple, *Nature, Man and God* (Macmillan, London, 1934, and reprintings), ch. XIX, 'The Sacramental Universe'. For discussion of this idea in the general context of Temple's thought, see A. R. Peacocke, 'The New Biology and *Nature, Man and God*', in *The Experience of Life: science and religion*, ed. F. K. Hare (Univ. of Toronto Press, 1983), pp. 27–88, esp. pp. 27–31.

13   Bernard J. Cooke, *The Distancing of God* (Fortress Press, Minneapolis, 1990).

14   Ch. 15, section 2.

15   Ch. 15, n. 32.

16   John D. Zizioulas, *Being as Communion* (Darton, Longman and Todd, London, 1985).

17   This 'new biological hypostasis of man' he describes as a human existence seen 'as personal not on the basis of the laws of nature, but on the basis of a relationship with God which is identified with what Christ in freedom and love possesses as Son of God with the Father' (ibid., p. 56).

18   In, respectively: *SCE*, pp. 174–6, *CWS*, pp. 308–11; and *CWS*, pp. 305–11, 315–7, 350, 355.

19   Or, better, 'co-creating creatures'?

20   Philip Hefner, *The Human Factor: evolution, culture, technology, and religion in theological perspective* (Fortress Press, Minneapolis, 1993); 'The Evolution of the Created Co-Creator', in *Cosmos as Creation*, ed. Ted Peters (Abingdon Press, Nashville, 1989), pp. 211–233.

21   See ch. 12 section 8, p. 247 and n. 172 for references.

22   Symeon Lash, article on 'Deification' in *NDCT*, p. 148. N.B., the distinction traditionally made in the Orthodox theology between God's essence and his energies (cf., ch. 10, p. 185, above). The whole approach is too important and profound to deal with adequately here – reference is inevitable to V. Lossky's classical treatment [1968] of Orthodox theology: *The Mystical Theology of the Eastern Church* (e.g., in the edition of James Clarke, Cambridge, 1991), esp. chs. 4 and 5. See also *CWS*, pp. 251–2.

I find this kind of understanding of the results of the operation of divine grace in completing human nature more congenial to an evolutionary perspective than the traditional, often Western, language of redemption, salvation, sanctification, etc.

23   ibid., p. 148.

24   *CWS*, pp. 348–9.

25   Quoting Lewis Ford, in *Hope and the Future of Man*, ed. E. H. Cousins (Garnsone Press, London, 1973 (Fortress Press, Philadelphia, 1972]), p. 136.

26   For a fuller exposition and discussion, see *CWS* ch. VIII, on 'Creation and Hope', pp. 319–59.

27   Freeman Dyson, *Disturbing the Universe* (Pan Books, London,

1981 [1979]).

28 F. J. Tipler, 'The Omega Point Theory: a model of an evolving God', in *Physics, Philosophy and Theology*, eds. R. J. Russell and W. R. Stoeger (Univ. Notre Dame Press, Notre Dame, Ind., 1988), pp. 313–331; *Zygon* 24 (1989), pp. 217–253. (See also ch. 14, n. 31, last para.).

29 See also J. Polkinghorne, *Reason and reality*, (SPCK, London, 1991) for comments on these views from a Christian perspective.

30 T. S. Eliot, *Little Gidding*, V.

Postscript

1 The experience of God as Trinity in prayer is particularly well expressed in a valuable section (ch. 7, based on a paper of Dr Sarah Coakley), entitled 'God as Trinity: an approach through prayer', in *We Believe in God* (A Report of the Doctrine Commission of the Church of England, Church House Publishing, London, 1987). It is an 'attempt to indicate an experience of prayer from which the pressure towards trinitarian thinking might arise . . . it is clear that we do not here begin with two perfect and supposedly fixed points, Father and Son, external to our selves and wholly transcendent, with the Spirit then perhaps (rather unconvincingly) characterized as that which relates them . . . Rather, we start with the recognition of a vital, though mysterious, divine dialogue within us, through which the meaning and implications of being 'in Christ' become gradually more vivid and extensive. Thus the Trinity ceases to appear as something abstract or merely propositional. It is not solely to do with the internal life of God, but has also to do with us. The flow of trinitarian life is seen as extending into every aspect of our being, personal and social, and beyond that to the bounds of creation' (p. 111).

2 Sometimes also called the 'immanent' Trinity, a usage to be distinguished from the sense of 'immanence' and its cognates elsewhere in this book, referring to God's presence in the world, etc.

3 For useful discussions of both the tradition(s) and the contemporary situation, with bibliographies, see: *The Forgotten Trinity*, Report of the British Council of Churches Study Commission on Trinitarian Doctrine Today (BCC, London, 1989); and articles on the 'Essential Trinity' and the 'Doctrine of the Trinity' by J. P. Mackey, in *NDCT*, pp. 186–7 and 581–9, respectively.

4 Ch. 8, section 1(a), (b), pp. 102–3.

5 The emphasis on 'personal' here is intended as a reminder of those pointers we have heeded, in Part II, to God's being and becoming as 'at least personal' and to distance ourselves from the view that the

underlying unity of the Godhead, of the *personae* of the Trinity, is in some *impersonal* substance or substratum (see the discussion in section 5.2, especially on pp. 32–3, of the BCC's *The Forgotten Trinity*).

6   The relations (1')–(3') correspond, respectively, on our time-scale, to the activity of God: (1″) in initiating and bringing into existence the whole cosmic process; (2″) focussed in the life, death and resurrection/exaltation of Jesus the Christ; (3″) continuing creating in and through the cosmic process, in general, and in the life of the church 'in Christ', in particular.

7   Note the more apophatic position of J. P. Mackey who, after referring to 'a more ancient piece of Christian (and Greek) wisdom which said that God's inner essence or being remained veiled from us while *in via*, in a way in which God's outreach did not', goes on to suggest that 'from that more ancient point of view it seems best to say that trinities (or binities) primarily, to the extent that they are or were at all successful, point to God's being in outreach to us and as such suggest some self-differentiation in God which, however, we are quite unable to describe.' (ibid., n. 2, above, p. 187).

8   ibid., p. 589.

9   Related by F. C. Copleston, *Aquinas* (Penguin Books, London, 1955), p. 10.

INDEX (of the main text and of extended notes)